Infant Development
The Essential Readings

Edited by Darwin Muir and Alan Slater

BLACKWELL
Publishers

Copyright © Blackwell Publishers Ltd 2000
Editorial matter and organization copyright ©
Darwin Muir and Alan Slater 2000

First published 2000

2 4 6 8 10 9 7 5 3 1

Blackwell Publishers Ltd
108 Cowley Road
Oxford OX4 1JF
UK

Blackwell Publishers Inc.
350 Main Street
Malden, Massachusetts 02148
USA

British Library Cataloguing in Publication Data

A CIP catalogue record for this book is available from the British Library.

Library of Congress Cataloging-in-Publication Data has been applied for.

ISBN 0 631 21746 0 (hbk)
0 631 21747 9 (pbk)

Typeset in $10\frac{1}{2}$ on 13 pt Photina
by Best-set Typesetter Ltd., Hong Kong
Printed in Great Britain by MPG Books Ltd, Bodmin, Cornwall.

This book is printed on acid-free paper

   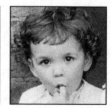

Martin Davies
*Senior
Commissioning
Editor*

Siobhán
Pattinson
*Publishing
Assistant*

Ally Dunnett
*Editorial
Services*

Lisa Eaton
Production

Books are to be returned on or before
the last date below.

0 2 MAY 2003

- 8 MAY 2003

1 9 MAY 2003

2 6 SEP 2003

1 6 OCT 2003

23 1 0 03

' DEC 2003

LIBREX —

Essential Readings in Developmental Psychology

Series Editors: Alan Slater and Darwin Muir
Queen's University, Kingston, Ontario and the University of Exeter

In this brand new series of nine books, Alan Slater and Darwin Muir, together with a team of expert editors, bring together selections of readings illustrating important methodological, empirical and theoretical issues in the area of developmental psychology. Volumes in the series and their editors are detailed below:

Infant Development	*Darwin Muir and Alan Slater*
Childhood Social Development	*Wendy Craig*
Childhood Cognitive Development	*Kang Lee*
Adolescent Development	*Gerald Adams*
The Psychology of Aging	*William Gekoski*
The Nature/Nurture Issue	*Stephen J. Ceci and Wendy M. Williams*
Educational Attainment	*Charles Desforges*
Language Development	*Elizabeth Bates and Michael Tomasello*
Developmental Disorders	*Wendy M. Williams, Stephen J. Ceci, Alan Slater and Darwin Muir*

Each of the books is introduced by the volume editor with a rationale behind the chosen papers. Each reading is then introduced and contextualized within the individual subject debate as well as within the wider context of developmental psychology. A selection of further readings is also assigned, making each volume an ideal teaching resource for both classroom and individual study settings.

Contents

Preface

Discoveries by infant researchers are some of the most exciting and important to be found in the study of human development, and they have been the subject of intense speculations and theorizing. Despite the fact that, as adults, we can remember little about the times and places when we acquired knowledge early in life, that information does remain with us for the rest of our lives (see chapter 1). The aim of this collection of readings is to introduce the reader to the field of infancy research and to some of the current, lively controversies within the areas investigated.

Several criteria have been used for the selection of articles included in the book. First, the articles should reflect the dynamic and changing nature of the subject and the current "state of the art." Thus, all but three of the papers have been published in the 1990s and most in the latter part of this decade: the three earlier papers are classic and highly cited papers. Second, the articles should reflect the diversity of research and thinking in infancy research. A third consideration is that the articles selected should be accessible, and make sense, to students at all levels of their studies in psychology. We have, therefore, not included lengthy, complex articles that would only be understood by specialists in infancy research.

The readings are organized into four Parts to illustrate research into major areas of thinking and development: Theoretical Issues; Sensation and Perception; Cognitive Development; and Social Development and Communication. For each part and for each paper the Introductions put each reading into context, and occasionally provide additional information where we feel that this might be helpful.

Any choice of articles in a field as extensive and dynamic as infancy research, where many hundreds of original articles are published each year, is bound to be somewhat idiosyncratic. We acknowledge that different editors may have made different choices and that we have left out brilliant papers by many international authorities in infancy research due to necessary space limitations for a single volume. However, we feel that our selection of readings represents some of the best thinking and research in the different areas of investigation.

Many of our authors have been kind enough to let us have photos of themselves as they are now, and when they were infants – long before they ever realized that they would become experts in infant development! We would like to thank Martin Davies of Blackwell Publishers who encouraged the development of this series of *Essential Readings* and for his enthusiasm throughout, and to those at Blackwell Publishers who have helped in the development of the series.

Darwin Muir
Alan Slater

Acknowledgments

The editors and publishers gratefully acknowledge the following for permission to reproduce copyright material:

Photograph

Gary Larson, "Fuel . . . check lights . . . ." The Far Side © 1985 Farworks Inc.,/Dist. by Universal Press Syndicate." Reprinted with permission. All rights reserved.

Text

Ahmed, A., & Ruffman, T., "Why do infants make A Not B errors in search task, yet show memory for the location of hidden objects in a non-search task?" *Developmental Psychology* 34, 1998. Copyright (1998) by the American Psychological Association. Reprinted with permission.

Bahrick, L., "The role of amodal information in infant learning of inter-modal information." (Original paper, based on talk at ICIS, 1998.)

Baillargeon, R., "How do infants learn about the physical world?" *Current Directions in Psychological Science* 3, 1994.

Benoit, D. & Parker, K., "Stability and transmission of attachment across three generations." *Child Development* 65, 1994 © Society for Research in Child Development, Inc.

Carpenter, M., Akhtar, N. & Tomasello, M., "Fourteen-through 18-month-old infants differentially imitate intentional and accidental actions." *Infant Behavior and Development* 21, 1998. Reprinted with permission from Elsevier Science.

Charman, T., Swettenham, J., Baron-Cohen, S., Cox, A., Baird, G. & Drew, A. "An experimental investigation of social-cognitive abilities in infants with autism: Clinical implications." *Infant Mental Health Journal* 19, 1998. Copyright Michigan Association for Infant Mental Health.

Kisilevsky, B. S., Muir, D. W. & Low, J. A., "Maturation of human fetal responses to vibroacoustic stimulation" *Child Development* 63, 1992 © Society for Research in Child Development, Inc.

Mareschal, D., "Connectionist modelling and infant development." (Original article.)

Meltzoff, A. N., & Moore, M. K. "Imitation of facial and manual gestures by human neonates." Reprinted with permission from *Science* 198, 1977. Copyright (1977) American Association for the Advancement of Science.

Meltzoff, A. N. & Moore, M. K. "Resolving the debate about early imitation" from A. Slater & D. Muir (eds.), *The Blackwell Reader in Developmental Psychology* (Blackwell Publishers, Oxford, 1999).

Muir, Darwin & Slater, Alan "Infancy Research: History and Methods." (Original article.)

Papoušek, M., Bornstein, M. H., Nuzzo, C., Papoušek, H., & Symmes, D., "Infant responses to prototypical melodic contours in parental speech." *Infant Behavior and Development* 13, 1990. Reprinted with permission from Elsevier Science.

Rovee-Collier, C. "Shifting the focus from what to why." *Infant Behavior and Development* 19, 1996. Reprinted with permission from Elsevier Science.

Sigman, M., Cohen, S. E. & Beckwith, L., "Why does infant attention predict adolescent intelligence?" *Infant Behavior and Development* 20, 1997. Reprinted with permission from Elsevier Sicence.

Slater, A. "Visual perception in the young infant: Early organization and rapid learning," based on Slater A., "Visual perception" from G. Bremmer and A. Fogel (eds.) *The Blackwell Handbook of Infancy*.

Sorce, J. F., Emde, R. N., Campos, J. & Klinnert, M. D. "Maternal emotional signaling: Its effect on the visual cliff behavior of 1-year-olds." *Developmental Psychology* 21, 1985. Copyright (1985) by the American Psychological Association. Reprinted with permission.

Spelke, E. S. "Nativism, Empiricism, and the origins of knowledge." *Infant Behavior and Development* 21, 1998. Reprinted with permission from Elsevier Science.

Symons, L. A., Hains, S. M. & Muir, D. W., "Look at me. Five-month-old infants" sensitivity to very small deviations in eye-gaze during social interactions." *Infant Behavior and Development* 21, 1998. Reprinted with permission from Elsevier Science.

Tincoff, R. & Jusczyk, P. W. "Some beginnings of word comprehension in 6-month-olds" *Psychological Science* 10, 1999.

Werker, J. F., "Becoming a native listener." *American Scientist* 77, 1989.

Wynn, K., "Addition and subtraction by human infants.' *Nature* 358, 1992.

The publishers apologize for any errors or omissions in the above list and would be grateful to be notified of any corrections that should be incorporated in the next edition or reprint of this book.

Introduction
Infancy Research:
History and Methods

Darwin Muir and Alan Slater

Alan Fogel (1997) asked ". . . ever wondered about the details of your own birth? Do you remember learning to crawl or to walk?" If you can answer "yes" to any of these questions, Fogel suggests that you probably heard about these experiences from your parents. Gavin Bremner (1994) points out that "the entymological definition of infant is 'unable to speak', and this certainly marks infancy as a distinct period at least from the point of view of methodology" (p. 1). Infants cannot talk about their experiences and later, when they can talk, they do not seem to remember them. Thus, we have no direct measures from children and adults of what they saw, heard, felt and understood when they were infants. Researchers have had to design clever experiments and methodologies to reveal the nature of the development of perceptual, cognitive and social abilities during infancy, and this book contains a representative sample of their work.

Two basic world views, organismic and mechanistic, have been used to characterize different types of developmental theories and research (e.g., Berk, 1998). Lerner (1986) defines a world view ("paradigm" or "model") as "a philosophical system of ideas that serves to organize a set or family of scientific theories and associated scientific methods" (p. 42). Its basic principles are *assumed* to be true rather than being empirically derived (see Lerner, 1986, chapter 2 for details, and Hultsch and Deutsch, 1981, for a concise summary). Here, we briefly summarize the organismic and mechanistic world views, and the nativist perspective (the view that certain abilities are either present at birth or emerge later through some "intrinsic growth processes"), and give examples of developmental functions associated with each viewpoint, drawn in part from articles in this reader.

Developmental functions are patterns of behavioral change as a function of age. Examples are shown in figure 1; the vertical (Y) axis represents the dependent variable – a behavioral/physical index; the horizontal (X) axis represents the passage of time (age). These functions, describing how infants typically grow and change with age, are of both theoretical and practical use. Clinical psychologists use them as a base-line (norms) against which they can: (1) identify infants with an abnormal developmental course (e.g., developmental delay) and; (2) evaluate the success of their intervention programs. Developmental functions are also used to evaluate theoretical predictions associated with different world views. This Introduction ends with a review of the strengths and weaknesses of various methods that infancy researchers use to derive developmental functions.

Note that to save space all cross-references in this chapter to papers included in the book are in italics and omitted from the reference section.

Organismic World View

The organismic world view represents the infant as being inherently active and continually engaged in interactions with the environment. It emphasizes the interaction between maturation and experience that leads to the development of new physical and psychological (mental) structures. According to this view, development progresses in a stage-like manner. Lerner (1986) states: "The Organismic model stresses the integrated structural features of the organism. If the parts making up the whole become reorganized as a consequence of the organism's active construction of its own functioning, the structure of the organism may take on a new meaning; thus qualitatively distinct principles may be involved in human functioning at different points in life. These distinct, or new, levels of organization are termed stages . . ." (p. 57). An analogy is the qualitative change that occurs when molecules of two gases – hydrogen and oxygen – combine to form a liquid – water. The point is that each new stage cannot be reduced to the

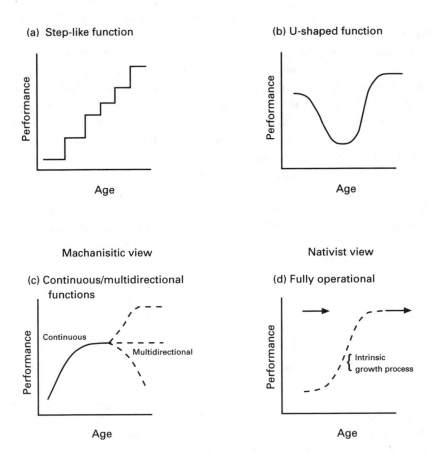

Figure 1 Four types of schematic developmental functions: stage-like (a) and U-shaped (b) functions represent an organismic world view; continuous and multidirectional functions (c) reflect a mechanistic world view; and mature behavior at birth or emerging later, following an intrinsic growth process independent of experience (d), reflect a nativist orientation

components of the previous stage; instead, a structural metamorphosis (reorganization) has occurred which has characteristics not present in the previous stage. A stage-like developmental function is shown in figure 1(a).

Developmental functions reflecting stages

A clear example of structural stages occurs during fetal development. In this case the Y-axis (vertical axis) in figure 1(a) represents increasingly complex structural organizations which appear at successive ages in a *step-like developmental function*. In the germinal stage (first few weeks after conception) cells multiply and form clusters; in the embryonic stage (2 to about 8 weeks post conception) the major body parts are formed by cell multiplication, specialization, and migration as well as cell death. In the last, fetal stage the body parts mature and begin to operate in an organized manner (e.g., arm extensions and grasping, thumb sucking, startling to loud noises).

Stage-like progressions have also been described for the development of motor skills. In this case, the Y-axis could be distance traveled (in feet or metres) by an infant during a given period of time. This distance suddenly increases at different points in time matching the relatively abrupt onset of different types of mobility. Infants are relatively immobile during the first few months of life, begin to crawl around 6–8 months of age, stand up and toddle around furniture a few months later, and begin to walk on their own between 12–18 months of age. These mobility milestones represent qualitatively different types of locomotion, suggesting a stage-like progression.

Stages in the development of psychological processes have been postulated by many theorists including Freud and Piaget. Piaget described four major stages in cognitive development corresponding in time to infancy, pre-school, school age, and adolescence (see Piaget, 1962, in Slater and Muir, 1999). Only the first stage, the sensory-motor period, is relevant here. Piaget suggested that infants progress through a series of 6 sub-stages during the sensory-motor period. For example, in stage 1 newborns make non-integrated reflex responses to stimulation in different sensory modalities (e.g., eye flicks directed towards a blinking light; arm movements to a touch). In stage 2 these reflexes become coordinated with other patterns of activity in repetitive cycles where the goal is to repeat action sequences (e.g., repetitively reaching out and touching their faces). This experience leads to coordination between the senses (e.g., the discovery that objects can be seen and heard at the same time). By the third stage, infants' responses to stimulation become reorganized into volitional responses to multidimensional objects in an integrated perceptual space (e.g., they begin to reach for objects at particular spatial locations). In the next stage, they begin to form mental representations (memories) of objects that disappear from sight (object permanence), and by stage 5 they are able to solve problems by trial and error. By the end of the sensory-motor period, around 18 months of age, they can imitate novel actions of other people and are beginning to use symbols, such as words, to represent objects. This, very brief account, describes only a few of the changes that take place from one stage to the next, and is intended simply to illustrate the point that qualitatively different behaviors are found in the different stages.

A major point made by Piaget was that the shift from one stage to the next occurs in a step-like fashion that leads to successively higher levels of functioning. For example, infants rather suddenly begin to search for hidden objects around 8 months of age. However, at this age, when the object is hidden in a new location (B), they search for it at the old location (A). This "A-not B" error is solved a few months later. The relatively universal timing of the onset of successive stages of object permanence fits Piaget's stage model. In this book, a number of papers have challenged Piaget's ideas concerning the stages of intersensory coordination (e.g., *Bahrick, 1999; Slater, 1999*) and his interpretation of infants' failures on object permanence tasks (e.g., *Mareschal, 1999; Baillargeon, 1994; Ahmed and Ruffman, 1998*).

U-shaped developmental functions

These functions, illustrated in figure 1(b), also have been related to stage shifts in infancy. Certain abilities present early in life may disappear temporarily and then reappear at a later age in a more complex form. One example would be the alternating stepping of the legs and feet that can be elicited from newborns who are properly supported. This response disappears after a few months and reappears when infants begin to stand and walk, around 9–12 months of age (see Thelen and Ulrick, 1991, for a more detailed discussion). Another U-shaped function occurs in the development of auditory localization responses. Newborns readily turn their heads and eyes towards off-centered sounds. They stop turning towards the same sounds around 5–6 weeks of age, and turn to sounds again around 4 months of age. The timing of this U-shaped function coincides with the onsets of Piaget's first three sensory-motor sub-stages and may reflect the shift from reflexive directional responses to a sound's location (stage 1), which is temporarily suppressed (in the second stage), and then emerges when infants begin to search for objects at a particular location in space (in the third stage). The timing is also related to the maturation of different structures in the visual cortex. Various interpretations for these U-shaped and stage-like functions are discussed by Muir et al. (1994; reprinted in Slater and Muir, 1999).

Infant researchers who subscribe to the organismic world view have the job of determining what variables, processes, and/or laws represent differences in psychological operations at each stage, and when each stage begins to operate.

Mechanistic World View

The mechanistic world view uses a machine model (e.g., computer) analogy to represent human behavior. The infant is thought of as being inherently passive until stimulated by the environment. Human behavior can be reduced to the operation of fundamental behavioral units, such as habits, that are acquired and refined gradually in a relatively continuous growth function. American behaviorists such as John B. Watson and B. F. Skinner represent this world view. Donald Baer (1970), a prominent behaviorist, defined development as behavior change *over time* which involves "learning procedures: patterns of reinforcement, punishment, extinction, differentiation and discrimination, in general . . . development is behavior change which requires programming; and programming requires time, but not enough of it to call it age" (p. 245).

Baer rejected the methods used by developmental psychologists, such as Piaget, who simply observed infant behavior, catalogued the age at which infants began to perform various tasks, and then explained these age differences as being due to the onset of operations using new structures (both physical and mental). To illustrate the behaviorist's position, Baer (1970) described an experiment by Jeffrey (1958) in which children were given the task of learning to name a stick figure "Jack" when it was pointing to the left and "Jill" when it was pointing to the right. Seven-year-olds learned this task rapidly while 4-year-olds failed to learn it at all after many trials. Jeffrey eliminated this age difference by training 4-year-olds to push a button on the left for the left-pointing figure and on the right for the right-pointing one. They learned this motor association task quickly and when they returned to the first, verbal association task they solved it easily as well. Thus, earlier training on the motor task primed, or cued the children so that they were then able to understand the demands of the more difficult verbal task.

Baer's point is that the process of development can be revealed by providing the proper sequence of learning experiences that might take several years to occur under poorly constructed natural conditions. He argued that "Age" *per se* is not a useful concept and that developmentalists should study the environmental factors, or principles of learning, which determine the way organisms respond to stimulation.

Developmental functions reflecting the mechanistic viewpoint

The frequency (and skill) of behavior can increase with age (time) due to various learning processes (e.g., classical and operant conditioning, and observational learning). The most common developmental function found in textbooks that matches the behaviorist's viewpoint is the *continuous developmental function* shown in figure 1(c) (the initial component that simply increases with age). An example is the development of precision in reaching for and grasping objects that gradually increases throughout the first year of life, as infants practice and obtain feedback from their errors.

Behaviorists also postulate *multidirectional developmental functions*. After reaching an asymptote, performance may remain stable if contingencies remain consistent, increase if the contingencies become more attractive (higher reward values), or decrease if the behavior no longer has any functional consequence (extinction) or is punished. These different developmental functions are also illustrated in figure 1(c). It should be noted that learning theorists could explain U-shaped developmental functions as the result of changes in contingency. In the auditory localization example given above, head turning may be extinguished by exposure to non-contingent sound sources (e.g., a radio or TV or voice from another room) and may reappear once the infant is reinforced for reaching for sound sources.

The job of the behaviorist is to determine the nature of the contingencies that control infant behavior and produce the different developmental functions. Researchers have invented sensitive behavioral measures to test the ability of infants to respond to a variety of stimuli. For example, newborns will learn to change their patterns of sucking or visual attention to produce recordings of adult speech (see *Slater, 1999;*

Kisilevsky et al., 1992). Another example is *Werker's (1989)* observation that infants' universal phonetic sensitivity declines around 12 months of age so that they lose the ability to make many phonemic discriminations that are not used to differentiate words in their own native language, perhaps due to extinction or lack of use (see *Werker, figure 8.3*). *Baillargeon (1994)* discusses how an "innate learning mechanism" might lead to the development of successively more complex reasoning about objects that disappear from view. Finally, *Mareschal (1999)* provides a modern learning perspective with his formal computational model (computer model), based in part on our knowledge of how the brain is wired (neuroscience), to simulate the infant's development of categorical perception and object permanence.

The Nativist Perspective

Nativists characterize infants as being pre-programmed to process faces, language, space, numerosity, and social interaction (see Karmiloff-Smith, 1996, in Slater and Muir, 1999). These abilities may be revealed at birth, or they may appear later when the structures needed to display the ability mature (e.g., the motor coordination necessary to reach and grasp; the vocal apparatus needed to articulate consonant-vowel combinations, etc.). Historically, a strong nativist viewpoint was held by Gestalt psychologists in the 1930s. As Murray and Farahmand (1998) point out, Koffka (1935) postulated an "innate" perceptual organization (i.e., present at birth) for object discrimination (figure-ground), face perception, and speech perception (including maternal voice recognition). *Spelke (1998)* presents a detailed discussion of the logic behind the Nativist's position.

The developmental functions for nativism are shown in figure 1(d). The ability is either present at birth or emerges later through some "intrinsic growth processes." *Spelke (1998)* states: "there is some evidence for innate knowledge, embodied in structures that develop in advance of their function and in advance of relevant perceptual contacts with the objects of knowledge" (p. 193). The nativist's job is to design appropriate tests to uncover the young infant's innate perceptual, cognitive and social predispositions. Examples in this reader of newborn competence include *Slater's (1999)*, and *Meltzoff and Moore's (1977; 1999)* demonstrations of various *visual* perceptual abilities, and

Kisilevsky, et al.'s (1992) and Werker's (1989) descriptions of early *auditory* abilities. Also, *Wynn (1995)* shows that very young infants are capable of simple addition and subtraction.

Developmental Methods

Dependent measures (deriving values on the Y-axis)

Researchers have developed a variety of techniques to assess the abilities of non-verbal infants, many of which are described in this book. Body movements and heart-rate responses of fetuses and very young infants have been measured to assess their sensitivity to visual and auditory stimulation (e.g., *Kisilevsky et al., 1992*). Newborns also have been tested by measuring changes in their sucking patterns to auditory stimulation (e.g., DeCasper and Fifer, 1980). However, measures of visual attention have become the most common index for assessing perceptual and cognitive development and are used in most of the studies in this reader. Even newborns display visual preferences; they look at some visual stimuli longer than others (*Slater, 1999*). The visual preferences of newborns and older infants can be manipulated using visual reinforcement (*Werker, 1989*), auditory stimulation (*Papousek et al., 1990; Tincoff and Jusczyk, 1999*) and visual habituation procedures (*Bahrick, 1999; Baillargeon, 1994; Slater, 1999*). For example, in a habituation procedure, when infants are repeatedly presented with the same target their fixation times decline over trials, and when a novel target is presented they look at it longer than the familiar one. This visual preference (a preference for novelty) can be used to determine how sensitive infants are to various dimensions of stimulus change. Also, young infants may have an expectation for how objects and people behave; they appear to show "surprise" (usually indexed by increased visual attention) when an unusual, or impossible event occurs (*Baillargeon, 1994; Wynn, 1992*).

The development of inexpensive videotape equipment has allowed researchers to measure a number of additional dependent variables, especially variables of interest to researchers studying infant social development. In these studies, infants are videotaped while they are engaged in a variety of tasks such as face-to-face interactions with an adult (*Meltzoff and Moore, 1977; Symons et al., 1998*), social referencing tasks (when adults try to direct the infant's attention, *Charman et al., 1998; Sorce et al., 1985*), and the "Strange Situation" test (where various infant responses to the mother's departure are used to classify the infant's security of attachment, *Benoit and Parker, 1994*). The frequency and duration of a variety of infant behaviors including facial gestures (e.g., tongue protrusions), expressions of affect (e.g., smiling and grimacing), and pointing and looking at objects and people, can be scored by several observers who are blind to the experimental hypotheses. The use of videotape records aids in controlling for experimenter bias, and gives a clear documentation of procedural details that researchers can use if they wish to replicate and/or extend the work.

We have only considered a few of the measurement techniques described in this book. In all cases, the emphasis is on obtaining reliable, accurate, objective, and valid measures of the operation of some psychological process. However, it is important to remember that when infants fail a test, it could be because they do not have the ability to process the information, or because they do not have the skills necessary to demonstrate their knowledge.

Plotting the X-axis: changes with age

Infant researchers use a variety of methods to collect the data to plot developmental functions similar to those shown in figure 1. In all cases, they employ some variation of either the *longitudinal* or *cross-sectional* methods.

Conceptually, the simplest example of a longitudinal method is the *case study* – the repeated observation of the same person over time (when the subject of the observations is an infant, such case studies are often called *baby biographies*). A classic case study is Darwin's biographical sketch (1877, reprinted in Slater and Muir, 1999) of his eldest child's (William Erasmus Darwin) development of different skills and aptitudes in infancy. Piaget also developed most of the basic concepts for his stage theory of infant development by using case studies of his own children. He presented them with various stimuli (e.g., a moving light, object on a string) or problems (e.g., hiding objects in various places), and carefully recorded their responses.

Although case studies can provide a rich source of ideas and insights, and can document important, rare events (such as the first time an infant smiles or speaks), they also have serious limitations including:

(1) lack of generalizability – one or two children clearly do not constitute a representative sample of the population; (2) lack of systematic
observations; (3) the use of retrospective observations (i.e, sometimes
describing events long after their occurrence); and (4) experimenter bias
(a close relative may not be the most objective observer of an infant's
behavior and development). Another drawback may be that because
baby biographers usually have strong theoretical views that led them to
study their own children, they may only note anecdotes supporting their
own theories.

The generalization problem of case studies can be solved by conducting *longitudinal studies* in which a number of infants are tested systematically and repeatedly at different ages. Longitudinal data are often
summarized by plotting the average performance as a function of age.
If all infants have the same developmental function, stage-like and continuous growth functions can be distinguished (e.g., both types are
given in *Kisilevsky et al., 1992*). However, when the age of onset varies
among individuals, averaging the data at each age could result in a con-
tinuous-looking growth function (i.e., as more infants show the shift in
performance, the overall average performance increases steadily with
age). Thus, it may be necessary to examine each individual's growth
function to distinguish stage-like (as in figure 1(a)) from continuous or
more complex developmental functions (as in figures 1(b) and (c)). The
longitudinal method also allows researchers to study individual differences. Continuity or change in an individual's performance over age,
relative to his/her peers, can be determined (e.g., *Sigman et al.'s, 1997*
prediction of IQ scores at 18 years of age from a test of newborn visual
attention).

Although the longitudinal method seems ideal for plotting developmental functions, it also has limitations. It is expensive to run and takes
a long time to complete; its length equals the age span being tested. This
is not as serious a problem for infancy researchers (given a maximum
age span of about 2 years) as it is for those who study older age groups
(especially life-span researchers). However, it is very difficult to schedule
repeated visits and the drop-out rate of participants can be high. Parents
of infants who perform poorly on the tasks may withdraw from the study,
and the selective survivorship that results from this drop-out can give an
inflated indication of the "true" average development over age. Infants'
performance also can improve on successive tests because of practice
or familiarity with the procedure. These effects limit the generality of

the results and complicate their interpretation. Finally, the results of a longitudinal study may only be true for the particular age *cohort* tested (i.e., infants born at about the same time). For example, changes in medical technology, hospital prenatal care, and publicity about infant abilities can influence infant well-being, and parenting activities, and are some of the potential factors that may produce a cohort effect. For these, and other changes that occur over time, the results from one cohort may not be applicable to different cohorts born at different times; thus a cohort effect is another population bias that may limit the generality of the findings.

In the *cross-sectional method* infants of different ages are tested once; the developmental function is described by plotting the average for each age group as a function of age. This method provides a quick and inexpensive way to estimate the shape of a developmental function. It is the most common method used by infancy researchers, including those in this reader (e.g., *Rovee-Collier's, 1996*, development function for infant memory in figure 1.10; *Werker's, 1989*, developmental function for the loss of discriminations of some non-native phonemic contrasts in speech perception in figure 8.3; and *Bahrick's, 1999*, contrasting developmental functions for changes in sensitivity to variations in synchrony versus composition of associated auditory-visual events in figure 6.2). However, the cross-sectional method only shows age differences. As noted above, stage-like functions may appear by plotting average performance if infants shift at the same age. However, if the individuals' timing of their step-like functions varies, averaging the data could produce a continuous looking function. Only longitudinal data can ensure against this possibility. Finally, because different groups are tested at each age, the developmental function could be due to either age or to non-age differences (i.e., cohort effects discussed above) between groups.

Cohort effects can be examined using a *sequential design* that simply combines cross-sectional and short-term longitudinal methods (e.g., Berk, 1998). Although sequential designs are not often used in infancy research, they are a cost-effective way to provide a measure of individual differences and to ensure that the results of longitudinal and cross-sectional studies agree. *Kisilevsky et al. (1992, figure 4.6)* give an example in which the developmental functions for fetal sensitivity to vibroacoustic stimulation derived from the two methods match.

Summary

The organismic and mechanistic world views, and the nativist perspective have been summarized to provide a general framework for placing the various types of research included in this book, and elsewhere. The organismic world view leads infancy researchers to identify infant abilities which emerge at different stages during infancy (e.g., different levels of object permanence). Investigators subscribing more to the mechanistic world view have invented clever behavioral technologies to measure how various aspects of infant memory, face processing, and social and other behaviors develop. Those with a more nativist orientation look for evidence that certain abilities are present at birth, or emerge through an intrinsic growth process.

The job of the infant researcher is to describe the developmental functions for various processes and to generate theories to explain their patterns. Some developmental function may reflect, and give support, to a particular perspective (e.g., some abilities are present at birth, others appear suddenly in a stage-like progression, while others show a relatively continuous pattern of growth or decline. Others are complex, such as the U-shaped functions). We acknowledge that it will not be appropriate to define all the research described in this reader as a derivative of a particular viewpoint. For example, the developmental function for speech perception suggests that some phonetic discriminations which are innate (nativist), are lost through lack of use (a mechanistic extinction process), at about the time when infants begin to speak (a possible language stage process reflecting both maturation (nativist) and experience (organismic view). When developmental functions are plotted on the same figure, depending on the timing of the shifts in behavior, we may be able to establish causal relationships between different processes. A more comprehensive picture of development will arise as more developmental functions are described and compared.

Acknowledgments

The authors would like to thank Larry Symons for producing figure 1 and Ann Muir for proofreading the manuscript.

References

Baer, D. (1970). An age-irrelevant concept of development. *Merrill-Palmer Quarterly, 16,* 238–45.

Berk, L. E. (1998). *Development Through the Life Span.* Needham Heights, MA: Allyn & Bacon.

Bremner, J. G. (1994). *Infancy, 2nd Edition.* Oxford: Blackwell.

Darwin, C. (1877). A biographical sketch of an infant. *Mind: A Quarterly Review of Psychology and Philosophy, 7,* 285–94.

DeCasper, T., & Fifer, W. (1980). Of human bonding: newborns prefer their mothers' voices. *Science, 208,* 1174–6.

Fogel, A. (1997). *Infancy: Infant, Family, and Society, 3rd Edition.* St Paul, MN: West.

Hultsch, D. & Deutsch, F. (1981). *Adult Development and Aging: A Life-Span Perspective.* New York: McGraw-Hill.

Jeffrey, W. (1958). Variables in early discrimination learning: I. Motor responses in the training of left-right discrimination. *Child Development, 29,* 269–75.

Karmiloff-Smith, A. (1996). The connectionist infant: would Piaget turn in his grave? *SRCD Newsletter, Fall 1996,* 1–3, 10.

Koffka, K. (1935). *Principles of Gestalt Psychology.* London: Routledge & Kegan Paul.

Lerner, R. (1986). *Concepts and Theories of Human Development.* (2nd ed.). New York: Random House.

Muir, D., Humphrey, D., & Humphrey, K. (1994). Pattern and space perception in young infants. *Spatial Vision, 8,* 141–65.

Murray, D. J., & Farahmand, B. (1998). Gestalt theory and evolutionary psychology. In R. W. Rieber and K. D. Salzingers (eds.), *Psychology: Theoretical-Historical Perspectives, 2nd Edition* (pp. 255–87). Washington, DC: American Psychological Association.

Piaget, J. (1962). The stages of the intellectual development of the child. *Bulletin of the Menninger Clinic, 26,* 120–8.

Slater, A., & Muir, D. (1999). *The Blackwell Reader in Developmental Psychology.* Oxford: Blackwell.

Thelen, E., & Ulrick, B. (1991). Hidden skills: a dynamic systems analysis of treadmill stepping during the first year. *Monographs of the Society for Research in Child Development, 56* (1).

Carolyn Rovee-Collier

Andrew N. Meltzoff

Elizabeth S. Spelke

Karen Wynn

Denis Mareschal

Renée Baillargeon

Alan Slater

Ayesha Ahmed

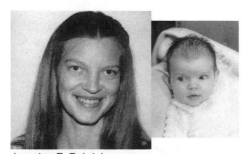

Lorraine E. Bahrick

Marian Sigman

Hanǔs Papoušek

Mechthild Papoušek

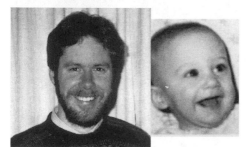

Lawrence A. Symons

Ruth Tincoff

Diane Benoit

Malinda Carpenter

Darwin Muir

Tony Charman

Barbara S. Kisilevsky

Janet F. Werker

Part I

Theoretical Issues

Introduction to Part I

Theoretical speculations are to be found in abundance in infancy research. The articles in Part I illustrate some of the current concerns. In chapter 1 Carolyn Rovee-Collier points out that infancy researchers have spent close to 40 years documenting *what* infants can do, and we have now reached sufficient maturity to ask *why* they do what they do. An abiding issue in developmental psychology, which is particularly germane to infant development, is the question of what is innately given to a species, and what is learned. In chapter 2 Elizabeth Spelke considers the nature-nurture issue and in particular considers several arguments against nativist interpretations of research on cognition in infancy. The final paper in this part, by Denis Mareschal, gives a brief account of connectionist modeling which is one of the most recent types of theoretical models that are being applied to infancy research.

ONE

Why Do Infants Do What They Do?

Introduction

Carolyn Rovee-Collier begins this article by pointing out that over the last 40 years we have been accumulating information about *what* infants can do – what they can hear, smell, learn, remember, and so on. It is now time to turn our focus to *why* they do what they do, when they do. The behavior that an infant displays is constrained by its niche in time (associated with age and abilities) and with its current habitat.

Thus, Rovee-Collier describes the infant's different "occupations" over time. The infant begins life as a *Body Builder* (from 0–9 weeks from birth), when its task is to minimize activity in order to convert calories to optimal growth. In order to do this the infant maximizes caloric intake and minimizes caloric expenditure. It is perhaps not surprising that the best evidence of learning in this early period of life is through the experimental manipulation of behaviors that are normally associated with the ingestion of food (sucking and rooting) and those which require minimal energy expenditure (such as looking). High-energy activities, such as foot-kicking, are difficult to train in infants of this age, but are readily trained in older infants. The very young infant, therefore, works to acquire energy and minimize energy loss.

Around 10–24 weeks the infant can be described as an *Inventory Control Officer*. The infant is now liberated from its previous energy-preserving niche and is able to expend large amounts of energy in order to learn about its environment. Infants now pick up huge amounts of information about the world around them, often "with uncanny rapidity," even though there is no specific reinforcement for doing so. One constraint on learning is that it tends to be context-specific – associations learned in one room tend not to be available when the room is changed. Thus, infants who learn to control the movements of a mobile in one place or room, appear not to recognize the mobile when it (and they) are put in a new place.

As soon as infants become able to self-locomote – by crawling, scooting, and walking – they enter the next developmental niche, that of *Map Maker*. The infant is now able to learn spatial relationships and construct cognitive maps. Memories of events that occur in different locations now become associated with each other, and memories are no longer context-specific. An intriguing issue is that of *infantile amnesia*, which refers to the fact that we (as adults) cannot remember the events of early childhood. Rovee-Collier points out that while we cannot remember where and when we first encoded a particular memory in childhood, *"adults actually can and do remember what was experienced early in life* – that is, the *origin* of the memories is lost, but the information is retained.

One of the themes running throughout this paper is that infants are different organisms than adults, and they are perfectly adapted at every point in ontogeny. If we look at infants in relation to their changing occupations we may get a clearer understanding of why they do the things that they do.

Shifting the Focus From What to Why

Carolyn Rovee-Collier

The title of this presentation, "Shifting the Focus From What to Why," summarizes its take-home message: infant researchers have spent 40 years gathering data on What; the time has now come to turn our focus from What infants can do to Why they do it when they do.

First, some background. The Modern Age of Infancy was officially launched in 1958 with the inauguration of a national prospective study, carried on at 16 different sites across the country. The goal of the study was to catalog the various abilities of newborns, who would then be followed until adolescence to determine whether anything measured during infancy predicted any outcomes later on. To meet this goal, researchers had to document exactly *what* infants could do; for example, could they smell? Or hear? Or see? If so, then what could they smell or hear or see? And when could they first do it? The common finding over succeeding generations of researchers was that infants could do a lot and that they could do it quite early on. My own work followed this pattern. Initially, my students and I asked if infants could show operant learning; then, we asked what did they learn and when could they learn it? Finally, we got around to asking the Big Question – *why* did they learn – particularly since they presumably could not remember it anyway? That question launched a new career. Initially, we asked if infants could remember. Then, we asked what infants could remember. Then, we asked when could infants remember what and for how long. Now, we have returned full cycle to the Big Question – *why* do infants remember what they do for the length of time that they do, and *why* do they forget what they do – if they forget at all?

How do we go about answering the Why question? First, we must recognize that infants are not just incomplete adults who get better with age. Rather, infants are different organisms altogether. Second, we must appreciate the evolutionary fact that parents have an enormous economic and genetic investment in an offspring, who typically is a singleton, has already exploited the mother's resources for 9 months by the time of birth, and will remain dependent for its essential resources until adolescence, when the problem shifts to the Society for Adolescent Research. (I note parenthetically that many mammals chase their offspring from the nest when they reach 35 percent of their adult body weight. As the mother of five sons, I have on occasion thought that this was a pretty good idea.) Third, we must recognize that throughout most of human history, the infancy period has occupied about one third of the life span. Some survival advantage must have been incurred by such a long introduction to the rest of the species.

Given these considerations, our Why answer begins with differentiating between a niche and a habitat. Hutchinson (1959) described a *niche* as a species' occupation or profession and a *habitat* as its address. Although the human adult is usually characterized as a generalized social omnivore. the human infant occupies a very different niche – even, perhaps, a *series* of different niches. Figure 1.1 lists the different professions of infants in their first year of life as they appear in the "Dictionary of occupational titles," along with their accompanying job descriptions. The behavior an infant will display at any point in time – including what the infant will learn and remember – is constrained by its niche and current habitat.

Today, I will focus on the infant's first two niches because they encompass the ages on which my research has concentrated. Consider the first one – *Body-Builder*. For approximately the first 9 weeks of life, infants are incapable of physiological regulation and must depend upon behavioral regulation for survival. Adolph (1968) characterized the newborn's regulatory arrangements and their interactions as the major constraint on infant behavior and the environmental conditions that it can tolerate. This is best understood in terms of the *energy budget* (see figure 1.2).

The major problem facing all newborn mammals is to grow, which requires converting as many calories as possible into tissue (Kennedy,

---

The dictionary of occupational titles

Body-Builder
  Job description: Age 0–9 weeks. Part-time work days and nights acquiring energy and minimizing energy expenditure. Variable hours. Persistence required; strong suck and cry desirable. Net energy income will be invested in fueling growth. Around-the clock protection and personal shopper service available.

Inventory Control Officer
  Job description: Age 10–24 weeks. Full-time days/occasional nights maintaining and controlling inventory of people and objects, what goes with what, and what happens where and in what order. Must be adept at soliciting caregiving and social interactions. Regular hours, benefits.

Map Maker, Level I
  Job description: Age 25–40 weeks. Full-time days, weekends; no nights. Regular hours. Acquisition of preliminary cognitive map; some babbling, receptive language skills desired. Beginning-level crawling a must.

Map Maker, Level II
  Job description: Age 41–52 weeks. Full-time days, weekends; no nights. Regular hours. Self-starter. Navigational and receptive language skills required. Must know when who and what are where, and how to get there.

Figure 1.1   The dictionary of occupational titles

The energy budget

Caloric income   Caloric expenditure

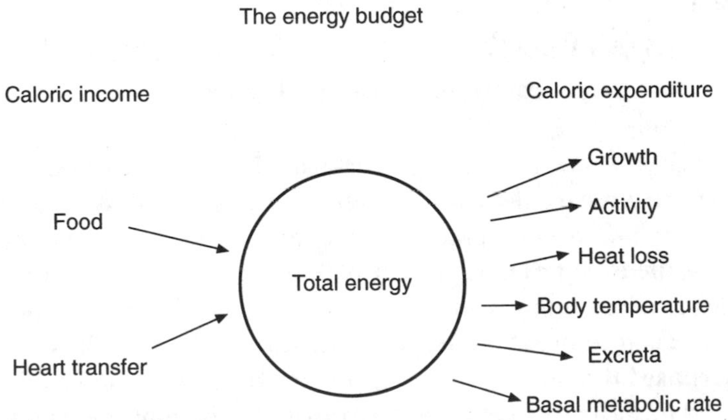

Figure 1.2   The energy budget, showing (*left*) the ways organisms can acquire energy and (*right*) spend it. Expending more energy on one activity requires either spending less energy on others or increasing the total energy income

1967). The optimal solution to this problem is to maximize caloric income and minimize caloric expenditure. As you can see at the left, there are only two ways to gain calories – through ingestion and heat transfer from a warmer body – but, as you can see at the right, there are many ways to spend them. To maximize the number of calories available to spend on growth requires minimizing the number of calories spent elsewhere. Thus, calories can be saved by minimizing activity of all forms, reducing heat loss, maintaining a lower body temperature, lowering the basal metabolic rate, and becoming more feed-efficient. While behaviors such as clinging, rooting, and sucking bear an obvious relation to caloric income, behaviors that reduce caloric expenditure, such as quiescence and postural adjustments that reduce the surface area from which heat is lost, are less obvious. The energy equation predicts that the Body-Builder will learn and remember whatever facilitates growth – either behaviors that increase energy income, shown at the left of the figure, or behaviors that decrease other sources of energy expenditure, shown at the right. However, if the target behavior in a learning experiment competes with behaviors that facilitate growth, then the Body-Builder either will not learn it or will not express it. Either way, the infant will appear to be unable to learn when, in fact, it would be biologically imprudent to do so.

Rule 1. Infants CAN Learn Many Different Relations, and They CAN Learn Them Early On, But What They Actually DO Learn (or Express) Are the Relations That Suit Their Needs

A number of years ago, Marcy Gekoski and I proposed that energy relations constrain early learning (Rovee-Collier and Gekoski, 1979). We argued that low-energy responses that permit exploration and manipulation of the infant's environment without competing with behavioral solutions to the infant's growth and regulatory problems should be learned readily, but high-energy responses should not. Thus, we were not surprised that Solkoff and Cotton (1975) failed to find evidence of learning in terms of increased footkicking in premature infants who were studied in the mobile conjugate reinforcement paradigm 4 to 6 weeks after birth. In contrast, Thoman and Ingersoll (1995) reported that premature infants did learn directional body movements that brought them into contact with a "breathing" Teddy Bear that had been placed in their isolette. In addition to showing an increased amount of contact with the bear, they located it more rapidly over time. Why did premature infants learn this? We can assume that infants would not have learned to find the bear had there been no net benefit for doing so. Thoman et al. (1991) previously reported that the rhythmic stimulation provided by the breathing bear increased the amount of quiet sleep in premies in the weeks following birth. Their finding suggests what one benefit might have been. This is an example, then, of a learned response that reduces energy expenditure.

As predicted by the energy budget, the very young infant also learns behaviors such as orienting, rooting, mouth opening, and sucking that are associated with the identification, procurement, and ingestion of milk (Blass et al., 1984; Lipsitt and Kaye, 1964; Marquis, 1931, 1941; Papousek, 1967). Because newborns cannot know beforehand what specific benefits will result if they exhibit these behaviors, these behaviors are ideal candidates for experimental studies of learning. Thus, Butterfield and Siperstein (1972) found that newborns sucked longer when their sucks were synchronized with music than when the music was synchronized with the pauses between sucks; DeCasper and Fifer (1980) showed that newborns sucked preferentially to hear the voice of their own mother versus that of a strange mother; and Eimas et al. (1971) showed that slightly older infants sucked to produce the speech sounds /p/ and /b/. Because none of the infants in these studies received milk for sucking, why did they learn these relations? Of course, we can observe that sucking is not very costly. The ultimate benefit, however, was originally suggested by Skinner. He wrote, "Any organism which is reinforced by its success in manipulating nature, apart from any deprivation, will be in a favored position when important consequences follow" (Skinner, 1953, p. 78).

There also are more specific benefits. Consider, for example, the DeCasper and Fifer (1980) finding that infants learn to suck selectively to hear their own mother's voice. DeCasper and Prescott (1984) subsequently eliminated postnatal experience as the underlying factor for their preference by exposing newborns postnatally to their father's voice and finding no preference for it. Then, French researchers put a microphone in the pregnant mother's uterus and discovered that it recorded only her speech sounds and not the speech sounds of others within a normal speaking range (Querleu et al., 1988; Versyp, 1985). Meanwhile,

Noirot and Algeria (1983) had reported that hungry breast-fed newborns root in the direction of their mother's voice irrespective of the arm in which they are held, that is, whether they must root to the left or to the right to locate the breast. Therefore, learning the mother's voice *in utero* increases the efficiency with which the newborn localizes a food source.

The facility with which newborns learn appetitive responses is matched only by the difficulty with which they acquire defensive ones. The biological advantage of anticipating an appetitive event is clear – infants can increase the efficiency with which they locate, procure, ingest, and process food. Moreover, newborns have the behavioral capacity to do this. In contrast, newborns are motorically incapable of escaping or avoiding aversive events signaled by cues in the environment. The conditioned eyeblink, a defensive response, is an exception (Little et al., 1984). Instead, the newborn's first line of defense is to cry, alerting a parent, who is biologically invested in providing around-the-clock protection. Not surprisingly, most of the successful examples of aversive conditioning in infants have been obtained after the age of independent locomotion, when the infant is more likely to be at a distance from the protection afforded by the parent. This is reflected, for example, in the timing of the onset of fear of strangers (Kagan, 1979), social referencing (Sorce et al., 1985), and fear of the visual cliff (Bertenthal and Campos, 1990).

In addition, very young infants lack shut-down mechanisms for some response systems, such as the response system associated with ingestion. This should not be viewed as a maturational deficit but as the result of *selection pressures that have favored behavioral persistence* in some response systems critical to the survival of the very young, particularly when the optimal stimulus for responding is present, such as a nipple in the mouth. A baby lamb, for example, will continue to take milk from a bottle even while milk is dribbling out of the sides of its mouth. Likewise, nursing rat pups will not acquire a taste aversion if a flavor in the dam's milk is paired with an injection of LiCl that makes them sick but will continue nursing from the dam (Martin and Alberts, 1979). For preweanlings, however, the dam is the sole source of food, and it would obviously be maladaptive for pups to avoid nursing. However, preweanlings who are made sick while ingesting the flavored milk will display the learned taste aversion later, after they have been weaned, avoiding a solid food that is saturated with the same flavor (Gubernick and

Alberts, 1983). We conclude, then, that nursing rat pups could learn and did learn the relation between a novel flavor and sickness, but they simply could not express this learning until they had other ingestive options.

On the other hand, *selection pressures have also favored behavioral shut-down* in response systems associated with reducing energetic costs, such as the inhibition of distress (Gekoski et al., 1983).

Rule 2. Infants are Perfectly Adapted at Every Point in Ontogeny

Adolph (1968) speculated that over the course of evolution, selection pressures operated most strongly early in development and concluded that infants are perfectly adapted at every point in ontogeny. This is an important point to remember. Just as we consider the adaptive benefit of various kinds of learning, we should also view a learning failure – not as cognitive deficit (in, for example, habituation, aversive conditioning, and discrimination learning) – but in terms of the disadvantage that a particular kind of learning or its expression might confer.

Let me cite one final instance of the Why question vis-à-vis the newborn's niche. In 1972, the Introductory Psychology text I was teaching from proclaimed that "newborns' sense of smell is rudimentary at best." I knew from my own dissertation research years earlier (Rovee, 1969) that newborns' sense of smell is probably better than it ever will be again in their lifetime. But, *why* is their smell so good? Teicher and Blass (1977) showed that when a chemical found in the amniotic fluid is wiped on a mother rat's nipples, as it normally is when she cleans off her newborn pups and then licks her ventrum, the pups use this olfactory information to find her nipples and attach to them. If the mother's nipples are washed first, the pups will never attach to them.

Macfarlane (1975) reported that newborn humans could discriminate the odor of their own mother's breast from the odor of another lactating mother and preferred it. In addition, breast-fed infants exhibited behavioral calming to a breast pad that had been worn by their own mother but not to a breast pad worn by another lactating mother (Schaal et al., 1980). Porter and his colleagues (Porter et al., 1988) asked if bottle-fed infants whose mothers were not lactating could likewise recognize maternal odors. To this end, they simultaneously

presented infants with two gauze pads that had been worn in the underarm area by the mother and an unfamiliar adult. Although breast-
feeding infants oriented preferentially to their mother's underarm pad,
nonbreast-feeders did not. In ancient hunter-gatherer societies, of
course, all infants were breast-fed. Their ability to recognize their own
mother and discriminate her by her odor from others in their extended
family was clearly adaptive. The finding that mothers can also recognize
their own infant's odor – as can other closely related family members –
suggests that olfaction may subserve the more general function of kin
recognition (Porter et al., 1988).

Next, consider the infant's second niche – *Inventory Control Officer*
(see figure 1.1). Marcy Gekoski and I had also proposed that when the
infant's physiological regulations became functional, usually by 9 weeks
of age, the infant would be liberated from the energetic constraints on
its behavior and could acquire energetically more costly responses
(Rovee-Collier and Gekoski, 1979). In fact, infants who occupy this
niche learn a vast amount of information about their environment as
well as how to control significant features of it – including their caregivers. Thus, for example, infants quickly learn to cry when their
wind-up mobile has wound down, apparently so that their mother will
appear rapidly to rewind it – which they usually do. Infants also pick up
information about their environment by visually exploring it. As a
result, they quickly discover that they can produce "interesting specta-
cles" in it.

Thus, Siqueland and DeLucia (1969) reported that 4-month-olds
more than doubled the proportion of their high-amplitude sucks within
4 minutes when they were conjugately reinforced with colored slides
of geometric forms, cartoon figures, and human faces (see figure 1.3),
and we found that 3-month-olds learned with equal rapidity when their
footkicks were conjugately reinforced by the movement of a crib mobile
(see figure 1.4; Rovee and Rovee, 1969). Although 8-week-olds also
learned the mobile task, their kick rate was decidedly lower (Davis and
Rovee-Collier, 1983; Vander Linde et al., 1985).

As Inventory Control Officers, infants must also acquire information
when there is no specific reinforcement contingency for doing so. In two
studies of feature binding, for example, 3-month-olds were trained with
a six-block mobile containing three blocks each of two sets of feature
combinations (Bhatt and Rovee-Collier, 1994, 1996). The two sets of
feature combinations were *black As on red blocks* and *yellow 2s on green*

Figure 1.3   A 1-month-old infant producing conjugate illumination of a visual target by means of high-amplitude sucks (photograph courtesy of E. R. Siqueland)

blocks. These two training combinations are shown on the pair of blocks at the upper left of figure 1.5. Groups were tested with a mobile on which a single feature from one of these two sets was switched with the corresponding feature from the other set, while the two remaining features in each set were unchanged. The test recombinations – a switch in figure color, in figure form, in block color, or a block–color/figure–color reversal – are shown in the right column of figure 1.5.

During testing 1 day later, infants discriminated every recombination except the figure–block chromatic reversal (the recombination that is most apparent to adults), which they discriminated after 1 hour (Bhatt and Rovee-Collier, 1994). After 3 days, they had forgotten which figure color went with which block color but still discriminated which figure form went with which block color; after 4 days, they had forgotten this relation as well. Even after this delay, however, they still recognized the original colors and figure forms they had been trained with, and discriminated if a novel figure color, a novel form, or a novel block color was substituted for one of the original features on the test mobile (Bhatt and Rovee-Collier, 1996). These data reveal that infants learn feature correlations earlier than previously thought. Learning exactly which

Figure 1.4   A 3-month-old infant performing a differentiated response of the
left leg to produce mobile conjugate reinforcement

features go with which others, *even though there is no specific reinforcement for doing so,* is just part of the job of an Inventory Control Officer.

In her dissertation, Boller (1993) showed that infants also pick up
information about correlations in their environment *before* they have
ever learned anything about the significance of this information. In
figure 1.6, the left column shows the typical delayed recognition performance of 6-month-olds who are trained and tested with the same
mobile in the same context; the middle column shows the typical recognition failure of infants who are trained and tested with the same mobile
in a different context; and the far right column shows the test performance of infants who had been simultaneously exposed to two contexts,
Context A and Context B, for 1 hour daily for 7 days. (The context was
defined in terms of the immediate visual surround – a distinctively
colored and patterned cloth that was draped over the sides of the

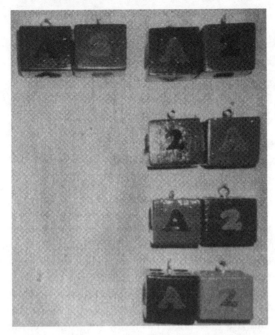

Figure 1.5   The two sets of combinations, shown on the blocks at the left, with which all 3-month-olds were trained. These were a black A on a red block or a yellow 2 on a green block. The test recombinations are shown in the right column. They were a switch in *figure color*, in *figure form*, in *block color*, or a *block–color/figure–color* reversal (from Bhatt and Rovee-Collier, 1994, 1996)

playpen during training.) Later, infants in the latter group learned to kick to move a mobile in one of these contexts (Context A) and then were tested in the context (Context B) that had previously been paired with it. Apparently, when infants had been exposed to the two contexts simultaneously, Context A had been associated with Context B. As a result, the infants were subsequently able to recognize the mobile in a context different from the one in which they were trained (see figure 1.6, right panel). Infants who had been initially familiarized with the two contexts for the same amount of time but separately, at different times of day, did not recognize the mobile in Context B after training in Context A, behaving like infants in the middle column of figure 1.6. This example illustrates the important fact that infants had learned that Context A and

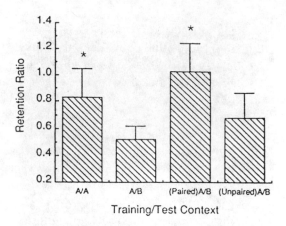

Figure 1.6 Mean retention ratios of four groups of 6-month-olds who were trained in Context A (a distinctly colored-and-patterned playpen liner) and tested in either the same context or a different one. *Groups A/A and A/B* received no preexposure treatment. *Group (Paired) A/B* was simultaneously exposed to Contexts A and B (i.e., paired) for 1 hour/day for 7 days before being trained in A and then tested in B. *Group (Unpaired) A/B* was successively exposed to Contexts A and B a different times a day (i.e., unpaired) for a total of 1 hour/day for 7 days before being trained in A and tested in B. The letters before and after the slash indicate the training and testing contexts, respectively. An asterisk indicates that the group exhibited significant 24-hour retention (*M* baseline ratio significantly > 1.00). Vertical bars indicate ± 1 *SE* (from Boller, 1993, Experiment 1)

Context B went together long before they were given an occasion to *express* this knowledge on a transfer test. Again, this learning occurred in the absence of a specific contingency.

It seems clear that the preceding examples are only the tip of the proverbial iceberg in terms of the kind and amount of information that infants who occupy this niche spontaneously pick up from their environment but are given no opportunity to express. Recent research by Baillargeon and her students (e.g., Baillargeon, 1995; Needham et al., 1997) has revealed more of this information.

Just like 6-month-olds, 3-month-olds also "pick up" information from their environment simply by passively observing it, and they do so with uncanny rapidity. In a series of studies, we found that if infants learned to kick to move a particular mobile and, at some point within the next few days, they were briefly shown a novel mobile or another object in motion, then they would treat that new object as if they had actually been trained with it and would attempt to move it later by kicking (Greco et al., 1990; Rovee-Collier et al., 1994; Rovee-Collier et al., 1993; Rovee-Collier et al., 1993). Note that this also occurred even though infants *were never reinforced* for kicking in its presence and *had never practiced* doing so. If the passively exposed object was not moving when infants saw it, however, then they did not kick when tested with it later. The latter result eliminates stimulus generalization as an account for their subsequent test behavior. Apparently, because the new object *functioned* like an object infants had already learned to control, they did not have to learn how to control it; instead, they simply associated it with the old object in memory. This example also reveals how infants' prior memories are updated and expanded – clearly an adaptive capacity for very young organisms who encounter more things that are novel than are not. I will return to this issue later.

Deferred imitation is another example of learning by passive observation. Here, instead of seeing a novel object display an action that they already know how to produce and do so the next time they see the object, infants see a person display an action on a novel object and imitate it the next time they see the object. Meltzoff and Moore (1994) asked why infants display deferred imitation of an individual who models an action such as sticking out his tongue. Their answer is intriguing. They proposed that infants label the person's social identity in terms of this act. Later, when the infants display deferred imitation, they are asking the modeler, in effect, "Are you the person who sticks out his tongue?" Deferred imitation is just another of the many activities of an Inventory Control Officer.

Inventory Control Officers must also keep track of temporal-order information, or What happens When, and place information, or What happens Where. They do both. In the case of temporal-order information, 6-month-olds who were trained with a list of three mobiles for 2 minutes each on 3 days displayed a classic primacy effect (see figure 1.7, left panel) when tested on the fourth day with a single mobile from either the first, second, or third serial position (Merriman et al., 1997). When the length of the list was increased to five mobiles, infants recognized all of the mobiles on the list and discriminated a novel test mobile, but they no longer displayed a serial position effect. Apparently, they had learned item information but not order information when the list was

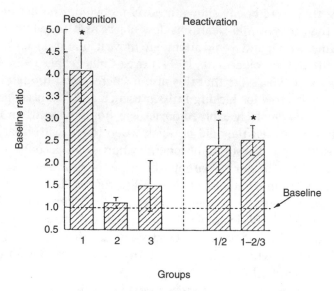

Figure 1.7 *Left panel*: Six-month-olds displaying a classic primacy effect in a 24-hour recognition test with mobiles from serial positions 1, 2, and 3 on a training list. *Right panel*: Facilitated 24-hour recognition of mobiles from serial positions 2 and 3 immediately following priming by the mobile(s) preceding the test mobile on the training list. Asterisks indicate significant retention (*M* baseline ratio significantly > 1.00); vertical bars indicate ± 1 *SE* (from Gulya and Rovee-Collier, 1996)

longer. As a direct test of whether infants in the original study had learned the serial order of the three-mobile list, new groups were again trained with a three-mobile list and were tested with the mobile from serial position 2 or 3, but this time they were primed immediately before the recognition test with the mobile from the immediately preceding serial position. Excerpts of these data are shown in the right panel of figure 1.7. Infants recognized the mobile from serial position 2 if they were primed with the mobile from serial position 1 but not if they were primed with the mobile from serial position 3. Infants tested with the mobile from serial position 3 recognized it only if they were successively primed with the mobile from serial position 1 and then with the mobile from serial position 2 (Gulya and Rovee-Collier, 1996).

In the case of place information, even 3-month-olds know when they are in the crib or in the place where they had played the mobile game (Hayne et al., 1991). Undoubtedly, they know other place information as well, such as the changing table, the feeding chair, and other significant places associated with specific kinds of activities. We know this because if infants learn to move the mobile or a miniature train in one place and then the location is changed at the time of testing, then they do not recognize the mobile or the train in the new place – even though they readily recognize it in the old one. That is, infants do not recognize a familiar object "out of context." In one study, 3-month-olds were trained in a portacrib in their bedrooms, allowed to forget the task, and then were reminded in the kitchen – a familiar room but not where they were trained (Hayne et al., 1991). Even though the portacrib was draped with a distinctively colored and patterned cloth liner during both training and reminding, the reactivation treatment failed to recover the memory in the different room. Apparently, differences in the remote place cues that were visible above the portacrib precluded memory reactiviation.

We obtained the same result at 6 months when infants learned a train task in one room and were later reminded with the same train in a different room in their house (Hartshorn and Rovee-Collier, 1997). The reminder did not work there, although it did in the original room. Even if they had been reminded in the original room, however, infants who were tested in a different room the next day failed to recognize the original train (see figure 1.8, far right column). In contrast, their retention was excellent if they were tested the next day in the same room (figure 1.8, second column from left).

Although the retrieval context constrains early memory, once infants are able to self-locomote, either by crawling or scooting about in a walker, their definition of context seems to change. Before this time, they know what happens in what place, but they do not know how to get there, Once they can get there without being carried, however, they acquire spatial relations along with their new navigational skills and begin to construct a congnitive map. This behavior characterizes infants' next niches – *Map Maker, Levels I and II* (see figure 1.1). As shown in figure 1.9, a Level-I Map Maker learns to *fill in the arrows between the places it had previously learned about*. This is particularly important because *once these different places become related to each other, the memories of events that transpired in those places also become associated with each other*.

For infants who occupy these niches, changing the room where they learned the train task no longer impairs retention. This is true both at

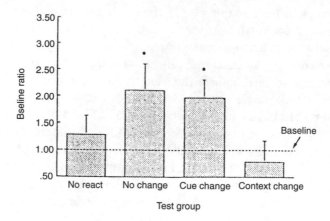

Figure 1.8 The memory performance of 6-month-olds 1 day after successful reactivation treatment (3 weeks after the end of training) showing that recognition was impaired when the place where infants were trained was changed at the time of testing. *Group No change* was tested with the original cue (a miniature train set) in the original context (a room in the infant's house); *group Cue change* was tested with a different cue in the original context; *group Context change* was tested with the original cue in a different context; and *group No react* (a forgetting control) was tested without having received the reactivation treatment 1 day earlier. Asterisks indicate significant retention (*M* baseline ratio significantly > 1.00); vertical bars indicate ± 1 *SE* (from Hartshorn and Rovee-Collier, 1997)

9 and 12 months (Aaron et al., 1994). Similarly, 14-month-olds who saw actions modeled in either the laboratory or the day-care center readily produced those actions a few days later when they were tested at home (Hanna and Meltzoff, 1993). Obviously, infants in the latter study had not learned to drive themselves from home to the day-care center by this age, but they had clearly acquired a memory link between "here" and "there."

Rule 3. Infant Learning and Memory is a Problem of Economics, Not Capacity

The preceding data suggest that what infants learn and remember is a problem of economics, not cognitive capacity. First, consider capacity.

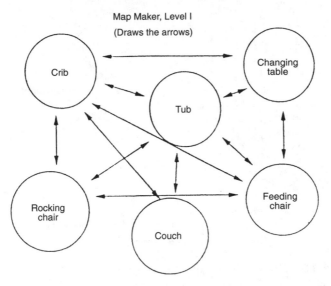

Figure 1.9 Once an infant begins to locomote, the infant becomes a Map Maker, Level I (see figure 1.1). Infants who occupy this niche learn the spatial relations or links (i.e. they draw the arrows) between the places they had previously learned about. Once these places are linked or associated, so too are the memories of events that transpired in them. The result is an apparent cognitive leap because a memory that was encoded in one place can now be indirectly activated or brought to mind by directly activating another memory that was encoded in a different place

Figure 1.10 shows that the maximum duration of retention of infants trained and tested in a standardized procedure with standardized parameters increases monotonically over the first year of life. These data were collected from 2- to 6-month-olds trained for 2 days in the mobile conjugate reinforcement paradigm (Rovee and Rovee, 1969; Sullivan et al.) and from 6- to 18-month-olds trained for 2 days in a new task (Hartshorn and Rovee-Collier, 1997) that we developed for infants too old for the mobile task. In this new task, each lever press briefly moves a miniature train around a circular track within a fairly complex stimulus display.

There are several important points to notice in figure 1.10. First, at 6 months of age, infants' memory performance in the two tasks is identical (Hartshorn and Rovee-Collier, 1997). Second, there is no indication that memory changes abruptly in the last part of the first year,

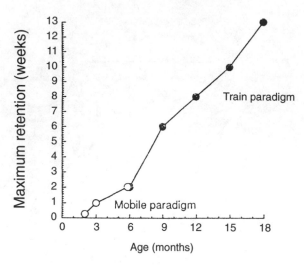

Figure 1.10   The maximum duration (in weeks) of retention exhibited by infants over the first 18 months of life. Infants were trained under standardized conditions with task parameters calibrated to yield equivalent immediate retention; independent groups were tested in increments of 1 week until they exhibited a baseline level of performance for 2 consecutive weeks. Two-, 3-, and 6-month-olds were trained and tested in mobile conjugate reinforcement paradigm (*open circles*); 6-, 9-, 12-, 15-, and 18-month-olds were trained and tested in a miniature-train paradigm (*filled circles*). Long-term retention at 6 months was identical irrespective of task (from Hartshorn and Rovee-Collier, 1997)

when a qualitatively different memory system has been hypothesized to emerge (Kagan and Hamburg, 1981; C. A. Nelson, 1995; Schacter and Moscovitch, 1984). Third, there is no indication that memory changes qualitatively with the appearance of language (K. Nelson, 1989). In addition, the degree of brain maturation is *not* the rate-limiting step in infant memory. Although this figure shows that 2-month-olds remember for only 2 days, they will remember for 2 weeks – just like 6-month-olds – if their same total training time is distributed into three 6-minute sessions instead of the standard two 9-minute sessions, shown here. Likewise, 3-month-olds typically remember for approximately 1 week; yet, they will remember for at least 6 weeks – just like 9-month-olds – if they are simply exposed to a brief reminder on two different occasions (Hayne, 1990). The standardized retention function shown here is not

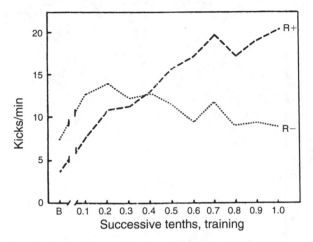

Figure 1.11 Mean kick rates reinforced (R+) and nonreinforced (R–) feet during baseline (B) and over successive tenths of training (vincentized scores) of 3-month-olds (from Rovee-Collier et al., 1978, Experiment 2)

unique to my particular paradigm. Similar durations of retention have been reported with paradigms that are vastly different, including the deferred imitation paradigm (e.g., Bauer and Shore, 1987) and the reenactment paradigm (Hudson, 1994; Sheffield and Hudson, 1994).

So much for capacity. Next, consider economics. As we saw earlier, infants learn what pays off. If the cost of learning exceeds the benefit of doing so, then they will not learn it. If the benefit exceeds the cost, they will. Thus, new-borns will not learn to kick to move a mobile, but they will learn to suck at a high rate to turn on a recording of their mother's voice. Even after they have been behaviorally liberated from energetic constraints, however, infants will continue to behave economically. For example, 3-month-olds initially learn to move the mobile by kicking both feet. After playing the game for 30 minutes or so, however, they begin to kick the foot without the ankle ribbon less often, even though there is no specific contingency for doing so – the mobile will move whether one or both feet move, as long as the foot with the ankle ribbon moves (see figure 1.11).

We were surprised when we first noticed this response differentiation because infants were thought to be bilateral at this age. Yet, like college undergraduates, infants expend the minimum amount of effort

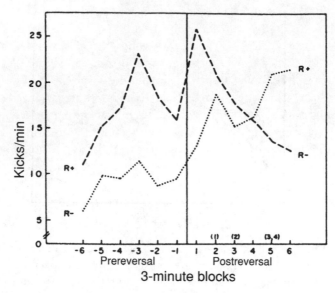

Figure 1.12 Mean kick rates of reinforced (R+) and nonreinforced (R–) feet over successive 3-min blocks preceding and following a switch of the mobile to the second (previously empty) mobile stand. Both legs were connected by an ankle ribbon to an overhead mobile stand, but the mobile was hung from only one of them. Data from the 4 infants (of 5) who successfully mastered the reversal are shown; the numbers in parentheses indicate the successive blocks at which each infant first exhibited the reversal behaviorally (from Rovee-Collier et al., 1978, Experiment 2)

necessary to produce a desired outcome. In the preceding case, they reduced their energy cost by decreasing the activity of the second leg. Morrongiello subsequently demonstrated that when control of the mobile was shifted to the other foot, its kick frequency increased, and kicks of the original foot decreased (see figure 1.12). Moreover, infants learned this reversal more rapidly than the original response differentiation, again in the absence of an experimenter-imposed contingency (Rovee-Collier et al., 1978). Thus, what young infants will and will not learn is determined by the economics of learning it.

I began this presentation by asking the Why question: *why* do infants remember what they do for the length of time that they do, and *why* do they forget what they do? This leads to a consideration of *infantile amnesia*. Little more than a decade ago, scientists thought that infants' memories were highly transient, and infantile amnesia was attributed to this (Moscovitch, 1984). When researchers found that infants could encode, store, and retrieve information after relatively long periods of time, however, it became patently clear that the earlier account of infantile amnesia was wrong. Many of us then attempted to account for infantile amnesia by appealing to changes in context between encoding and retrieval, a developmental shift from visual to linguistic encoding, changes in the brain mechanisms thought to be responsible for long-term memory, and so forth. None of these attempts has proven satisfactory.

Over time, I have come to view the question of infantile amnesia, "Why do adults not remember events from early childhood – before the age of 3 or 4?" as being much like the question, "Have you stopped beating your wife lately?" That is, *the basic premise of the question is wrong*. I propose that *adults actually can and do remember what was experienced early in life*, particularly if they have periodically re-experienced it in the meantime. Moreover, I think that adults use much of this long-maintained information on a regular basis.

One reason adults think that they cannot remember their early memories is that they have lost access to the particular memory attributes that represent when and where they first encoded a particular memory; as a result, they cannot pinpoint the *origin* of these memories. This does not mean, however, that the memories did not originate early on. In fact, our research has shown that the memory attributes which represent place information are quite fragile: they are "washed out" if the memory is retrieved in a variety of different contexts (Amabile and Rovee-Collier, 1991; Rovee-Collier and DuFault, 1991). They are also "washed out" even if the memory is repeatedly retrieved in the original context, if the retention intervals are long enough. Hitchcock, for example, found that a memory which was forgotten, reactivated in the original context, and then forgotten again was already context-free by the second time it was reactivated (Hitchcock and Rovee-Collier, 1996).

The second reason adults may fail to identify a memory as having originated early in life is that its *content* has probably been updated – perhaps many times – to reflect more recent circumstances. This reason is addressed in detail below.

Rule 4. There is a Logical Relation Between Learning and Memory

Twenty years ago, Bob Bolles (1976) wrote that there is a logical relation between learning and memory: were it not for learning, members
of the animal kingdom would have nothing to remember; and were it
not for memory, they would never be able to learn in the first place. As
the infant's niche changes, what the infant learns also changes. From
this, it follows that the infant's memories must change as well. this
occurs, for example, when the behavior that is appropriate in a given situation at one age becomes inappropriate at another. However, the infant
need not relearn everything anew. It is, in fact, much more economical
to simply update a prior memory than to acquire a completely new one.
And, such updating is more likely to occur more often when organisms
are young and in periods of rapid change than when they are older.

   Updating memories to reflect changing circumstances does not mean
the loss of the original memory. We have found that the updating
process can either *replace* one of the original memory attributes or supplement them (Boller et al., 1995; Boller and Rovee-Collier, 1992, 1994;
Boller et al., 1996; Muzzio and Rovee-Collier, 1996; Rovee-Collier et al.,
1994; Rovee-Collier et al., 1993; Rovee-Collier et al., 1993). Which of
these occurs depends on the age of the infant, whether the new information is central or peripheral to the original event, and the interval
between encoding and updating. Not surprisingly, the shorter the interval, the more likely is the new information to supplement the old; the
longer the interval, the more likely is the new information to replace
the old.

Rule 5. A Rose By Any Other Name is Still a Rose

Even if a memory that originated in infancy or early childhood has
undergone so many transformations that it is no longer recognized as
such, it is still the same early memory. An analogous scenario is played
out as an infant is transformed into a child or young adult – slight
changes in the infant from one day or week to the next are not notice-
able, but if a person has not seen the child for awhile, the change is quite
obvious – in fact, the person may not recognize the child at all! Yet, the
child is the very same individual who once was the infant. In short, *those*

seeking to explain infantile amnesia are trying to explain a phenomenon that does not exist.

> "It's a poor sort of memory that only works backwards," the Queen remarked.
> (Lewis Carroll: *Alice's Adventures in Wonderland and Through the Looking Glass*)

The function of memory is reflected in this remark made by the Queen of Hearts to Alice. The Queen was describing the advantages of having a memory that works both ways – in the future as well as in the past. In fact, as records of our past experiences, our memories function as the data base that informs our present and future behavior (see also Bruner, 1964). Today, I have argued that the time has come to move beyond the search for *mechanism* and consider the *function* of infant behavior. I have also argued that answers to the Why question will ultimately rest on an evolutionarily based understanding of the infant's ecological niche. Although I have focused on early learning and memory, this is only one small piece of the puzzle.

Currently, the field of infancy is fractionated into highly specialized areas such as face recognition, attachment, play, symbolic development, sensory and motor development, categorization, imitation, spatial learning, object search, perceptual development, language development, emotional development, social development, and so forth. Each of these areas is an important piece of the puzzle and was originally obtained by asking the What question. The Big Picture of this puzzle, however, will emerge only when *all* of its pieces are fit together. As researchers in these areas of specialization and others, we have now arrived at a point in our science where each of us can begin to ask the Why question and contemplate how our own, separate pieces might fit into the puzzle to yield the Big Picture. In this way, we can begin to achieve an understanding of infant behavior and development that is broader, richer, and more integrated – as well as a greater sense of community – than the current situation permits.

Shifting the focus from What to Why should not be taken to mean that we should stop asking What. In fact, asking the Why question will lead to many new What questions that we had not before thought to ask. Also, although some of our initial Why answers may turn out to be less than satisfactory, we still must see how the pieces fit together so that we can determine what pieces we are still missing. In the process, the

The Far Side   By Gary Larson

"Fuel ... check. Lights ... check. Oil pressure...
check. We've got clearance. Ok, Jack – let's get
this baby off the ground."

Figure 1.13   The Far Side © 1985 far Works Inc./Dist. by Universal Press
Syndicate. Reprinted with permission. All rights reserved

notions that we entertain and the hypotheses that they generate can
open entirely new avenues of inquiry. In short . . . *it's time to get this baby
off the ground and see if it flies.*

References

Aaron, F., Hartshorn, K., Klein, P., & Rovee-Collier, C. (1994, November). *Developmental changes in the specificity of memory retrieval cues.* Paper presented at
the meeting of the International Society for Developmental Psychobiology,
Islamorada, FL.

Adolph, E. F. (1968). *Origins of physiological regulations*. New York: Academic.

Amabile, T. A., & Rovee-Collier, C. (1991). Contextual variation and memory retrieval at six months. *Child Development, 62,* 1155–1166.

Baillargeon, R. (1995). A model of physical reasoning in infancy. In C. Rovee-Collier & L. P. Lipsitt (Eds.), *Advances in infancy research* (Vol. 9, pp. 305–371). Norwood, NJ: Ablex.

Bauer, P. J., & Shore, C. M. (1987). Making a memorable event: Effects of familiarity and organization in young children's recall of action sequences. *Cognitive Development, 2,* 327–338.

Bertenthal, B. I., & Campos, J. J. (1990). A systems approach to the organizing effects of self-produced locomotion during infancy. In C. Rovee-Collier & L. P. Lipsitt (Eds.), *Advances in infancy research* (Vol. 6, pp. 1–60). Norwood, NJ: Ablex.

Bhatt, R. S., & Rovee-Collier, C. (1994). Perception and 24-hour retention of feature relations in infancy. *Developmental Psychology, 30,* 142–150.

Bhatt, R. S., & Rovee-Collier, C. (1996). Infants' forgetting of correlated attributes and object recognition. *Child Development, 67,* 172–187.

Blass, E. M., Ganchrow, J. R., & Steiner, J. E. (1984). Classical conditioning in newborn humans 2–48 hours of age. *Infant Behavior and Development, 7,* 223–235.

Boller, K. (1993). *Preexposure effects on memory in 6-month-olds.* Unpublished doctoral dissertation, Rutgers University, New Brunswick, NJ.

Boller, K., Grabelle, M., & Rovee-Collier, C. (1995). Effects of postevent information on infants' memory for a central target. *Journal of Experimental Child Psychology, 59,* 372–396.

Boller, K., & Rovee-Collier, C. (1992). Contextual coding and recoding of infant memory. *Journal of Experimental Child Psychology, 52,* 1–23.

Boller, K., & Rovee-Collier, C. (1994). Contextual updating of infants' reactivated memories. *Developmental Psychobiology, 27,* 241–256.

Boller, K., Rovee-Collier C., Gulya, M., & Prete, K. (1996). Infants' memory for context: Timing effects of postevent information. *Journal of Experimental Child Psychology.*

Bolles, R. C. (1976). Some relationships between learning and memory. In D. L. Medin, W. A. Roberts, & R. T. Davis (Eds.), *Processes of animal memory* (pp. 21–48). Hillsdale, NJ: Erlbaum.

Bruner, J. (1964). The course of cognitive growth. *American Psychologist, 19,* 1–15.

Butterfield, E. C., & Siperstein, G. N. (1972). Influence of contingent auditory stimulation upon non-nutritional suckle. In J. Bosma (Ed.), *Third symposium on oral sensation and perception: The mouth of the infant* (pp. 313–334). Springfield, IL: C. C. Thomas.

Carroll, L. (1989). *Alice's adventures in Wonderland and through the looking glass* (Rev. ed). Chicago: Wellington Publishing.

Davis, J., & Rovee-Collier, C. (1983). Alleviated forgetting of a learned contingency in 8-week-old infants. *Developmental Psychology, 19*, 353–365.

DeCasper, A. J., & Fifer, W. P. (1980). Of human bonding: Newborns prefer their mothers' voices. *Science, 208*, 1174–1175.

DeCasper, A. J., & Prescott, P. A. (1984). Human newborns' perception of male voices: Preference, discrimination, and reinforcing value. *Developmental Psychobiology, 17*, 481–491.

Eimas, P. D., Siqueland, E., Jusczyk, P., & Vigorito, J. (1971). Speech perception in infants. *Science, 171*, 303–306.

Gekoski, M. J., Rovee-Collier, C. K., & Carulli-Rabinowitz, V. (1983). A longitudinal analysis of inhibition of infant distress: The origins of social expectations? *Infant Behavior and Development, 6*, 339–351.

Greco, C., Hayne, H., & Rovee-Collier, C. (1990). The roles of function, reminding, and variability in categorization by 3-month-old infants. *Journal of Experimental Psychology: Learning, Memory, and Cognition, 16*, 617–633.

Gubernick, D. J., & Alberts J. R. (1983). A specialization of taste aversion learning during suckling and its weaning-associated transformation. *Developmental Psychobiology, 17*, 613–628.

Gulya, M., & Rovee-Collier, C. (1996, April). *Memory for serial order at 6 months of age*. Paper presented at the International Conference on Infant Studies, Providence, RI.

Hanna, E., & Meltzoff, A. N. (1993). Peer imitation by toddlers in laboratory, home and day-care contexts: Implications for social learning and memory. *Developmental Psychology, 29*, 701–710.

Hartshorn, K., & Rovee-Collier, C. (1997). Infant learning and long-term memory at 6 months: A confirming analysis. *Developmental Psychobiology*.

Hayne, H. (1990). The effect of multiple reminders on long-term retention in human infants. *Developmental Psychobiology, 23*, 453–477.

Hayne, H., Rovee-Collier, C., & Borza, M. (1991). Infant memory for place information. *Memory and Cognition, 19*, 378–386.

Hitchcock, D. F. A., & Rovee-Collier, C. (1996). The effect of repeated reactivations on memory specificity in infants. *Journal of Experimental Child Psychology, 62*, 378–400.

Hudson, J. (1994, August). *Reinstatement off toddlers' event memory: A matter of timing*. Paper presented at the Practical Aspects of Memory Conference, College Park, MD.

Hutchinson, G. F. (1959). Homage to Santa Rosalia or why there are so many kinds of animals. *The American Naturalist, 93*, 145–149.

Kagan, J. (1979). Growing by leaps: The form of early cognitive development. *The Sciences, 19*, 8–12, 39.

Kagan, J., & Hamburg, M. (1981). The enhancement of memory in the first year. *Journal of Genetic Psychology, 138,* 3–14.

Kennedy, G. C. (1967). Ontogeny of mechanisms controlling food and water intake. In C. F. Code (Ed.), *Handbook of physiology (Section 6). Alimentary canal: Control of food and water intake* (Vol. 1, pp. 337–351). Washington, DC: American Physiological Society.

Lipsitt, L. P., & Kaye, H. (1964). Conditioned sucking in the human newborn. *Psychonomic Science, 1,* 29–30.

Little, A. H., Lipsitt, L. P., & Rovee-Collier, C. K. (1984). Classical conditioning and retention of the infant's eyelid response: Effects of age and interstimulus interval. *Journal of Experimental Child Psychology, 37,* 512–524.

Macfarlane, A. (1975). Olfaction in the development of social preferences in the human neonate. In *Parent–infant interaction* (Ciba Foundation Symposium, 33, pp. 103–113). New York: Elsevier.

Marquis, D. P. (1931). Can conditioned responses be established in the newborn infant? *Journal of Genetic Psychology, 39,* 479–492.

Marquis, D. P. (1941). Learning in the neonate: The modification of behavior under three feeding schedules. *Journal of Experimental Psychology, 29,* 263–282.

Martin, L. T., & Alberts, J. R. (1979). Taste aversions to mother's milk: The age-related role of nursing in acquisition and expression of a learned association. *Journal of Comparative and Physiological Psychology,* 93, 430–445.

Meltzoff, A. N. & Moore, M. K. (1994). Imitation, memory, and the representation of persons. *Infant Behavior and Development, 17,* 83–89.

Merriman, J., Rovee-Collier, C., & Wilk, A. (1997). Developmental changes in within-session categorization. *Infant Behavior and Development.*

Moscovitch, M. M. (Ed.). (1984). *Advances in the study of communication and affect; Vol. 9. Infant memory.* New York: Plenum.

Muzzio, I. A., & Rovee-Collier, C. (1996). Timing effects of postevent information on infant memory. *Journal of Experimental Child Psychology, 63,* 212–238.

Needham, A., Baillargeon, R., & Kaufman, L. (1997). Object segregation in infancy. In C. Rovee-Collier & L. P. Lipsitt (Eds.), *Advances in infancy research* (Vol. 11). Norwood, NJ: Ablex.

Nelson, C. A. (1995). The ontogeny of human memory: A cognitive neuroscience perspective. *Developmental Psychology, 31,* 723–738.

Nelson, K. (1989). Remembering: A functional developmental perspective. In P. R. Solomon, G. R. Goethals, C. M. Kelley, & R. B. Stephens (Eds.), *Perspectives on memory* (pp. 127–150). New York: Springer-Verlag.

Noirot, E., & Algeria, J. (1983). Neonate orientation towards human voice differs with type of feeding. *Behavioral Processes, 8,* 65–71.

Papousek, H. (1967). Experimental studies of appetitional behavior in human newborns and infants. In H. W. Stevenson, E. H. Hess, & H. L. Rheingold (Eds.), *Early behavior: Comparative and developmental approaches* (pp. 249–277). New York: Wiley.

Porter, R. H. Balogh, R. D., & Makin, J. W. (1988). Olfactory influences on mother-infant interactions. In C. Rovee-Collier & L. P. Lipsitt (Eds.). *Advances in infancy research* (Vol. 5, pp. 39–68). Norwood, NJ: Ablex.

Querleu, D., Renard, X., Versyp, F., Paris-Delrue, L., & Crespin, G. (1988). Fetal hearing. *European Journal of Obstetrics and Gynecology and Reproductive Biology, 29,* 191–212.

Rovee, C. K. (1969). Psychophysical scaling of olfactory response to the aliphatic alcohols in human neonates. *Journal of Experimental Child Psychology, 7,* 245–254.

Rovee, C. K., & Rovee, D. T. (1969). Conjugate reinforcement of infant exploratory behavior. *Journal of Experimental Child Psychology, 8,* 33–39.

Rovee-Collier, C., Adler, S. A., & Borza, M. A. (1994). Substituting new details for old? Effects of delaying postevent information on infant memory. *Memory and Cognition, 22,* 644–656.

Rovee-Collier, C., Borza, M. A., Adler, S. A., & Boller, K. (1993). Infants' eyewitness testimony: Effects of postevent information on a prior memory representation. *Memory and Cognition, 21,* 267–279.

Rovee-Collier, C., & DuFault, D. (1991). Multiple contexts and memory retrieval at 3 months. *Developmental Psychobiology, 24,* 39–49.

Rovee-Collier, C., & Gekoski, M. J. (1979). The economics of infancy: A review of conjugate reinforcement. In H. W. Reese & L. P. Lipsitt (Eds.), *Advances in child development and behavior* (Vol. 13, pp. 195–255). New York: Academic.

Rovee-Collier, C., Greco-Vigorito, C., & Hayne, H. (1993). The time window hypothesis: Implications for categorization and memory modification. *Infant Behavior and Development, 16,* ʾ49–176.

Rovee-Collier, C., Morrongiello, B. A., Aron M., & Kupersmidt, J. (1978). Topograhical response differentiation in three-month-old infants. *Infant Behavior and Development, 1,* 323–333.

Schaal, B., Montagner, H., Hertling, E., Bolzoni, D., Moyse, A., & Quichon, R. (1980). Les stimulations olfactives dans les relations entre l'enfant el la mere. *Reproduction, Nutrition, et Development, 20,* 843–858.

Schacter, D. L., & Moscovitch, M. (1984). Infants, amnesics, and dissociable memory systems. In M. Moscovitch (Ed.), *Advances in the study of communication and affect; Vol. 9. Infant memory* (pp. 173–216). New York: Plenum.

Sheffield, E. G., & Hudson, J. A. (1994). Deactivation of toddlers' event memory. *Memory, 2,* 447–465.

Siqueland, E. R., & DeLucia, C. A. (1969). Visual reinforcement of nonnutritive sucking in human infants. *Science, 165,* 1144–1146.

Skinner, B. F. (1953). *Science and human behavior.* New York: Macmillan.

Solkoff, N., & Cotton, C. (1975). Contingency awareness in premature infants. *Perceptual and Motor Skills, 41,* 709–710.

Sorce, J., Emde, R., Campos, J., & Klinnert, M. (1985). Maternal emotional signaling: Its effect on the visual cliff behavior of 1-year-olds. *Developmental Psychology, 21,* 195–200.

Sullivan, M. W., Rovee-Collier, C., & Tynes D. M. (1979). A conditioning analysis of infant long-term memory. *Child Development, 50,* 152–162.

Teicher, M. H., & Blass, E. M. (1977). First suckling response of the newborn albino rat: The roles of olfaction and amniotic fluid. *Science, 198,* 635–636.

Thoman, E. B., & Ingersoll, E. W. (1995). Learning in pre-mature infants. *Developmental Psychology, 29,* 692–700.

Thoman, E. B., Ingersoll, E. W., & Acebo, C. (1991). Premature infants seek rhythmic stimulation, and the experience facilitates neurobehavioral development. *Journal of Developmental and Behavioral Pediatrics, 12,* 11–18.

Vander Linde, E., Morrongiello, B. A., & Rovee-Collier, C. K. (1985). Determinants of retention in 8-week-old infants. *Developmental Psychology, 21,* 601–613.

Versyp, F. (1985). *Transmission intra-amniotique des sons et des voix humaines.* Theses pour le Doctorat en Medecine, Lille, France.

TWO

The Origins of Knowledge: Nature versus Nurture

Introduction

Questions about the origins of knowledge have "been central to a dialogue that has spanned more than 2000 years of intellectual history." Nativist and empiricist views are at the extremes of this dialogue, the former asserting that much knowledge, or knowledge structures, is innately provided and guides subsequent learning, the latter asserting that knowledge is acquired as a result of experience.

In this article Elizabeth Spelke considers the nativism/empiricism debate in the context of studies of infant cognition, and considers several arguments against nativist interpretations of research on cognition in infancy. This paper was originally presented in a debate at the meeting of the Society for Research in Child Development, Washington, DC, April 1997, and stands in opposition to the views put forward in the same meeting by Marshall Haith. The reader who wishes to gain a wider perspective on the debate is advised to read Haith's (1998) article.

Reference

Haith, M. M. (1998). Who put the cog in infant cognition? Is rich interpretation too costly? *Infant Behavior and Development, 21,* 167–179.

Nativism, Empiricism, and the Origins of Knowledge

Elizabeth S. Spelke

What aspects of knowledge emerge in children prior to their first contacts with the objects of their knowledge, and what aspects emerge through the shaping effects of experience with those objects? What aspects of knowledge are constant over human development from the moment that infants begin to make sense of the world, and what aspects change as children grow and learn? What aspects of knowledge are universal, and what aspects vary across people in different cultures or with different educational backgrounds? Finally, what aspects of knowledge can people change in themselves or their children with sufficient insight or effort, and what aspects are invariant?

These questions are central to a dialogue that has spanned more than 2000 years of intellectual history. Contributors to the dialogue have raised the questions in order to shed light on larger concerns about human nature, child development, education, science, and society. Although contributors have tended to be labeled "nativists" or "empiricists" according to the kinds of answers they thought most plausible, most have viewed these questions as empirical matters to be resolved not by ideology but by studies of the origins and development of knowledge. Research on cognition in infancy remained a dormant enterprise throughout most of the history of the nativist-empiricist dialogue, however, because the tools then used to probe human knowledge were not appropriate for young children.

Today, the study of early cognitive development has overcome this longstanding barrier to progress. A number of tools have been developed over this century for investigating human cognitive states and processes, and some of these tools have been adapted for studies of preverbal children. New tools of enormous promise are appearing, moreover, with the rapid development of cognitive neuroscience. For the first time, these tools allow developmental scientists to use studies of infancy to shed light on the central questions of the nativist-empiricist dialogue.

As ancient obstacles have been overcome, however, new obstacles have arisen. Countering the advance of research are intellectual attitudes that impede studies of cognition in infancy and undermine the larger questions those studies address. Investigations of infant cognition are sometimes dismissed on the grounds that young infants are known *a priori* to be incapable of true knowledge or cognitive processes, and investigators are sometimes handicapped by demands that no empirical enterprise can meet. The questions of the nativist-empiricist dialogue have lost much of their allure, moreover, because of widespread arguments that claims for innate knowledge are incoherent, false, or dangerous to society.

In this article, I argue that our intellectual ancestors were right to ask the questions of the nativist-empiricist dialogue, and that developmental scientists should address these questions vigorously through research on early cognitive development. My defense of the dialogue is divided into three parts. First, I discuss one example of research on cognition in infancy – studies of object representation – in hopes of showing how this research is advancing understanding of the origins and development of knowledge. [Because of space limitations it is not possible to reproduce here Professor Spelke's account of object representation. The interested reader is directed to the original article for her account of this important area of infancy research. Second, I consider some contemporary critiques of this research.] Arguing that the criticisms are based on skewed interpretations and impossible standards, I suggest a different set of standards against which all research on early cognitive development could productively be evaluated. Third, I consider some popular, contemporary arguments against the nativist-empiricist dialogue, focusing in particular on arguments against any claim that knowledge can emerge through intrinsic growth processes, without prior shaping by encounters with the objects of knowledge. I conclude that the arguments are mistaken and that the concerns that motivated them instead should lead developmental scientists to embrace the dialogue and pursue research on the origins of knowledge.

Challenges to the Study of Cognition in Infancy

Like all empirical research, studies of cognition in infancy can thrive only in an environment in which investigators are open to any discoveries their research might yield, including evidence for knowledge in the mind that did not arise through the shaping effects of sensory contact with the things that are known. A number of students of development are persuaded, however, that such openness is inappropriate, and that the field should reject either the questions at the center of the nativist-empiricist dialogue or any answer to those questions short of extreme empiricism. When minds are closed, research can only suffer. Here, I consider a family of skeptical attitudes to research on infant cognition, first discussing skeptical reactions to specific research findings and then discussing the prevalent attitude of wariness toward nativist claims.

Standards for research on cognition in infancy

Anyone who has conducted research on perception or cognition in infants has likely encountered colleagues, science writers, and others who have expressed disbelief at his or her findings. Evidence for perceptual and cognitive capacities in infants strains the beliefs of many people because it conflicts with prevalent conceptions about infants and intuitions about cognitive development. Haith (1997) states this conflict clearly and casts his lot on the side of intuition, criticizing students of infant cognition for "asserting that young infants know things about objects, events and people far earlier than seems reasonable."

When data conflict with intuition, however, intuition is rarely the best guide for advancing understanding. Intuition has proved to be an especially poor guide to understanding human perception and cognition. Cognitive psychologists and cognitive neuroscientists have repeatedly made discoveries that either violated prevailing intuitions or that intuition never would have contemplated: recent examples include the evidence for implicit memory, for multiple representations of objects, and for separate visual coding of surface color and motion. If human intuitions are not a trustworthy source of knowledge about the cognitive processes of adults, they are hardly likely to be more trustworthy guides to knowledge about cognition in infants. The intuitions and preconceptions of scientists can never be eliminated from science, but they should not be used to filter the evidence that research brings.

Related to this skeptical reaction is a tendency to judge the findings of studies of cognition in infancy against an impossible standard. For example, Haith (1997) claims that investigators who use preferential looking methods to probe infants' cognitive capacities "must fend off every possible perceptual interpretation of differences [in looking times] to entertain default cognitive interpretations." That is, no evidence for any cognitive ability in infants can be accepted until every sensory and perceptual interpretation of the evidence, *however implausible and empirically unsupported*, has been eliminated.

For example, Haith (1997) considered Wynn's (1992, 1995) experiments, in which the looking patterns of infants who viewed a succession of occlusion events on a single stage provide evidence that the infants represented two objects on the stage, even though only one object was visible at a time. He argued that infants' looking patterns should not be interpreted as evidence for object representations, because there is an alternative interpretation that has not been eliminated: infants' looking patterns could be produced by extremely long-term sensory persistence evoked by each object before it was occluded. Haith's alternative interpretation is implausible, because abundant research with adults provides evidence that sensory persistence in lighted environments is at least an order of magnitude shorter than this argument would require (e.g., Sperling, 1960). His interpretation also has no empirical support: no evidence for prolonged sensory persistence has been provided by any studies of sensory processes in infants. These considerations have no force, however, if Haith's default rule is accepted. Even the most implausible and unsupported sensory interpretation of data from infant studies is preferable, by this rule, to any cognitive interpretation.

The requirement that claims of cognitive competence be proved by the elimination of every alternative claim, however implausible and unsupported, sets an impossible standard for research on cognition in infancy. Like any other branch of science, the study of cognitive development is not an exercise in logic resulting in irrefutable conclusions:

hypotheses can be rejected or supported by evidence but can never be proven correct. Because there are an infinite number of alternative interpretations of any finding in any area of science, empirical progress requires that scientists select and evaluate interpretations in accord with evidence, not in accord with *a priori* preferences for some interpretations over others. No hypothesis can be held to be true or false until *proven* otherwise.

A third problem facing investigators of cognition in infancy is a tendency of some critics to consider individual studies in isolation, rather than to develop unitary and principled accounts for a larger body of research. One example of this tendency is discussed in note[1]. As a second example, Haith's (1997) suggestion that sensory persistence accounts for apparent cases of object representation is framed in the context of a discussion of studies in which infants view stationary objects that first are fully visible and then are occluded for several seconds (e.g., Baillargeon and Devos, 1991; Wynn, 1992). This suggestion cannot account for the findings of numerous studies presenting much longer occlusion times (e.g., Baillargeon and Graber, 1988; Wilcox et al., 1994), occluded objects that move or change (e.g., Rochat and Hespos, 1996; Koechlin et al., 1997; Simon et al., 1995), or objects with surfaces that are never visible (e.g., Johnson and Aslin, 1995; Kellman and Spelke, 1983; Van de Walle and Spelke, 1996). Although separate explanations could be proposed for the findings of each of these studies, our understanding of infant cognition is not likely to advance if we propose new explanations for each new set of findings. Requiring all rival accounts of cognitive development to be responsive to all experimental findings would help to place discussions on a firmer foundation, focusing attention on areas where serious alternative explanations exist and where further research would be most productive.

I do not claim that every study of perception and cognition in infancy has been correctly interpreted by its authors, or that every skeptical reaction to this research impedes progress. On the contrary, the development of competing accounts of findings can be extremely helpful to the field when the accounts are developed in a principled manner and tested by further research. Healthy progress has come, for example, from Cohen's studies of the sources of infants' reactions to violations (and interesting non-violations) of object solidity (Cohen, 1995; Cohen et al., 1996) and Oake's studies of limits to infants' sensitivity to contact-mechanical motions (Oakes, 1994) and to gravity (Kannass and Oakes,

1997). Further progress may come from Bogartz's new methodological and statistical approaches to preferential looking research, although the sensitivity of these approaches remains to be demonstrated (see note[1]). Finally, progress is coming from studies revealing surprising limits to infants' representation of occlusion events (e.g., Chiang and Wynn, 1996; Huntley-Fenner and Carey, 1995; Xu and Carey, 1996). To advance understanding of early cognitive development, those who are skeptical of current accounts of cognitive in infancy should not ignore their skepticism but submit it to test, adhering to guidelines that all investigators can follow. I suggest four guidelines:

1   Theories should be evaluated in relation to evidence, not compatibility with intuition.
2   No hypothesis should be considered "guilty until proven innocent" or the reverse.
3   All accounts of the findings of infant studies require evidence. In particular, those who would explain infants' performance by appealing to sensory or motor processes must provide evidence for those processes, on a par with those who would explain infants' performance in terms of perceptual or cognitive processes.
4   All theories of early cognitive development must encompass all the relevant data. In particular, explanations of infants' performance that appeal to sensory-motor processes, motivational processes, perceptual processes, and cognitive processes must all be held to the same standard; no account merits attention if it is based on a small subset of findings and ignores contrary results.

Arguments Against Nativist Claims

It is worth asking why the intuitions of many investigators have favored extreme empiricist theories and skewed standards for evaluating research. A number of arguments in support of these intuitions and standards have been offered. Here, I consider six arguments against any nativist interpretations of research on cognition in infancy, according to which such interpretations are incoherent, false, unparsimonious, empty, denying of flexibility, or socially dangerous. In each case, I suggest the arguments are misplaced, and that the considerations motivating them should lead investigators in a different direction.

Nativism is incoherent

As developmental biologists have shown in exquisite detail, all development involves a process of interaction between genes and environment.
Without the right physical and chemical environment, genes are inert
and no development happens. From this finding, some developmental
psychologists have concluded that it is incoherent to imagine that any
knowledge of the world could have its source solely in the organism (e.g.,
Oyama, 1985; Thelen and Smith, 1994).

The problem with this argument is that the nativist-empiricist dialogue is not about the interaction of genes and their environment, but
about whether knowledge of things in the external world develops on
basis of encounters with those things. Do we learn to perceive depth by
looking at three-dimensional scenes? Do we learn to see objects by
looking at and manipulating objects? Alternatively, do structures
for representing three-dimensional scenes furnished with bounded
objects develop independently of perceptual encounters with those
scenes and objects? These questions are not addressed by research on
interactions between genes and gene products but by research on the
emerging and changing capacities of children in interaction with their
surroundings.

Construed appropriately, the questions about the sources of human
knowledge are not incoherent but well-formed, and some of them are
straightforwardly testable. Psychologists who study animals can and
have asked whether a dark-reared rat perceives depth on first encoun-
tering the light, and whether a newborn chick represents an occluded
object the first time it sees an object being hidden. Psychologists who
study humans can and have asked whether a newborn infant with no
visual experience perceives depth, distinguishes faces from other kinds
of patterns, or represents occluded objects. Investigators also have asked
about the role of specific experiences such as locomotion in the development of perception and representation: a very fruitful contribution to
the dialogue (e.g., Bertenthal and Campos, 1990). The fascinating
advances in research in neurobiology do not undermine these questions. At its best, research in neurobiology suggests mechanisms by
which cognitive structures can develop in advance of sensory contact
with the external world, as well as mechanisms by which these structures can be shaped and modified by such contact.[2]

Nativism is false

When the findings of studies of early cognitive development are scrutinized with appropriate rigor, some investigators argue, they yield no evidence for knowledge of things preceding experience with those things. Rather, the evidence suggests that all knowledge results wholly from dynamic interactions with the external environment (Elman et al., 1996; Munakata et al., 1997; Thelen and Smith, 1994).

This conclusion rests in part on skewed interpretations of studies of cognition in infancy, as discussed above, and it is further nourished by a general error of interpretation of developmental data. Faced with evidence for a developmental change in some capacity, investigators are apt to conclude that the cause of the change is learning, ignoring two alternative possibilities. First, the capacity may be constant over development but the ability to express it may change because of other developmental changes (see Banks and Shannon, 1988; Thelen, 1984, for examples). Second, the capacity may emerge over development but the cause of its emergence may be maturation or triggering rather than shaping by experience (see Held, 1985, for an example). This error of interpretation fosters the conclusion that knowledge has been acquired through learning when all that is known is that behavior on some task has changed.

Instead of drawing empiricist conclusions automatically, students of cognitive development should conclude that learning has taken place only when there is evidence for learning, from research revealing that different knowledge emerges under different environmental conditions. If one bases conclusions only on evidence, then I believe that studies of infants suggest that development is not strongly skewed toward either pole of the nativist-empiricist dialogue. There is some evidence for innate knowledge, embodied in structures that develop in advance of their function and in advance of relevant perceptual contacts with the objects of knowledge. (This evidence seems to me strongest in the cases of depth perception and face processing.) There is also some evidence for learning, from situations where children's knowledge varies with, and because of, variations in their experience. (This evidence seems to me strongest in the cases of speech perception and certain spatial representations.) Finally, there are vast areas of ignorance, where the contributions of innate structures and learning have not been disentangled. Students of development should not be surprised or discouraged by the extent of our ignorance, because the experimental study of cognition in infancy is a young enterprise and it *is* progressing. Above all, investigators should not be discouraged from conducting research to reduce that ignorance by skewing their interpretations of the evidence already at hand.

Nativism is unparsimonious

Some investigators have granted that questions about the origins of knowledge are meaningful and empirical. Because existing research does not yet resolve these questions in many cases, they argue, the most parsimonious assumption is that knowledge is lacking early in development. Until the evidence forces one to a different conclusion, on this view, one should assume that young infants lack all knowledge and cognitive processes.

This argument rests, I believe, on misunderstandings of the role of parsimony considerations in science and of the nature of developmental theories. First, parsimony is appropriately invoked in cases where a rich body of evidence is consistent with two or more detailed theories. When evidence is sparse and theories are sketchy, as in the study of cognitive development, scientists need to collect further evidence, not jump to conclusions on grounds of parsimony. Second, theories of development aim to describe and explain how the capacities of adults come to be. Parsimony arguments apply to these theories *as wholes*: the most parsimonious theory of cognitive development is the theory providing the simplest account of the development of mature knowledge, not the simplest description of the young infant. Because all theories must arrive at the same end state of mature knowledge, accounts with simpler characterizations of the initial state will tend to have more complex characterizations of developmental change. If one focuses on the simplicity of developmental theories as wholes, rather than the simplicity of the pieces of those theories characterizing the initial state, then parsimony considerations do not automatically favor one voice over others in the nativist-empiricist dialogue.

Nativism is empty

Perhaps the most common argument against nativist claims is that they do not explain development: to say that a given aspect of knowledge is innate is not to account for its emergence or its form. Nativist claims, it is argued, only shift the burden of explaining development to some other discipline, such as developmental biology.

This argument misconstrues the nature of explanation in developmental psychology. All theories of cognitive development have the dual task of characterizing the initial state of knowledge and the processes that transform this initial state into mature knowledge. In extreme empiricist theories, the initial state typically is held to consist of a set of innate sensory transducers and one or more mechanisms of learning; in other theories, the initial state and developmental mechanisms are characterized differently. Because all theories across the nativist-empiricist spectrum have the same general form, the explanatory value of each theory depends only on how well it accounts for the phenomena of development and on theory-internal qualities such as completeness and consistency. A theory's explanatory value does *not* depend on the content it assigns to the initial state.

To build good explanatory theories, students of cognitive development must seek the most complete, consistent, and empirically adequate account of the initial state and subsequent growth of knowledge. As psychologists learn more about cognition in infancy, the constraints on all theories grow and the explanatory virtues of different theories will become clearer. Developing better explanatory theories requires vigorous programs of research addressing the questions at the center of the nativist-empiricist dialogue; it is not aided by *a priori* rejection of one side of the dialogue.

Nativism denies flexibility

Investigators of cognitive development sometimes characterize initial knowledge as a set of "constraints on learning" (e.g., Gelman, 1990; Keil, 1981; Spelke, 1990). This terminology is in some ways unfortunate, for it appears to imply that innate knowledge prevents people from learning (see Quartz and Sejnowski, 1997). In fact, innate structures have traditionally been proposed in order to explain how it is possible for humans to learn anything. They do not deny human flexibility but instead participate in attempts to understand both human flexibility and its limits.

For example, theories positing initial knowledge have been proposed to explain how is it possible for human children to learn any human culture's language, motor skills, and object taxonomies, or formal belief systems (e.g., Chomsky, 1975; Hirschfeld and Gelman, 1994). Theories that posit unlearned systems of knowledge have even been proposed to account for the development of humans' most flexible, formal belief systems (e.g., Carey and Spelke, 1994, 1996; Sperber, 1994). Debates between nativists and empiricists are not denials and assertions of flexibility but contrasting accounts of the sources and the nature of humans' often flexible cognitive performance.

Nativism is dangerous

Perhaps the most serious argument against nativist claims focuses on the impact of these claims on society. The thesis that certain systems of knowledge are innate in our species is sometimes said to go naturally with the thesis that some people are inherently more capable thinkers and knowers than others. As is well known, this second thesis has underpinned social evils such as racist immigration policies, it serves to rationalize social injustice, and it threatens to foster further, regressive social changes. By this argument, nativist claims should be shunned so as to avoid these social consequences (Elman et al., 1996; Fischer and Bidell, 1994).

The problem with this argument lies in its first premise: the question whether any knowledge is innate in our species is entirely different from the question whether there are any innate *differences* between people in knowledge or cognitive ability. Consider, for example, a scientist who believes that a system of knowledge of objects is innate in all people, and who asks why adults differ in the extent to which they go beyond this system: why one student of physics gets an A whereas another gets a C, or why one athlete-in-training consistently hits baseballs whereas another consistently misses. It is completely open to this scientist to believe that all differences between people stem from differences in their experiences: their differing opportunities to extend their knowledge and abilities in classrooms or on athletic fields. Consider now a second scientist who believes that all knowledge of objects is learned and who asks the same question about the sources of individual differences in adults. It is entirely open to this scientist to believe that differences among physics students and baseball players stem from differences in people's innately given learning capacities.[3] For better or worse, claims about the sources of the knowledge that all people share do not bear questions about the sources of the abilities that distinguish one person from another.

The Nativist-Empiricist Dialogue in a Larger Social Perspective

Although studies of cognition in infancy do not reveal the sources of individual differences in ability or achievement, I believe that they cast a valuable new perspective on those differences. When experiments reveal systems of knowledge that emerge early in human development and that persist and grow in common ways over all children, they suggest that the cognitive differences between people are not as great as many current discussions imply. Debates over the genetics of IQ and over cultural differences in language and thinking tend to overlook the cognitive capacities and attainments that all people share, because most of our common cognitive endowment is obscure to intuition whereas differences between people are salient. Studies of the origins and early development of knowledge serve to increase awareness of the vast common ground uniting all human thinkers, helping us to understand what it is to be a human thinker and knower in any culture and in any set of circumstances. Much of the heat in the controversies over IQ and multiculturalism may dissipate as this understanding grows.

Research guided by the nativist-empiricist dialogue does not, however, deny human differences. On the contrary, it sheds light on the particular circumstances that lead different people to extend their knowledge and skills in different directions. Where knowledge is found to vary across people in different cultures or circumstances, that variability teaches us something about our own potential and that of others. This information can guide choices about how to educate children and structure societies, and it can help everyone to view the differing accomplishments of different people with understanding and respect.

These are not new reasons for asking about the origins and growth of knowledge, for they trace back to the beginnings of the nativist-empiricist dialogue. What is new are the advances in cognitive science that now allow students of cognitive development to address these questions empirically. By pursuing that work and overcoming old prejudices, our understanding of human knowledge and human nature may grow considerably in the coming years, enriching and informing long-standing social dialogues on human nature, human differences, and human development.

Notes

1   Bogartz and Shinskey (1998) recently reported a divergent finding. Like the five sets of investigators cited above, Bogartz and Shinskey habituated one group of infants to a center-occluded object and then tested them with a fully visible continuous object and with an object with a gap. In contrast to the infants in the above studies, these infants showed equal looking times to the two test displays. In further conditions similar to two control conditions reported by Kellman and Spelke (1983, Experiments 2 and 4), Bogartz and Shinsky habituated two further groups of infants either to a fully visible continuous object or to a fully visible object with a gap and then tested them with the same two fully visible displays. In contrast to the infants in Kellman and Spelke's (1983) control conditions, these infants also showed equal looking times to the two test displays. Bogartz and Shinsky based their discussion only on their own findings and those of one condition of Kellman and Spelke's (1983) first experiment, without citing any other experimental conditions or investigators. They suggested that infants fail to show novelty preferences when tested with the method and displays of Kellman and Spelke, but the findings reported by Kellman and Spelke (1983, Experiments 2, 3, and 4), Slater et al. (1990, Experiment 4), Johnson and Aslin (1996, Experiments 1 and 2), and Needham (1994) provide evidence against this suggestion. It is not clear why Bogartz and Shinskey's method failed to elicit novelty preferences; their use of small numbers of infants and test trials, a larger number of test stimuli, and older infants are differences worthy of test. Because they did not observe novelty preferences for one fully visible object after habituation to another fully visible object, however, the absence of novelty preferences after habituation to a center-occluded object cannot be taken either as evidence for any specific limitation to infants' perception of partly occluded objects or as any challenge to the findings of Kellman (Kellman and Spelke, 1983, Kellman et al., 1986, 1987), Johnson (Johnson and Aslin, 1995, 1996; Johnson and Nañez, 1995), Jusczyk et al. (1997), Needham (1994), or Slater et al. (1990).

2   Spelke and Newport (1998) discuss possible neurobiological mechanisms for the development of object representations.

3   Claims that all knowledge is learned frequently accompany claims that differences in cognitive ability are innate; see Herrnstein and Murray (1994) for a recent example.

References

Baillargeon, R., & DeVos, J. (1991). Object permanence in young infants: Further evidence. *Child Development, 62,* 1227–1246.

Baillargeon, R., & Graber, M. (1988). Evidence of location memory in 8-month-old infants. *Cognition, 20,* 191–208.

Banks, M. S., & Shannon, E. (1993). Spatial and chromatic visual efficiency in human neonates. In C. E. Granrud (Ed.), *Visual perception and cognition in infancy* (pp. 1–46). Hillsdale, NJ: Erlbaum.

Bertenthal, B. I., & Campos, J. J. (1990). A systems approach to the organizing effects of self-produced locomotion during infancy. In C. Rovee-Collier and L. P. Lipsitt (Eds.), *Advances in infancy research,* (Vol. 6, pp. 1–60). Norwood, NJ: Ablex.

Bogartz, R. S., & Shinskey, J. L. (1998). On perception of a partially occluded object in 6-month-olds. *Cognitive Development.*

Carey, S., & Spelke, E. S. (1994). Domain-specific knowledge and conceptual change. In L. Hirschfeld & S. Gelman (Eds.), *Mapping the mind: Domain-specificity in cognition and culture* (pp. 169–200). Cambridge: Cambridge University Press.

Carey, S., & Spelke, E. S. (1996). Science and core knowledge. *Philosophy of Science, 63,* 515–533.

Chiang, W.-C., & Wynn. K. (1996). Eight-month-old infants' reasoning about collections (abstract). *Infant Behavior and Development, 19,* 390.

Chomsky, N. (1975). *Reflections on language.* NY: Pantheon.

Cohen, L. B. (1995, April). *How solid is infants' understanding of solidity?* Paper presented at the meeting of the Society for Research in Child Development, Indianapolis.

Cohen, L., Gilbert, K., & Brown, P. (1996). Infants' understanding of solidity: Replicating a failure to replicate (abstract). *Infant Behavior and Development, 19,* 398.

Elman, J., Bates, E., Johnson, M., Karmiloff-Smith, A., Parisi, D., & Plunkett, K. (1996). *Rethinking innateness: A connectionist perspective on development.* Cambridge. MA: MIT Press.

Fisher, K. W., & Bidell, T. (1994). Constraining nativist inferences about cognitive capacities. In S. Carey & R. Gelman (Eds.), *The epigenesis of mind: Essays on biology and cognition* (pp. 199–236). Hillsdale, NJ: Erlbaum.

Gelman, R. (1990). Structural constraints on cognitive development: Introduction. *Cognitive Science, 14,* 3–9.

Haith, M. M. (1997, April). *Who put the cog in infant cognition?* Invited debate presented at the meeting of the Society for Research in Child Development, Washington, DC.

Held, R. (1985). Binocular vision: Behavioral and neural development. In

Theoretical Issues

J. Mehler and R. Fox (Eds.). *Neonate cognition* (pp. 279–296). Hillsdale, N: Erlbaum.

Herrnstein, R. J., & Murray, C. A. (1994). *The bell curve: intelligence and class structure in American life*. New York: Free Press.

Hirschfeld, L. A., & Gelman, S. A. (1994). *Mapping the mind: Domain-specificity in cognition and culture.* Cambridge: Cambridge University Press.

Huntley-Fenner, & Carey, S. (1995, April). *Physical reasoning in infancy: The representation of nonsolid substances.* Paper presented at the meeting of the Society for Research in Child Development, Indianapolis, IN.

Johnson, S. P., & Aslin, R. N. (1995). Perception of object unity in 2-month-old infants. *Developmental Psychology, 31,* 739–745.

Johnson, S. P., & Aslin, R. N. (1996). Perception of object unity in young infants: The roles of motion, depth, and orientation. *Cognitive Development, 11,* 161–180.

Johnson, S. P., & Nañez, J. E. Sr. (1995). Young infants' perception of object unity in two-dimensional displays. *Infant Behavior and Development, 18,* 133–143.

Jusczyk, P., Johnson, S., Spelke, E., Kennedy, L., & Smith, C. (1997, April). *Does synchronous change over time specify object unity for infants?* Poster presented at the meeting of the Society for Research in Child Development, Washington, DC.

Kannass, K. N., & Oakes, L. M. (1997, April). *Downhill vs. uphill: Infants' sensitivity to gravitational constraints on object motion.* Poster presented at the meeting of the Society for Research in Child Development, Washington, DC.

Keil, F. C. (1981). Constraints on knowledge and cognitive development. *Psychological Review, 88,* 197–227.

Kellman, P. J., Gleitman, H., & Spelke, E. S. (1987). Object and observer motion in the perception of objects by infants. *Journal of Experimental Psychology: Human Perception and Performance, 13,* 586–593.

Kellman, P. J., & Spelke, E. S. (1983). Perception of partly occluded objects in infancy. *Cognitive Psychology, 15,* 483–524.

Kellman, P. J., Spelke, E. S., & Short, K. R. (1986). Infant perception of object unity from translatory motion in depth and vertical translation. *Child Development, 57,* 72–86.

Koechlin, E., Dehaene, S., & Mehler, J. (1997). Numerical transformations in five-month-old human infants. *Mathematical Cognition.*

Munakata, Y., McClelland, J. L., Johnson, M. H., & Siegler, R. S. (1997). Rethinking infant knowledge: Toward and adaptive process account of successes and failures in object permanence tasks. *Psychological Review, 104,* 686–713.

Needham, A. (1994). Infants' use of perceptual similarity when segregating partly occluded objects during the fourth month of life (abstract). *Infant Behavior and Development, 17,* 163.

Oakes, L. M. (1994). The development of infants' use of continuity cues in their perception of causality. *Developmental Psychology, 30,* 869–879.

Oyama, S. (1985). *The ontogeny of information: Development systems and evolution.* Cambridge: Cambridge University Press.

Quartz, S. R., & Sejnowski, T. J. (1997). The neural basis of cognitive development: A constructivist manifesto. *Behavioral and Brain Sciences, 20,* 537–596.

Rochat, P., & Hespos, S. J. (1996). Tracking and anticipation of invisible spatial transformations by 4- to 8-month-old infants. *Cognitive Development, 11,* 3–17.

Simon, T., Hespos, S., & Rochat, P. (1995). Do infants understand simple arithmetic? A replication of Wynn (1992). *Cognitive Development, 10,* 253–269.

Slater, A., Morison, V., Somers, M., Mattock, A., Brown, E., & Taylor, D. (1990). Newborn and older infants' perception of partly occluded objects. *Infant Behavior and Development, 13,* 33–49.

Spelke, E. S. (1990). Principles of object perception. *Cognitive Science, 14,* 29–56.

Spelke, E. S., & Newport, E. L. (1998). Nativism, empiricism, and the development of knowledge. In W. Damon (Series Ed.) & R. Lerner (Vol. Ed.), *Handbook of Child Psychology: Vol. 1. Theoretical Models of Human Development.* (5th ed., pp. 275–340). New York: Wiley.

Sperber, D. (1994). The modularity of thought and the epidemiology of representations. In L. Hirschfeld & S. Gelman (Eds.), *Mapping the mind: Domain-specificity in cognition and culture* (pp. 39–67). Cambridge: Cambridge University Press.

Sperling, G. (1960). The information available in brief visual presentations. *Psychological Monographs, 74*(11).

Thelen, E. (1984). Learning to walk: Ecological demands and hylogenetic constraints. In L. P. Lipsitt & C. Rovee-Collier (Eds.), *Advances in Infancy Research* (Vol. 3, pp. 214–250). NY: Ablex.

Thelen, E., & Smith, L. B. (1994). *A dynamical systems approach to the development of cognition and action.* Cambridge, MA: Bradford/MIT Press.

Van de Walle, G. A., & Spelke, E. S. (1996). Spatiotemporal integration and object perception in infancy: Perceiving unity vs. form. *Child Development, 67,* 2621–2640.

Wilcox, T., Rosser, R., & Nadel, L. (1994). Representation of object location in 6.5-month-old infants. *Cognitive Development, 9,* 193–210.

Wynn, K. (1992). Addition and subtraction in infants. *Nature, 358,* 749–750.

Wynn, K. (1995). Infants possess a system of numerical knowledge. *Current Directions in Psychological Science, 4,* 172–177.

Xu, F., & Carey, S. (1996). Infants' metaphysics: The case of numerical identity. *Cognitive Psychology, 30,* 111–153.

THREE

Connectionist Modeling

Introduction

Connectionist models are computer models, loosely based on the principles of neural information processing, which can offer insights into the ways in which development takes place by positing a set of mechanisms for learning, and exploring whether the model can mirror, and perhaps explain, real learning and development in neurally plausible terms. Computer models of development and learning have been around for some 40 years, but it is only recently that they have begun to be used to explore infant development. As Denis Mareschal puts it, "This is surprising because infancy is a rich period of development . . . "

Following an introduction to some of the characteristics of connectionist computational models, Mareschal gives two examples of ways in which such models can be used to explain aspects of infant development. The first example concerns a fundamental cognitive activity, our ability to categorize objects and events. In the course of development infants form categories of natural objects, so that they may appreciate that all cats belong in one category, dogs in another, that dogs and cats (and other animals) belong in a more global category of four-legged-animals, and so on.

When 3- and 4-month-olds are shown pictures of different cats it seems that they will form a category of CAT that *excludes* dogs. However, when shown pictures of different dogs the category DOG *includes* cats. This asymmetry is possibly attributable to the fact that there is much greater variation between different dogs' appearances than between different cats', and hence cats (particularly cat faces) share more of the characteristics of dogs, than dogs do of cats. Mareschal describes a model whose networks also developed CAT and DOG categories with the same asymmetry as found with the 3- to 4-month-old infants. What is important is that the model is able to make predictions about other aspects of categorization, and these predictions are often borne out by experimental evidence with infants.

Mareschal's second example concerns a curious developmental lag in infants' behavior with respect to hidden objects. Infants as young as 3.5 months have some understanding of hidden objects in that they will show surprise (measured by increased *looking*) when a physical property, such as solidity, of a hidden object is violated. However, it is not until they are over 7 months that they will show this understanding by *reaching* for an object that has been hidden by a screen. Mareschal's connectionist solution to this apparent paradox is developed from recent anatomical, neurophysiological, and psychophysical evidence which suggests that there are two different processing routes for visual object information in the cortex. In order simply to be *aware* of the continued existence of a hidden object (as shown by surprise) the infant needs access only to one cortical representation, whereas to *search* for the object requires a coordination of the two representations. In the model "A developmental lag appeared between retrieval and surprise-based tasks because of the added cognitive demands of accessing two object representations simultaneously."

Connectionist modeling goes hand-in-hand with rigorous empirical work: "modeling and empirical work form a symbiotic partnership." The models can offer insights into the ways in which development takes place. They can also help to guide decisions about future research, and can suggest critical experiments to develop our understanding in particular domains of development. What is certain is that connectionist accounts of development are here to stay! Such models give insights into what might develop, and how changes in behavior and thinking might occur. They can often suggest critical experiments, and they challenge existing models of the course of cognitive development.

Further reading

Elman, J., Bates, E., Karmiloff-Smith, A., Johnson, M., Parisi, D., and Plunkett, K. (1996). *Rethinking Innateness: Development in a Connectionist Perspective*. Cambridge, MA: MIT Press.

Connectionist Modelling and Infant Development

Denis Mareschal

The real challenge for developmental psychology is to explain *how* and *why* behaviours emerge. The traditional approach has been to describe infant competence across different domains in great detail, in the hopes that by establishing the milestones of development a causal explanation will emerge from a synthesis of the data. This chapter presents a very different approach. The alternative approach consists in positing a set of mechanisms for learning, and implementing these mechanisms in a working computer model (a computer program). The model then provides a tool for exploring whether specific behaviours can emerge or be caused by the interaction of this well-defined set of mechanisms with some equally well-defined learning environment.

Although the use of computer modelling in developmental psychology is not new (e.g., Simon, 1962; Papert, 1963; Young, 1976; Klahr and Wallace, 1976; Boden, 1980; McClelland, 1989; Shultz et al., 1995; Mareschal and Shultz, 1996) it remains relatively rare. Until recently there have been few attempts to model infant development. This is surprising because infancy is a rich period of development in which many behaviours are closely tied to perceptual and motor development. The close link between behaviour and perceptual-motor skills makes it easier to posit mechanisms without the need to appeal to poorly defined metacognitive skills.

Why Connectionist Computational Models?

Connectionist models are computer models loosely based on the principles of neural information processing (Rumelhart and McClelland,
1986; Elman et al., 1996; McLeod et al., 1998). However, they are not
intended to be neural models. Instead, they attempt to strike the balance
between importing some of the key ideas from the neurosciences while
maintaining sufficiently discrete and definable components to allow
questions about behaviour to be formulated in terms of high-level computational concepts.

From a developmental perspective, connectionist networks are ideal
for modelling because they develop their own internal representations
as a result of interacting with an environment (Plunkett and Sinha,
1992). However, these networks are not simply *tabula rasa* empiricist
learning machines. The representations they develop can be strongly
pre-determined by initial constraints. These constraints can take the
form of different associative learning mechanisms attuned to specific
information in the environment (e.g., temporal correlation or spatial
correlation), or they can take the form of architectural constraints that
guide the flow of information in the system. Although connectionist
modelling has its roots in associationist learning paradigms, it has
inherited the Hebbian rather than the Hullian tradition. That is, what
goes on *inside* the box (inside the network) is as important in determining the overall behaviour of the networks as is the correlation between
the inputs (stimuli) and the outputs (responses).

Connectionist Information Processing

Connectionist networks are made up of simple processing units (idealized neurons) interconnected via weighted communication lines (idealized synapses). Units are often represented as circles and the weighted
communication lines, as lines between these circles. Activation flows
from unit to unit via these connection weights. Figure 3.1(a) shows a
generic connectionist network in which activation can flow in any direction. However, most applications of connectionist networks impose constraints on the way activation can flow.

Figure 3.1(b) shows a typical feed-forward network. Activation
(information) is constrained to move in one direction only. Some units

(a)   (b)

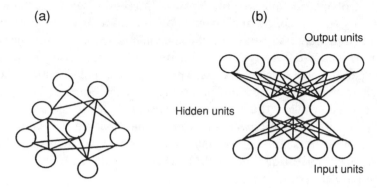

Figure 3.1   Schema of (a) a generic and (b) a feedforward connectionist
network

(those units through which information enters the network) are called
input units. Other units (those units through which information leaves
the network) are called *output units*. All other units are called *hidden
units*. In a feed-forward, network information is first encoded as a
pattern of activation across the bank of input units. That activation
then filters up through a first layer of weights until it produces a pattern
of activation across the band of hidden units. The pattern of activation
produced across the hidden units constitutes an *internal re-representation*
of the information originally presented to the network. The activation
at the hidden units continues to flow through the network until it
reaches the output unit. The pattern of activation produced at the
output units is taken as the network's response to the initial input.

Each unit is a very simple processor that mimics the functioning of
an idealized neuron. The unit sums the weighted activation arriving into
it. It then sets its own level of activation according to some non-linear
function of that weighted input. The non-linearity allows the units to
respond differentially to different ranges of input values. The key idea of
connectionist modelling is that of collective computations. That is,
although the behaviour of the individual components in the network is
simple, the behaviour of the network as a whole can be very complex.
It is the behaviour of the network as a whole that is taken to model different aspect of infant behaviours.

The network's global behaviour is determined by the connection
weights. As activation flows through the network, it is transformed by

the set of connection weights between successive layers in network. Learning (i.e., adapting one's behaviour) is accomplished by tuning the connection weights until some stable behaviour is obtained. *Supervised* networks adjust their weights until the output response (for a given input) matches a target response. That target can come from an active teacher, or passively through observing the environment, but it must come from outside the system. *Unsupervised* networks adjust their weights until some internal constraint is satisfied (e.g., maximally different input must have maximally different internal representations). *Backpropagation* (Rumelhart et al., 1986) is a popular training algorithm for supervised connectionist networks.

Many connectionist network models are very simple and only contain some 100 units. This does not imply that the part of the brain solving the corresponding task only uses 100 neurones. It is important to understand that these models are not neural models but information processing models of behaviour. The models provide examples of how systems with similar computational properties to the brain can give rise to the behaviours observed in infants. As such, they constitute possible *explanations* of those behaviours in terms of neurally plausible mechanisms. Sometimes, individual units are taken to represent pools of neurones or cell assemblies rather than single neurones. According to this interpretation, the activation level of the units corresponds to the proportion of neurones firing in the pool (e.g., Changeux and Dehaene, 1989).

Two examples of how connectionist modelling is used to explain behaviours are described below. The first is a model of novelty preference that is used to explain infants' categorization bahaviours. The second is a model of visual object processing that is used to explain object permanence behaviours.

A General Model of Novelty Preference

Many infant categorization tasks rely on preferential looking or habituation techniques based on the finding that infants direct more attention to unfamiliar or unexpected stimuli. The standard interpretation of this behaviour is that infants are comparing an input stimulus to an internal representation of the same stimulus (e.g., Solokov, 1963; Charlesworth, 1969; Cohen, 1973). As long as there is a discrepancy

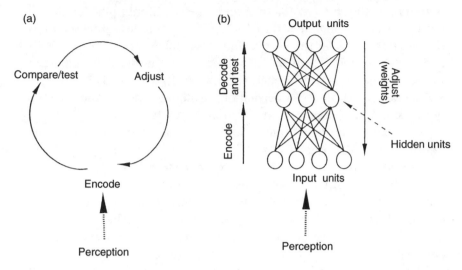

Figure 3.2   Novelty preference as a process of representation construction in
(a) infants and (b) connectionist autoencoder networks

between the information stored in the internal representation and the
visual input, the infant continues to attend to the stimulus. While
attending to the stimulus the infant updates its internal representation.
When the information in the internal representation is no longer dis-
crepant with the visual input, attention is directed elsewhere. This
process is illustrated in Figure 3.2(a). When a familiar object is presented there is little or no attending because the infant already has a
reliable internal representation of that object. In contrast, when an
unfamiliar or unexpected object is presented, there is more attending
because an internal representation has to be constructed or adjusted.
The degree to which a novel object differs from existing internal representations determines the amount of adjusting that has to be done, and
hence the duration of attention.

Connectionist autoencoder networks have been used to model the
relation between sustained attention and representation construction
(Mareschal and French, 1997; Mareschal and French, in press;
Mareschal et al., submitted; Schafer and Mareschal, submitted). An
autoencoder is a feed-forward connectionist network with a single layer
of hidden units (Figure 3.2(b)). It is called an autoencoder because it
associates an input with itself. The network learns to reproduce on the

output units the pattern of activation across the input units. It relies on a supervised learning algorithm, but because the input signal serves as the training signal for the output units no teacher other than the environment is hypothesized. In an autoencoder, the number of hidden units is smaller than the number of input or output units. This produces a bottleneck in the flow of information through the network forcing the network to develop a more compact internal representation of the input (at the hidden unit level) that is sufficiently rich to reproduce all the information in the original input. Information is first compressed into an internal representation and then expanded to reproduce the original input. The successive cycles of training in the autoencoder are an iterative process by which a reliable internal representation of the input is developed. The reliability of the representation is tested by expanding it, and comparing the resulting predictions to the actual stimulus being encoded.

This approach to modelling novelty preference assumes that infant looking times are positively correlated with the network error. The greater the error, the longer the looking time because it takes more training cycles to reduce the error. The degree to which error (looking time) increases on presentation of a novel object depends on the similarity between the novel object and the familiar object. Presenting a series of similar objects leads to a progressive error drop on future similar objects.

An unusual asymmetry has been observed in natural category formation in infants (Quinn et al., 1993; Quinn and Eimas, 1996). When 3- to 4-month-olds are initially exposed to a series of pictures of cats they will form a category of cat that excludes dogs. However, when they are exposed to a series of pictures of dogs, they will form a category of dog that does include cats. We used the autoencoder network above to explain this bahaviour. The original cat and dog pictures were measured along 10 dimensions and presented to the networks for categorization. The same presentation procedure was used as with the infants. These networks developed CAT and DOG categories with the same exclusivity asymmetry as the 3- to 4-month-olds. Moreover, the model predicted that learning DOG after CAT would disrupt the prior learning of CAT whereas as learning CAT after DOG would not disrupt the prior learning of CATS. A subsequent study with 3- to 4-month-olds found this to be true of infants as well (Mareschal et al., submitted).

The asymmetry was explained in terms of the distribution of cat and dog feature values in the stimuli presented to the infants. Most cat values fell within the range of dog values but the converse was not true. Thus for a system that processes the statistical distribution of features of a stimulus, the cats would appear as a subset of the dog category. Further analyses revealed that these networks could parse the world into distinct categories according to the correlation of feature values, in the same way that 10-month-olds have been shown to do (Younger, 1995; Mareschal and French, in press).

Object Directed-behaviours

Newborns possess sophisticated object-oriented perceptual skills (Slater, 1995) but the age at which infants are able to reason about *hidden* objects remains unclear. Using *manual search* to test infants' understanding of hidden objects, Piaget concluded it was not until 7.5 to 9 months that infants understand that hidden objects continue to exist because younger infants do not successfully reach for an object hidden behind an occluding screen (Piaget, 1952, 1954) More recent studies using a violation of expectancy paradigm have suggested that infants as young as 3.5 months do have some understanding of hidden objects. These studies rely on non-search indices such as surprise instead of manual retrieval to assess infant knowledge (e.g., Baillargeon et al., 1985; Baillargeon, 1993). Infants *watch* an event in which some physical property of a hidden object is violated (e.g., solidity). Surprise at this violation (as measured by increased visual inspection of the event) is interpreted as showing that the infants know: (a) that the hidden object still exists, and; (b) that the hidden object maintains the physical property that was violated (Baillargeon, 1993). The nature and origins of this developmental lag between *understanding* the continued existence of a hidden object and *searching* for it remains a central question of infant cognitive development.

Mareschal et al. (1995; 1999) describe a model designed to address this question (Figure 3.3). Clues may be found in recent work on cortical representation of visual object information. Anatomical, neurophysiological, and psychophysical evidence points to the existence of two processing routes for visual object information in the cortex (Ungerleider and Mishkin, 1982; Van Essen et al., 1992; Goodale, 1993;

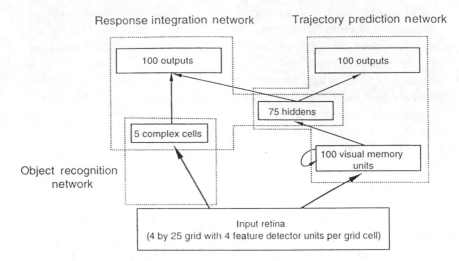

Figure 3.3   Schema of object processing model

Milner and Goodale, 1995). Although the exact functionality of the two routes remains a hotly debated question, it is generally accepted that they contain radically different kinds of representations. The dorsal (or parietal) route processes spatial-temporal object information, whereas the ventral (or temporal) route processes object feature information.

The Mareschal et al. model is more complex than the simple autoencoder networks described above. Rather than drawing individual units as above, each box represents a layer of units and each arrow represents a full set of connections between successive layers. The dotted lines delimit separate modules. Information enters the networks via a simplified retina. The object recognition network develops a spatially invariant feature-based representation of the object (compare the functions of the ventral cortical route) whereas as the trajectory prediction network develops a spatial temporal representation of the object (compare the functions of the dorsal cortical route). The response integration network recruits and co-ordinates these representations as and when required by an active, voluntary response.

Like infants, the model also showed a developmental lag. Active tasks such as retrieval of a desired hidden object required the integration of information across the multiple object representations, whereas surprise or dishabituation tasks may only have required access to one of the representations separately. A developmental lag appeared between retrieval and surprise-based tasks because of the added cognitive demands of accessing two object representations simultaneously in an active response task. The model predicted that dishabituation tasks that required infants to access cortically separable representations would also show a developmental lag as compared to tasks that only required access to one cortical representation.

Conclusions

This chapter began with an introduction to connectionist computational modelling and reviewed two applications of connectionist modelling to understanding infant behaviours. Although connectionist models can explain infant behaviours in terms of neural information processing, this is not to say that they supersede rigorous empirical work with infants. On the contrary: a model is only as good as the empirical data it is based on. In turn, the model can be used to guide decisions about future research. Modelling and empirical work form a symbiotic partnership. Each partner feeds off the other with the ultimate benefit of increasing our understanding of infant behaviour. It is important to remember that building a model of infant behaviours does not mean building an infant. Any model necessarily embodies a number of approximations and simplifications. The degree to which any approximation is justified depends on the nature of the task being modelled and the degree to which it is already understood.

References

Baillargeon, R. (1993). The object concept revisited: New directions in the investigation of infants' physical knowledge. In C. E. Granrud (Ed.). *Visual perception and cognition in infancy* (pp. 265–315). London, UK: LEA.

Baillargeon, R., Spelke, E. S., & Wasserman, S. (1985). Object permanence in 5-month-old infants. *Cognition, 20,* 191–208.

Boden, M. A. (1980). Artificial intelligence and Piagetian theory. In M. Boden (Ed.), *Minds and mechanisms: Philosophical psychology and computational models* (pp. 236–261). Ithaca: Cornell University Press.

Changeux, J. P., & Dehaene, S. (1989). Neuronal models of cognitive function. *Cognition, 33,* 63–109.

Charlesworth, W. R. (1969). The role of surprise in cognitive development. In

D. Elkind, & J. Flavell (Eds.), *Studies in cognitive development. Essays in honor of Jean Piaget* (pp. 257–314). Oxford, UK: Oxford University Press.

Cohen, L. B. (1973). A two-process model of infant visual attention. *Merrill-Palmer Quarterly, 19*, 157–180.

Elman, J. L., Bates, E. A., Johnson, M. H., Karmiloff-Smith, A., Parisi, D., & Plunkett, K. (1996). *Rethinking innateness: A connectionist perspective on development*. Cambridge, MA: MIT Press.

Goodale, M. A. (1993). Visual pathways supporting perception and action in the primate cerebral cortex. *Current Opinion in Neurobiology, 3*, 578–585.

Klahr, D., & Wallace, J. G. (1976). *Cognitive development: An information processing view*. Hillsdale, NJ: Erlbaum.

Mareschal, D., & French, R. M. (1997). A connectionist account of interference effects in early infant memory and categorization. In M. G. Shafto, & P. Langley (Eds.), *Proceedings of the 19th annual conference of the Cognitive Science Society* (pp. 484–489). Mahwah, NJ: Erlbaum.

Mareschal, D., & French, R. M. (in press). Mechanisms of Categorization in Infancy. *Infancy, 1*.

Mareschal, D., French, R. M., & Quinn, P. C. (submitted). A Connectionist Account of Asymmetric Category Learning in Early Infancy.

Mareschal, D., Plunkett, K., & Harris, P. (1995). Developing object permanence: A connectionist model. In J. D. Moore & J. F. Lehman (Eds.), *Proceedings of the Seventeeth Annual Conference of the Cognitive Science Society* (pp. 170–175). Mahwah, JN: Lawrence Erlbaum Associates.

Mareschal, D., Plunkett, K., & Harris, P. (1999). A computational and neuropsychological account of object-oriented behaviours in infancy. *Developmental Science, 2*, 306–317.

Mareschal, D., & Shultz, T. R. (1996). Generative connectionist networks and constructivist cognitive development. *Cognitive Development, 11*, 571–603.

McClelland, J. L. (1989). Parallel distributed processing: Implications for cognition and development. In Morris, R. G. M. (Ed.), *Parallel distributed processing: Implications for psychology and neurobiology* (pp. 8–45). Oxford: Oxford University Press.

McLeod, P., Plunkett, K., and Rolls, E. T. (1998) *Introduction to connectionist modeling of cognitive processes*. Oxford: Oxford University Press.

Milner, A. D., & Goodale, M. A. (1995). *The Visual Brain in Action*. Oxford, UK: Oxford University Press.

Papert, S. (1963). Intelligence chez l'enfant et chez le robot. In L. Apostel, J. Grize, S. Papert, & J. Piaget. La filiation des structures. *Etudes D'Epistemologie Génétiques, 15*, 131–194.

Piaget, J. (1952). *The Origins of Intelligence in the Child*. New York: International Universities Press.

Piaget, J. (1954). *The Construction of Reality in the Child*. New York: Basic Books.

Plunkett, K., & Sinha, C. (1992). Connectionism and developmental theory. *British Journal of Developmental Psychology, 10*, 209–254.

Quinn, P. C., & Eimas, P. D. (1996). Perceptual organization and categorization in young infants. *Advances in Infancy Research, 10*, 1–36.

Quinn, P. C., Eimas, P. D., & Rosenkrantz, S. L. (1993). Evidence for representations of perceptually similar natural categories by 3-month-old and 4-month-old infants. *Perception, 22*, 463–475.

Rumelhart D. E., & McClelland J. L. (1986). *Parallel distributed processing: Explorations in the microstructure of cognition, Vol. 1*. Cambridge, MA: MIT Press.

Rumelhart, D. E., Hinton, G. E., & Williams, R. J. (1986). Learning representations by back-propagating errors. *Nature 323*, 533–536.

Schafer, G., & Mareschal, D. (submitted). Qualitative shifts in behavior without qualitative shifts in processing: the case of speech sound discrimination and word learning in infancy.

Shultz, T. R., Schmidt, W. C., Buckingham, D., & Mareschal, D. (1995). Modeling cognitive development with a generative connectionist algorithm. In T. Simon, & G. Halford (Eds.), *Developing Cognitive Competence: New Approaches to Process Modeling* (pp. 347–362). Hillsdale, NJ: Erlbaum.

Simon, H. A. (1962), An information processing theory of intellectual development. *Monograph of the Society for Research in Child Development, 27* (2, Serial No. 82).

Slater, A. (1995). Visual perception and memory at birth. *Advances in Infancy Research, 9*, 107–162.

Solokov, E. N. (1963). *Perception and the conditioned reflex*. Hillsdale, NJ: Erlbaum.

Ungerleider, L. G., & Mishkin, M. (1982). Two cortical visual systems. In D. J. Ingle, M. A. Goodale, and R. J. W. Mansfield (Eds.), *Analysis of visual behavior* (pp. 549–586). Cambridge, MA: MIT Press.

Van Essen, D. C., Anderson, C. H., & Felleman, D. J. (1992). Information processing in the primate visual system: An integrated systems perspective. *Science, 255*, 419–423.

Young, R. (1976). *Seriation by children: An artificial intelligence analysis of a Piagetian task*. Basel: Birkhauser.

Younger, B. A. (1985). The segregation of items into categories by ten-month-old infants. *Child Development, 56*, 1574–1583.

Part II

Sensation and Perception

Introduction to Part II

In order to begin to make sense of the world the infant has to perceive it! The study of sensation and perception occupies a central role in infancy research, and the papers in this section have been selected to give an account of some of the different areas of investigation. We know that sensitivity to sensory stimulation and, indeed, learning about aspects of stimulation, begins in the womb. Researchers have become sophisticated in developing ways of investigating fetal behavior, and in chapter 4 Kisilevsky et al. give an account of fetal sensitivity to touch stimulation. Vision is unique among the senses in that there is no opportunity for its use prior to birth, but, as Slater makes apparent in chapter 5, the visual world of the newborn baby is organized and, from birth, learning about the visual world is rapid. In chapter 6 Bahrick gives an account of learning about information provided by more than one sensory modality when she investigates the development of intermodal perception.

Perceptual abilities allow infants to learn about the world, and this is illustrated in chapters 7 and 8. In chapter 7 Symons et al. demonstrate that young infants are very sensitive to an important cue that is crucial in social interactions, that of knowing when someone is looking at them or not. In chapter 8 Werker describes how infants, in their first year of life, become acutely attuned to the characteristics of their native language.

FOUR

Fetal Sensitivity to Touch

Introduction

Does birth signal the onset of human experience, making newborn testing ideal for addressing the nature-nurture issue? The answer to this question is a resounding "No". Of course, the fetus lives in a relatively dark uterine environment, with little or no patterned visual stimulation. However, fetal experience does include variations in tactile, auditory, and chemical stimulation throughout gestation. Any or all of this experience could influence both fetal development and ultimately newborn behavior. There is indeed evidence that fetal experience has an impact on newborns. In a classic study Anthony DeCasper and William Fifer (1980; reprinted in Slater and Muir, 1999) had newborns suck on a nonnutritive nipple in an operant conditioning paradigm. By lengthening or shortening the interval between sucking bursts, these infants produced a recording of their mother's voice reciting a nursery rhyme. By changing the interval in the opposite direction they produced a stranger's voice reading the same passage. Infants rapidly learned to alter their sucking pattern to produce their mother's voice more often than the stranger's voice. Given that they were only a few hours old, this preference presumably was generated by the familiarity of the mother's voice heard during gestation.

Newborns also appear to be affected by sounds from external sources – they may even listen to TV and radio programs. Peter Hepper (1988) reported that newborns of mothers who were "addicted" to relaxing and watching the soap opera "Neighbors" on a daily basis also appeared to "relax" (i.e., stop crying and become quiet) when he played them the soap opera's theme song. Infants of mothers who did not watch the soap opera were not affected by the theme song. However, these studies do not directly test fetal responses to intrauterine stimulation.

It has been known for a long time that late in gestation, fetuses will respond to loud acoustic stimuli. For example, Sontag and Wallace

(1936) used a stethoscope to listen to fetal heart beats and reported reliable increases in fetal heart rate to loud sounds. Even earlier, Peiper (1925) rested his hand on a pregnant woman's abdomen and reported feeling fetal movements when he honked the horn of a car a few feet away. For many years, pregnant women have reported feeling their fetuses move in response to external stimulation. Now highly advanced ultrasound technology allows researchers to make accurate recordings of fetal heart rate and fetal body movements in response to a variety of auditory and tactile stimuli (see reviews by Lecanuet et al., 1995; Kisilevsky and Low, 1998). Indeed, many of today's pregnant mothers (and their family and friends) have watched their fetuses growth and noted their behavioral development during routine obstetric ultrasound examinations.

This paper, by Kisilevsky et al. (1992), on fetal sensitivity to vibroacoustic stimulation was selected to illustrate a number of points. First, it is one of the few papers in the literature that reports both fetal heart rate and body movement responses during stimulus and no-stimulus control trials. Second, the design includes both cross-sectional and longitudinal data (the cross-sequential design discussed in chapter 1). This allowed the authors to describe the developmental function for the onset of fetal sensitivity to a particular type of vibroacoustic stimulation. Third, when the developmental functions for heart rate acceleration and body movement responses are compared, a different picture emerges. The heart rate data suggest that the onset of vibroacoustic sensitivity appears suddenly (stage-like) at around 29 weeks' gestational age, while the body movement responses to the same stimulus begin around 26 weeks' gestation and increase in strength steadily for the next 6 weeks, reflecting a more continuous function. It is important to note that the shape of some developmental functions may depend on the response measure used and that on occasion, as here, different response measures can give a different indication of the underlying behavioral development.

References

DeCasper, A. J., and Fifer, W. P. (1980). Of human bonding: Newborns prefer their mothers' voices. *Science, 208*, 1174–6.

Hepper, P. G. (1988). Fetal "soap" addiction. *The Lancet, 1*, 1347–8.

Kisilevsky, B. S., and Low, J. A. (1998). Human fetal behavior: 100 years of study. *Developmental Review, 18*, 1–29.

Lecanuet, J.-P., Granier-Deferre, C., and Busnel, M.-C. (1995). Human fetal auditory perception. In J.-P. Lecanuet, W. P. Fifer, N. A. Krasnegor, and W. P. Smotherman (eds.) *Fetal Development: A Psychobiological Perspective* (pp. 239–62). Hillsdale, NJ: Erlbaum.

Peiper, A. (1925). Sinnesempfindungen des kindes vor seiner geburt. *Monatsschrift Fur Kinderheikunde, 29,* 236–41.

Slater, A., and Muir, D. (eds.) (1999). *The Blackwell Reader in Developmental Psychology.* Blackwell: Oxford, UK.

Sontag., L. W., and Wallace, R. F. (1936). Changes in the rate of the human fetal heart in response to vibratory stimuli. *American Journal of Diseases of Children, 51,* 583–9.

Maturation of Human Fetal Responses to Vibroacoustic Stimulation

Barbara S. Kisilevsky, Darwin W. Muir,
and James A. Low

The full-term human fetus, 37–42 weeks' gestational age, responds to sound and vibration with fetal heart rate (FHR) accelerations and body movements (e.g., Grimwade et al., 1971; Kisilevsky and Muir, 1991; Leader et al., 1982; Sontag and Wallace, 1936). However, to date, little is known about the maturation of these responses. Such information would increase our understanding of the development of sensory abilities and identify the period when sensory stimulation may influence functional development.

Limited information concerning maturation comes from prenatal studies of elicited body movements/startles. Birnholz and Benacerraf (1983) observed fetal blink-startle responses following vibroacoustic stimulation and noted that movement was first elicited in a small number of fetuses at 24–25 weeks gestational age and was present consistently after 28 weeks. Although they failed to control for spontaneous activity, others replicated and extended these findings, observing a response latency of 1–2 sec; habituation of body movement, but not eye-blink, as early as 30–31 weeks (e.g., Kuhlman et al., 1988); and an increase in the percentage of fetuses responding from 30% at 24 weeks to 95% at 37 weeks (Crade and Lovett, 1988). The results of these initial studies indicate that responding to sensory stimuli changes as gestation advances, but they provide little information concerning the nature of the developmental change. For example, whether changes are continuous or discontinuous and whether the onset and response pattern are the same for all fetuses is not known.

Gagnon and colleagues (e.g., Gagnon et al., 1987a, 1987b; Gagnon et al., 1988; Gagnon et al., 1986) provide the most extensive analysis of maturation of selected cardiac response measures. In a series of studies employing an artificial larynx to deliver a 5-sec vibroacoustic stimulation, cardiac changes during 10-min intervals were measured for up to 1 hour following stimulation. Latency, duration, and magnitude of the first FHR acceleration of at least 15 beats per minute (BPM) also were reported. Examining the first FHR acceleration, which could have occurred between 0 and 134 sec following stimulus onset (Gagnon et al., 1986), Gagnon et al. (1988) noted that reliable FHR changes occurred from about 30 weeks; a shorter latency and duration and a greater peak magnitude were observed (Gagnon et al., 1986) from 30 to 40 weeks. Using the first 15 BPM FHR acceleration criterion, they reported reliable responses from 100% of subjects at 36–40 weeks, 67% of subjects at 30–32 weeks, and 25% of subjects at 26–28 weeks. Using a less stringent 10 BPM criterion, responses occurred in 100% of subjects from 30 to 40 weeks and 75% of subjects at 26–28 weeks (Gagnon et al., 1988). Looking at cardiac changes during 10-min intervals, the mean baseline FHR did not change between 26 and 28 weeks. However, an increase was observed during the first 10 min following stimulation from 30 weeks gestation and remained above baseline level for at least an hour in fetuses from 33 to 40 weeks (Gagnon et al., 1987a). Although there were no changes in the number of responses occurring 0–10 min after stimulation, at 36–40 weeks there was in increase in the number of FHR accelerations (Gagnon et al., 1987b) between 10 and 20 min. From these findings, Gagnon and colleagues conclude that the cardiac response to vibroacoustic stimulation first appears at a narrow window in time between 28 and 30 weeks gestational age and becomes fully mature by 30 weeks; they note that this developmental function may be related to maturation of the fetal autonomic nervous system (Gagnon et al., 1988). Unfortunately, in this series of studies, immediate and delayed responses were not separated. The stimulus-induced behavioral changes lasting up to 60 min in some cases that were found when measurements were analyzed over 10-min windows may reflect the effects of state transition. These findings need to be replicated by examining immediate FHR changes controlling for time of stimulus onset.

We have shown (Kisilevsky and Muir, 1991) that a large, reliable FHR acceleration can be elicited within seconds of stimulation in the full-term fetus and that it is continuous with the neonatal response. Thus, the present study was designed to characterize further the nature of the immediate changes in FHR and movement responses as the "healthy" fetus matures from 23 to 36 weeks. Specifically, we addressed the questions of: (1) the age of onset of responding, (2) the pattern of change with increasing gestation, and (3) the concordance between longitudinal and cross-sectional age effects. Furthermore, we predicted, based on the literature, that the age at which a response first appeared would vary depending on the response measure. An earlier onset of the motor compared to the cardiac acceleration response has been demonstrated in studies with humans (see above) and other species (e.g., Gottlieb, 1971). Thus, a reliable movement response was expected to occur first around 25 weeks, while a reliable cardiac acceleration response was not expected until 29–31 weeks. We also expected that response patterns would vary with response measure. Earlier reports of increasing numbers of subjects responding at increasing gestational age suggested that maturation of movement responses occurred in a continuous fashion, increasing gradually and steadily over time. In contrast, if Gagnon and colleagues were replicated, the pattern of FHR change may be a more discontinuous function, with a sudden change from no response to mature response between 28 and 30 weeks. The comparability of age effects in longitudinal and cross-sectional studies is unknown.

Given the paucity of information concerning human fetal response to external sensory stimulation, selection of an "ideal" stimulus with which to examine maturation is difficult. Most investigators have used a vibroacoustic rather than an airborne sound stimulus, probably because of salience. Vibroacoustic elicited response rates are between 75% and 100% (e.g., Gagnon et al., 1988), compared to airborne sound rates of 30% to 60% (e.g., Kisilevsky et al., 1989, and Schmidt et al., 1985). Typically, an artificial larynx is used to deliver a vibroacoustic stimulus. However, reports that it induces tachycardia (Gagnon et al., 1988), a high occurrence of increased baseline FHR, unusual FHR patterns (Thomas et al., 1989), and a disorganization of behavioral states (Visser et al., 1989) make one question its suitability for examining FHR responses. In addition, because of its high sound intensity (recorded in air at 100 dB), its safety for use with the preterm fetus during cochlear development has been questioned (Gerhardt, 1989). To overcome these problems, we chose a vibroacoustic stimulus with a less intense auditory component (64 dB SPL recorded in air) previously shown to elicit movement and/or FHR acceleration responses from 92% of term fetuses with no significant response decrement over eight repeated trials (Kisilevsky and Muir, 1991). It was assumed that the intensity of the auditory component of our stimulus was at/near threshold for our youngest fetuses (Starr et al., 1977), and that there was no attenuation when the stimulus was delivered directly to the maternal abdomen (Oliver, 1989). We recognize that employing a single stimulus limits our ability to differentiate between maturity of sensory and response systems.

Method

Subjects

Sixty pregnant Caucasian women attending prenatal clinics at a community teaching hospital gave informed, written consent to participate in a study examining the usefulness of spontaneous and stimulus-induced fetal behavioral measures in the assessment of fetal well-being. Given the universal health care system in Canada, information regarding socioeconomic status is not obtained. The present data were collected as part of a larger study, following a 1-hour recording of spontaneous behavior. At the time of testing, there were 12 fetuses in each of the following five age ranges (weeks:days gestation): 23:0–25:6, 26:0–28:6, 29:0–31:6, 32:0–34:6, and 35:0–36:6. Gestational age was calculated from the first day of the last menstrual period (accuracy rate 75%–85%) or from early ultrasound scan (SD = 1 week). Also, a sequential design (mixed cross-sectional and longitudinal methods) was used. Six fetuses in each of the three youngest age groups were retested at subsequent age levels (i.e., 23–25 and 26–28 weeks, 26–28 and 29–31 weeks, 29–31 and 32–34 weeks). Neonatal outcome measures confirmed the gestational age and good health of the fetuses studied. All infants (28 females, 32 males) had a gestational age >37 weeks, birth weight >2,500 grams,

Apgar 6–10 at 5 min, cord artery buffer base >34 mMol/L (if obtained), and a diagnosis of healthy term infant on the first day physical examination.

Stimuli/Equipment. The low-frequency (broad-band 50–1,250 Hz, with peaks at 125 and 160 Hz) vibroacoustic stimulus was produced by a cylindrical shaped (3.5 × 25.2 cm), hand-held, battery-powered, commercial vibrator (Allied Traders Limited) whose spectral characteristics have been described previously (Kisilevsky and Muir, 1991). The intensity of the vibrator's sound in air was 64 dB SPL (C scale; Bruel & Kjaer Impulse Precision Sound Level Meter measured at a distance of 10 cm). At the onset of each stimulus trial, the researcher turned on the vibrator and applied its tip to the maternal abdomen over the site of the fetal head (confirmed by ultrasound scan).

During the procedure, continuous FHR recordings were obtained using a Hewlett-Packard fetal monitor (Model 8040A) with an event marker to indicate trial onset on each record. The FHR monitor produces a record of instantaneous heart rate for each beat. To smooth the output and obtain an FHR for each second, records were scored using a Numonics digitizer and a Zenith 151 computer. A scorer, blind to stimulus and control trial status, traced over each FHR recording using the digitizer. The data consisted of a computer record of the FHR in BPM at 1-sec intervals beginning 10 sec prior to trial onset and ending 20 sec following onset for every trial. Finally, a difference score for each trial was obtained by subtracting the FHR at each second from the FHR at trial onset. The peak FHR acceleration score for each trial was the maximum difference score obtained within the 20 sec following trial onset.

Fetal movements were observed and recorded within 5 sec of trial onset by a trained research assistant, blind to vibrator or control trial occurrence. Judgments were made from an image of a cross-section of the fetal trunk, which may or may not have included limbs, viewed with a real-time ultrasound scanner (Siemens LX). Because current scanning techniques permit only a partial view of the fetus, a dichotomous movement score, either yes = 1 or no = 0, was recorded on each trial. Trials were grouped into three-trial blocks to permit the use of analysis of variance (ANOVA) tests (Hsu and Feldt, 1969). Ninety-seven percent agreement was obtained between the scores of the trained assistant and the researcher, who also scored movement at the time of testing; thus, only scores from the trained assistant were used in the analyses.

BMDP and SPSSx statistical software packages were used for data analyses. Conservative probabilities using Huynh-Feldt adjusted degrees of freedom are reported for repeated-measures analyses.

Procedure. During the 10-min procedure, each fetus received three stimulus and three no-stimulus control trials, intermixed and randomly presented. A stimulus trial consisted of the activated vibrator being applied to the maternal abdomen for approximately 2.5 sec. A control trial consisted of the vibrator being turned on for approximately 2.5 sec and placed over the site of the fetal head without touching the maternal abdomen. The minimum interstimulus interval was set at 1 min, with the restriction that trials were begun only when the heart rate was judged to be stable and no movements were seen on ultrasound scan. The same procedure was used for repeat testing.

Results

FHR – change over first 10 sec from stimulus onset

FHR change over the first 10 sec following stimulus onset was examined to describe the immediate cardiac response. Initial analyses were limited to the first 10 sec of the first stimulus and control trial because previous work (Kisilevsky et al., 1989) had shown significant FHR acceleration over this time period with no differences in responding across three trials. A three-way ANOVA with one between factor (age – five groups) and two within factors (stimulus condition – vibrator vs. control; seconds – 1 to 10) demonstrated that all main effects and interactions were significant (p's < .0001). Looking at figure 4.1, it can be seen that FHR acceleration was the typical response from 29 weeks' gestational age. Orthogonal contrasts comparing responding across age groups showed that significantly greater FHR accelerations occurred in the three older age groups compared to the two younger ones. There were: (1) greater FHR accelerations at 29–31, 32–34, and 35–36 weeks' gestational age compared to 23–25 and 26–28 weeks, $F(1, 55) = 41.25$, $p < .00001$; (2) no differences in responding at 29–31 and 32–34 weeks, $F(1, 55) = 1.77$, N.S.; and (3) significantly greater responding at

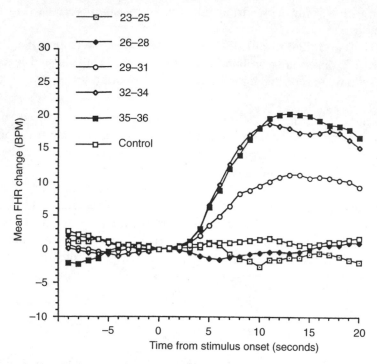

Figure 4.1 Mean FHR change (BPM) as a function of time from stimulus onset at the 0 sec fetuses at 23–25, 26–28, 29–31, 32–34, and 35–36 weeks' gestational age. Control trial responding is the average of the first control trial across gestational ages

29–31 compared to 26–28 weeks, $F(1, 55) = 10.25$, $p < .01$. Although there were no significant differences in the magnitude of the FHR acceleration at 29–31 and 32–34 weeks when responding over condition and seconds was compared, as illustrated in figure 4.1, from 3 to 20 sec poststimulus onset, the average magnitude of the FHR acceleration in the 29–31-week group was always below that of the 32–34- and 35–36-week fetuses (Sign Test, $p < .05$).

The significant age × stimulus condition × second interaction, $F(36, 495) = 8.95$, $p < .00001$, indicated that there was a difference over seconds and stimulus condition and that difference varied with age. It would follow that either a vibrator-induced FHR response occurred at some age(s) and not others or that there was a qualitatively different response at some age(s). To sort out this complex interaction, first, a two-way ANOVA with one between factor (age – five groups) and one within factor (seconds – 1 to 10) was used to examine responding on the first control trial. No differences in responding were found as a function of age or seconds, and there were no interactions, indicating that there were no differences in spontaneous activity among the different age groups and that spontaneous activity did not vary over time; the control data were averaged over groups for display in figure 4.1. Since there were no differences on control trial responding over age or time, the differences had to occur on the stimulus trial. A one-way ANOVA (simple effects analysis; Keppel, 1982) with one within factor (seconds – 1 to 10) and trend analyses for the first vibrator trial for each age group revealed that FHR changes were qualitatively different across age groups. There was a significant effect of time (p's < .00001) and a significant linear trend (p's < .001–.00001) for each of the three older age groups and a significant quadratic trend, $F(1, 11) = 5.43$, $p < .05$, for the 26–28-week group. In these younger fetuses, eight out of 12 fetuses showed a small FHR deceleration.

FHR – mean peak FHR acceleration within 20 sec of stimulus onset

Peak FHR acceleration within 20 sec of trial onset on the first testing was examined to compare our results with those of other investigators. To determine the earliest age at which a vibroacoustic stimulus elicits a reliable FHR acceleration response, a three-way ANOVA with one between factor (age group – five levels) and two within factors (stimulus condition – vibrator vs. control; trials – 1 to 3) was used. A main effect of age group, $F(4, 55) = 26.74$, $p < .00001$, and stimulus condition, $F(1, 55) = 134.49$, $p < .00001$, is qualified by a condition × age interaction, $F(4, 55) = 25.26$, $p < .00001$, clearly shown in figure 4.2(a); the mean peak FHR acceleration was greater on vibrator compared to control trials from 29 weeks. An analysis of simple effects demonstrated significantly greater FHR acceleration ($p < .00001$) on vibrator compared to control trials at 29–31, 32–34, and 35–36 weeks. There were no differences in cardiac responding between the two

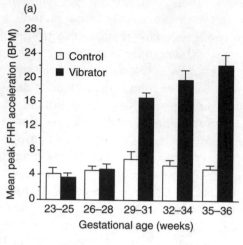

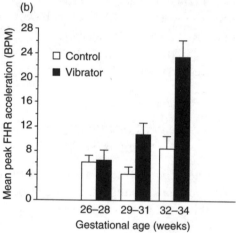

Figure 4.2 Mean peak FHR acceleration (BPM) as a function of gestational age (a) at the initial testing ($n = 12$) and (b) at repeat testing ($n = 6$). Responding across three stimulus and three control trials was grouped for display purposes. Vertical bars indicate standard error of the mean (SEM)

subsamples within each age group (i.e., those tested only once vs. those tested twice). Because there were no differences in responding across trials, the three stimulus and three control trials were grouped together for display purposes in figure 4.2(a).

Movement – within 5 sec of stimulus onset

The results for the three-trial block movement measure were similar to those found for FHR. A two-way ANOVA with one between factor (age group) and one within factor (stimulus condition) demonstrated main effects for age, $F(4, 55) = 5.97$, $p < .0001$, and stimulus condition, $F(1, 55) = 125.14$, $p < .00001$, and a significant condition × age interaction, $F(4, 55) = 7.30$, $p < .0001$. This interaction is shown in figure 4.3(a); movements were greater on vibrator compared to control trial blocks from 26 through 36 weeks' gestation. This difference in the older four age groups was confirmed by simple effects analysis. Significantly greater movement occurred on vibrator compared to control trials (p's $< .01$) at 26–28, 29–31, 32–34, and 35–36 weeks. Furthermore, there were no differences in movement responding between the two subsamples within each age group (i.e., those tested once vs. those tested twice).

Percentage of subjects responding

To determine whether the FHR and movement scores, which represented averaged data, were an accurate reflection of individual subject behavior, we looked at both the percentage of subjects responding on the first trial with an FHR acceleration of at least 10 BPM (figure 4.4(a)) or movement (figure 4.4(b)). As can be seen, individual fetal behavior and averaged data give the same picture. From 29 weeks' gestation, 83%–100% of subjects responded with an FHR acceleration on the first stimulus trial; there was an 83%–92% response rate across all vibrator trials. Percentages of subjects responding with movement on the first vibrator trial increased from 58% at 26–28 weeks to 92%–100% at 32–36 weeks; the movement response rate across all vibrator trials increased from 53% to 94% from 26–28 to 35–36 weeks.

Evidence for maturation: cross-sectional and longitudinal comparisons

FHR changes and movements observed during the second testing session were analyzed exploiting both the cross-sectional and longitudinal

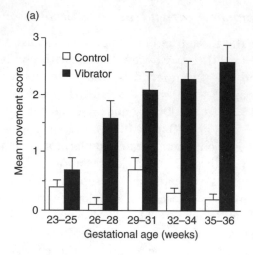

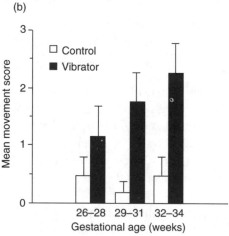

Figure 4.3   Mean movement score over three-trial blocks as a function of gestational age (a) at the initial testing ($n = 12$) and (b) at repeat testing ($n = 6$). Vertical bars indicate SEM

nature of the data. From a cross-sectional perspective, the findings from the first testing (i.e., those relating to the mean peak FHR acceleration within 20 sec and movement within 5 sec of stimulus onset) were replicated when the initial analyses were repeated with the data from the second testing. For the FHR acceleration response, there was a main effect of age group (three levels – 26–28, 29–31, and 32–34 weeks),

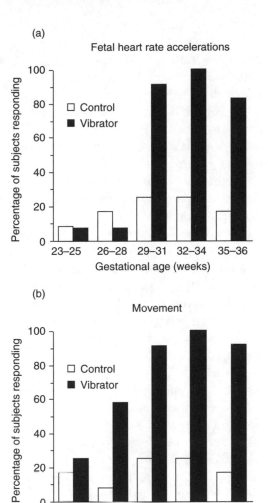

Figure 4.4 Percentage of subjects responding with (a) an FHR acceleration of at least 10 BPM and (b) a movement on the first vibroacoustic and first control trial. Vertical bars indicate SEM. Note: in (b) the control bar for the 35–36-week age group indicates no responding

$F(2, 15) = 7.41$, $p < .01$, and stimulus condition (vibrator vs. control), $F(1, 15) = 26.55$, $p < .0001$, which was qualified by a condition × age interaction, $F(2, 15) = 9.26$, $p < .01$, shown in figure 4.2(b). Analysis of simple effects confirmed greater FHR acceleration on vibrator compared to control trials in the 29–31- ($p < .05$) and the 32–34-week ($p < .01$) fetuses. For the movement data, there was only a main effect of stimulus condition (vibrator vs. control), $F(1, 15) = 22.16$, $p < .001$. Figure 4.3(b) illustrates that there is more movement on stimulus compared to control trials in all three age groups. Analyses of both the first and second testing showed that the magnitude of FHR accelerations was significantly greater on vibrator compared to control trials from 29 weeks and that significantly more movements occurred on vibrator compared to control trials from 26 weeks. Thus, subsequent analyses were limited to responding on stimulus trials.

From a sequential perspective, we examined the longitudinal data to determine whether FHR accelerations were observed first at 29–31 weeks gestation and movement responses were observed first at 26–28 weeks, as they had been with the cross-sectional analyses. As would be expected from the previous analyses, three separate two-way ANOVAs with two within factors (age – 23–25 vs. 26–28, 26–28 vs. 29–31, and 29–31 vs. 32–34; trials – 1 to 3) used to determine FHR changes on vibrator trials with advancing gestation showed no differences in responding for those fetuses tested at 23–25 and then 26–28 or for those tested at 29–31 and then 32–34 weeks. Fetuses tested at 26–28 and then 29–31 weeks showed a significant increase in mean peak FHR acceleration on the second testing, $F(1, 5) = 6.48$, $p = .05$. However, looking at figure 4.5, it can be seen that the average magnitude of the FHR acceleration for those fetuses retested at 29–31 weeks was significantly lower compared to those tested for the first time at this age. This was confirmed in a two-way ANOVA with one between factor (number of testings – one vs. repeated, $F(1, 16) = 10.65$, $p < .01$) and one within factor (trials). Perhaps there is a repeated-measures effect during this transition period from an FHR deceleration to an acceleration response at 29–31 weeks.

Finally, looking at figure 4.6, it can be seen that when one uses a movement score obtained over a series of trials, responsivity increases steadily from 26 to 36 weeks' gestation. Three separate one-way ANOVAs with one within factor (age – 23–25 vs. 26–28, 26–28 vs. 29–31, and 29–31 vs. 32–34) showed no differences in responding over the 3-week period between the first and second testing.

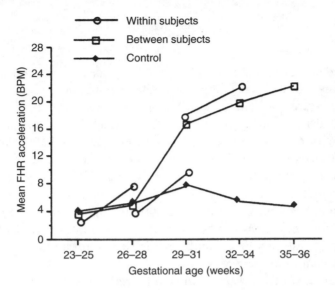

Figure 4.5 Mean FHR acceleration (BPM) as a function of gestational age measured longitudinally and cross-sectionally. Mean FHR acceleration during control trials measured cross-sectionally is displayed

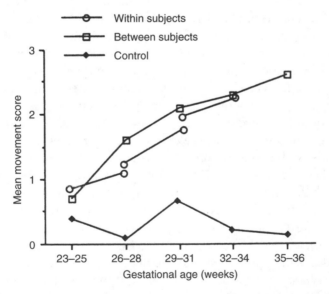

Figure 4.6 Mean movement score as a function of gestational age longitudinally and cross-sectionally. Mean movement score during control trials measured cross-sectionally is displayed

Discussion

Our prediction that age at onset of fetal response to vibroacoustic stimulation would vary depending on whether movements or cardiac accelerations were measured was confirmed. The onset of reliable
stimulus-driven movements occurred by 26 weeks' gestation, preceding
the onset of reliable cardiac accelerations at 29 weeks. Furthermore, as
expected, developmental functions also varied depending on the
response measured. Responding to vibroacoustic stimulation increased
in a gradual, continuous fashion when movements were plotted as a
function of gestational age. Looking at both longitudinal and cross-sectional data, the number of movements across stimulus trials and the
number of subjects responding on the first stimulus trial increased
steadily from 26 to 36 weeks.

The present FHR acceleration results were consistent with those of
previous researchers when we employed similar response criteria. For
example, using either mean peak FHR accelerations on stimulus compared to control trials or the number of subjects responding with FHR
accelerations of at least 10 BPM on the first stimulus trial, the results
were comparable with those of Gagnon and co-workers (see the beginning of this chapter). The FHR response pattern reflected a discontinuous function with a rather abrupt change from no response to a
relatively mature response between 29 to 31 weeks gestation. However,
upon closer inspection of FHR performance, a more complex maturational profile for cardiac responses to vibroacoustic stimulation was
revealed, and the apparent discrepancy between the age at onset of
movement and cardiac response systems was resolved. The first observ-
able cardiac response was a deceleration at 26–28 weeks. Although the
magnitude of the deceleration response was small, it appears to be reliable, indicating that a cardiac response to vibroacoustic stimulation
emerges at the same age as movement response. Although we were skeptical of this finding, there are three compelling reasons why we are
forced to take it seriously. First, it has been replicated in a separate group
of high-risk fetuses (Kisilevsky et al., 1990). Second, it appears at a time
in gestation when spontaneous decelerations are the most common FHR
change (Wheeler and Murrills, 1978). And third, small FHR decelerations have been reported in response to low intensity auditory stimuli
(Lecanuet et al., 1989).

The change from an FHR deceleration to acceleration response observed in this lab needs to be replicated at other sites. At present, we have no definitive explanation to account for this change. However, because of its importance, we offer several possible explanations, recognizing that they are purely speculative. For example, the change may be the result of a simple shift in the locus of control in the autonomic nervous system (i.e., the shift results from ontogenetic changes in the neural systems mediating aspects of the cardiac response). Although later in gestation there is a more complex interplay in the systems mediating FHR accelerations and decelerations (e.g., see overview by Martin, 1978), at mid-gestation, FHR deceleration is controlled by the parasympathetic nervous system, an earlier developing structure than the sympathetic nervous system that exerts control over FHR acceleration (Sampson et al., 1980). Observations of spontaneous FHR changes indicate that decelerations are common in the very premature fetus, representing 97% of FHR changes between 20 and 22 weeks, and decrease to 34% by 28–30 weeks (Sorokin et al., 1982). On the other hand, FHR accelerations are first observed at about 25 weeks and represent 36% of changes by 28–30 weeks (Sorokin et al., 1982; Wheeler and Murrills, 1978). Perhaps vibroacoustic stimuli initially elicit a parasympathetic-mediated FHR deceleration followed by a sympathetic-mediated FHR acceleration. If such is the case, we would expect disorganization and decreased stability in the response during the transition period, similar to that shown during the development of other response systems (e.g., auditory localization – Muir et al., 1989; newborn stepping – Thelen and Cooke, 1987). Perhaps the decreased magnitude of FHR acceleration (see figure 4.1) in our 29–31-week group represents disorganization during transition. Although the present results may reflect both the system controlling the response at age of onset and the time when control changes from one system to another, speculations about autonomic nervous system control do not tell us what triggers the change or why it should occur.

The cardiac change also may indicate a shift in the effectiveness of the stimulus, reflecting an increase in vibroacoustic sensitivity. For example, with an airborne sound, we know that fetal response, at term, is related to stimulus intensity (e.g., Kisilevsky et al., 1989). However, we do not know whether the younger fetuses in this study are showing FHR decelerations because perception of the stimulus was less intense owing to immaturity or because FHR deceleration was the only response operational. In this study, from 26 to 36 weeks, 58 of 60 fetuses (97%) responded with movement and/or cardiac change on the first vibroacoustic trial. With increasing gestational age, moreover, the magnitude and frequency of response increased. These changes across gestation may reflect maturation of the response systems. Alternatively, they may reflect a change in the amodal sensitivity of the sensory systems with stimuli perceived as lower intensity eliciting an attention/orienting response and stimuli perceived as higher intensity eliciting an arousal/defensive response similar to that which has been described in infants (e.g., Graham and Clifton, 1966). It must be emphasized that this study was not designed to untangle the loci of developmental trends that were uncovered. Nevertheless, our results set the stage for future work aimed at determining the mechanisms underlying the response.

Given that we used a multimodal stimulus, the mechanisms underlying the shift in the FHR response may be much more complex than simply a change in locus of control or vibroacoustic sensitivity as the organism matures. Possibly, a change in the sensitivity of both the tactile and auditory systems occurs in parallel, and when both systems are stimulated the response is additive. Alternatively, the shift from FHR deceleration to acceleration may reflect a change from a tactile to an auditory response or from a unimodal (tactile) to a multimodal (auditory-tactile) sensory response. Because we used a compound stimulus, we cannot identify which component(s) of the tactile and auditory systems drive the fetal response.

As stated in the introduction, we choose a vibroacoustic stimulus to begin our investigation of the maturation of fetal sensory responses because of its reported salience when used in the assessment of fetal well-being from 25 weeks to term. Also, we knew that both the tactile and auditory systems are operational by 26 weeks. The tactile system matures very early in fetal development, with evidence of head bending as early as 7.5 weeks (e.g., Hooker, 1952). Although the auditory system develops later, with histological development completed by 28–36 weeks (e.g., Pujol et al., 1990), studies employing auditory evoked potentials in babies born preterm demonstrate that cochlear function begins as early as 25 weeks and that the threshold intensity for such responses at this age is 65 dB SPL (Starr et al., 1977). Furthermore, studies using vibroacoustic stimuli report much higher response rates than those using either mechanical vibration or airborne sound alone. For example, at term, response rates for ballottement range from 0% to 58% (e.g., Kisilevsky and Muir, 1991; Richardson et al., 1981; Visser et al., 1983), and those for airborne sound range from 30% to 60% (see introduction). For the compound vibroacoustic stimulus used in this study, response rates near term, 35–36 weeks, varied from 83% to 92%, replicating earlier reports (see introduction). Given that both the tactile and auditory systems are operational by 26 weeks and that response rates appear to be much higher for multimodal than unimodal sensory stimuli, perhaps in the fetus, the salience of the stimulus results from an interaction between the two modalities. Such an effect was demonstrated in newborns when a somatosensorily evoked response was enhanced by the addition of noise to touch (Wolff et al., 1974).

Our findings lead to more questions than answers. However, several directions for future research on the maturation of fetal responses to vibroacoustic stimuli are clearly indicated. First, additional longitudinal studies are required to identify the shape of developmental functions. We began our investigation using a sequential design. The repeated-measures effect found for the cardiac measure at 29–31 weeks suggests that the results of a longitudinal study may be complex, perhaps because of greater variability characteristic of transition periods (e.g., Thelen, 1989). Of course, given our small sample size, this suggestion is tentative. Second, studies to differentiate further FHR acceleration from movement responses are essential early in development to determine whether these responses are independently controlled. Certainly, this was the case in the present study at 26–28 weeks. Third, movement responses need to be investigated in younger fetuses. Investigators (e.g., Gottlieb, 1971; Jackson and Rubel, 1978) employing auditory stimuli to examine maturational changes in motor responses during embryonic development in other species have found that the initial response is a decrease in activity. In particular, Jackson and Rubel found in the chick embryo that a pure tone initially elicited an inhibition in motor activity followed by a transition period of unreliable responding which was replaced by an increase in motor activity. These authors speculated that the shift from inhibition to excitation might result from ontogenetic changes in neural systems mediating motor aspects of response. In the present study, we noted only an increase in stimulus-induced movement with age. However, the design of our study did not allow for a decrease. Stimuli were presented only when there was no fetal movement. Thus, activity was at a floor and no decrease could be observed. It may be that stimulation of younger fetuses during movement would result in an attentional or orienting response manifested by a decrease in activity. Finally, vibrotactile sensitivity functions need to be obtained from young fetuses, similar to the acoustic sensitivity function derived from the term fetus (e.g., Kisilevsky et al., 1989). Varying the stimulus intensity might reveal shifts from FHR deceleration to acceleration within each age group.

References

Birnholz, J. C., & Benacerraf, B. R. (1983). The development of human fetal hearing. *Science, 222,* 516–518.

Crade, M., & Lovett, S. (1988). Fetal response to sound stimulation: Preliminary report exploring use of sound stimulation in routine obstetrical ultrasound examinations. *Journal of Ultrasound Medicine, 7,* 499–503.

Gagnon, R., Hunse, C., Carmichael, L., Fellows, F., & Patrick, J. (1987a). Human fetal responses to vibratory acoustic stimulation from twenty-six weeks to term. *American Journal of Obstetrics and Gynecology, 157,* 1375–1381.

Gagnon, R., Hunse, C., Carmichael, L., Fellows, F., & Patrick, J. (1987b). External vibratory acoustic stimulation near term: Fetal heart rate and heart rate variability responses. *American Journal of Obstetrics and Gynecology, 156,* 323–327.

Gagnon, R., Hunse, C., & Patrick, J. (1988). Fetal responses to vibratory acoustic stimulation: Influence of basal heart rate. *American Journal of Obstetrics and Gynecology, 159,* 835–839.

Gagnon, R., Patrick, J., Foreman, J., & West, R. (1986). Stimulation of human fetuses with sound and vibration. *American Journal of Obstetrics and Gynecology, 155,* 848-851.

Gerhardt, K. J. (1989). Characteristics of the fetal sheep sound environment. *Seminars in Perinatology, 13,* 362–370.

Gottlieb, G. (1971). *Development of species identification in birds.* Chicago: University of Chicago Press.

Graham, F. K., & Clifton, R. K. (1966). Heart-rate change as a component of the orienting response. *Psychological Bulletin, 65,* 305–320.

Grimwade, J. C., Walker, D. W., Bartlett, M., Gordon, S., & Wood, G. (1971). Human fetal heart rate change and movement in response to sound and vibration. *American Journal of Obstetrics and Gynecology, 109,* 86–90.

Hooker, D. (1952). *The prenatal origin of behavior.* Lawrence: University of Kansas Press.

Hsu, T. C., & Feldt, L. S. (1969). The effect of limitations on the number of criterion score values on the significance level of the *F*-test. *American Educational Research Journal, 6,* 515–527.

Jackson, H., & Rubel, E. W. (1978). Ontogeny of behavioral responsiveness to sound in the chick embryo as indicated by electrical recordings of motility. *Journal of Comparative and Physiological Psychology, 92,* 682–696.

Keppel, G. (1982). *Design and analysis: A researcher's handbook* (2d ed.). Englewood Cliffs, NJ: Prentice-Hall.

Kisilevsky, B. S., & Muir, D. W. (1991). Human fetal and subsequent newborn responses to sound and vibration. *Infant Behavior and Development, 14,* 1–26.

Kisilevsky, B. S., Muir, D. W., & Low, J. A. (1989). Human fetal responses to sound as a function of stimulus intensity. *Obstetrics and Gynecology, 73,* 971–976.

Kisilevsky, B. S., Muir, D. W., & Low, J. A. (1990, February). *Comparison of responses elicited by a vibroacoustic stimulus in "healthy" and "hospitalized" human preterm fetuses.* Poster presented at the Second International Conference on Sound and Vibration in Pregnancy, Gainesville, FL.

Kuhlman, K. A., Burns, K. A., Depp, R., & Sabbagha, R. E. (1988). Ultrasound imaging of normal fetal response to external vibratory acoustic stimulation. *American Journal of Obstetrics and Gynecology, 158,* 47–51.

Leader, L. R., Baillie, P., Martin, B., & Vermeulen, E. (1982). Fetal habituation in high risk pregnancies. *British Journal of Obstetrics and Gynaecology, 89,* 441–446.

Lecanuet, J. P., Granier-Deferre, C., & Busnel, M. C. (1989). Differential fetal auditory reactiveness as a function of stimulus characteristics and state. *Seminars in Perinatology, 13,* 421–429.

Martin, C. B. (1978). Regulation of the fetal heart rate and genesis of FHR patterns. *Seminars in Perinatology, 2,* 131–146.

Muir, D. W., Clifton, R. K., & Clarkson, M. G. (1989). The development of a human auditory localization response: A U-shaped function. *Canadian Journal of Psychology, 43,* 199–216.

Oliver, C. (1989). Sound and vibration transmission in tissues. *Seminars in Perinatology, 13,* 354–361.

Pujol, R., Lavigne-Rebillard, M., & Uziel, A. (1990). Physiological correlates of development of the human cochlea. *Seminars in Perinatology, 14,* 275–280.

Richardson, B., Campbell, K., Carmichael, L., & Patrick, J. (1981). Effects of external physical stimulation on fetuses near term. *American Journal of Obstetrics and Gynecology, 139,* 344–352.

Sampson, M. B., Mudaliar, N. A., & Lele, A. S. (1980). Fetal heart rate variability as an indicator of fetal status. *Postgraduate Medicine, 67,* 207–215.

Schmidt, W., Boos, R., Gnirs, J., Auer, L., & Schulze, S. (1985). Fetal behavioral states and controlled sound stimulation. *Early Human Development, 12,* 145–153.

Sontag, L. W., & Wallace, R. F. (1936). Changes in the rate of the human fetal heart in response to vibratory stimuli. *American Journal of Diseases of Children, 51,* 583–589.

Sorokin, Y., Dierker, L. J., Pillay, S. K., Zador, I. E., Schreiner, M. L., & Rosen, M. G. (1982). The association between fetal heart rate patterns and fetal movements in pregnancies between 20–30 weeks' gestation. *American Journal of Obstetrics and Gynecology, 143,* 243–249.

Starr, A., Amlie, R. N., Martin, W. H., & Sanders, S. (1977). Development of auditory function in newborn infants revealed by auditory brainstem potentials. *Pediatrics, 60,* 831–839.

Thelen, E. (1989). Self-organization developmental processes: Can systems approaches work? In M. R. Gunnar, & E. Thelen (Eds.), *Minnesota Symposia on Child Psychology* (Vol. 22, pp. 77–119). Hillsdale, NJ: Erlbaum.

Thelen, E., & Cooke, D. W. (1987). Relationship between newborn stepping and later walking: A new interpretation. *Developmental Medicine and Child Neurology, 29,* 380–393.

Thomas, R. L., Johnson, T. R. B., Besinger, R. E., Rafkin, D., Treanor, C., & Strobino, D. (1989). Preterm and term fetal cardiac and movement responses to vibratory acoustic stimulation. *American Journal of Obstetrics and Gynecology, 161,* 141–145.

Visser, G. H. A., Mulder, H. H., Wit, H. P., Mulder, E. J. H., & Prechtl, H. F. R. (1989). Disturbed fetal behaviour following fibroacoustic stimulation. In G. Gennser, K. Marsal, N. Svenningsen, & K. Lindstrom (Eds.), *Fetal and neonatal physiological measurements III* (pp. 355–358). Malmoe, Sweden: Flenhags Tryckeri.

Visser, G. H. A., Zeelenberg, H. J., deVries, J. I. P., & Dawes, G. S. (1983). External physical stimulation of the human fetus during episodes of low heart rate variation. *American Journal of Obstetrics and Gynecology, 145,* 579–584.

Wheeler, T., & Murrills, A. (1978). Patterns of fetal heart rate during normal pregnancy. *British Journal of Obstetrics and Gynaecology, 85,* 18–27.

Wolff, P., Matsumiya, Y., Abroms, I. F., Van Velzer, C., & Lombroso, C. T. (1974). The effect of white noise on the somatosensory evoked responses in sleeping newborn infants. *Electroencephalography and Clinical Neurophysiology, 37,* 269–274.

FIVE

Early Visual Perception

Introduction

In this chapter Alan Slater discusses the ways in which the visual world of the newborn, and young infant, is structured and organized. Early theories of visual development argued persuasively that infants had to learn to see. Thus, the influential Canadian psychologist Donald Hebb (1949) suggested that perception of even very simple shapes, such as a triangle (the example he used) is the result of complex learning: "The idea that one has to learn to see a triangle must sound extremely improbable" (p. 31), but the best available evidence at the time suggested that this was the case.

Slater describes some of the earlier theoretical views, and presents experimental evidence which convincingly demonstrates that the visual world of the newborn and young infant is highly organized, and that infants are "born to see." He illustrates this view with an account of experiments on size and shape constancy and other visual organizing tendencies – the conclusion from many studies is that "young infants organize the visually perceived world in a similar manner to that of adult perceivers."

Slater's account of early visual abilities continues with a discussion of infants' perception of human faces, and of face-like stimuli. Young infants are attracted to faces more than to any other visual stimulus, and there may, indeed, be some innately-provided propensity to respond to faces *as faces*, rather than merely as collections of visual elements.

What is also becoming clear is that infants learn about their visual world with great rapidity – "at birth visual processing begins with a vengeance" (Karmiloff-Smith, 1996, p. 10) – and this theme is illustrated with respect to newborn infants' learning about connections between the information provided by different sensory modalities, particularly those of seeing and hearing.

Two themes are apparent from Slater's chapter. One is that the newborn and young infant is highly competent in the way(s) in which they perceive the world – there is no going back to the notion of the incompetent infant. The other is that, while we understand some aspects of the starting point of visual perception, we still have a lot to learn!

References

Hebb, D. O. (1949). *The Organization of Behavior*. New York: Wiley.
Karmiloff-Smith, A. (1996). The Connectionist Infant: Would Piaget Turn in his Grave? *SRCD Newsletter* (Fall issue), 1–10.

Further readings

Kellman, P. J. and Arterberry, M. E. (1998). *The Cradle of Knowledge: Development of Perception in Infancy*. Cambridge, Massachusetts: MIT Press.
Slater, A. (ed.) (1998). *Perceptual Development: Visual, Auditory, and Speech Perception in Infancy*. Hove, UK: Psychology Press.

Visual Perception in the Young Infant: Early Organization and Rapid Learning

Alan Slater

Introduction

The major characteristic of perception, which applies to all the sensory modalities, is that it is organized. With respect to visual perception, the world that we experience is immensely complex, consisting of many entities whose surfaces are a potentially bewildering array of overlapping textures, colours, contrasts and contours, undergoing constant change as their position relative to the observer changes. However, as adults we do not perceive a world of fleeting, unconnected retinal images; rather, we perceive objects, events and people that move and change in an organized and coherent manner. For hundreds of years there has been speculation about the development of the visual system and of the perception of an organized visual world; however, answers to the many questions awaited the development of sensitive methods to test infants' perceptual abilities. Many such procedures are now available and, since the 1960s, many relevant infant studies have been reported. The findings from some of these studies are described in this paper.

First, the Theoretical Overview gives a brief account of some of the theories of visual development that have helped shape our understanding of the infant's perceived world. Next Visual Organization at and Near Birth is described. This research has investigated the intrinsic organization of the visual world, including size and shape constancy, subjective contours, and Gestalt organizational principles. Several lines of evidence converge to suggest that infants are born with some representation of the human face, and it has become apparent that infants rapidly learn about their visually perceived world. These themes are discussed under the headings Newborn Infants' Representation of the Human Face and Early Experience and Learning.

Theoretical Overview

Until recent times the majority of theories of visual perception emphasized the extreme perceptual limitations of the newborn and young infant. For example, the "father of modern psychology" William James claimed (1890, Vol. 1, p. 488), in one of the most memorable phrases in developmental psychology, that "the baby, assailed by eyes, ears, nose, skin and entrails at once, feels it all as one great blooming, buzzing confusion." Piaget argued that visual perception is exceptionally impoverished at birth and suggested that its development is a consequence of intensive learning in the months and years from birth: "Perception of light exists from birth (but) All the rest (perception of forms, sizes, positions, distances, prominence, etc.) is acquired through the combination of reflex activity with higher activities" (1953, p. 62). Piaget did not discuss visual development in any detail; however, his constructionist approach suggested that perception becomes structured, in a sequence of stages, as the infant becomes able to coordinate more and more complex patterns of activity. Thus, many perceptual abilities, such as intersensory coordination, size and shape constancy, object permanence (an understanding that hidden objects continue to exist), and the understanding of space and objects, develop relatively late in infancy.

The obvious alternative to a perceptual learning account of visual development is to adopt a nativist view that the ability to perceive a stable, organized visual world is an innate property of the visual system. A coherent and influential Gestalt theory of perception was developed by three psychologists, Max Wertheimer (1890–1943), Kurt Koffka (1886–1941), and Wolfgang Kohler (1887–1967). These Gestalt psychologists listed rules of perceptual organization that describe how groups of stimuli spontaneously organize themselves into meaningful patterns, and they argued that visual organization is a natural characteristic of the human species that is innately provided. Although not of the Gestalt persuasion Zuckerman and Rock (1957) argued on logical grounds that adaptive evolution would have provided the newborn infant with a visual system that was organized: "perceptual organization must occur *before* experience . . . can exert any influence" (p. 294).

The distinguished American psychologist J. J. Gibson (1904–1979) was for many years a leading critic of the empiricist and constructivist position. Gibson (for example, 1979) argued that the senses, or "perceptual systems," have evolved over evolutionary time to detect perceptual invariants directly, and without the need for additional supplementation by experience: "Perception is not a matter of constructing a three-dimensional reality from the retinal image, either in development or in the perceptual acts of adults. The structure of the environment is 'out there' to be picked up, and perception is a matter of picking up invariant properties of space and object" (Bremner, 1994, p. 118). Gibson was not a nativist. However, when researchers began to discover perceptual abilities in young infants that could not be explained by recourse to empiricist, learning, and constructivist views, it was appealing to interpret findings in terms of Gibson's views: since perception is direct and does not need to be enhanced by experience, then Gibson's theory was the only "grand theory" able to accommodate the findings.

The theoreticians mentioned here were presenting their views when there was little experimentation into perceptual development in infancy, and as Zuckerman and Rock (1957) pointed out, "One can hardly take a dogmatic position in an area where, as yet, there exists so little decisive experimentation" (p. 293). However, as soon as research into infant perceptual abilities began in earnest, from the early 1960s, it became apparent that extreme empiricist views were untenable. As early as 1966 Bower concluded that "infants can in fact register most of the information an adult can register but can handle less of (it)" (p. 92). Research over the last 40 years has given rise to conceptions of the "competent infant," who enters the world with an intrinsically organized visual world that is adapted to the need to impose structure and meaning on the people, objects and events that are encountered.

Visual Organization at and Near Birth

The visual information detected by newborn infants is poor compared with that of the adult, and many important visual functions, including scanning abilities, acuity, contrast sensitivity, depth perception and stereopsis, and colour discrimination, are limited at birth. However, visual development is rapid, and many visual functions approach adult standards 3 or 4 months from birth. Even the poor vision of very young infants does not hamper their development: there is "little indication that young infants are handicapped by their purported primitive visual abilities" (Hainline, 1998, p. 5). Young infants do not need to scrutinize the fine print in a contract, or to see things clearly at a distance. The most important visual stimuli are to be found in close proximity, and better acuity, which would allow infants to focus on distant objects that are of no relevance to their development, might well hinder (i.e., distract them), rather than promote, their development. Hainline (1998, p. 9) summarizes it rather nicely: "visually normal infants have the level of visual functioning that is required for the things that infants need to do."

It is clear that the visual system is functioning at birth, and that newborns have many ways in which to make sense of the visually perceived world. This section considers several types of visual organization that are found in early infancy.

Shape and size constancy

As objects move, they change in orientation, or slant, and perhaps also their distance, relative to an observer, causing constant changes to the image of the objects on the retina. However, we do not experience a world of fleeting, unconnected retinal images, but a world of objects that move and change in a coherent manner. Such stability, across the constant retinal changes, is called perceptual constancy. Perception of an object's real shape regardless of changes to its orientation is called shape constancy, and size constancy refers to the fact that we see an object as the same size regardless of its distance from us. If these constancies were not present in infant perception the visual world would be extremely confusing, perhaps approaching James's "blooming, buzzing confusion," and they are a necessary prerequisite for many other types of

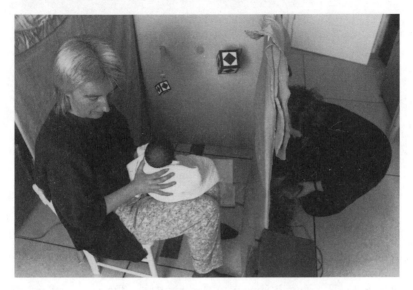

Figure 5.1   A newborn infant being tested in a size constancy experiment

perceptual organization. This view of the newborn as having little in the way of perceptual organisation contrasts with E. J. Gibson's (1969) suggestion that shape and size constancy are present early in life:

> *I think, as is the case with perceived shape, that an object tends to be perceived in its true size very early in development, not because the organism has learned to correct for distance, but because he sees the object as such, not its projected size or its distance abstracted from it.* (p. 366)

Recent experiments give clear evidence that Gibson was correct. In fact, these constancies are present at birth. In a study of size constancy, Slater et al. (1990) used preferential looking (PL) and familiarization procedures. The stimuli in their experiments were two cubes, one twice as large as the other, and a newborn infant being tested is shown in figure 5.1. In the PL experiment they presented pairs of cubes of different sizes at different distances, and it was found that newborns preferred to look at the cube which gave the largest retinal size, regardless of its distance or its real size. These findings are convincing evidence that newborns can base their responding on retinal size alone.

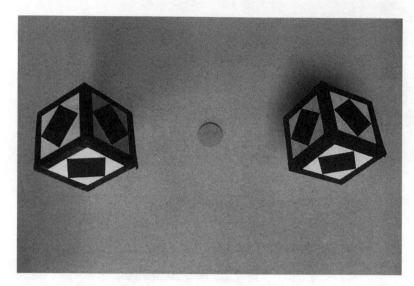

Figure 5.2 The stimuli shown to the infants on the post-familiarization test trials. This photograph, taken from the babies' viewing position, shows the small cube on the left at a distance of 30.5 cm, and the large cube on the right at a distance of 61 cm

In their second experiment each infant viewed either a small cube or a large cube during 6 familiarization trials: each infant was exposed to the same-sized cube shown at different distances on each trial: for example, the baby might see the cube at a distance of 23 cm on one trial, at 53 cm on the next, at 38 cm on the next, and so on. Both distance, and the size of the cube's retinal image, varied from trial to trial. After familiarization, the infants were shown both cubes side-by-side, the small cube nearer and the large cube farther, such that their retinal images were the same size (figure 5.2). All the infants tested looked longer at the cube they were not familiarized with (consistent with the novelty preferences commonly observed in habituation studies). This indicates that the neonates differentiated the two cube sizes despite the similarities of the retinal sizes, and had abstracted the familiar cube's constant, real size over the changes in distance and retinal image sizes presented on the familiarization trials.

Slater and Morison (1985) described experiments on shape constancy and slant perception, using a similar methodology to that used in testing for size constancy, and obtained convincing evidence both that newborn infants detect, and respond systematically to, changes in objects' slants, and also that they could respond to an object's real shape, regardless of its slant. Their results demonstrate that newborn babies have the ability to extract the constant, real shape of an object that is rotated in the third dimension: that is, they have shape constancy.

The findings of these studies demonstrate that shape and size constancy are organizing features of perception that are present at birth.

Subjective contours and Gestalt organizational principles

Many organizational principles contribute to the perceived coherence and stability of the visual world. In addition to size and shape constancy, several other types of visual organization have been found in young infants, and by way of illustration two of these are discussed here: subjective contours and some Gestalt principles.

Subjective contours are contours that are perceived "in the absence of any physical gradient of change in the display." Such contours were described in detail by Kanizsa (1979) and the Kanizsa square is shown as pattern A in figure 5.3: the adult perceiver usually "completes" the contours of the figures, despite the fact that the contours are physically absent. Convincing evidence that 3- and 4-month-old infants perceive subjective contours was provided in a series of experiments by Ghim (1990), from whose work figure 5.3 is derived. In one experimental condition infants were found to discriminate between the pattern containing the subjective contour (SC, pattern A) and any of the patterns B, C and D which do not produce subjective contours. However, they seemed unable to discriminate between the non-subjective (NSC) contour patterns: thus, having been habituated to one of the NSC patterns they did not recover attention when presented a different NSC pattern. This leads to the conclusion that "... the difference between patterns with and without subjective contours is greater than the difference between patterns without subjective contours" (Ghim, 1990, p. 225). This, and the other experiments described by Ghim, lead to the conclusion that "infants have knowledge of the complete form and its components after viewing patterns that produce forms with subjective contours" (p. 244).

Figure 5.3   Pattern A (a Kanizsa square) produces subjective contours and is seen as a square. Patterns B, C and D contain the same four elements but do not produce subjective contours

One of the main contributions of the Gestalt psychologists was to describe a number of ways in which visual perception is organized. Quinn et al. (1993) report evidence that 3-month-old infants group patterns according to the principle of similarity. Two of the stimuli they used are shown in figure 5.4. Adults reliably group the elements of such stimuli on the basis of lightness similarity and represent the figure on the left as a set of rows, and the other as a set of columns. Three-month-olds do the same, in that those habituated to the columns pattern generalize to vertical lines and prefer (perceive as novel) horizontal lines, while those habituated to the rows prefer the novel vertical lines. In recent experiments (Simion, personal communication), using similar stimuli, it is clear that newborn infants also group by similarity.

Quinn et al. (1997) describe experiments using an habituation-novelty testing procedure, to determine if 3- and 4-month-old infants can organize visual patterns according to the Gestalt principles of good continuation and closure. The stimuli they used are shown in figure 5.5.

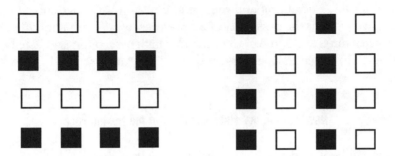

Figure 5.4   Stimuli used by Quinn et al. (1993) with 3-month-olds and by Simion (personal communication) with newborns. Infants, like adults, group by similarity and perceive the pattern on the left as rows, and that on the right as columns

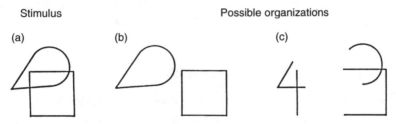

Figure 5.5   Patterns used by Quinn et al. (1997)

Following familiarization to pattern (a) in figure 5.5, tests revealed that the infants parsed the pattern into a square and teardrop (b) rather than into the "less-good" patterns shown in (c): that is, they had parsed the familiarized figure into the two separate shapes of a square and a teardrop in the same way that adults do.

Overview

The above is just a sample of the many studies which demonstrate that young infants organize the visually perceived world in a similar manner to that of adult perceivers. But the newborn and young infant's world is very different from ours; obviously, their perceptual worlds lack

experience, associations and meaning derived from experience. In the
next two sections the possibility of early representations that might guide
early learning, and some of the ways in which perception is affected and
changed by experience and learning in infancy are discussed.

Newborn Infants' Representation of the Human Face

Several lines of evidence converge to suggest that newborn infants come
into the world with some innately specified representation of faces.
Goren et al., 1975, and M. Johnson and Morton, 1991, present evidence
that newborn infants are more likely to track (follow with their eyes)
face-like patterns than non-face-like patterns. Johnson and Morton
argue for the existence of an innate face-detecting device they call
"Conspec" (short for conspecifics), which may be equivalent to three
dark patches in a triangle, corresponding to eyes and mouth, and which
serves to direct the newborn infant's visual attention to faces.

Imitation

Other evidence suggests that the hypothesized innate facial representation might be more detailed than simply a template that matches three
dots. In particular it has been demonstrated that newborn (and older)
infants will imitate a variety of facial gestures they see an adult model
performing. One of the first published reports of imitation by newborn
and older infants was by Meltzoff and Moore (1977), and there are now
many reports of such imitation (e.g., Meltzoff and Moore, in chapter 9
of this book). Meltzoff (1995) suggests that "newborns begin life with
some grasp of people" (p. 43) and that their ability to recognize when
their facial behaviour is being copied implies that "there is some representation of their own bodies" (p. 53). Infants can see the adult's face,
but of course they cannot see their own. This means that in some way
they have to match their own, unseen but felt, facial movements with
the seen, but unfelt, facial movements of the adult. Meltzoff and Moore
(for example, chapter 9 of this book) propose that they do this by a
process of "active intermodal matching."

A fundamental question is "What is the motive for imitation in the
newborn?" No man, and no baby, is an island, and one suggestion is that

babies are born with a deep-seated need to communicate (Kugiumutza-kis, 1993). A complementary interpretation is offered by Meltzoff and Moore (1998) who claim that imitation is an act of social cognition which serves to help the infant identify, understand and recognize individuals.

Infants prefer attractive faces

Several experimenters have found that infants prefer to look at attractive faces when these are shown paired with faces judged to be less attractive (for example, Langlois et al., 1991; Samuels et al., 1994). The "attractiveness effect" seems to be robust in that it is found for stimulus faces that are infant, adult, male, female, and of two races (African-American and Caucasian), and babies also preferred attractive to symmetrical faces when these two dimensions were varied independently. Recently, Rhodes et al. 1999, confirmed this latter effect with adults: adults' facial attractiveness ratings are based on averageness, and not symmetry. The attractiveness effect has recently been found with newborn infants, who averaged less than 3 days from birth at the time of testing (Slater et al., 1998).

A frequently expressed interpretation of the attractiveness effect is in terms of prototype formation and a cognitive averaging process. The origins of this interpretation can be traced back to more than a hundred years ago. In the 19th century Charles Darwin received a letter from Mr A. L. Austin of New Zealand (Galton, 1907, p. 227). The letter read:

> *Although a perfect stranger to you, and living on the reverse side of the globe, I have taken the liberty of writing to you on a small discovery I have made in binocular vision in the stereoscope. I find by taking two ordinary carte-de-viste photos of two different persons' faces, the portraits being about the same sizes, and looking about the same direction, and placing them in a stereoscope, the faces blend into one in a most remarkable manner, producing in the case of some ladies' portraits, in every instance, a decided improvement in beauty.*

Darwin passed the discovery to his half cousin, Francis Galton, who confirmed the effect. Galton went further and was the first scientist to average faces, which he did photographically by underexposing each individual picture. In recent times such averaging can be done by computer, and the resulting "average" or prototypical face is typically seen as more attractive than the individual faces that combine to produce it. For this reason, averageness has been claimed to be an important ingredient of attractiveness. According to this interpretation, therefore, attractive faces are seen as more "face-like" because they match more closely the prototype that infants have formed from their experience of seeing faces: thus, "Infants may prefer attractive or prototypical faces because prototypes are easier to classify as a face" (Langlois and Roggman, 1990, p. 119). It is possible that newborn infants' preferences for attractive faces result from an innate representation of faces that infants bring into the world with them. Alternately, it is possible that even the newborn's preference for attractive faces is a preference for an image similar to a composite of the faces they have seen in the few hours from birth prior to testing.

Overview

It seems now to be reasonably well agreed that "there does seem to be some representational bias . . . that the neonate brings to the learning situation for faces" (Karmiloff-Smith, 1996, p. 10). This representational bias is likely to be something more elaborate than simply a tendency to attend to stimuli that possess three blobs in the location of eyes and mouth ("Conspec"). It is possible that evolution has provided the infant with a more detailed blueprint of the human face. This possibility is suggested by newborn infants' ability to imitate the facial gestures produced by the first face they have ever seen (Reissland, 1988), and also, perhaps, by newborn infants' preferences for attractive faces. It is perhaps likely that experiences *in utero* (for example, proprioceptive feedback from facial movements) contribute to the newborn infant's representation of faces, which might therefore result from evolutionary biases in interaction with prenatal experiences.

Early Experience and Learning

Infants learn rapidly about their visually-encountered world: as Karmiloff-Smith (1996, p. 10) has put it, "At birth visual processing starts with a vengeance." This rapid learning is apparent in the ease with which even newborn infants will habituate to visual stimuli and

Figure 5.6 A face as it might appear to a newborn (left) and to us

subsequently recover attention to novelty. In this section some clear examples of early visual learning in infancy are discussed, under the headings of face perception, intermodal perception, and perception of object unity.

Face perception

As a rough guide, figure 5.6 gives an indication of how the mother's face might look to a newborn infant, and how she might look to us: while the image is degraded and unfocused for the newborn, enough information is potentially available for the infant to learn to recognize the mother's face, and to detect many facial features. The representational bias for faces discussed in the previous section ensures that newborn infants have a predisposition to attend to faces, and it is clear that soon after birth they learn to distinguish between individual faces, particularly between the mother's and a stranger's face. (for example, Bushnell et al., 1989). Apparently, this recognition is not dependent solely on facial features. The effect disappears if the women's hairlines are covered with a scarf (Pascalis et al., 1995). Thus, attention to outer contours seems to contribute to neonates' face recognition abilities.

Such remarkable early learning might result from a face-specific learning mechanism, or it might be a product of a more general pattern-processing system that assists the infant in learning about complex visual stimuli.

Intermodal perception

Most of the objects and events that we experience are intermodal in that they provide information to more than one sensory modality. Such inter-modal information can be broadly categorized into two types of relation, amodal and arbitrary. Amodal perception is where two (or more) senses provided information that is equivalent in one or more respects, and many types of amodal perception have been demonstrated in early infancy. For example, newborn infants reliably turn their heads and eyes in the direction of a sound source, indicating that spatial location is given by both visual and auditory information (Butterworth, 1983; Muir and Clifton, 1985; Wertheimer, 1961).

Many intermodal events give both amodal and arbitrary information. For instance, when a person speaks the synchrony of voice and mouth provides amodal information, whereas the pairing of the face and the sound of the voice is arbitrary. In several publications Bahrick (for example, chapter 6 of this book) has provided strong evidence that learning about arbitrary intermodal relations is greatly assisted if there is accompanying amodal information: "detection of amodal invariants precedes and guides learning about arbitrary object-sound relations by directing infants' attention to appropriate object-sound pairings and then promoting sustained attention and further differentiation" (Bahrick and Pickens, 1994, p. 226).

There is evidence that newborn babies are easily able to learn arbi-trary intermodal relations, but only if the intermodal stimuli are accom-panied by amodal information which specifies that they "go together." Such information can include spatial co-location (sight and sound are found at the same place), temporal synchrony (lips and voice are syn-chronized), temporal microstructure (a single object striking a surface produces a single impact sound, but a compound object, consisting of several elements, will produce a more complex, prolonged sound). Mor-rongiello et al. (1998) found that newborn infants learned toy-sound pairs when the two stimuli were spatially co-located, but not when they were presented in different locations.

Slater et al. (1999) tested newborn infants in two conditions. In their *auditory-noncontingent* condition 2-day-old infants were familiarized to

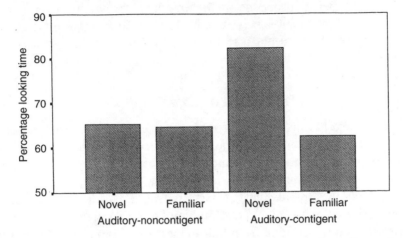

Figure 5.7 Percentage looking at familiar and novel auditory-visual combinations on the test trials. Only in the auditory-contingent condition have the newborn infants learned the auditory-visual combination, and hence look more at the novel combination

two alternating visual stimuli, each accompanied by its "own" sound: when each visual stimulus was presented its sound was continuously presented, independently of whether the infant looked at the visual stimulus. In the *auditory-contingent* condition the auditory stimulus was presented only when the infant was looking at the visual stimulus: thus, presentation of the sound was contingent upon the infant looking at the target.

On the post-familiarization test trials they found that their newborn infants learned the arbitrary auditory-visual associations when the amodal *contingent* information was present, but not when it was absent: in the auditory-contingent condition attention recovered strongly to a novel auditory-visual combination, but in the auditory-noncontingent condition attention remained low, and indistinguishable from attention to one of the familiar combinations. These findings are shown in figure 5.7, and give strong support to Bahrick's views. It is clear that rapid learning about intermodal events occurs from birth, and that the presence or absence of amodal information acts both as a powerful facilitator and a constraint on learning. It is of interest to note that when the mother speaks to her infant the amodal information of temporal synchrony of voice and lips is quite likely to facilitate learning to associate her face and voice, and it seems likely that this learning occurs very soon after birth.

Perception of object unity

The visual world that we experience is complex, and one problem confronting the young infant is knowing how to segregate objects, and knowing when one object ends and another begins. Sometimes changes to color, contour, contrast, etc., are found within a single object. For example, many animals have stripes, spots, changes to coloring, etc.; people wear different colored clothing, and there are natural color and contrast changes, perhaps from hair to forehead, from eyes to face, and so on, but these changes of course are all part of the same person. Sometimes, similar appearance is found for different objects, as when two or more similar objects are perceived. Thus, there is no simple rule that specifies that an abrupt or gradual change in appearance indicates one or more objects.

How do infants respond to the apparently bewildering variety of visual cues that confront them, in order to parse the optic array into coherent objects? One way in which this question has been addressed is in studies of *object unity*. Object unity is where we appreciate that there is only one object, despite breaks in the perceptual display. For example, when a person sits behind a desk, our view of the person is partially blocked by the desk, but we naturally infer that the person is connected behind the desk! That is, we perceive a whole person.

A clear difference has been found in infants' perception of object unity in the age range birth to 4 months. In a series of experiments Kellman and his colleagues (e.g., Kellman and Spelke, 1983), habituated 4-month-olds to a partly blocked rod that moved back and forth behind a central block, or occluder, so that only the top and bottom parts of the rod were visible (as in the upper part of figure 5.8). On the posthabituation test trials the infants recovered attention to the two rod pieces, but not to the complete rod (shown in the lower part of figure 5.8) suggesting that they had been perceiving a complete rod during habituation and that the rod pieces were novel. One of the critical cues in allowing the infants to perceive the rod as a whole was the movement

Habituation display

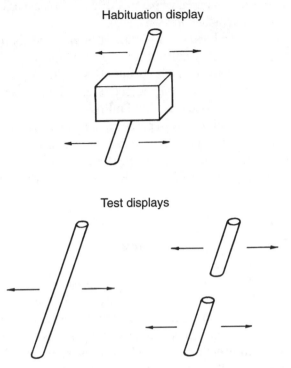

Test displays

Figure 5.8 Habituation and test displays shown to infants to test perception of object unity. During habituation the rod, and during test trials the rod and rod parts, moved back and forth undergoing common motion

of the two visible parts of the rod. When the partly blocked rod pieces were not moving the 4-month-olds appeared not to perceive a single complete rod behind the block (they did not look longer at either of the test displays). Thus, common motion is an important indication that visible parts of a partly concealed object are connected.

When the cues were made optimal, for instance by including movement, and making the occluding block very narrow so that more of the rod could be seen, infants as young as 2 months can perceive the continuity of partially occluded objects (S. P. Johnson, 1997). However, when newborn babies have been tested with similar displays they look longer on the test trials at the *complete* rod (e.g., Slater et al., 1990). Thus, neonates appear not to perceive partly occluded objects as consisting of both visible and nonvisible portions.

It appears that newborn infants cannot infer more about a partially concealed object than they can see: that is, they appear to respond only to what they see directly. Thus, it appears that an understanding of the completeness, or unity, of partly occluded objects begins around 2 months from birth. Based on other findings S. P. Johnson, 1997, suggests that infants rapidly learn to perceive object boundaries, depth and occlusion: "By the middle of the first year of life, infants seem to view objects in their surroundings in much the same way as do adults, by exploiting a variety of the visual cues available to them in the optic array" (p. 6).

Conclusions

Basic visual functions such as scanning abilities, acuity, contrast sensitivity, depth perception, and color discrimination are limited in neonates. However, as Hainline and Abramov (1992, pp. 40–41) put it, "While infants may not, indeed, see as well as adults do, they normally see well enough to function effectively in their roles as infants." Thus, despite their sensory limitations, it is clear that newborn infants have several means with which to begin to make sense of the visual world. Newborn infants can clearly remember what they see, and they demonstrate rapid learning about their perceived world (e.g., Pascalis and de Schonen, 1994).

One prerequisite for object knowledge is distinguishing proximal from distal stimuli. The proximal stimulus is the sensory stimulation – in this case, the pattern of light falling on the retina. The distal stimulus consists of what is represented by the pattern of stimulation – the object itself. Neonates distinguish proximal from distal stimuli when they demonstrate size and shape constancy: the object is perceived accurately, despite changes to its retinal image. The picture of visual perception in early infancy that is emerging is complex: some aspects of visual perception (e.g., depth and object perception) are very immature, whereas others appear to be remarkably advanced at birth. Newborn babies have, literally, a head-start, in that it is becoming clear that they are born with a preference for, and representation of the human face. It is also clear that the young infant's visual world is, to a large extent, structured and coherent as a result of the intrinsic organization of the visual system.

However well-organized the visual world of the young infant may be, it lacks the familiarity, meaning, and associations that characterize the world of the mature perceiver. Inevitably, some types of visual organization take time to develop. An appreciation of the underlying unity, coherence and persistence of occluded objects is not present at birth, and a proper understanding of the physical properties of objects emerges only slowly as infancy progresses. At birth, "visual processing begins with a vengeance" (Karmiloff-Smith, 1996, p. 10), and this processing can be seen in the rapidity with which newborn infants learn about faces, and about other types of stimuli and events. The newborn infant has an enormous amount to learn and it is reasonable that such learning should be constrained and guided by the contingencies that are found within the environment. This theme is illustrated by research on newborn infants' learning about arbitrary auditory-visual combinations: the presence or absence of amodal information (information that specifies what intermodal combinations do, or do not, belong together) acts both as a powerful facilitator and a constraint on learning. Meltzoff and Moore (1998, p. 229) offer the premise that evolution has . . . bequeathed human infants . . . with initial mental structures that serve as 'discovery procedures' for developing more comprehensive and flexible concepts." As development proceeds, the innate and developing organizational mechanisms are added to by experience, which assists the infant in making sense of the perceived world.

Acknowledgments

The author's research described in this paper has been supported by research grants RC00232466, and R000235288/237709 from the Economic and Social Research Council. Earlier versions of some of the material contained in this chapter have appeared in Vital-Durand, Atkinson and Braddick (eds.), *Infant vision* (Oxford University Press, 1996), Bremner, Slater and Butterworth (eds.), *Infant development: recent advances* (Psychology Press, 1997), Slater (ed.), *Perceptual development: visual, auditory and speech perception in infancy*, (Psychology Press, 1998), and Bremner and Fogel (eds.), *Handbook of infant development*, (Blackwell Publishers, Ltd).

114 *Sensation and Perception*

References

Bahrick, L. E., & Pickens, J. N. (1994). Amodal relations: the basis for intermodal perception and learning in infancy. In D. J. Lewkowicz & R. Lickliter (eds.) *The development of intersensory perception: comparative perspectives*. Hillsdale, NJ: Erlbaum, pp. 205–233.

Bower, T. G. R. (1966). The visual world of infants. *Scientific American, 215(6)*, 80–92.

Bremner, J. G. (1994). *Infancy*. Oxford, UK: Blackwell Publishers Ltd.

Bushnell, I. W. R., Sai, F., & Mullin, J. T. (1989). Neonatal recognition of the mother's face. *British Journal of Development Psychology, 7*, 3–15.

Butterworth, G. E. (1983). Structure of the mind in human infancy. In L. P. Lipsitt & C. K. Rovee-Collier (eds.) *Advances in Infancy Research*, Ablex Publishing Corpn., Norwood, New Jersey.

Galton, F. (1907). *Inquiries in human faculty and its development*. London: J. M. Dent & Sons Ltd.

Ghim, H.-R. (1990). Evidence for perceptual organization in infants: Perception of subjective contours by young infants. *Infant Behavior and Development, 13*, 221–248.

Gibson, E. J. (1969). *Principles of perceptual learning and development*. New York: Appleton-Century-Crofts.

Gibson, J. J. (1979). *The ecological approach to visual perception*. Boston, MA: Houghton Mifflin.

Goren, C. C., Sarty, M., & Wu, P. Y. K. (1975). Visual following and pattern discrimination of face-like stimuli by newborn infants. *Pediatrics, 56*, 544–549.

Hainline, L. (1998). The development of basic visual abilities. In A. Slater (ed.), *Perceptual development: visual, auditory and speech perception in infancy*. Hove: Psychology Press.

Hainline, L., & Abramov, I. (1992). Assessing visual development: Is infant vision good enough? In C. Rovee-Collier & L. P. Lipsitt (eds.) *Advances in Infancy Research*, (Vol 7). Norwood, NJ: Ablex.

James, W. (1890). *Principles of psychology*. New York: Henry Holt.

Johnson, M. H., & Morton, J. (1991). *Biology and cognitive development: the case for face recognition*. Oxford: Blackwell Publishers.

Johnson, S. P. (1997). Young infants' perception of object unity: implications for development of attentional and cognitive skills. *Current Directions in Psychological Science, 6*, 5–11.

Kanizsa, G. (1979). *Organization in vision: essays on gestalt perception*. New York: Praeger.

Karmiloff-Smith, A. (1996). The connectionist infant: Would Piaget turn in his grave? *SRCD Newsletter*, Fall issue, 1–3 and 10.

Kellman, P. J., & Spelke, E. S. (1983). Perception of partly occluded objects in infancy. *Cognitive Psychology, 15*, 483–524.

Kugiumutzakis, G. (1993). Intersubjective vocal imitation in early mother-infant interaction. In J. Nadel & L. Camioni (eds.), *New perspectives in early communicative development* (pp. 23–47) London & New York: Routledge.

Langlois, J. H., Ritter, J. M., Roggman, L. A., & Vaughn, L. S. (1991). Facial diversity and infant preferences for attractive faces. *Developmental Psychology, 27*, 79–84.

Langlois, J., & Roggman, L. A. (1990). Attractive faces are only average. *Psychological Science, 1*, 115–121.

Meltzoff, A. N. (1995). Infants' understanding of people and things: from body imitation to folk psychology. In J. L. Bermudez, A. Marcel, & N. Eilan (eds.), *The body and the self* (pp. 43–69). Cambridge, MA, and London: MIT Press.

Meltzoff, A. N., & Moore, M. K. (1977). Imitation of facial and manual gestures by human neonates. *Science, 198*, 75–78.

Meltzoff, A. N., & Moore, M. K. (1998). Object representation, identity, and the paradox of early permanence: steps toward a new framework. *Infant Behavior and Development, 21*, 201–235.

Morrongiello, B. A., Fenwick, K. D., & Chance, G. (1998). Crossmodal learning in newborn infants: inferences about properties of auditory-visual events. *Infant Behavior and Development, 21*, 543–553.

Muir, D. W., & Clifton, R. (1985). Infants' orientation to the location of sound sources. In G. Gottlieb & N. Krasnegor (eds.), *The measurement of audition and vision during the first year of life: a methodological overview*. Norwood, NJ: Albex, pp. 171–194.

Pascalis, O., & de Schonen, S. (1994). Recognition memory in 3- to 4-day-old human neonates. *NeuroReport, 5*, 1721–1724.

Pascalis, O., de Schonen, S., Morton, J., Deruelle, C., & Fabre-Grenet, M. (1995). Mother's face recognition by neonates: A replication and an extension. *Infant Behavior and Development, 18*, 79–85.

Piaget, J. (1953). *The origins of intelligence in the child*. London: Routledge & Kegan Paul.

Quinn, P. C., Brown, C. R., & Streppa, M. L. (1997). Perceptual organization of complex visual configurations by young infants. *Infant Behavior and Development, 20*, 35–46.

Quinn, P. C., Burke, S., & Rush, A. (1993). Part-whole perception in early infancy: Evidence for perceptual grouping produced by lightness similarity. *Infant Behavior and Development, 16*, 19–42.

Reissland, N. (1988). Neonatal imitation in the first hour of life: observations in Rural Nepal. *Developmental Psychology, 24*, 464–469.

Rhodes, G., Sumich, A., & Byatt, G. (1999). Are average facial configurations attractive only because of their symmetry? *Psychological Science, 10,* 52–58.

Samuels, C. A., Butterworth, G., Roberts, T., & Graupner, L. (1994). Babies prefer attractiveness to symmetry. *Perception, 23,* 823–831.

Slater, A., Mattock, A., & Brown, E. (1990). Size constancy at birth: Newborn infants' responses to retinal and real size. *Journal of Experimental Child Psychology, 49,* 314–322.

Slater, A., & Morison, V. (1985). Shape constancy and slant perception at birth. *Perception, 14,* 337–344.

Slater, A., Morison, V., Somers, M., Mattock, A., Brown, E., & Taylor, D. (1990). Newborn and older infants' perception of partly occluded objects. *Infant Behavior and Development, 13,* 33–49.

Slater, A., Quinn, P., Brown, E., & Hayes, R. (1999). Intermodal perception at birth: Intersensory redundancy guides newborn infants' learning of arbitrary auditory-visual pairings. *Developmental Science, 3,* 333–338.

Slater, A., von der Schulenburg, C., Brown, E., Badenoch, M., Butterworth, G., Parsons, S., & Samuels, C. (1998). Newborn infants prefer attractive faces. *Infant Behavior and Development, 21,* 345–354.

Wertheimer, M. (1961). Psychomotor coordination of auditory and visual space at birth. *Science, 134,* 1692.

Zuckerman, C. B., & Rock, I. (1957). A reappraisal of the roles of past experience and innate organizing processes in visual perception. *Psychological Bulletin, 54,* 269–296.

SIX

Intermodal Perception

Introduction

Most of the objects and events that we experience are *intermodal* in that they provide information to more than one sensory modality. Such intermodal information can be broadly categorized into one of two types of relations, amodal and arbitrary. Amodal information is where two (or more) senses provide information that is equivalent in one or more respects – thus, the temporal synchrony between the voice and the facial movements of a speaker are amodal. However, many of the intermodal relationships that we perceive appear to be quite arbitrary. For instance, there is no information specifying *a priori* that a particular animal makes a certain sound, that a particular voice is associated with a particular face, or that an object makes a certain sound on making contact with a certain surface.

In this paper Lorraine Bahrick presents evidence in support of three basic principles concerning the domain of intermodal learning. The first is that global, abstract, intermodal relations are detected developmentally prior to more specific nested relations. Global relations include shared temporal synchrony (for example, the sight and sound of a hammer hitting the ground are synchronized), and rhythm and tempo. All of these occur together when someone speaks, and the sight of their face and sound of their voice specifies a unitary event – the person talking. Nested relations are more specific and indicate more detail about the stimulation: thus, a single object makes a single sound when striking a surface, while a compound object (such as a tray of cutlery) makes a more complex set of sounds.

A second principle is that amodal relations are detected developmentally prior to arbitrary relations. A person's voice is always synchronized with their mouth movements, and hence the synchrony provides amodal information; however, the precise sound of the voice cannot be specified in advance and is arbitrary. Similarly, it is not possible to predict, for instance, the sound that a red object would make if dropped or struck.

The third principle is that the detection of amodal relations guides and constrains perceptual learning about arbitrary relations. For example, if infants detect the synchrony between a person's face and voice they are likely to learn the unique (arbitrary) pitch and sound of the voice and associate it with that person. However, if there is no amodal information, as when a face is seen and a voice heard, but if the two are not synchonized, then the association will not be learned.

These principles act both as powerful constraints on, and guides to, learning. The young infant has an enormous amount to learn, and it would be a complex and chaotic world if infants associated all arbitrary pairing of sights and sounds, and other intermodal combinations, and clearly they do not. As Bahrick concludes, "selective attention to global, amodal, relations in the first months of life can provide a means of organizing, guiding, and constraining perceptual experience in a way that ultimately leads to the intermodal knowledge of the adult perceiver."

Increasing Specificity in the Development of Intermodal Perception

Lorraine E. Bahrick

Increasing Specificity in the Development of Intermodal Perception

The infant is born into a world of objects and events that present a vast array of information to all the senses. Research now clearly demonstrates that young infants are adept perceivers of this multimodal stimulation (for a review, see Lewkowicz and Lickliter, 1994). They are able to perceive coherent, unitary multimodal events, even in the first months of life. For example, 2- to 5-month-olds are able to perceive a relationship between a person's face and their voice on the basis of temporal synchrony and shared rhythm between the movements of their mouth and the timing of their speech (Dodd, 1979; Lewkowicz, 1996a; Walker-Andrews, 1986) as well as between the shape of the lips and the corresponding vowel sound (Kuhl and Meltzoff, 1982, 1984). By 5- to 7-months, infants can match faces and voices on the basis of the age and gender of speaker (Bahrick et al., 1998; Walker-Andrews et al., 1991) as well as affective expression (Caron et al., 1988; Walker, 1982; Walker-Andrews, 1986, Walker-Andrews and Lennon, 1991). Young infants are also able to recognize information specifying the self by detecting amodal invariant relations. They can match their own body motion, experienced proprioceptively, with a visual display of the motion, on the basis of shared temporal and spatial information (Bahrick and Watson, 1985; Bahrick 1995; Rochat 1995; Rochat and Morgan, 1995; Schmuckler, 1996). For example, when 5-month-old infants view a live video display of their own legs moving, alongside that of another infant's legs, they can discriminate the two and prefer to watch the novel display of the other infant. Young infants are also able to detect the visually and acoustically specified substance and composition of an object striking a surface, as well as the synchrony, rhythm and tempo of impacts common across the senses (Bahrick, 1983, 1987, 1988, 1992; Bahrick and Lickliter, submitted; Lewkowicz, 1996b; Spelke, 1979). With no prior knowledge to guide selectivity, infants are able to make sense of this multimodal array and perceive intermodal relations across a wide range of natural events. However, we currently know little about how and in what developmental sequence, infants detect these intermodal relations. In this chapter, I present evidence that this process of perceptual development is set in motion and guided by the detection of amodal invariant relations and occurs in order of increasing specificity.

Amodal Information and the Principle of Increasing Specificity

Amodal information is information that is not specific to a particular sense modality, but is completely redundant across two or more senses (see Bahrick and Pickens, 1994; Gibson, 1969). For example, the sights and sounds of hands clapping share a synchrony relation, a common tempo of action and a common rhythm. The same rhythm and tempo can be picked up visually or acoustically. According to Gibson (1969), infants come into the world with a unified perceptual system, equipped to abstract amodal relations. Detection of amodal relations focuses attention on meaningful, unitary multimodal events and, at the same time buffers against learning inappropriate relations (Bahrick, 1992, 1994; Bahrick and Pickens, 1994). For example, if the infant detects temporal synchrony, shared rhythm and tempo between the sounds of a person's voice and the sight of their moving face, the infant will necessarily be focusing on a unitary event; the person talking. During that time, the infant would not attend to sights that are unrelated to the audible voice such as the nearby movements of colorful objects or the activities of other people.

Objects and events have hierarchically organized properties. Some properties are nested within others. Gibson (1969) has proposed a principle of *increasing specificity* suggesting that global, abstract relations are detected developmentally prior to more specific, nested relations. I have applied and tested this principle in the domain of intermodal learning about audible and visible events. In this chapter, I present evidence from several series of studies that illustrate this principle. Together, these studies reveal three basic principles about how perception becomes increasingly more specific with development. First, they demonstrate that global amodal relations, such as temporal synchrony, are detected developmentally prior to nested amodal relations (in this case, information specifying object composition). Second, research from several domains demonstrates that amodal relations are detected developmentally prior to arbitrary relations. Third, evidence suggests that detection of amodal relations guides and constrains perceptual learning about arbitrary relations.

For the purpose of this research, audio-visual relations were defined as having different levels of specificity:

1   Amodal *temporal synchrony* between the sights and sounds of an object hitting a surface was defined as the most global level. Synchrony specifies the unity of audible and visible stimulation.
2   Amodal *temporal microstructure* is a more specific and embedded kind of audio-visual relation that characterizes the nature of each synchronous impact. There is a temporal structure common to the type of sound and type of motion that can tell us about the object's substance, its composition, weight, size, or number. In the case of object composition, a single object striking a surface produces a single, abrupt impact sound with a single, abrupt change in visual trajectory. In contrast, a compound object (composed of many smaller elements) produces a more prolonged sound with a more gradual onset and a correspondingly gradual change in visual trajectory. This internal temporal structure is common across vision and audition and specifies the object's composition.
3   Modality-specific or *arbitrary* audio-visual relations (such as the relation between the pitch of a sound and the color of the object) were defined as the most specific level. Arbitrary audio-visual relations are context specific and not united by common information common across the different sense modalities.

Global Amodal Relations are Detected Developmentally Prior to Nested Amodal Relations

One series of studies (Bahrick, 1996; Bahrick, submitted) explored the developmental progression of infants' sensitivity to global, amodal synchrony versus nested, composition relations. Would infants detect temporal synchrony developmentally prior to amodal information for object composition, consistent with an increasing specificity view?

Four pairs of events were created to illustrate the synchrony and embedded composition relations (see figure 6.1). They each depicted an object striking a surface in an erratic temporal pattern. One member of each pair was a large, single object, which produced a single, discrete impact sound, and the other was a similar looking compound object (comprised of many smaller elements), which produced a more prolonged, complex impact sound. There were two categories of objects, plastic fruit and metal hardware. The plastic objects were abruptly hit against the two wooden surfaces by an unseen hand from behind. The metal objects were suspended from a string and abruptly dropped against the wooden surface. Pairs of objects within the same category differed from one another in terms of color and shape (e.g., pears versus tomatoes), but were comprised of the same substance (plastic or metal) and were moved in the same manner.

Infants were habituated, in an infant controlled procedure (see Bahrick, 1992, 1994; Horowitz et al., 1972), to a single and a compound event in an alternating sequence from one of the two pairs of metal objects. Each event was accompanied by its natural synchronized sounds. After infants met the habituation criterion (a 50% decrement in looking on two successive trials with respect to the infant's initial interest level), they received two test trials depicting either a change in synchrony or a change in composition relations. For the synchrony change test, each visual event was presented out of synchrony with its soundtrack. Thus, the only change from habituation to test, was the synchrony relation between the films and soundtracks. For the composition change test, the wrong sounds were played in synchrony with the object's motions. That is, the motions of the single object were synchronized with the sounds of the compound object and the motions of the compound object were synchronized with the sounds of the single object. Thus, the only change from habituation to test was the

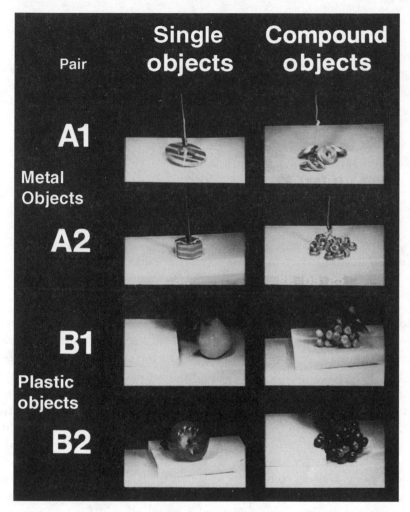

Figure 6.1 Photograph of the stimulus events (from Bahrick, 1992)

pairing of the objects and sounds. Visual recovery to the change in relationship between the objects and sounds was measured for each type of test.

Ninety six infants were tested, 48 at 11-weeks, 28 at 7-weeks, and 20 at 4-weeks of age. Half the infants in each age group participated in the synchrony change condition and half in the composition change.

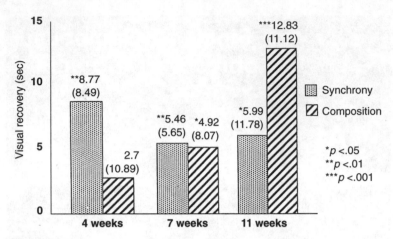

Figure 6.2 Visual recovery to the change in temporal synchrony and temporal microstructure specifying object composition a 4-, 7-, and 11-weeks of age (from Bahrick, submitted)

Results (depicted in figure 6.2) demonstrated significant visual recovery to the change in temporal synchrony at all ages, according to single sample *t*-tests. However, visual recovery to the change in composition relations was significant only at the two older ages, and not at 4-weeks of age. In fact, at 11-weeks of age, recovery to the change in composition was significantly greater than recovery to the change in synchrony ($p < .05$). A trend analysis also revealed a significant linear increase in sensitivity to composition information across age ($p = .01$), but no change in sensitivity to synchrony across age. Thus, these results indicate that by 4-weeks, sensitivity to synchrony was already present and it remained fairly stable across age. And by 7-weeks, sensitivity to object composition emerged, and increased dramatically, so that at 11-weeks it was more salient than synchrony. Further, a control study demonstrated that 3 to 4-week-olds were in fact able to discriminate both the visual and acoustic changes specifying object composition (see figure 6.3). That is, within each pair of events, they could discriminate between the single and compound moving objects, and they could discriminate between the single and compound impact sounds. Thus, even by 3-weeks of age, infants were able to discriminate unimodal information for object composition, but they did not relate this information across modalities before the age of 7-weeks.

Loan Receipt
Liverpool John Moores University
Learning and Information Services

Borrower ID: 21111107195117

Loan Date: 29/04/2009
Loan Time: 3:21 pm

Infant development :
31111010236105

Due Date: 06/05/2009 23:59

Please keep your receipt
in case of dispute

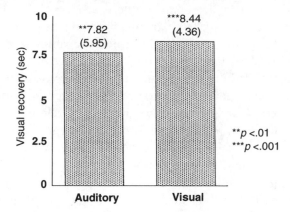

Figure 6.3 Visual recovery to the change in visual versus acoustic information specifying a single versus a compound event at 3–4 weeks of age (from Bahrick, submitted)

These findings reveal evidence of infants' sensitivity to amodal synchrony and composition information at much younger ages than previously thought. More importantly, they demonstrate a changing sensitivity to amodal information across age, consistent with the principle of increasing specificity. Infants detect global amodal relations prior to nested amodal relations. This pattern is adaptive. By first detecting temporal synchrony, infants can focus on unitary events and further differentiation will be appropriately constrained. The initial focus on global, synchrony relations creates a natural buffer against processing unrelated streams of visual and acoustic stimulation. By ensuring that attention is first focused on audible and visible stimulation that belongs together, further processing of multimodal events can proceed in an economical and veridical way.

Amodal Relations are Detected Developmentally Prior to Arbitrary Relations

Multimodal events make a variety of intermodal relations available. Some are amodal and redundant across the senses, such as synchrony, rhythm, tempo, and information specifying object composition. Other information is modality-specific and arbitrarily related across the senses. For example, the relation between the unique sound of a person's voice and the sight of their face or hair style is arbitrary; so is the relation between the color or shape of a moving object and the pitch of its impact sound; or the appearance of an object and the verbal label we give it. Although amodal relations can be directly perceived, arbitrary relations must be learned. Although amodal relations are context-free, arbitrary relations may vary from one context or event to another. Thus, arbitrary relations are considered the most specific type of relation because they are context specific whereas amodal relations are not. For example, in the case of amodal relations, a compound sound always goes with a compound object and a single sound is always produced by a single object. The sights of an erratic rhythm always specify the sounds of an erratic rhythm. However, arbitrary pairings can vary from one context or event to another. A dull, low-pitched sound only sometimes goes with a yellow, round object; a happy, lilting voice only sometimes goes with mommy's face. Because of this, it would be maladaptive for infants to learn arbitrary relations that vary from one context to the next, prior to learning about amodal relations that can be appropriately generalized across contexts. Thus, another way of evaluating the principle of increasing specificity is to ask whether infants would detect amodal relations developmentally prior to detecting arbitrary audio-visual relations.

In one study (Bahrick, 1992), I explored this issue by assessing infants' sensitivity to the amodal synchrony and composition relations in the metal and plastic events (see figure 6.1), as well as to an arbitrary, modality-specific relation provided by the same events. The arbitrary relation was one between the pitch of an impact sound and the color/shape of the object. All objects that impact a surface can be characterized as having a particular color and shape and a sound of a particular pitch. An auditory signal processor was used to raise or lower the pitch of the object's natural impact sounds. Three-month-old infants were again habituated with the single and compound events as before (either the plastic or metal objects) producing natural synchronous sounds of either the high or low pitch. Then they received test trials in which the relation between the visual and acoustic information was mismatched, to assess whether they detected the change from habituation. Infants received the synchrony and composition change tests just like in the prior study, as well as an arbitrary change test. In the arbitrary change test, infants received trials where the object with the high-pitched sound now was synchronized with the low-pitched impact

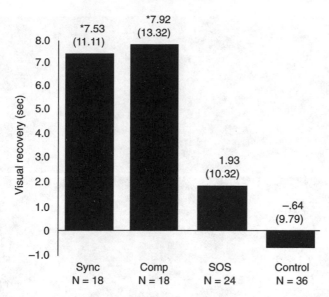

Figure 6.4 Mean visual recovery to a change in synchrony (Sync), composition (Comp), and pitch-color/shape (SOS; specific object-sound) relations, as compared with no-change controls (from Bahrick, 1992) (*$p \leq .01$ with respect to controls)

sound, and vice versa. Results are depicted in figure 6.4. They demonstrated that infants showed significant visual recovery to the change in both synchrony and composition relations, but not to the change in the relation between the pitch of the impact sound and the color/shape of the object, relative to the performance of control subjects who received no changes. Two further control studies demonstrated that 3-month-olds could, in fact, discriminate all the color/shape and pitch changes used. A further study (Bahrick, 1994) extending the test for arbitrary relations to infants of 5- and 7-months demonstrated that only the 7-month-olds were able to detect the arbitrary color/shape-pitch relations used.

These findings, taken together with the studies described earlier (Bahrick, 1996; Bahrick, submitted), suggest that prior to 3-months, infants were already sensitive to the amodal relations, but they were not able to detect the arbitrary pitch color/shape relations until much later. This suggests there may be a developmental lag between the detection

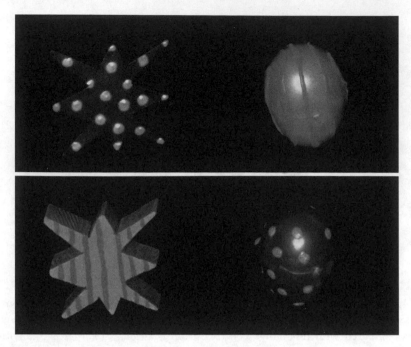

Figure 6.5   Three-dimensional objects presented for visual-tactual exploration (from Hernandez-Reif and Bahrick, submitted)

of amodal and arbitrary relations from a given set of events. It appears
that the detection of amodal relations developmentally precedes and
constrains detection of arbitrary relations in a given domain.

Converging evidence for this developmental lag comes from another
set of studies we conducted in the area of visual-tactual perception of
objects (Hernandez-Reif and Bahrick, submitted). Amodal information for object shape was detected by infants of 4- and 6-months of age.
However, only the 6-month-olds were able to detect the arbitrary
relation between the haptically experienced shape of the object and its
color and pattern. Infants were given two objects, one at a time, to
explore visually (above a bib) and haptically (below a bib) during familiarization trials (see figure 6.5). Each object had a distinctive color and
pattern. Then infants received test trials where the two objects were
displayed visually, side by side, while they haptically explored one of
the objects at a time below the bib. Results (see figure 6.6) indicated

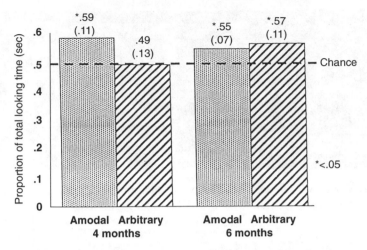

Figure 6.6 Proportion of total looking time to the visual display that matched the object in the infant's hand (from Hernandez-Reif and Bahrick, submitted) (*$p \leq .05$)

that infants at both 4- and 6-months looked significantly more to the object that matched the shape of the one in their hands, demonstrating matching on the basis of amodal information for shape across vision and touch. In contrast, when infants were given test trials assessing matching on the basis of the arbitrary relation between the color and pattern of the object and its haptically experienced shape, only the 6-month-olds, but not the 4-month-olds showed matching. That is, when two flat posterboards displaying the distinctive color/patterns were displayed side by side (see figure 6.7) while infants haptically explored the three-dimensional object under the bib, only the 6-month-olds looked more to the color/pattern that matched the object in their hands. The younger infants showed no evidence of detecting the arbitrary relation between the haptically experienced shape and the visually given color-pattern.

These findings converge with those on audio-visual event perception and demonstrate a developmental lag between the detection of amodal and arbitrary relations across the senses. This developmental lag is likely to be adaptive in promoting the development of veridical object and event perception. By detecting amodal relations first, infants can develop intermodal knowledge about persistent properties of object and events

Figure 6.7   Two-dimensional displays of color and pattern information (from Hernandez-Reif and Bahrick, submitted)

prior to acquiring knowledge about more idiosyncratic, arbitrary relations that often vary from one context or event to another. By first detecting amodal relations, infants will avoid making inappropriate generalizations about unrelated or context-bound aspects of events.

Detection of Amodal Relations Guides and Constrains Learning about Arbitrary Relations

Evidence from at least two sets of studies (Gogate and Bahrick, 1998; Hernandez-Reif and Bahrick, submitted) suggests that detection of amodal relations not only developmentally precedes detection of arbitrary relations, but amodal relations can provide a basis for detecting and learning about arbitrary relations as well. In the series of studies on visual-tactual matching described above (Hernandez-Reif and Bahrick, submitted), another experiment was conducted exploring the basis for the 6-month-olds' ability to match the tactually experienced shape with the arbitrarily paired color/pattern information. It asked if amodal information for shape were eliminated during the familiarization trials, would infants no longer be able to match on the basis of the arbitrary shape-color/pattern relations during the test trials. Thus, instead of receiving an identical three-dimensional object of a particular shape above the bib for visual inspection and below the bib for haptic exploration, infants haptically explored the three-dimensional object below

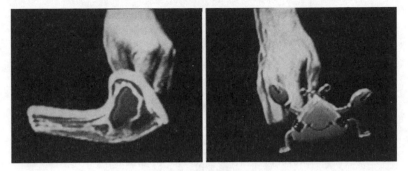

Figure 6.8   Objects used in the study of speech sound-object relations (from Gogate and Bahrick, 1998)

the bib while viewing the flat two-dimensional posterboard displaying the distinctive color/pattern above the bib. In this way the visual information for three-dimensional shape was eliminated during the familiarization trials, while still presenting the color/pattern information. Test trials were identical to those described earlier with the flat posterboards. Results indicated that 6-month-olds no longer showed matching of the haptically experienced shape and the color/pattern during the test trials. These findings suggest that the common shape information provided to touch and sight during familiarization was necessary for successful performance in the arbitrary matching task. Six-month-old infants apparently related the object's color/pattern with its shape by first detecting the shape common to the two modalities. Thus, detection of amodal shape information must have guided learning about arbitrary shape-color/pattern relations.

A recent set of studies on the perceptual precursors to language learning (Gogate and Bahrick, 1998) also suggests that detection of amodal relations provides a basis for detecting and learning about arbitrary relations. Seven-month-old infants were taught arbitrary relations between two verbal labels ("a" versus "i") and two distinctive looking objects under one of three conditions during a habituation procedure. In one condition (the amodal condition) there was synchrony relating the motions of the objects with the timing of the speech sounds (like showing and naming the object simultaneously; see figure 6.8). In a second condition the objects were moved out of synchrony with the

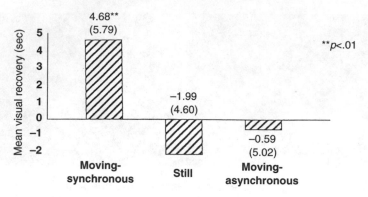

Figure 6.9   Mean visual recovery to the change in vowel-object relations in the moving-synchronous, still, and moving-asynchronous conditions (from Gogate and Bahrick, 1998) (**$p < .01$)

speech sounds, and in the third condition, the objects were still while the speech sounds were presented. Each object was presented along with its corresponding vowel sound, in an alternating sequence, until the infant was habituated. Then infants received test trials where the relationship between the sound and the object was switched. Visual recovery reflected detection of the change in object-sound relations. Results (figure 6.9) demonstrated significant visual recovery to the change in object-sound relations only in the amodal condition where temporal synchrony united the motions of the objects with the speech sounds. Infants showed no evidence of learning to relate the speech sounds and objects when there was asynchrony, or when the objects were still. These findings suggest that arbitrary associations between speech sounds and objects are best learned on the basis of amodal synchrony at first. Prior research had failed to demonstrate learning of arbitrary speech sound-object relations in infants so young, presumably because multimodal synchrony was not present. As infants mature and learn that sounds can stand for objects, synchrony is apparently no longer necessary for learning new object-sound relations. In fact, further research (Gogate et al., submitted) has demonstrated that mothers use synchrony to teach their young infants new names for objects, but the use of synchrony decreases as the infants become older and more lexically competent. Thus, the mother's use of temporal synchrony parallels the infant's changing reliance on it. These finding converge with those in the area of visual-tactual perception to demonstrate how detection of amodal information can guide and constrain detection of arbitrary relations across the senses.

Conclusions

In this chapter, I have reviewed evidence from a number of studies supporting three developmental principles that show how perception becomes increasingly more specific with development. Infants appear to detect intersensory relations in a particular order developmentally. When multimodal events make both amodal and arbitrary relations available, as is typical in the natural environment, infants first differentiate global amodal synchrony relations. Later, developmentally, they differentiate nested amodal relations such as information specifying object composition. Finally, they detect the arbitrary relations between aspects of the object's visual appearance and its sound or touch. There appears to be a developmental lag between the detection of global amodal, nested amodal, and arbitrary relations within a given domain or set of events.

How might this lag develop? Amodal relations appear to be perceptually more salient to infants because they create redundancy across the senses (see Bahrick and Lickliter, submitted). Amodal properties convey the same information to two senses simultaneously. Redundant stimulation captures infant attention at first, and becomes "foreground" while other, non-redundant properties become "background". Thus, when stimulation is multimodal, the attentional salience of intersensory redundancy can lead to a processing priority for amodal relations. This processing priority is illustrated in a recent study. Bahrick and Lickliter (submitted) showed 5-month-old infants films of a hammer tapping out one of two distinctive rhythms. Results demonstrated that infants could distinguish between the two rhythms when they were presented bimodally (visually and acoustically), but not when they were presented in either modality alone. Further, the advantage of bimodal audio-visual stimulation over unimodal stimulation was only evident when the films and soundtracks were temporally synchronous and not when they were presented asynchronously. Apparently, the attentional salience of amodal information presented redundantly across two senses creates a processing advantage and in turn creates a developmental lag between detection of properties that are bimodally specified and those that are not. Thus, the developmental lag between detection of amodal and arbitrary intersensory relations is result of the attentional salience of redundant stimulation. This developmental lag is adaptive because it fosters infant learning of consistencies and regularities across the senses that are context independent. It fosters appropriate generalization and minimizes learning of inappropriate, context bound relations. Thus, detection of amodal relations can guide and constrain learning of nested amodal and arbitrary relations.

Together, the findings reported here provide converging evidence for the principle of increasing specificity. Through perceptual experience, infants come to differentiate increasingly more specific levels of stimulation, from global synchrony, to nested amodal relations, to modality-specific arbitrary, associations. Detection of each level constrains and guides further perceptual selectivity. In this way, selective attention to global, amodal, relations in the first months of life can provide a means of organizing, guiding, and constraining perceptual experience in a way that ultimately leads to the intermodal knowledge of the adult perceiver.

References

Bahrick, L. E. (1983). Infants' perception of substance and temporal synchrony in multimodal events. *Infant Behavior and Development, 6,* 429–451.

Bahrick, L. E. (1987). Infants' intermodal perception of two levels of temporal structure in natural events. *Infant Behavior and Development, 10,* 38–416.

Bahrick, L. E. (1988). Intermodal learning in infancy: Learning on the basis of two kinds of invariant relations in audible and visible events. *Child Development, 59,* 197–207.

Bahrick, L. E. (1992). Infants' perceptual differentiation of amodal and modality-specific audio-visual relations. *Journal of Experimental Child Psychology, 53,* 180–199.

Bahrick, L. E. (1994). The development of infants' sensitivity to arbitrary intermodal relations. *Ecological Psychology, 6,* 111–123.

Bahrick, L. E. (1995). Intermodal origins of self-perception (pp. 349–373). In P. Rochat (Ed.) *The self in infancy: Theory and research.* Amsterdam: North Holland-Elsevier.

Bahrick, L. E. (1996, April). Increasing specificity in the development of infants' sensitivity to two nested amodal relations. Presented at the *International Conference on Infant Studies,* Providence, RI.

Bahrick, L. E. (submitted). Increasing specificity in the development of perception: Detection of nested levels of temporal structure in multimodal events.

Bahrick, L. E., Netto, D., & Hernandez-Reif, M. (1998). Intermodal perception of adult and child faces and voices by infants. *Child Development, 69,* 1263–1275.

Bahrick, L. E., & Lickliter, R. (submitted). Intersensory redundancy guides attentional selectivity and perceptual learning in infancy.

Bahrick, L. E., & Pickens, J. N. (1994). Amodal relations: The basis for intermodal perception and learning. In D. Lewkowicz and R. Lickliter (Eds.), *The development of intersensory perception: Comparative perspectives,* (205–233). Hillsdale, NJ: Lawrence Erlbaum Associates.

Bahrick, L. E., & Watson, J. S. (1985). Detection of intermodal proprioceptive-visual contingency as a potential basis of self-perception in infancy. *Developmental Psychology, 21,* 963–973.

Caron, A. J., Caron, R. F., & MacLean, D. J. (1988). Infant discrimination of naturalistic emotional expressions: The role of face and voice. *Child Development, 59,* 604–616.

Dodd, B. (1979). Lip reading in infants: Attention to speech presented in- and-out of synchrony. *Cognitive Psychology, 11,* 478–484.

Gibson, E. J. (1969). *Principles of perceptual learning and development.* New York: Appleton-Century-Crofts.

Gogate, L. J., & Bahrick, L. E. (1998). Intersensory redundancy facilitates learning of arbitrary relations between vowel sounds and objects in seven-month-old infants. *Journal of Experimental Child Psychology, 69,* 1–17.

Gogate, L. J., Bahrick, L. E., & Watson, J. (submitted). A cross-cultural study of multimodal motherese: The use of temporal synchrony in maternal communication to infants.

Hernandez-Reif, M., & Bahrick, L. E. (submitted). The development of visual-tactual perception of objects: Amodal relations provide the basis for learning arbitrary relations.

Horowitz, F., Paden, L., Bhana, K., & Self, P. (1972). An infant-control procedure for studying infant visual fixations. *Developmental Psychology, 7,* 90.

Kuhl, P. K., & Meltzoff, A. N. (1982). The bimodal perception of speech in infancy. *Science, 218,* 1138–1141.

Kuhl, P. K., & Meltzoff, A. N. (1984). The intermodal representation of speech in infants. *Infant Behavior and Development, 7,* 361–381.

Lewkowicz, D. J. (1996a). Infants' response to the audible and visible properties of the human face: 1. Role of lexical-syntactic content, temporal synchrony, gender, and manner of speech. *Developmental Psychology, 32,* 347–366.

Lewkowicz, D. J. (1996b). Perception of auditory-visual temporal synchrony in human infants. *Journal of Experimental Psychology: Human Perception and Performance, 22,* 1094–1106.

Lewkowicz, D. J., & Lickliter, R. (1994). *The development of intersensory perception: Comparative perspectives.* Hillsdale, NJ: Lawrence Erlbaum Associates.

Rochat, P., & Morgan, R. (1995). Spatial determinants in the perception of self-produced leg movements in 3- to 5-month-old infants. *Developmental Psychology, 31,* 626–636.

Rochat, P. (1995). *The self in infancy: Theory and research.* Amsterdam: North Holland-Elsevier.

Schmuckler, M. (1996). Infants' visual-proprioceptive intermodal perception. *Infant Behavior and Development, 19,* 221–232.

Spelke, E. S. (1979). Perceiving bimodally specified events in infancy. *Developmental Psychology, 15,* 626–636.

Walker, A. S. (1982). Intermodal perception of expressive behaviors by human infants. *Journal of Experimental Child Psychology, 33,* 514–535.

Walker-Andrews, A. (1986). Intermodal perception of expressive behaviors: Relation of eye and voice? *Developmental Psychology, 22,* 373–377.

Walker-Andrews, A. S., & Lennon, E. (1991). Infants' discrimination of vocal expressions: Contributions of auditory and visual information. *Infant Behavior and Development, 14,* 131–142.

Walker-Andrews, A., Bahrick, L. E., Raglioni, S. S., & Diaz, I. (1991). Infants' bimodal perception of gender. *Ecological Psychology, 3,* 55–75.

SEVEN

Social Perception

Introduction

Have you ever noticed how disconcerting it is when someone looks over your shoulder while you are talking to them? When you look at a sea of faces, either live or in pictures, do you notice how the ones looking in your direction tend to stand out from the group? As adults, we are exceptionally sensitive to eye-contact, particularly during face-to-face conversations when eye-contact helps us determine that the message is meant for us. Well, the same thing seems to be true for very young infants.

This paper in part II, by Symons, Hains and Muir, bridges infancy research in perceptual (part II) and social (part IV) development. Social perception concerns the perception of people (and other living things) as opposed to objects. Symons et al. examine how sensitive young infants are to one social cue, adult eye-direction. There are several important differences between this selection and others in part II that should be noted. First, a certain degree of stimulus control (the use of standard pictures, or recorded sounds, that can be precisely described and used in any laboratory to replicate and extend the work) is sacrificed. Symons et al. tested infants using a more natural context designed to engage their "social perception system." The procedure is based on the discovery that when adults engage infants as young as 3-months of age in brief (1–2 minute) face-to-face interactions, the infants appear to respond in a "reciprocal" manner. Of course these young infants do not actually talk, but they do look and smile at the adult, move their arms and legs, and sometimes vocalize during the interaction, even when the infants and adults are looking at each other on TV monitors (like using a videophone).

The trick is to introduce (instruct) infants to the task by first engaging them in a normal face-to-face interaction for 1–2 minutes. Next, the adult's behavior is altered for 1–2 minutes, followed by another normal interaction period. Using this general procedure, one can test how sensitive infants are to various alterations in adult social signals. For example, a big effect occurs when the adult terminates the social interaction by adopting a neutral still-face; almost every infant stops looking and smiling at the adult. This "still-face" effect is social because it occurs for people but not objects – infants rarely smile at non-human looking "interacting" objects, although they find them very interesting to look at. Also, the adult needs to respond in a contingent manner to the infant's signals. Both infant visual attention and positive affect drop substantially, relative to normal contingent interaction periods, when a *noncontingent*, video replay of a stranger's TV interaction with another infant is presented.

Less dramatic responses are generated by changes in other cues adults respond to. In fact, an important methodological point is that the conventional measures of visual attention (i.e., the amount of looking at a stimulus) may be entirely insensitive to a variety of important adult social signals. For example, smiling, but not visual attention, declines when the adult shifts from happy to sad expressions, or looks away from the infant during contingent interactions (in the latter case, by viewing the infant on a TV monitor hidden from the infant – for details on these and other manipulations of adult "social" behavior, see Muir and Nadel, 1998). The present paper shows that a small, but reliable drop in both visual attention (not found in other studies) and positive effect (found in several studies) does occur when an adult breaks eye-contact and looks at one of the infant's ears. Pay particular attention to the comparisons of the size of the effect for visual attention and smiling measures in figure 7.2, which summarizes the results from several studies that use different methods. There are two remarkable things about the results of Symons et al's. study: the high degree of infant sensitivity to very small shifts in adult eye-direction, and the lack of response to an equivalent shift in the vertical direction. Why should infants be so sensitive to adult eye-contact, and why should their response vary as a function of the orientation of the adult's shift in eye direction?

Reference

Muir, D. W., and Nadel, J. (1998). Infant social perception. In A. Slater (ed.) *Perceptual development: Visual, auditory, and speech perception in infancy* (pp. 247–286). East Sussex, UK: Psychology Press.

Look at Me: Five-Month-Old Infants' Sensitivity to Very Small Deviations in Eye-Gaze During Social Interactions

Lawrence A. Symons, Sylvia M. J. Hains, and Darwin W. Muir

Eye contact is an integral part of adult communication and plays an important role in infant-adult interaction (Kleinke, 1986). It has been suggested that infants' sensitivity and responses to eye-gaze information may also be crucial for social and cognitive development (Baron-Cohen, 1994; Robson, 1967). This proposal is supported by the findings of a number of studies demonstrating that infants are sensitive to the presence of eyes and the direction of another person's gaze. For example, using stationary stimuli, Mauer and Salapatek (1976) showed that 2-month-olds fixate the eye region of a face more than other areas. Caron et al. (1973) used an habituation task to demonstrate that the eyes were more salient than the mouth area for 3-month-olds. Vecera and Johnson (1995) reported that 4-month-olds could distinguish between a face with frontal eye gaze and one with averted gaze in a preferential looking task, although no preference for frontal eye gaze was found. While these studies indicate attentiveness to eye-like stimuli, they do not address the issue of the relevance of eye direction for the infant.

Muir et al. (1994) have suggested that eye-gaze information is a social cue which is best assessed with paradigms that emphasize the social context of the information. As well, they suggested that measures of infant affect (e.g. smiling) may be more sensitive for revealing differential responses to social stimuli than classic measures of attention such as looking time. A few studies have examined infant sensitivity to direction of an interactor's gaze in a social setting. Zeifman, Delaney and Blass (1996) recently demonstrated that whereas 2-week-olds were calmed by oral infusion of sucrose alone, by 4-weeks-of-age, infants were calmed only when the oral sucrose was accompanied by adult eye contact. Lasky and Klein (1979) had an adult engage in face-to-face interactions with 5-month-olds, while looking directly at the infant or above the infant's head; infants gazed longer when the adult made eye contact. Hains and Muir (1996) demonstrated that infants as young as 3-months-of-age smiled less when an adult did not make eye contact during a social interaction. In their paradigm, an adult interacted with an infant over four 1-minute periods. In the first and third periods, eye-contact with the infant was maintained during the interaction; in the second and fourth periods, eye-contact was broken by shifting the gaze 20 degrees to look at a TV display of the baby (Hains and Muir, 1996 – Experiment 2). By viewing the TV monitor, the interactor could maintain a social interaction during the eyes-away periods. The infants displayed decreased positive affect (as measured by smiling) during the eyes-away periods, but showed no change in looking time (a measure of infant attention).

While eye contact appears to mediate infant social responses during face-to-face interactions, little is known about the limits of infant sensitivity to shifts in eye gaze, as all of the studies described above used relatively large shifts in the interactor's or model's gaze. If eye-gaze plays an important role in social and cognitive development, it might be expected that even small shifts in an interactor's gaze would be noticed by infants. The present experiment assessed infant sensitivity to a small shift of an interactor's eye gaze (approximately 5 degrees) using a four-period social interaction paradigm similar to that used by Hains and Muir (1996). During the eyes-away periods, the interactor shifted her gaze to look at one of the infant's ears (Horizontal condition) or the top of the infant's head or chin (Vertical condition). If infants are sensitive to this small shift in an adult's gaze, they should show qualitatively similar effects to those found by Hains and Muir (1996). This small shift in eye gaze is detectable by adult observers (Gibson and Pick, 1962), and is within the range of infant acuity for the ages tested (Dobson and

Teller, 1978) but allows the interactor to maintain contingent social responses with the infant.

Forty-five infants identified from birth announcements in a local newspaper were recruited for this study. All children were non-Hispanic Whites. The parents' income, occupations and educational status were not recorded. The mothers were contacted by phone and informed consent was obtained before testing. Data for 5 subjects were lost due to excessive fussing, resulting in a total of 40 infants (18 girls, 22 boys), average age = 21.3 weeks ($SD = 3.6$), remaining in the study.

During the face-to-face interactions, infants were secured in an infant seat approximately 65 cm from the adult. A camera behind the adult was trained on the infant; a second camera recorded the adult. Two adult females were trained to interact with infants. Assignment to inter-actor was made on an *ad hoc* basis with approximately the same number of infants interacting with each adult. All infants interacted with one of the adults for four 60 s periods of contingent, social interaction. The adult's activity and responses were contingent on the behavior of the infant and consisted of smiling and infant-directed conversational speech without physical contact; (see Hains and Muir, 1996 for a fuller description). Timing of the periods was measured by stopwatch and the periods were separated by 15 s. Infants were randomly assigned to con-dition. For the Horizontal condition (*H*); the adult interacted while maintaining eye-contact in the first and third periods. During the second period, the adult looked at one of the infant's ears and in the fourth period, she looked at the other ear while maintaining normal contingent interactions. For the Vertical group (*V*), the adult interacted while main-taining eye-contact in the first and third periods, and during the second and fourth periods she looked at the top of the infant's head in one period and the chin in the other period. The direction of looking was counterbalanced across infants.

Frame-by-frame analyses of the videotaped behaviors of the infants and adults were scored by two independent observers. The adult's side of the split-screen was covered so that the observers were naive to the experimental conditions. The infant behaviors measured included dura-tion of looking and smiling. Looking was defined as looking towards the adult's face; smiling was defined as an upward movement of the corners of the mouth. For a behavior to be scored, it had to last at least 0.5 s. Durations of behaviors were measured from a timeline that had been superimposed on the videotape record and had a resolution of $\frac{1}{30}$th of a second. The duration of each behavior was expressed as a percentage of the total period for the analyses. Inter-observer reliabilities were calculated by comparing the scoring of the two experienced observers on six records they both scored: values of the kappas (0.89 for smile and 0.96 for looking) were acceptable.

We hypothesized that the infants' behaviors would decline in the eyes away periods (2 and 4) relative to the eyes toward periods (1 and 3). This result would be supported by a significant cubic trend in an analysis of the means across periods. Thus, the data were analyzed using analysis of variance with linear, quadratic and cubic trends on the period effect. As shown in figure 7.1, both smiling and looking time declined during the eyes away periods for the H condition, but not for the V condition. For looking, there was no main effect of group but there was a marginally significant period effect, $F(3,114) = 2.62$, $p = .054$, which had a linear component, $F(1,38) = 5.24$, $p < .01$. The groups did not differ on the linear trend but differed on the cubic component of the period effect, $F(1,38) = 3.95$, $p < .05$.

For smile duration, there was no main effect of group but there was a period effect, $F(3,114) = 3.62$, $p < .01$ with a linear component, $F(1,38) = 5.98$, $p < .01$, but the groups did not differ on this effect. However, the groups differed on the cubic component of the period effect, $F(1,38) = 4.77$, $p < .05$. For both dependent measures, the infants in the H group showed a reduction when the adult averted her eyes in Periods 2 and 4, while the V group showed no effect of the manipulation. More importantly, the reduction shown in Period 2 by the H group was accompanied by a recovery in Period 3, indicating that these effects were not the result of habituation.

The results of this study demonstrate that infants are sensitive to very small horizontal shifts in an interactor's gaze and smile more for an adult who maintained eye contact. These results confirm Muir et al.'s (1994) suggestion that the dyadic interaction is a powerful vehicle for examining infant perceptual capacities. Muir et al. (1994) suggested that the sensitivity should be especially pronounced when one assessed measures of affect, as this measure has been shown to be a reliable indicator of infant perception of various perturbations in adult behavior patterns (e.g., Ellsworth et al., 1993, Hains and Muir, 1996). However, in the present study, unlike previous research using this paradigm (e.g. Hains and Muir, 1996), there appeared to be a shift in infant attention as well. It should be noted, though, that Hains and Muir's (1996)

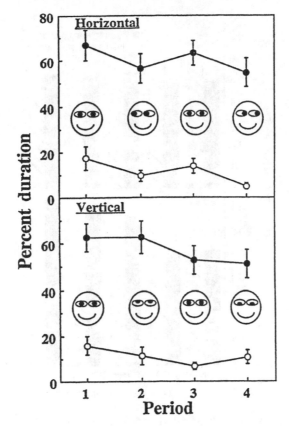

Figure 7.1 *Top panel*: Infants' looking (closed circles) and smiling duration (open circles) to eye-contact (Periods 1 and 3) and averted gaze (Periods 2 and 4) in the Horizontal condition. *Bottom panel*: Infants' looking and smiling duration to vertical shifts in gaze. Data points represent the mean duration of each period the behavior was exhibited, expressed as a percentage of that period. Error bars represent 1 standard error of the mean

attention data show a non-significant trend similar to that in the present study.

For the purposes of comparison, figure 7.2 shows the relative size of the effects of eye-gaze shifts on infant affect in the present experiment and the conditions reported in Hains and Muir (1996). The present effect for smiling was slightly less than that obtained by Hains and Muir

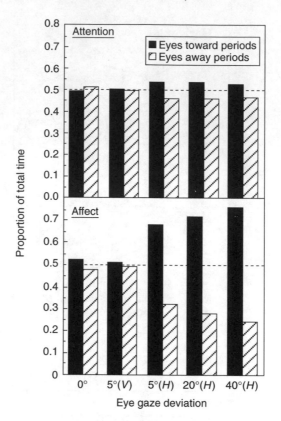

Figure 7.2   A comparison of the present results (5 degrees vertical and 5 degrees horizontal) with those of Hains and Muir (1996 – no change controls (0 degrees), 20 degrees and 40 degrees horizontal). *Top panel*: Looking. *Bottom panel*: Smiling. Each bar represents the proportion of the total amount of infant looking or smiling exhibited in the eyes toward or eyes away periods(e.g. eyes Toward periods = (sum of looking duration for eyes toward periods (1 and 3) / (sum of looking duration for all periods (1, 2, 3, and 4))

(1996). The loss of smiling appears to increase with greater shifts in eye direction. However, in the present study, the horizontal group showed a substantial sensitivity to the lack of eye contact by the adult, even when the eye aversion was only 5 degrees. In an analysis comparing the data from the present experimental conditions with those from the control infants from Hains and Muir (1996), the *H* group showed a significant cubic trend x group interaction for smiling, $F(1,31) = 6.53$, $p < 0.05$. but not for gaze. No significant differences were found in comparing the V group with these control infants.

The lack of effect for vertical shifts in the interactor's eye-gaze was somewhat surprising. There are at least two possibilities for the difference between horizontal and vertical sensitivities to eye direction. First, it is possible that vertical shifts in gaze do not disrupt the normal social interaction. Considerable information concerning emotional expression is derived from the brow and mouth areas of the face, so it is not unreasonable for people to shift their gaze to these areas during face-to-face interactions. However, little social information can be derived from the ears, so a shift in gaze to this area may represent a reliable break in the social interaction to the infant. Thus, the difference between vertical and horizontal shifts of gaze may be due to learning the permissible changes in eye direction in the normal social interactions the infant has previously encountered.

The second possibility is more perceptual in nature. Anstis et al. (1969), in assessing accuracy in determining the direction of a looker's gaze, found that adults were extremely accurate at mapping vertical shifts, but tended to show overextensions in horizontal shifts. Thus, if the looker was gazing at the participant's ear, the participant reported a gaze to his or her shoulder. In the present experiment, the differential infant responses to vertical and horizontal shifts in gaze may be similar to the phenomenon demonstrated by Anstis et al. (1969).

Whereas the results of studies using nonsocial stimuli as described above (e.g., Maurer and Salapatek, 1976; Vecera and Johnson, 1995) may be sufficient to demonstrate that infants can discriminate between face-like stimuli, the role attributed to mutual eye-contact in the social development of infants (e.g., Baron-Cohen, 1994; Wolff, 1987), requires a demonstration of the importance of eye-contact within a social context. Although Lasky and Klein (1979) and Hains and Muir (1996) have demonstrated that infants interact less with an adult when large eye-direction deviations are used, the present study is the first to demonstrate that young infants are less responsive to adults who make a very small deviation in eye direction. The extreme sensitivity of young infants to small deviations in an interactor's eye gaze suggests that eye-gaze information is a crucial cue used by infants in the development of their social interactions.

References

Anstis, S. M., Mayhew, J. W., & Morley, T. (1969). The perception of where a face or television "portrait" is looking. *American Journal of Psychology, 82,* 474–489.

Baron-Cohen, S. (1994). How to build a baby that can read minds: Cognitive mechanisms in mind-reading. *Cahiers de Psychologie Cognitive, 13,* 513–552.

Caron, A., Caron, R., Caldwell, R., & Weiss, S. (1973). Infant perception of the structural properties of the face. *Developmental Psychology, 9,* 385–400.

Dobson, V., & Teller, D. Y. (1978). Visual acuity in human infants: A review and comparison of behavioral and electrophysiological studies. *Vision Research, 18,* 1469–1483.

Ellsworth, C. P., Muir, D. W., & Hains, S. M. J. (1993). Social competence and person-object differentiation: An analysis of the still-face effect. *Developmental Psychology, 29,* 63–73.

Gibson, J., & Pick, A. (1962). Perception of another person's looking behavior. *American Journal of Psychology, 76,* 386–394.

Hains, S. M. J., & Muir, D. W. (1996). Infant sensitivity to adult eye direction information. *Child Development, 67,* 1940–1951.

Kleinke, C. L. (1986). Gaze and eye contact: A research review. *Psychological Bulletin, 100,* 78–100.

Lasky, R. E., & Klein, R. E. (1979). The reactions of five-month-olds to eye contact of the mother and of a stranger. *Merrill-Palmer Quarterly, 25,* 163–170.

Maurer, D., & Salapatek, P. (1976). Developmental changes in the scanning of faces by young infants. *Child Development, 47,* 523–527.

Muir, D. W., Hains, S. M. J., & Symons, L. A. (1994). Baby and me: Infants need minds to read! *Cahiers de Psychologie Cognitive, 13,* 669–682.

Robson, K. S. (1967). The role of eye-to-eye contact in maternal-infant attachment. *Journal of Child Psychology and Psychiatry, 8,* 13–25.

Vecera, S. P., & Johnson, M. H. (1995). Gaze detection and the cortical processing of faces: Evidence from infants and adults. *Visual Cognition, 2,* 59–87.

Wolff, P. H. (1987). *The development of behavioral states and the expression of emotions in early infancy.* The University of Chicago Press, Chicago.

Zeifman, D., Delaney, S., & Blass, E. M. (1996). Sweet taste, looking, and calm in 2- and 4-week-old infants: The eyes have it. *Developmental Psychology, 6,* 1090–1099.

EIGHT

Speech Perception

Introduction

Some 30 years ago there was little knowledge about the origins and development of speech perception in infants, and the general view was that infants learned to discriminate speech sounds, in part by listening to their own speech productions in babbling, and in part by listening to the speech they hear around them. However, when methodologies were developed to investigate speech perception in infants, it became apparent that they are able to make a whole range of speech discriminations well before they produce speech-like sounds. As discussed in chapter 4, we now know that speech perception begins in the womb, and that infants are sensitive to speech sounds in the last trimester of fetal life: near-term fetuses can make a number of auditory discriminations, including that between male and female voices. And, soon after birth, newborn infants will prefer to listen to their mother's voice (DeCasper and Fifer, 1980). According to Moon et al., (1993) two-day-old infants can even discriminate between their native and a foreign language – they prefer to listen to their native tongue!

Infant speech research began in earnest with the findings of Peter Eimas and his colleagues (for example, Eimas et al., 1971) that 1-month-olds could discriminate the subtle phonetic contrast between [ba] and [pa], and evidence has accumulated to demonstrate that young infants are extremely sensitive to small differences in phonemes – the basic units of sound that distinguish one word from another. It seems that young infants can discriminate almost every phonetic contrast from all of the world's languages, even phonemes that are not used in their own language. However, it is clearly the case that the sound structures of different languages vary considerably, and infants therefore have to learn about the sound patterns of their native language.

In this article Janet Werker reviews her own, and others', research which shows clearly that as they get older, and particularly as they begin

to utter meaningful words, infants *lose* the ability to make many phonetic discriminations that are not used to differentiate words, or contrast
meaning, in their native language. As she puts it, the infant is "becoming a native listener."

References

DeCasper, A. J. and Fifer, W. P. (1980). Of human bonding: newborns prefer
their mother's voices. *Science, 208*, 1174–1176.

Eimas, P. D., Siqueland, E. R., Jusczyk, P. W. and Vigorito, J. (1971). Speech
perception in infants. *Science, 171*, 303–306.

Moon, C., Cooper, R. P. and Fifer, W. P. (1993). Two-day-olds prefer their native
language. *Infant Behavior and Development, 16*, 495–500.

Further reading

A. Slater (ed.), (1998). *Perceptual development: visual, auditory and speech perception in infancy*. Hove, UK: Psychology Press.

Becoming a Native Listener
Janet F. Werker

The syllables, words, and sentences used in all human languages are formed from a set of speech sounds called phones. Only a subset of the phones is used in any particular language. Adults can easily perceive the differences among the phones used to contrast meaning in their own language, but young infants go much farther: they are able to discriminate nearly every phonetic contrast on which they have been tested, in cluding those they have never before heard. Our research has shown that this broad-based sensitivity declines by the time a baby is one year old. This phenomenon provides a way to describe basic abilities in the young infant and explore the effects of experience on human speech perception.

To put infants' abilities in perspective, adult speech perception must be understood. The phones that distinguish meaning in a particular language are called phonemes. There is considerable acoustic variability in the way each individual phoneme is realized in speech. For example, the phoneme /b/ is very different before the vowel /ee/ in "beet" from the way it is before the vowel /oo/ in "boot." How do adults handle this variability? As first demonstrated in a classic study by Liberman and his colleagues (1967), they treat these acoustically distinct instances of a single phoneme as equivalent. This equivalency is demonstrated in the laboratory by presenting listeners with a series of pairs of computer-synthesized speech stimuli that differ by only one acoustic step along a physical continuum and asking them first to label and then to try to discriminate between the stimuli. Adult listeners are able to discriminate reliably only stimuli that they have labeled as different – that is, they cannot easily discriminate between two acoustically different stimuli that they labeled /pa/, but they can discriminate between two similar stimuli if one is from their /ba/ category and one from their /pa/ category.

The phenomenon by which labeling limits discrimination is referred to as categorical perception. This has obvious advantages for language processing. It allows a listener to segment the words he hears immediately according to the phonemic categories of his language and to ignore unessential variations within a category.

Given that adults perceive speech categorically, when do such perceptual capabilities appear? To find out, Eimas and his colleagues (1971) adapted the so-called high-amplitude sucking procedure for use in a speech discrimination task. This procedure involves teaching infants to suck on a pacifier attached to a pressure transducer in order to receive a visual or auditory stimulus. After repeated presentations of the same sight or sound, the sucking rate declines, indicating that the infants are becoming bored. The infants are then presented with a new stimulus. Presumably, if they can discriminate the new sight or sound from the old, they will increase their sucking rate.

In Eimas's experiment, infants one and four months old heard speech sounds that varied in equal steps from /ba/ to /pa/. Like adults, they discriminated between differences in the vicinity of the /ba/-/pa/ boundary but were unable to discriminate equal acoustic changes from within the /ba/ category. Rather than having to learn about phonemic categories, then, infants seem capable of grouping speech stimuli soon after birth.

Experiments in the 17 years since Eimas's original study have shown that infants can discriminate nearly every phonetic contrast on which they are tested but are generally unable to discriminate differences within a single phonemic category (for a review, see Kuhl 1987). That is, like adults, infants perceive acoustically distinct instances of a single phoneme as equivalent but easily discriminate speech sounds from two different categories that are not more acoustically distinct.

Of special interest are demonstrations that young infants are even able to discriminate phonetic contrasts not used in their native language. In an early study, Streeter (1976) used the high-amplitude sucking procedure to test Kikuyu infants on their ability to discriminate the English /ba/-/pa/ distinction, which is not used in Kikuyu. She found that the infants could discriminate these two syllable types. Similar results have been obtained from a variety of laboratories using other nonnative phonetic contrasts (Lasky et al. 1975; Trehub 1976; Aslin et al. 1981; Eilers et al. 1982). This pattern of results indicates that the ability to discriminate phones from the universal phonetic inventory may be present at birth.

Developmental Changes

Given these broad-based infant abilities, one might expect that adults would also be able to discriminate nearly all phonetic contrasts. However, research suggests that adults often have difficulty discriminating phones that do not contrast meaning in their own language. An English-speaking adult, for example, has difficulty perceiving the difference between the two /p/ phones that are used in Thai (Lisker and Abramson 1970). So too, a Japanese-speaking adult initially cannot distinguish between the English /ra/ and /la/, because Japanese uses a single phoneme intermediate between the two English phonemes (Miyawaki et al. 1975; MacKain et al. 1981). This pattern of extensive infant capabilities and more limited capabilities in the adult led to the suggestion that infants may have a biological predisposition to perceive all possible phonetic contrasts and that there is a decline in this universal phonetic sensitivity by adulthood as a function of acquiring a particular language (Eimas 1975; Trehub 1976).

My work has been designed to explore this intriguing possibility. In particular, I wanted to trace how speech perception changes during development. Are infants actually able to discriminate some pairs of speech sounds better than adults, or have they simply been tested with more sensitive procedures? If infants do have greater discriminative capacities than adults, when does the decline occur and why?

The first problem that my colleagues and I faced was to find a testing procedure which could be used with infants, children of all ages, and adults. We could then begin a program of studies comparing their relative abilities to perceive the differences between phonetic contrasts of both native and nonnative languages.

The testing routine we chose is a variation of the so-called infant head turn procedure (for a complete description, see Kuhl 1987). Subjects are presented with several slightly different versions of the same phoneme (e.g., /ba/) repeated continuously at 2-sec intervals. On a random basis every four to twenty repetitions, a new phoneme is introduced. For example, a subject will hear "ba," "ba," "ba," "ba," "ba," "da," "da." Babies are conditioned to turn their heads toward the source of the sound when they detect the change from one phoneme to another (e.g., from "ba" to "da"). Correct head turns are reinforced with the activation of a little toy animal and with clapping and praise from the experimental assistant. Figure 8.1 shows a baby being tested. Adults and children are tested the same way, except that they press a button instead of turning their heads when they detect a change in the phoneme, and the reinforcement is age-appropriate.

In the first series of experiments, we compare English-speaking adults, infants from English-speaking families, and Hindi-speaking adults on their ability to discriminate the /ba/-/da/ distinction, which is used in both Hindi and English, as well as two pairs of syllables that are used in Hindi but not in English (Werker et al. 1981). The two pairs of Hindi syllables were chosen on the basis of their relative difficulty. The first pair contrast two "t" sounds that are not used in English. In English we articulate "t" sounds by placing the tongue a bit behind the teeth at the alveolar ridge. In Hindi, there are two different "t" phonemes. One is produced by placing the tongue on the teeth (a dental t – written /t/). The other is produced by curling the tip of the tongue back and placing it against the roof of the mouth (a retroflex t – written /T/). This contrast is not used in English, and is in fact very rare among the world's languages.

The second pair of Hindi syllables involves different categories of voicing – the timing of the release of a consonant and the amount of air released with the consonant. Although these phonemes, called /t^h/ and /d^h/, are not used in English, we had reason to believe that they might be easier for English-speaking adults to discriminate than the /t/-/T/ distinction. The timing difference between /t^h/ and /d^h/ spans the English /t/-/d/ boundary. Moreover, this contrast is more common among the world's languages.

The results of this study, which are presented in figure 8.2, were consistent with the hypothesis of universal phonetic sensitivity in the young infant and a decline by adulthood. As expected, all subjects could discriminate /ba/ from /da/. Of more interest, the infants aged six to eight months performed like the Hindi adults and were able to discriminate both pairs of Hindi speech contrasts. The English-speaking adults, on the other hand, were considerably less able to make the Hindi distinctions, especially the difficult dental-retroflex one.

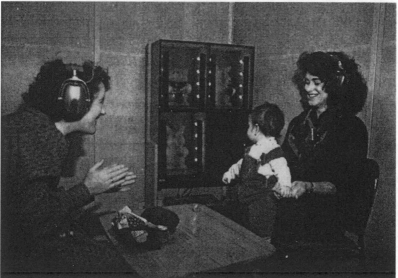

Figure 8.1 Human beings are born with the ability to recognize the speech sounds used in all the world's languages, even though only a portion of the sounds are used in any one language. As a baby listens to its own "native" tongue, it gradually loses the ability to discriminate sounds that are not used in that language. The author and her colleagues have elucidated this developmental change by testing infants, children, and adults with contrasting sounds in various languages. The infant shown here has learned to turn his head toward the source of the sounds when he hears a change in them. A correct head turn is reinforced by the activation of the toy animals as well as by clapping and praise of the experimental assistant (photographs by
Peter McLeod)

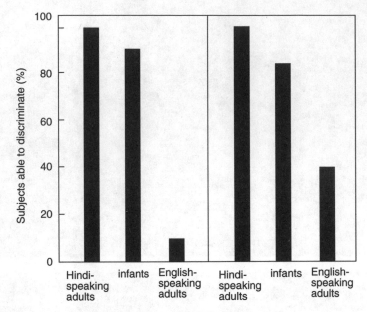

Figure 8.2   When tested on their ability to discriminate two Hindi syllables that are not used in English, six-to-eight-month-old infants from English speaking families do nearly as well as Hindi-speaking adults. English-speaking adults, however, have great difficulty with this discrimination task, depending on the degree of difference from English sounds. The graph on the left shows a contrast involving two "t" sounds, one dental (i.e., made with the tip of the tongue touching the upper front teeth) and the other retroflex (made with the tongue curled back under the palate). This contrast is rare in the world's languages. The contrast in the graph on the right involves two kinds of voicing, a phenomenon that is less unusual and thus somewhat more recognizable to English-speaking adults (after Werker et al., 1981)

Timing of Developmental Changes

The next series of experiments was aimed at determining when the decline in nonnative sensitivity occurs. It was originally believed that this decline would coincide with puberty, when, as Lenneberg (1967) claims, language flexibility decreases. However, our work showed that twelve-year-old English-speaking children were no more able to discriminate non-English syllables than were English-speaking adults (Werker and Tees 1983). We then tested eight- and four-year-old English-speaking children, and, to our surprise, even the four-year-olds could not discriminate the Hindi contrasts. Hindi-speaking four-year-olds, of course, showed no trouble with this discrimination.

Before testing children even younger than age four, we felt it was necessary to determine that the phenomenon of developmental loss extended to other languages. To this end, we chose a phonemic contrast from a North American Indian language of the Interior Salish family, called Nthlakapmx by native speakers in British Columbia but also referred to as Thompson.

North American Indian languages include many consonants produced in the back of the vocal tract, behind our English /k/ and /g/. The pair of sounds we chose contrasts a "k" sound produced at the velum with another "k" sound (written /q/) produced by raising the back of the tongue against the uvula. Both are glottalized – that is, there is an ejective portion (similar to a click) at the beginning of the release of the consonants.

Again, we compared English-speaking adults, infants from English-speaking families, and Nthlakapmx-speaking adults in their abilities to discriminate this pair of sounds (Werker and Tees 1984a). As was the case with the Hindi syllables, both the Nthlakapmx-speaking adults and the infants could discriminate the non-English phonemes, but the English-speaking adults could not.

We were now satisfied that there is at least some generality to the notion that young infants can discriminate across the whole phonetic inventory but that there is a developmental decline in this universal sensitivity. Our next series of experiments involved testing children between eight months and four years of age to try to determine just when the decline in sensitivity might start. It quickly became apparent that something important was happening within the first year of life. We accordingly compared three groups of infants aged six to eight, eight to ten, and ten to twelve months. Half of each group were tested with the Hindi (/ta/-/Ta/) and half with the Nthlakapmx (/ki/-/q̇i/) contrast.

As shown in figure 8.3, the majority of the six-to-eight-month-old infants from English-speaking families could discriminate the two non-English contrasts, whereas only about one-half of the eight-to-ten-month-olds could do so. Only two out of ten ten-to-twelve-month-olds could discriminate the Hindi contrast, and only one out of ten the Nthlakapmx. This provided strong evidence that the decline in universal phonetic sensitivity was occurring between six and twelve months of age. As a further test to see if this developmental change would be apparent within the same individuals, six infants from English-speaking

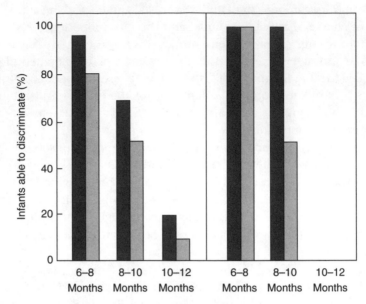

Figure 8.3 Infants show a decline in the universal phonetic sensitivity demonstrated in figure 8.2 during the second half of their first year, as shown here in the results of experiments performed with babies from English-speaking families and involving non-English syllables from Hindi (*dark gray bars*) and Nthlakapmx, a language spoken by some native Indians in British Columbia (*light gray bars*). The graph on the left gives results from experiments with three groups of infants aged six to eight months, eight to ten months, and ten to twelve months. The graph on the right gives results from testing one group of infants three times at the appropriate ages. None of the latter group were able to discriminate either of the non-English contrasts when they were ten to twelve months old (after Werker and Tees, 1984a)

families were tested at two-month intervals beginning when they were about six to eight months old. All six infants could discriminate both the Hindi and Nthlakapmx contrasts at the first testing, but by the third testing session, when they were ten to twelve months old, they were not able to discriminate either contrast.

To verify that the decline in nonnative sensitivity around ten to twelve months was a function of language experience, we tested a few infants from Hindi- and Nthlakapmx-speaking families when they reached eleven to twelve months old. As predicted, these infants were still able to discriminate their native contrasts, showing quite clearly that the decline observed in the infants from English-speaking families was a function of specific language experience. Since doing these studies, we have charted the decline between six and twelve months old using a computer-generated set of synthetic syllables which model another pair of Hindi sounds not used in English (Werker and Lalonde 1988).

How Does Experience Affect Development?

A theoretical model for considering the possible effects of experience on perceptual development was suggested by Gottlieb in 1976. As expanded by both Gottlieb (1981) and Aslin (1981), the model includes several roles experience might – or might not – play, as shown in figure 8.4.

Induction refers to cases in which the emergence and form of a perceptual capability depend entirely on environmental input. In this case, an infant would not show categorical perception of speech sounds without prior experience. Attunement refers to a situation in which experience influences the full development of a capability, enhancing the level of performance; for example, categorical boundaries between phonetic contrasts might be sharper with experience than without. In facilitation, experience affects the rate of development of a capability, but it does not affect the end point. If this role were valid, speech perception would improve even without listening experience, but hearing specific sounds would accelerate the rate of improvement. Maintenance/loss refers to the case in which a perceptual ability is fully developed prior to the onset of specific experience, which is required to maintain that capability. Without adequate exposure an initial capability is lost. Finally, maturation refers to the unfolding of a perceptual capability independent of environmental exposure. According to this hypothetical possibility, the ability to discriminate speech sounds would mature regardless of amount or timing of exposure.

Our work is often interpreted as an illustration of maintenance/ loss, since it suggests that young infants can discriminate phonetic contrasts before they have gained experience listening but that experience hearing the phones used in their own language is necessary to maintain the ability to discriminate at least some pairs of phones.

Support for this view was provided by another study in which we tested English-speaking adults who had been exposed to Hindi during the first couple of years of life and had learned their first words in Hindi but had

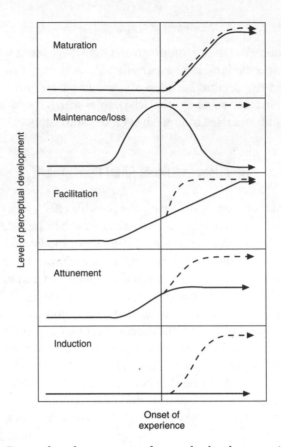

Figure 8.4 Researchers have suggested several roles that experience might – or might not – play in the development of particular perceptual capabilities. These possibilities are shown graphically here: broken lines represent development after the onset of experience, and solid lines represent development in the absence of experience. Induction refers to cases in which a capability depends entirely on experience. Attunement refers to a situation in which experience makes possible the full development of a capability. In facilitation, experience affects only the rate of development of a capability. Maintenance/loss refers to the ease in which a capability is fully developed before the onset of experience, but experience is necessary to maintain the capability. Maturation refers to the development of a capability independent of experience. The phenomenon of universal phonetic sensitivity followed by a narrowing of sensitivity to native language sounds appears to illustrate maintenance/loss, since it suggests that young infants can discriminate phonetic contrasts before they have gained experience listening but that experience with language is necessary to maintain the full ability (after Aslin 1981; Gottlieb 1981)

little or no subsequent exposure. These subjects could discriminate the Hindi syllables much more easily than other English-speaking adults, and performed virtually as well as native Hindi speakers on the discrimination task (Tees and Werker 1984). This is consistent with the view that early experience functions to maintain perceptual abilities, suggesting that no further experience is necessary to maintain them into adulthood.

Recovery of Sensitivity

Our early work led us to believe that the loss of nonnative sensitivity is difficult to reverse in adults. In one study, we tested English-speaking adults who had studied Hindi for various lengths of time. Adults who had studied Hindi for five years or more were able to discriminate the non-English Hindi syllables, but those who had studied Hindi for one year at the university level could not do so. In fact, even several hundred trials were insufficient to teach English-speaking adults to discriminate the more difficult Hindi contrasts (Tees and Werker 1984). This implies that while the ability is recoverable, considerable experience is required. Similar conclusions can be drawn from a study by MacKain and her colleagues (1981), who tested Japanese speakers learning English. Only after one year of intensive English training in the United States could they discriminate/ra/ from /la/.

The question still remained whether recovery of non-native sensitivity results from new learning in adulthood or from a latent sensitivity. To explore this question, we asked English-speaking adults to discriminate both the full syllables of the difficult Hindi and Nthlakapmx phonemes and shortened portions of the syllables which do not sound like speech at all but contain the critical acoustic information specifying the difference between the phonemes (Werker and Tees 1984b). Subjects were first tested on the shortened stimuli and then on the full syllables. To our surprise, they were able to discriminate the shortened stimuli easily but were still not able to discriminate the full syllables, even immediately after hearing the relevant acoustic information in shortened form. This finding reveals that the auditory capacity for discriminating the acoustic components of these stimuli has not been lost but that it is difficult to apply when processing language-like sounds.

In a further set of experiments, we attempted to make English-speaking adults discriminate the full-syllable non-native stimuli

(Werker and Logan 1985). One task involved presenting adults with pairs of stimuli and asking them to decide simply if the stimuli were the same or different, a test that proved to be much more sensitive than the head turn procedure. In this "same/different" task, listeners have to compare only two stimuli at a time. Moreover, if the interval between the two stimuli is short enough, listeners can hold the first stimulus in auditory memory while comparing it to the second. In the head turn task, on the other hand, listeners have to compare each stimulus to a whole set of variable stimuli and judge whether it is a member of the same category.

We found that English-speaking adults could discriminate the Hindi syllables when tested in the same/different procedure, particularly after practice. Thus there was evidence that adults can discriminate non-native contrasts if tested in a more sensitive procedure. Similar results have been reported by other researchers (Pisoni et al. 1982). This suggests that the developmental changes between infancy and adulthood should be considered a language-based reorganization of the categories of communicative sounds rather than an absolute loss of auditory sensitivity. The increasing reliance on language-specific categories accounts for the age-related decline, implying that maintenance has its effect at the level of linguistic categories rather than simple peripheral auditory sensitivity (see Best et al. 1988).

Parallels in Speech Production

It is interesting to compare our findings of developmental changes in speech perception to recent work on speech production. Although it is impossible to survey this substantial literature here, there appear to be systematic regularities in the repertoire of sounds produced at different stages of babbling. These regularities may reflect vocal tract and neuromuscular maturation, with phones appearing as a child develops the ability to articulate them (Locke 1983). In contrast to early work suggesting that the sounds produced during babbling gradually narrow to those that are used in the language-learning environment, recent research shows very little influence from the native language on vocal development during the babbling stage. This conclusion is particularly strong for consonants. However, it is clear that after the acquisition of the first word children's vocal productions start becoming differentiated on the basis of language experience. That is, once a child begins to talk, the sounds produced conform more and more closely to the subset of phones used in his native language. The stage at which these changes occur is consistent with our work showing universal sensitivity in early infancy followed by only language-specific sensitivity beginning around ten to twelve months.

This leads us to believe that just as a reorganization of language production is related to the emergence of the first spoken word, so too the reorganization of perceptual abilities may be related to the emergence of the ability to understand words. By the time he is one year old, a child understands a fair amount of spoken language, even though he may produce only a few words. We are currently conducting experiments to see if the reorganization of speech perception is related to the emerging ability to understand words. This work will add another piece to the solution of the puzzle of how early sensitivity to all language sounds becomes limited to the functional categories that are necessary for communicating in one's own language.

References

Aslin, R. N. 1981. Experiential influences and sensitive periods in perceptual development: A unified model. In *Development of Perception*, ed. R. N. Aslin, J. R. Alberts, & M. R. Petersen vol. 2, pp. 45–94. Academic Press.

Aslin, R. N., D. B. Pisoni, B. L. Hennessy, & A. J. Perey. 1981. Discrimination of voice onset time by human infants: New findings and implications for the effect of early experience. *Child Development* 52: 1135–45.

Eilers, R. E., W. J. Gavin, & D. K. Oller. 1982. Cross-linguistic perception in infancy: Early effects of linguistic experience. *Journal of Child Language* 9: 289–302.

Eimas, P. D. 1975. Developmental studies in speech perception. In *Infant Perception: From Sensation to Cognition*, ed. L. B. Cohen, & P. Salapatek, vol. 2, pp. 193–231. Academic Press.

Eimas, P. D., E. R. Siqueland, P. W. Jusczyk, & J. Vigorito. 1971. Speech perception in infants. *Science* 171: 303–06.

Gottlieb, G. 1976. The roles of experience in the development of behavior and the nervous system. In *Studies on the Development of Behavior and the Nervous System*, ed. G. Gottlieb, vol. 3, pp. 1–35, Academic Press.

———. 1981. Roles of early experience in species-specific perceptual development. In *Development of Perception*, ed. R. N. Aslin, J. R. Alberts, & M. R. Petersen, vol. 1, pp. 5–44. Academic Press.

Kuhl, P. K. 1987. Perception of speech and sound in early infancy. In *Handbook of Infant Perception*, ed. P. Salapatek, & L. Cohen, vol. 2, pp. 275–382. Academic Press.

Sensation and Perception

Lasky, R. E., A. Syrdal-Lasky, & R. E. Klein. 1975. VOT discrimination by four to six and a half month old infants from Spanish environments. *Journal of Experimental Child Psychology* 20: 215–25.

Lenneberg, E. H. 1967. *Biological Foundations of Language*. Wiley.

Liberman, A. M., F. S. Cooper, D. P. Shankweiler, & M. Studdert-Kennedy. 1967. Perception of the speech code. *Psychological Review* 431–61.

Lisker, L., & A. S. Abramson. 1970. The voicing dimension: Some experiments in comparative phonetics. In *Proceedings of the 6th International Congress of Phonetic Sciences*, pp. 563–67. Prague: Academia.

Locke, J. L. 1983. *Phonological Acquisition and Change*. Academic Press.

MacKain, K. S., C. T. Best, and W. Strange. 1981. Categorical perception of English /r/ and /l/ by Japanese bilinguals. *Appl. Psycholing.* 2: 269–90.

Miyawaki, K., et al. 1975. An effect of linguistic experience: The discrimination of [r] and [l] by native speakers of Japanese and English. *Perception and Psychophysics* 18: 331–40.

Pisoni, D. B., R. N. Aslin, A. J. Perey, and B. L. Hennessy. 1982. Some effects of laboratory training on identification and discrimination of voicing contrasts in stop consonants. *J. Exper. Psychol.: Human Percept. Perform.* 8: 297–314.

Streeter, L. A. 1976. Language perception of two-month old infants shows effects of both innate mechanisms and experience. *Nature* 259: 39–41.

Tees, R. C., & J. F. Werker. 1984. Perceptual flexibility: Maintenance or recovery of the ability to discriminate non-native speech sounds. *Canadian Journal of Psychology* 34: 579–90.

Trehub, S. 1976. The discrimination of foreign speech contrasts by infants and adults. *Child Development* 47: 466–72.

Werker, J. F., J. H. V. Gilbert, K. Humphrey, & R. C. Tees. 1981. Developmental aspects of cross-language speech perception. *Child Development* 52: 349–53.

Werker, J. F., & C. E. Lalonde. 1988. The development of speech perception: Initial capabilities and the emergence of phonemic categories. *Developmental Psychology* 24: 672–83.

Werker, J. F., & J. S. Logan. 1985. Cross-language evidence for three factors in speech perception. *Perception and Psychophysics* 37: 35–44.

Werker, J. F., & R. C. Tees. 1983. Developmental changes across childhood in the perception of non-active speech sounds. *Canadian Journal of Psychology* 37: 278–86.

——. 1984a. Cross-language speech perception: Evidence for perceptual reorganization during the first year of life. *Infant Behavior and Development* 49–63.

——. 1984b. Phonemic and phonetic factors in adult cross-language speech perception. *Journal of Acoustical Soc. Am.* 75: 1866–78.

Cognitive Development

Introduction to Part III

Cognition refers to knowledge and thought, and it includes all mental activity – memory, categorization, thinking, problem-solving, creating, learning, and so on. Mental processes involve almost everything that we do, including social awareness and language development. The distinctions between cognitive development and other aspects of development are ones of emphasis. It would be possible to include other chapters in this volume in this part on cognitive development and conversely to move chapters from this part to other parts!

The papers in this part are a sample of studies concerning some aspects of cognition in infancy. Chapter 9, by Meltzoff and Moore, concerns early imitation which, the authors argue (in their update, chapter 9(b)), is "a discovery procedure in understanding persons." Chapters, 10, 11 and 12 all have as their dependent measure the infant's looking at events or outcomes that are surprising. Thus, if sums don't "add up" (chapter 10), if objects don't obey physical laws (chapter 11), if objects appear from where they have not been hidden (chapter 12), infants will look longer at the "impossible" or implausible event that at events or outcomes that are likely or possible.

One abiding concern of developmental psychologists it to find if there is stability and continuity across development – do the biggest, brightest infants turn out to be the tallest, most intelligent adults? It seems that there is some degree of stability and chapter 13, by Sigman et al., consider some of the possible causes of this.

NINE

Newborn Imitation

Introduction

For over 50 years it has been known that 1-year-old infants can imitate facial gestures that they see adults producing. This is not particularly surprising since imitation is one of the ways in which infants, children, and adults learn, but it *is* surprising to find that much younger infants can also imitate. The first report of newborn infants imitating adult facial gestures was by Olga Maratos, one of Piaget's students, who reported to him that if she stuck out her tongue to a young baby, the baby would respond by sticking its tongue out at her. This goes counter to Piaget's views on imitation – according to his theory it should only emerge around 8 months of age, at the earliest. When Piaget was appraised of his student's findings he apparently sucked contemplatively on his pipe for a few moments and then commented "How rude."

The first scientific report of human newborns imitating adult facial (and manual) gestures was by Andy Meltzoff and Keith Moore in 1977, and this paper is reproduced here. When it was published it aroused considerable interest and controversy. The initial debate concerned the question "Can they do it?," and there were several papers reporting difficulty in replicating the findings. By now, however, at least 25 different studies have confirmed early imitation, and the questions asked have gone beyond "Can they do it?" (they can), to "Why is it done?"; "Does it develop"; and "Why should we care?" One suggestion is that babies are born with a deep-seated need to communicate (Kugiumutzakis, 1993). Meltzoff and Moore (for example, 1992) offer the view that imitation is an act of social cognition that serves to help the infant identify, understand, and recognize people: "infants use the nonverbal behavior of people as an identifier of who they (the people) are and use imitation as a means of verifying this identify" (p. 479).

Meltzoff and Moore bring the debate up to date and consider several questions about early imitation. Their account is given in their paper in chapter 9(b), Resolving the Debate about Early Imitation, which follows their 1977 paper. In the later paper in 9(b) they point the reader to new data and new theories, so that the interested student can chase down the references and be informed about the current debates.

One intriguing suggestion in their paper is that newborn imitation is the origin and the foundation for developing a "theory of mind." Certainly, older infants are much more likely to imitate adults' acts that they interpret as being intentional rather than accidental (Carpenter et al., 1998, reproduced here as chapter 17; Meltzoff, 1995).

References

Carpenter, M., Akhtar, N. and Tomasello, M. (1998). Fourteen- through 18-month-old infants differentially imitate intentional and accidental acts. *Infant Behavior and Development*, *21*, 315–330.

Kugiumutzakis, G. (1993). Intersubjective vocal imitation in early mother-infant interaction. In J. Nadel and L. Camioni (eds.), *New Perspectives in Early Communicative Development* (pp. 23–47). London and New York: Routledge.

Meltzoff, A. N. (1995). Understanding the intentions of others: Re-enactment of intended acts by 18-month-old children. *Developmental Psychology*, *66*, 838–850.

Meltzoff, A. N. and Moore, M. K. (1992). Early imitation within a functional framework: The importance of person identity, movement, and development. *Infant Behavior and Development*, *15*, 83–99.

Further reading

Meltzoff, A. N. and Moore, M. K. (1998). Object representation, identity, and the paradox of early permanence: Steps towards a new framework. *Infant Behavior and Development*, *21*, 201–235.

Imitation of Facial and Manual Gestures by Human Neonates

Andrew N. Meltzoff and M. Keith Moore

Piaget and other students of developmental psychology consider the imitation of facial gestures to be a landmark achievement in infant development. Infants are thought to pass this milestone at approximately 8 to 12 months of age. Infants younger than this have been postulated to lack the perceptual-cognitive sophistication necessary to match a gesture they see with a gesture of their own which they cannot see.[1] The experiments we report show that the infant's imitative competence has been underestimated. We find that 12- to 21-day-old infants can imitate both facial and manual gestures (figure 9(a).1). This result has implications for our conception of innate human abilities and for theories of social and cognitive development.

An experimental evaluation of the neonate's imitative competence raises several methodological difficulties. One consists of distinguishing true imitation from a global arousal response. For example, one can conclude nothing about imitation if an infant produces more tongue protrusions in response to a tongue protrusion demonstration than he does to the presentation of a neutral facial expression. It would be more parsimonious simply to conclude that a moving, human face is arousing for the infant and that increased oral activity is part of the infant's arousal response. A second issue involves controlling interactions between adult and infant that might shape the imitative response. We found that if parents were informed of the imitative tasks we planned to examine, they practiced these gestures with their infants before coming into the

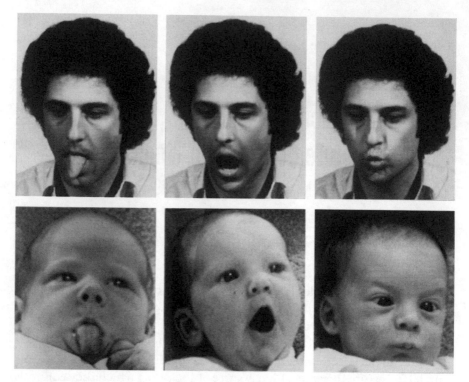

Figure 9(a).1 Sample photographs from videotape recordings of 2- to 3-week-old infants imitating (a) tongue protrusion, (b) mouth opening, and (c) lip protrusion demonstrated by an adult experimenter

laboratory so that their baby "would do well on the test." In reviewing films of preliminary work, we also noticed that the examiner tended to alter the rhythm of his tongue protrusion as a function of the response of the infant. These kinds of interactions would expose findings of imitation to a variety of explanations, including the possibility that the infants were merely being conditioned to imitate tongue protrusion. A third issue concerns the scoring of the infant's responses. The movements tested were not generally produced in a discrete, unambiguous fashion, and not surprisingly, there were gross differences in the scoring as a function of whether or not the observer knew which gesture had been demonstrated to the infant.

In the experiments we now report, these three issues are addressed as follows:

1   Each infant's response to one gesture is compared to his response to another similar gesture demonstrated by the same adult, at the same distance from the infant, and at the same rate of movement. For instance, we test whether infants produce more tongue protrusions after an adult demonstrates tongue protrusion than after the same adult demonstrates mouth opening, and vice versa. If differential imitation occurs, it cannot be attributed to a mere arousal of oral activity by a dynamic, human face.

2   Parents were not told that we were examining imitation until after the studies were completed; moreover, the experiments were designed to preclude the possibility that the experimenter might alter the rhythm of his demonstration as a function of the infant's response.

3   The infant's reactions were videotaped and then scored by observers who were uninformed of the gesture shown to the infant they were scoring.[2]

In experiment 1, the subjects were six infants ranging in age from 12 to 17 days ($\bar{X} = 14.3$ days). Three were male and three female. Testing began with a 90-second period in which the experimenter presented an unreactive, "passive face" (lips closed, neutral facial expression) to the infant. Each infant was then shown the following four gestures in a different random order: lip protrusion, mouth opening, tongue protrusion, and sequential finger movement (opening and closing the hand by serially moving the fingers). Each gesture was demonstrated four times in a 15-second stimulus-presentation period. This period was immediately followed by a 20-second response period for which the experimenter stopped performing the gesture and resumed a passive face. In order to allow for the possibility that the infants might not watch the first stimulus presentation, the procedure allowed a maximum of three stimulus presentations and corresponding response periods for any one gesture. Half the cases required only one stimulus presentation. In those cases necessitating more than one stimulus presentation, the 20-second response period used in assessing imitation was the one following the final presentation of the gesture. A 70-second passive-face period separated the presentation of each new type of gesture from preceding ones.

The videotape recordings of the response periods were scored in a random order by undergraduate volunteers. Two groups of six coders

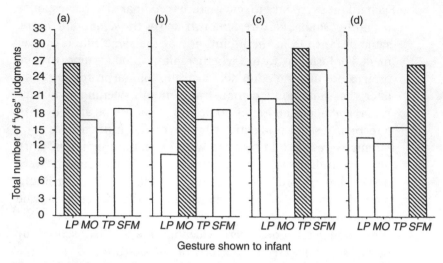

Figure 9(a).2 Distribution of "yes" judgments as a function of the gesture shown to the infant during experiment 1. The maximum possible number of judgments for each bar was 36 (six infants and six judges). Shaded bars indicate the imitative reaction. (a) Number of judgments that infants responded with lip protrusion (*LP*) to each of the four gestures shown them, (b) mouth-opening (*MO*) judgments, (c) tongue-protrusion (*TP*) judgments, and (d) sequential-finger-movement (*SFM*) judgments

were used. One group scored the infant's facial behavior; the other scored the manual responses. The face coders were informed that the infant in each videotaped segment was shown one of the following four gestures: lip protrusion, mouth opening, tongue protrusion, or passive face. They were instructed to order the four gestures by ranks from the one they thought it most likely the infant in each segment was imitating to the one they thought was least likely. No other training was given. The hand coders were treated identically, except that they were informed that the infant in each segment was presented with one of the following hand gestures: sequential finger movement, finger protrusion, hand opening, or passive hand.

For the purposes of analysis, the two highest ranks and the two lowest ranks were collapsed. This procedure yields dichotomous judgments of whether it was likely or unlikely (hereafter referred to as "yes" or "no") that the infants were imitating a particular gesture. The distribution of "yes" judgments for each infant gesture peaked when the corresponding gesture was demonstrated by the experimenter (figure 9(a).2). In all four instances, Cochran Q tests[3] reveal that the judged behavior of the

Condition	Baseline exposure	Baseline period (150 seconds)	Experimental exposure 1	Response period 1 (150 seconds)	Experimental exposure 2	Response period 2 (150 seconds)
Experimenter	Passive face	Passive face	Gesture 1	Passive face	Gesture 2	Passive face
Infant	Pacifier	No pacifier	Pacifier	No pacifier	Pacifier	No pacifier

Figure 9(a).3 Schematic illustration of the pacifier technique for assessing facial imitation in neonates in experiment 2. Half of the infants were exposed to the gestures in the order tongue protrusion, mouth opening; the other half were exposed to the gestures in the reverse order

infants varies significantly as a function of the gestures they are shown [lip protrusion, $P < .01$ (figure 9(a).2(a)); mouth opening, $P < .02$ (figure 9(a).2(b)); tongue protrusion, $P < .05$ (figure 9(a).2(c)); and sequential finger movement, $P < .001$ (figure 9(a).2(d))]. That this variation is attributable to imitation is supported by the fact that none of these effects is significant when the judgments corresponding to the imitative reaction (shaded columns in figure 9(a).2) are excluded from the analyses.

Experiment 1 avoided a prolonged stimulus-presentation period during which the experimenter might alter the timing of his gesturing as a function of the infant's responses. However, in adopting a fixed stimulus-presentation period as brief as 15 seconds, it was sometimes necessary to repeat the presentation to ensure that the infants actually saw the gesture they were to imitate. This procedure then opened the possibility that the experimenter might unwittingly have been prefiltering the data by readministering the stimulus presentations until the random behavior of the infant coincided with the behavior demonstrated. A second study was therefore designed which is not open to this potential objection.

The subjects in experiment 2 were 12 infants ranging in age from 16 to 21 days ($\bar{\bar{X}} = 19.3$). Six were male and six female. They were shown both a mouth opening and a tongue-protrusion gesture in a repeated-measures design, counter-balanced for order of presentation. The experimental procedure is illustrated in figure 9(a).3. Testing began with the insertion of a pacifier into the infant's mouth. Infants were allowed to suck on it for 30 seconds while the experimenter presented a passive face. The pacifier was then removed, and a 150-second baseline period was timed. After the baseline period, the pacifier was reinserted into the infant's mouth, and the first gesture was demonstrated until the experimenter judged that the infant had watched it for 15 seconds. The experimenter then stopped gesturing, resumed a passive face, and only then removed the pacifier. A 150-second response period, during which the experimenter maintained his passive face, was clocked. Immediately thereafter the pacificer was reinserted, and the second gesture was presented in an identical manner.[4]

Infants did not tend to open their mouths and let the pacifier drop out during the mouth-opening demonstration; nor did they push out the pacifier with their tongues during the tongue-protrusion demonstration. On the contrary, they sucked actively with the pacifier remaining firmly within their mouths during the stimulus-presentation period. Thus, the pacifier technique: 1 safeguards against the experimenter's altering his gesturing as a function of the imitative responses of the infant and; 2 permits the experimenter to demonstrate the gesture until the infant has seen it, while ensuring that the experimenter's assessment of this point is uncontaminated by any knowledge of the infant's imitative response.

The 36 videotaped segments (12 infants for 3 periods each) were scored in a random order by an undergraduate assistant who was uninformed of the structure of the experiment. The frequencies of tongue protrusions and mouth openings were tallied for each videotaped segment.[5] The results demonstrate that neonates imitate both tongue protrusion and mouth opening (figure 9(a).4). As assessed by Wilcoxon matched-pairs signed-ranks tests,[3] significantly more tongue-protrusion responses occurred after that gesture had been presented than during the baseline period ($P < .005$) or after the mouth-opening gesture ($P < .005$). Similarly, there were significantly more mouth-opening responses after that gesture had been demonstrated than during the baseline period ($P < .05$) or after the tongue-protrusion gesture ($P < .05$). It is noteworthy that under the present experimental conditions, the infants had to delay their imitation until after the gesture to be imitated had vanished from the perceptual field.

At least three different mechanisms could potentially underlie the imitation we report:

1 It could be argued that the imitation is based on reinforcement administered by either the experimenter or the parents. In order to prevent the experimenter from shaping the infant's imitative responding, the procedure directed that he maintain an unreactive,

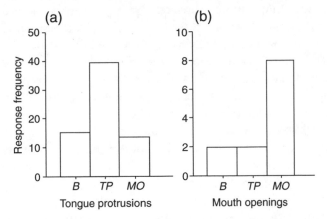

Figure 9(a).4 Total frequency of condition (a) tongue-protrusion and (b) mouth-opening responses for three conditions in experiment 2. Abbreviations: *B*, baseline period; *TP*, tongue protrusion response period; and *MO*, mouth-opening response period

neutral face during the response period. The experimenter's face was videotaped throughout both experiments in order to evaluate whether this procedure was followed. The videotaped segments were shown to observers whose task it was to score any reinforcements that the experimenter administered. No smiles or vocalizations were noted in any trial. Indeed, the only changes from the passive face occurred in three trials in experiment 1, when the experimenter was judged to "blink extremely rapidly." Considering only experiment 2, then, the experimental procedure does not appear to have been violated, and therefore, differential shaping of the mouth-opening and tongue-protrusion responses during the successive 150-second response periods is an unlikely source of the effects obtained. Since none of the parents were informed about the nature of the study, special practice on imitative tasks at home in preparation for the experiment was avoided. Further, informal questioning revealed that no parent was aware of ever having seen babies imitating in the first 21 days of life; indeed, most were astonished at the idea. Thus, a history of parental reinforcement seems an improbable basis for imitation at this very early age.

2 This early imitation might be based on an innate releasing mechanism such as that described by Lorenz and Tinbergen.[6] This view

would hold that tongue protrusion, mouth opening, lip protrusion, and sequential finger movement are each fixed-action patterns and that each is released by the corresponding adult gesture (sign stimulus). The overall organization of the infant's imitative response, particularly its lack of stereotypy, does not favor this interpretation. In addition, the fact that infants imitate not one, but four different gestures, renders this approach unwieldy.

3   The hypothesis we favor is that this imitation is based on the neonate's capacity to represent visually and proprioceptively perceived information in a form common to both modalities. The infant could thus compare the sensory information from his own unseen motor behavior to a "supramodal" representation of the visually perceived gesture and construct the match required.[7] In brief, we hypothesize that the imitative responses observed are not innately organized and "released," but are accomplished through an active matching process and mediated by an abstract representational system. Our recent observations of facial imitation in six new-borns – one only 60 minutes old – suggest to us that the ability to use intermodal equivalences is an innate ability of humans. If this is so, we must revise our current conceptions of infancy, which hold that such a capacity is the product of many months of postnatal development. The ability to act on the basis of an abstract representation of a perceptually absent stimulus becomes the starting point for psychological development in infancy and not its culmination.

Notes

1   For example, J. Piaget, *Play, Dreams and Imitation in Childhood* (Norton, New York, 1962); H. Werner and B. Kaplan, *Symbol Formation* (Wiley, New York, 1963); I. Uzgiris and J. Hunt, *Assessment in Infancy* (Univ. of Illinois Press, Chicago, 1975). See D. Parton [*Child Dev. 47*, 14 (1976)] for a recent review of the literature concerning infant imitation. Some reports are in conflict with these age norms. In the most extensive of these, O. Maratos [thesis, University of Geneva (1973)] noted imitation of two facial gestures by 1- to $2\frac{1}{2}$-month-old infants. However, the interpretation of her work is limited by the fact that the three factors discussed in the text were not controlled.

2   In addition, the following procedural details were held constant for both experiments. All infants were full term (40 ± 2 weeks gestation), of normal birth weight (3,400 ± 900 g), and born through an uncomplicated vaginal delivery with a minimum of maternal medication (for example, no general

anesthesia). The infants were tested when awake and alert, and they were supported in a semiupright posture by a well-padded infant seat. All the gestures were silently demonstrated 35 cm from the infant's eyes. They were presented against a white cotton backdrop and illuminated by a 20-watt spotlight placed directly above and behind the infant's head. The experimental room was kept as free as possible from auditory distraction and was maintained in subdued, indirect lighting.

3   S. Siegel, *Nonparametric Statistics* (McGraw-Hill, New York, 1956).

4   There was no significant difference ($P > .05$) between the duration of the presentation of the tongue protrusion ($\overline{X} = 67.6$ seconds) and mouth opening ($\overline{X} = 74.8$ seconds) gestures. Preliminary work revealed that infants continued to make sucking movements for about 3 seconds after a pacifier was removed. Therefore, in all cases, a 3-second interval was timed after the pacifier was removed and before the beginning of the 150-second baseline or response period. The infant's oral activity during this interval was not included in the analyses.

5   A tongue protrusion was scored only when the tongue was thrust clearly beyond the lips. A mouth opening was tallied only when the infant fully opened his mouth. Intraobserver agreement (number of agreements divided by the total number of agreements plus disagreements) was high for both tongue protrusion (93 percent) and mouth opening (92 percent).

6   K. Lorenz and N. Tinbergen, *Z. Tierpsychol. 2*, 1 (1938); N. Tinbergen, *A Study of Instinct* (Oxford Univ. Press, New York, 1951).

7   "Supramodal" is used, following T. Bower [*Development in Infancy* (Freeman, San Francisco, 1974)], to denote that the representation is not particular to one sensory modality alone.

Resolving the Debate about Early Imitation

Andrew N. Meltzoff and M. Keith Moore

Facial imitation presents a puzzle. Infants can see an adult's face but cannot see their own faces. They can feel their own faces move, but have no access to the feelings of movement in another person. Developmentalists have known for 50 years that 1-year-olds imitate facial gestures. In 1977, Meltzoff and Moore reported that neonates imitate facial gestures. The report engendered a lively debate, and basic findings of early imitation have now been replicated and extended in 25 different studies from 13 independent laboratories.[1]

The field has now moved on to address four questions: (a) How is it done? (b) Why is it done? (c) Does it develop? (d) Why should we care? A recent review of the literature has identified 10 characteristics of early imitation (table 9(b).1).[1] These can be used for addressing the foregoing questions.

How it is Done

The 1977 report considered three mechanisms that could potentially underlie early imitation – early learning from social interaction (EL), innate-releasing mechanisms (IRM), or active intermodal mapping (AIM). Further research excluded EL as an account, because studies demonstrated that newborns imitated.[1,2,3] The IRM view made three

Table 9(b).1   Ten characteristics of early imitation

1	Infants imitate a range of acts
2	Imitation is specific (tongue protrusion leads to tongue not lip protrusion)
3	Newborns imitate
4	Infants quickly activate the appropriate body part
5	Infants correct their imitative efforts
6	Novel acts can be imitated
7	Absent targets can be imitated
8	Static gestures can be imitated
9	Infants recognize being imitated
10	There is developmental change in imitation

Source: Table from Meltzoff and Moore (1997). The paper provides the references reporting each of the 10 characteristics.

predictions: (a) matching occurs for only a few evolutionarily-privileged gestures; (b) the form of the response is fixed and stereotypic; (c) the matching response is time-locked to the triggering display. Research has disconfirmed each of these. First, although it was once thought that only tongue protrusion was imitated, several new studies have documented imitation for a wide range of gestures, not only tongue protrusion.[1,3] Secondly, the imitative response is not fixed or stereotypic. Infants imitate novel facial acts and correct their initial attempts to home-in on an accurate match.[4] Finally, the response is not rigidly time-locked. Infants can imitate when the model is not perceptually present, with studies documenting deferred facial imitation after delays of up to 24 hours.[4,5]

The new findings support the third view, the AIM account (figure 9(b).1). On this view early imitation is intentional, goal-directed intermodal matching. The central notion is that imitation, even early imitation, is a matching-to-target process. The goal or behavioral target is specified visually. Infants' self-produced movements provide proprioceptive feedback that can be compared with the visually-specified target. AIM proposes that such comparison is possible because both perceived and performed human acts are represented within a common framework. This allows correction of imitative attempts toward a more faithful match. A paper elaborating the AIM account provides a detailed

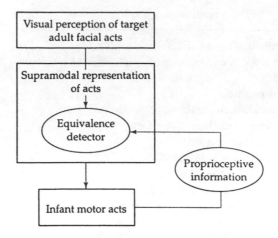

Figure 9(b).1   The "active intermodal mapping" account (AIM) (reprinted
from Meltzoff and Moore, 1997)

description of the metric infants use for establishing the intermodal
equivalence of human acts.[1]

Why it is Done

Any behavior as complex as imitation is multiply determined. However,
new findings have suggested that early imitation serves social and communicative functions. In particular, it has been argued that infants
deploy imitation to probe whether an encounter with a person is a *re-
encounter* with a familiar person or a new encounter with a stranger.[5]
Using imitation for this purpose serves a social-identity function.[4] On
this view, infants treat a person's non-verbal behavior as an identifier of
who the individual is, and use imitation as a means of verifying this
identity. The fundamental idea is that the distinctive behavior and
special interactive games of people serve as markers of their identity.
If infants are uncertain about the identity of a person, they will be
motivated to test whether this person has the same behavioral
properties as the old one by imitating her behavior and re-creating the
previous social interaction. In a recent paper, the social-identity
function of early imitation has been articulated in more detail and
related to infants' understanding of the identity and permanence of
inanimate objects.[6]

Development

A popular way of assimilating the 1977 article was to treat early imitation as a specialized phenomenon, disconnected from later forms of imitation. The idea was that early imitation existed, but then "dropped out" of the infant's repertoire until about 1 year of age. New empirical findings have shown there is no necessary drop out of early imitation. Studies showed that the apparent drop was not due to change in competence, but rather to performance changes that were easily reversed using novel designs that posed cognitive challenges to these older infants.[5]

Nonetheless, there are important developmental changes in imitation.[1,7] Whereas the newborn is focused on the act ("Can I do that?"), the 6-week-old treats facial displays as posing a problem about the identity of the actor ("Are you the individual who does behavior x, not y?").[2,4,5] Further development moves infants toward the more abstract notion of a matching relationship between actors. This change is illustrated by studies in which adults purposely imitate the infant, rather than the other way around. Fourteen-month-olds seem to recognize the interaction as a "matching game," and gleefully test whether they are being copied, by abruptly changing acts while staring at the adult to see what he will do.[8] Younger infants show no such testing behavior.

Subsequent development allows imitation of an inferred act. One study presented 18-month-olds with an adult who tried, but failed, to perform an act on an object.[7] Infants imitated what the adult was attempting to do, rather than what he did do. Imitation has developed to the point that infants no longer imitate what they literally see, but what the adult was striving to do. This moves beyond seeing other people solely in terms of behaviors to seeing them at a deeper level – in terms of the goals of their acts and the intentions they hold.[7,9]

Why we Should Care

Early imitation reveals a more sophisticated initial state than classical theories assumed. The 1977 article suggested that neonates were capable of: cross-modal matching, perceptual–motor coordination, and representation. Although these inferences were considered surprising 20 years ago, empirical discoveries by a host of researchers, using both people and things, have supported them. The modern empirical findings lend increasing support to the most far-reaching conclusion of the 1977 report: "The ability to act on the basis of an abstract representation of a perceptually absent stimulus becomes the starting point for psychological development in infancy and not its culmination" (p. 78).

Current debate in the field now concerns what is implied by such a rich initial state. One popular view is that the innate psychological structures are adult-like – what is built in and available to newborns remains essentially unchanged in the course of development. However, the developmental changes discussed above and elsewhere[6,10,11] do not support the view that infants are born with adult-like knowledge.

We favor an alternative to strong nativism. The notion is that evolution has bequeathed human infants not with adult concepts, but with initial mental structures that serve as "discovery procedures" for developing the more comprehensive and flexible concepts.[6,11] Imitation is deployed as a discovery procedure in understanding persons. Through interactions with others and the concomitant growth in self-understanding, infants are engaged in an open-ended developmental process. If one adopts this developmental view, it becomes tempting to hypothesize that the foundation for developing an "understanding of mind" may be grounded in the initial equivalence of "self" and "other" manifest by early imitation.[1,9] Moreover, the discovery procedures used for understanding of inanimate objects may be deeply connected with those used in the social world.[6,11]

References

1 Meltzoff, A. N., & Moore, M. K. (1997). Explaining facial imitation: A theoretical model. *Early Development and Parenting, 6,* 179–92.
2 Meltzoff, A. N., & Moore, M. K. (1983). Newborn infants imitate adult facial gestures. *Child Development, 54,* 702–9.
3 Meltzoff, A. N., & Moore, M. K. (1989). Imitation in newborn infants: Exploring the range of gestures imitated and the underlying mechanisms. *Developmental Psychology, 25,* 954–62.
4 Meltzoff, A. N., & Moore, M. K. (1994). Imitation, memory, and the representation of persons. *Infant Behavior and Development, 17,* 83–99.
5 Meltzoff, A. N., & Moore, M. K. (1992). Early imitation within a functional

framework: The importance of person identity, movement, and development. *Infant Behavior and Development, 15,* 479–505.

6 Meltzoff, A. N., & Moore, M. K. (1998). Object representation, identity, and the paradox of early permanence: Steps toward a new framework. *Infant Behavior and Development, 21,* 201–35.

7 Meltzoff, A. N. (1995). Understanding the intentions of others: Re-enactment of intended acts by 18-month-old children. *Developmental Psychology, 31,* 838–50.

8 Meltzoff, A. N. (1990). Foundations for developing a concept of self: The role of imitation in relating self to other and the value of social mirroring, social modeling, and self practice in infancy. In D. Cicchetti, & M. Beeghly (eds), *The Self in Transition: Infancy to Childhood* (pp. 139–64), Chicago: University of Chicago Press.

9 Meltzoff, A. N., & Moore, M. K. (1995). Infants' understanding of people and things: From body imitation to folk psychology. In J. Bermúdez, A. Marcel, & N. Eilan (eds), *The Body and the Self,* Cambridge, MA: MIT Press.

10 Kuhl, P. K., & Meltzoff, A. N. (1996). Infant vocalizations in response to speech: Vocal imitation and developmental change. *Journal of the Acoustical Society of America, 100,* 2425–38.

11 Gopnik, A., & Meltzoff, A. N. (1997). *Words, Thoughts, and Theories.* Cambridge, MA: MIT Press.

TEN

Infant Counting

Introduction

Karen Wynn shot to instant fame in developmental psychology with her report in *Nature* (1992) that infants can count! This paper is reproduced here. The basic experimental situation was to show the infant a small number of objects which were then covered by a screen; a hand then removed or added an object (the infant saw the taking away, or adding) and the screen was removed, revealing the display again. She found that young infants were "surprised" if the number of objects remaining did not match the change that had taken place (they looked more at the unexpected number of objects). This finding has been replicated (for example, Simon et al., 1995), and these reports of infant numerical abilities add to our understanding of the development of children's understanding of number from infancy onwards (this is reviewed by Bryant, 1995).

In later work Wynn has extended these findings and developed a detailed theory of infants' numerical competence. She suggests that "a system of numerical competence may be part of the inherent structure of the human mind" (1995, p. 172).

References

Bryant, P. (1995). Children and arithmetic. *Journal of Child Psychology and Psychiatry, 36,* 3–32.

Simon, T. J., Hespos, S. J., and Rochat, P. (1995). Do infants understand simple arithmetic? A replication of Wynn (1992). *Cognitive Development, 10,* 253–269.

Further reading

Wynn, K. (1995). Infants possess a system of numerical knowledge. *Current Directions in Psychological Science, 4*, 172–177.

Wynn, K. (1998). Psychological foundations of number: Numerical competence in human infants. *Trends in Cognitive Sciences, 2*, 296–303.

Addition and Subtraction by Human Infants

Karen Wynn

Human infants can discriminate between different small numbers of items,[1–4] and can determine numerical equivalence across perceptual modalities.[5,6] This may indicate the possession of true numerical concepts.[1,4–7] Alternatively, purely perceptual discriminations may underlie these abilities.[8,9] This debate addresses the nature or subitization, the ability to quantify small numbers of items without conscious counting.[10,11] Subitization may involve the holistic recognition of canonical perceptual patterns that do not reveal ordinal relationships between the numbers,[12] or may instead be an iterative or "counting" process that specifies these numerical relationships.[4,13] Here I show that 5-month-old infants can calculate the results of simple arithmetical operations on small numbers of items. This indicates that infants possess true numerical concepts, and suggests that humans are innately endowed with arithmetical abilities. It also suggests that subitization is a process that encodes ordinal information, not a pattern-recognition process yielding non-numerical percepts.

The experiments used a looking-time procedure that has become standard in studies of infant cognition.[14–17] Thirty-two infants participated in experiment 1. They were normal, full-term infants with a mean age of 5 months 1 day (range, 4 months 19 days to 5 months 16 days). Infants were divided randomly into two equal groups. Those in the "1 + 1" group were shown a single item in an empty display area. A small screen then rotated up, hiding the item from view, and the experimenter brought a second identical item into the display area, in clear view of the infant. The experimenter placed the second item out of the infant's sight behind the screen (figure 10.1). Thus, infants could clearly see the nature of the arithmetical operation being performed, but could not see the result of the operation. The "2 − 1" group were similarly shown a sequence of events depicting a subtraction of one item from two items (figure 10.1). For both groups of infants, after the above sequence of events was concluded, the screen was rotated downward to reveal either 1 or 2 items in the display case. Infants' looking time to the display was then recorded. Each infant was shown the addition or subtraction 6 times, the result alternating between 1 item and 2 items. Before these test trials, infants were presented with a display containing 1 item and a display containing 2 items and their looking time was recorded, to measure the baseline looking preferences for the two displays.

Infants look longer at unexpected events than expected ones, thus, if they are able to compute the numerical results of these arithmetical operations, they should look longer at the incorrect than at the correct results. The two groups should respond differently to results of 1 and 2 items: the "2 − 1" group should look longer than the "1 + 1" group when the result is 2 items than when it is 1 item, which is what is found (table 10.1). Pretest trials showed that infants in the two groups did not differ from each other in their baseline looking times to 1 or 2 objects. But in the test trials, infants in the two groups differed significantly − infants in the "1 + 1" group looked longer at 1, whereas infants in the 2 − 1 group looked longer at 2. Thus, both groups looked longer at the incorrect than at the correct outcomes (table 10.1).

Experiment 2 was a replication of experiment 1 with a smaller number of subjects (sixteen). Their mean age was 4 months 25 days (range, 4 months 18 days to 5 months 5 days). The same pattern of results was obtained; infants in each group looked longer at the incorrect outcome than at the correct outcome (table 10.1).

These results show that infants know that an addition or subtraction results in a change in the number of items. But the results are consistent with two distinct hypotheses: (1) that infants are able to compute the precise results of simple additions and subtractions and (2) that infants expect an arithmetical operation to result in a numerical change, but have no expectations about either the size or the direction of the change. They may simply expect that adding an item to an item will result in some number other than 1; and that subtracting an item from 2 items will result in some number other than 2. To determine whether

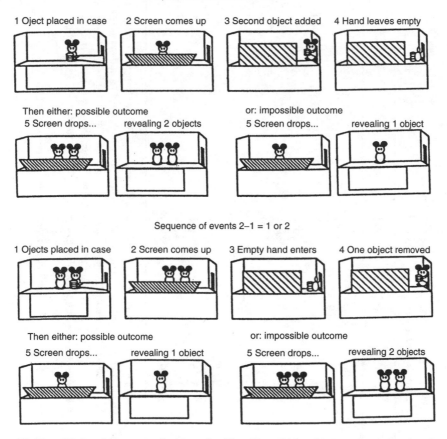

Figure 10.1 Sequence of events for '1 + 1' and '2 + 1' situations presented in experiments 1 and 2.

METHODS: Trials alternated between a 1-item and a 2-item result, half of the infants received the ordering (1, 2, 1, 2, 1, 2), the remainder receiving the reverse ordering. Infants sat facing the display; parents either stood out of sight behind and not touching the infant, or else gently touched the infant while facing away from the display. The experimenter was hidden behind the display, and manipulated the objects by means of a hidden trap door in the back wall of display. A hidden observer, unaware of the infant group and of the trial ordering, timed infants' looks to the display. In all experiments, infants were excluded if they became fussy or drowsy during the experiment (16 infants), if their test preference was more than 2.5 standard deviations away from the mean for that group (1 infant), or if they had a pretest preference of more than 10 s for either number (19 infants). The choice of 10 s does not affect the pattern of results (the analyses for experiments 1 and 2 combined give the same pattern even with no cutoff)

Table 10.1 Looking times and preference for 2 items over 1 item

Experiment	Trials	Group	LT(1)*	LT(2)*	P(2)*	d.f.	t	P
1	Pretest	1 + 1	20.06	20.80	0.74	30	0.649	>0.5
		2 − 1	17.99	19.61	1.62			
	Test	1 + 1	13.36	12.80	−0.53	30	2.078	<0.05
		2 − 1	10.54	13.73	3.19			
2	Pretest	1 + 1	11.12	10.62	−0.50	14	0.677	>0.5
		2 − 1	10.35	11.44	1.09			
	Test	1 + 1	12.08	9.45	−2.65	14	1.795	<0.05
		2 − 1	8.05	10.98	2.94			
1 + 2	Pretest	1 + 1	17.62	18.02	0.41	46	0.873	>0.35
		2 − 1	15.05	16.47	1.42			
	Test	1 + 1	13.01	11.89	−1.11	46	2.73	<0.005
		2 − 1	9.59	12.67	3.09			

Notes: Statistical significance was determined by between-group t-tests on infants' P(2) values. Probability values are 2-tailed for pretest comparisons, 1-tailed for test comparisons. In experiment 1, a trial concluded when an infant looked away for 2 consecutive seconds after looking at the display for at least 4 cumulative seconds, or had looked for 30 cumulative seconds. Experiment 2: same criteria, except that minimum cumulative looking time was only 2 s. The shorter mean looking times in experiment 2 are probably due to this procedural change. Times are lower in test than pretest trials because infants' looks decrease during the experiment as they become more familiar with the display. Experiment 2, 6 infants in the 1 + 1 group, 10 infants in the 2 − 1 group.

*P(2) = LT(2) − LT(1); where P(2), preference for 2: LT(1) and LT(2) are the mean looking times to 1 and 2 items (in seconds).

Table 10.2 Looking times and preferences for 3 items over 2

Condition	LT(2)*	LT(3)*	P(3)*	d.f.	t	P
Pretest	14.16	13.87	−0.29	15	−0.224	>0.5
Test	9.96	11.89	1.92	15	2.044	<0.03

Notes: Statistical significance was determined by t-tests comparing infants' P(3) values to the null hypothesis of no preference. Probability value for pretest comparison is 2-tailed; that for test comparison is 1-tailed. As in experiments 1 and 2, infants were excluded if they showed more than a 10-second pretest preference for one of the numbers; the pattern of results remains the same when these infants are included in the analyses. Experiment 3 used the same criterion for end-of-trial as that used in experiment 2.
*P(3) = LT(3) − LT(2), where P(3), preference for 3; LT(3) and LT(2) are the mean looking times to 3 and 2 items (in seconds).

infants are able to compute the precise results of simple arithmetical operations, I conducted a third experiment.

Experiment 3 tested 16 infants with a mean age of 4 months 18 days (range 4 months 4 days to 5 months 4 days). Infants were shown a "1 + 1" addition as before, except that the final number of objects revealed behind the screen was either 2 or 3. In both cases, the result is numerically different from the initial number of items. If infants are computing the exact numerical result of the addition, they would be expected to look longer at the result of 3 items than of 2 items. This pattern was indeed observed (table 10.2); infants significantly preferred 3 in the test trials, but not the pretest trials, showing that they were surprised when the addition appeared to result in 3 items. The results from the three experiments support the claim[7] that 5-month-old human infants are able to calculate the precise results of simple arithmetical operations.

There is an alternative explanation for infants' success in these experiments. Infants may be calculating the results of the addition and subtraction, not of a discrete number of items, but of a continuous amount of physical substance; infants may possess an ability to measure and operate on continuous quantities. But there are reasons to prefer the hypothesis that it is the number of items, not amount of substance, that infants are computing. It has been shown that infants are sensitive to small numerical changes,[1-4] but there is no evidence of a sensitivity to small differences in amount of physical matter. Infants are predisposed to interpret the physical world as composed of discrete, individual entities when perceiving spatial layouts,[14,15] and they represent the precise spatial locations and trajectories of individual objects relative to each other.[16,17] Thus, the notion of "individual entity" plays a prominent role in infants' conceptualization and representation of the physical world, and they have abilities that allow them to track distinct entities over time and space. This, together with infants' sensitivity to small numerical differences in collections of items, lends independent support to the hypothesis that infants possess a mechanism for quantifying collections of discrete entities. The most plausible explanation for the findings presented here is that infants can compute the results of simple arithmetical operations.

In sum, infants possess true numerical concepts – they have access to the ordering of and numerical relationships between small numbers, and can manipulate these concepts in numerically meaningful ways. This in turn indicates that the mental process giving rise to these concepts yields true numerical outputs that encode numerical relationships, not holistic percepts derived from a pattern-recognition process. The existence of these arithmetical abilities so early in infancy suggests that humans innately possess the capacity to perform simple arithmetical calculations, which may provide the foundations for the development of further arithmetical knowledge.[7,18]

References

1 Starkey, P., & Cooper, R. G. *Science 210*, 1033–1035 (1980).
2 Strauss, M. S., & Curtis, L. E. *Child Development 52*, 1146–1152 (1981).
3 Antell, S., & Keating, D. P. *Child Development 54*, 695–701 (1983).
4 van Loosbroek, E., & Smitsman, A. W. *Developmental Psychology 26*, 916–922 (1990).
5 Starkey, P., Spelke, E. S., & Gelman, R. *Science 222*, 179–181 (1983).
6 Starkey, P., Spelke, E. S., & Gelman, R. *Cognition 36*, 97–127 (1990).
7 Wynn, K. *Mind Lang.* (in the press).
8 Davis, H., Albert, M., & Barron, R. W. *Science 228*, 1222 (1985).
9 Cooper, R. G. in *Origins of Cognitive Skills* 157–192 (ed. Sophian, C.) (Erlbaum, Hillsdale, New Jersey, 1984).
10 Chi, M. T. H., & Klahr, D. *Journal of Experimental Child Psychology 19*, 434–439 (1975).
11 Silverman, I. W., & Rose, A. P. *Developmental Psychology 16*, 539–540 (1980).

12   Mandler, G., & Shebo, B. J. *Journal of Experimental Psychology: General 11*, 1–22 (1982).

13   Gallistel, C. R. *The Organization of Learning* 343–348 (MIT, Cambridge, Massachusetts, 1990).

14   Spelke, E. S. in *Perceptual Development in Infancy: Minnesota Symposia on Child Psychology* Vol. 20 (ed. Yonas, A.) 197–234 (Erlbaum, Hillsdale, New Jersey, 1988).

15   Spelke, E. S. *Cognitive Science 14*, 29–56 (1990).

16   Baillargeon, R. *Cognition 38*, 13–42 (1991).

17   Baillargeon, R., & DeVos, J. *Child Development 62*, 1227–1246 (1991).

18   Wynn, K. *Cognitive Psychology 24*, 220–251 (1992).

ELEVEN

Learning About the Physical World

Introduction

Renee Baillargeon begins her account of infants' understanding of the physical world by noting the developmental lag between *understanding* and *acting* in the world. It is possible, for example, for an infant to know that a hidden object continues to exist behind another, occluding object, while being unable to plan and execute an action sequence (e.g., reaching) in order to retrieve the object (see also chapter 3, this volume; and Willatts, 1997).

Her basic paradigm for exploring infant's physical knowledge is to present them with possible and impossible events: the impossible events violate some physical principle, relating to understanding gravity, support, solidity, occlusion, falling objects, continuity of motion, and so on. If infants understand the physical principle or belief being tested, then the assumption is that they will look longer at the impossible events than at the possible ones.

Baillargeon describes the possible nature and properties of infants' learning mechanisms and gives an outline of age differences in their developing understanding of the world of objects. The picture that is developing is of "infants as budding intuitive physicists, capable of detecting, interpreting, and predicting physical outcomes," whose "physical world . . . appears very similar to that of adults" (Baillargeon, 1993, p. 311).

References

Baillargeon, R. (1993). The object concept revisited: New directions in the investigation of infants' physical knowledge. In C. Granrud (ed.), *Visual Perception and Cognition in Infancy*. Hillsdale, NJ: Erlbaum Associates Ltd.

Willatts, P. (1997). Beyond the "couch potato" infant: How infants use their knowledge to regulate action, solve problems, and achieve goals. In G. Bremner, A. Slater and G. Butterworth (eds.), *Infant Development: Recent Advances*. Hove, UK: Psychology Press.

How Do Infants Learn About the Physical World?

Renée Baillargeon

Until recently, young infants were assumed to lack even the most fundamental of adults' beliefs about objects. This conclusion was based largely on analyses of young infants' performance in object manipulation tasks. For example, young infants were said to be unaware that an object continues to exist when masked by another object because they consistently failed tasks that required them to search for an object hidden beneath or behind another object.[1]

In time, however, researchers came to realize that young infants might fail tasks such as search tasks not because of limited physical knowledge, but because of difficulties associated with the planning and execution of action sequences. This concern led investigators to seek alternative methods for exploring young infants' physical knowledge, methods that did not depend on the manipulation of objects.

Infants' well-documented tendency to look longer at novel than at familiar events[2] suggested one alternative method for investigating young infants' beliefs about objects. In a typical experiment, infants are presented with two test events: a possible and an impossible event. The possible event is consistent with the expectation or belief examined in the experiment; the impossible event, in contrast, violates this expectation. The rationale is that if infants possess the belief being tested, they will perceive the impossible event as more novel or surprising than the possible event, and will therefore look reliably longer at the impossible than at the possible event.

Using this violation-of-expectation method, investigators have demonstrated that even very young infants possess many of the same fundamental beliefs about objects as adults do.[3,4] For example, infants aged 2.5 to 3.5 months are aware that objects continue to exist when masked by other objects, that objects cannot remain stable without support, that objects move along spatially continuous paths, and that objects cannot move through the space occupied by other objects.

The repeated demonstration of sophisticated physical knowledge in early infancy has led investigators in recent years to focus their efforts in a new direction. In addition to exploring what infants know about the physical world, researchers have become interested in the question of how infants attain their physical knowledge.

My colleagues and I have begun to build a model of the development of young infants' physical reasoning.[5–7] The model is based on the assumption that infants are born not with substantive beliefs about objects (e.g., intuitive notions of impenetrability, continuity, or force), as researchers such as Spelke[8] and Leslie[9] have proposed, but with highly constrained mechanisms that guide the development of infants' reasoning about objects. The model is derived from findings concerning infants' intuitions about different physical phenomena (e.g., support, collision, and unveiling phenomena). Comparison of these findings points to two developmental patterns that recur across ages and phenomena. We assume that these patterns reflect, at least indirectly, the nature and properties of infants' learning mechanisms. In this review, I describe the patterns and summarize some of the evidence supporting them.

First Pattern: Identification of Initial Concept and Variables

The first developmental pattern is that, when learning about a new physical phenomenon, infants first form a preliminary, all-or-none concept that captures the essence of the phenomenon but few of its details. With further experience, this *initial concept* is progressively elaborated. Infants slowly identify discrete and continuous *variables* that are relevant to the initial concept, study the effects of those variables, and incorporate this accrued knowledge into their reasoning, resulting in increasingly accurate predictions over time.

To illustrate the distinction between initial concepts and variables, I summarize experiments on the development of young infants' reasoning about support phenomena (conducted with Amy Needham, Julie DeVos, and Helen Raschke), collision phenomena (conducted with Laura Kotovsky), and unveiling phenomena (conducted with Julie DeVos).[3,5–7]

Support phenomena

Our experiments on young infants' ability to reason about support phenomena have focused on simple problems involving a box and a platform. Our results indicate that by 3 months of age, if not before, infants expect the box to fall if it loses all contact with the platform and to remain stable otherwise. At this stage, any contact between the box and the platform is deemed sufficient to ensure the box's stability. At least two developments take place between 3 and 6.5 months of age. First, infants become aware that the locus of contact between the box and the platform must be taken into account when judging the box's stability. Infants initially assume that the box will remain stable if placed either on the top or against the side of the platform. By 4.5 to 5.5 months of age, however, infants come to distinguish between the two types of contact and recognize that only the former ensures support. The second development is that infants begin to appreciate that the amount of contact between the box and the platform affects the box's stability. Initially, infants believe that the box will be stable even if only a small portion (e.g., the left 15%) of its bottom surface rests on the platform (see figure 11.1). By 6.5 months of age, however, infants expect the box to fall unless a significant portion of its bottom surface lies on the platform.

These results suggest the following developmental sequence. When learning about the support relation between two objects, infants first form an initial concept centered on a distinction between contact and no contact. With further experience, this initial concept is progressively revised. Infants identify first a discrete (locus of contact) and later a continuous (amount of contact) variable and incorporate these variables into their initial concept, resulting in more successful predictions over time.

Figure 11.1 Paradigm for studying infants' understanding of support phenomena. In both events, a gloved hand pushes a box from left to right along the top of a platform. In the possible event (*top*), the box is pushed until its leading edge reaches the end of the platform. In the impossible event (*bottom*), the box is pushed until only the left 15% of its bottom surface rests on the platform

Collision phenomena

Our experiments on infants' reasoning about collision events have focused on simple problems involving a moving object (a cylinder that rolls down a ramp) and a stationary object (a large, wheeled toy bug resting on a track at the bottom of the ramp). Adults typically expect the bug to roll down the track when hit by the cylinder. When asked how far the bug will be displaced, adults are generally reluctant to hazard a guess (they are aware that the length of the bug's trajectory depends on a host of factors about which they have no information). After observing that the bug rolls to the middle of the track when hit by a medium-size cylinder, however, adults readily predict that the bug will roll farther with a larger cylinder and less far with a smaller cylinder made of identical material.

Our experiments indicate that by 2.5 months of age, infants already possess clear expectations that the bug should remain stationary when not hit (e.g., when a barrier prevents the cylinder from contacting the bug) and should be displaced when hit. However, it is not until 5.5 to 6.5 months of age that infants are able to judge, after seeing that the

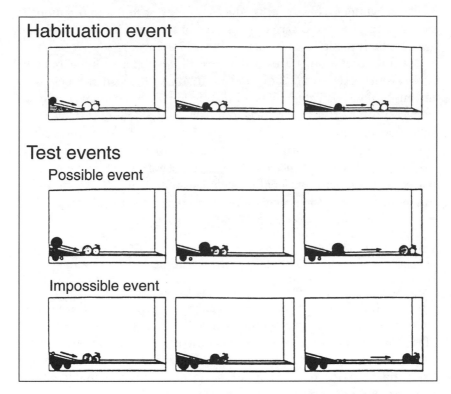

Figure 11.2 Paradigm for studying infants' understanding of collision phenomena. First, infants are habituated to (i.e. repeatedly shown) an event in which a blue, medium-size cylinder rolls down a ramp and hits a bug resting on one end of a track; the bug then rolls to the middle of the track. In the test events, two new cylinders are introduced, and the bug now rolls to the end of the track. The cylinder used in the impossible event is a yellow cylinder larger than the habituation cylinder; the cylinder used in the impossible event is an orange cylinder smaller than the habituation cylinder

medium cylinder causes the bug to roll to the middle of the track, that the bug should roll farther with the larger but not the smaller cylinder (see figure 11.2). Younger infants are not surprised to see the bug roll to the end of the track when hit by either the larger or the smaller cylinder, even though all three of the cylinders are simultaneously present in the apparatus, so that their sizes can be readily compared, and even though the infants have no difficulty remembering (as shown in other experiments) that the bug rolled to the middle of the track with the medium cylinder. These results suggest that prior to 5.5 to 6.5 months of age, infants are unaware that the size of the cylinder can be used to reason about the length of the bug's trajectory.

One interpretation of these findings is that when learning about collision events between a moving and a stationary object, infants first form an initial concept centered on a distinction between impact and no impact. With further experience, infants begin to identify variables that influence this initial concept. By 5.5 to 6.5 months of age, infants realize that the size of the moving object can be used to predict how far the stationary object will be displaced. After seeing how far a stationary object travels with a moving object of a given size, infants readily use this information to calibrate their predictions about how far the stationary object will travel with moving objects of different sizes.

Unveiling phenomena

Our experiments on unveiling phenomena have involved problems in which a cloth cover is removed to reveal an object. Our results indicate that by 9.5 months of age, infants realize that the presence (or absence) of a protuberance in the cover signals the presence (or absence) of an object beneath the cover. Infants are surprised to see a toy retrieved from under a cover that lies flat on a surface, but not from under a cover that displays a marked protuberance.

At this stage, however, infants are not yet aware that the size of the protuberance in the cover can be used to infer the size of the object beneath the cover. When shown a cover with a small protuberance, they are not surprised to see either a small or large toy retrieved from under the cover. Furthermore, providing infants with a reminder of the protuberance's size has no effect on their performance. In one experiment, for example, infants saw two identical covers placed side by side; both covers displayed a small protuberance (see figure 11.3). After a few seconds, a screen hid the left cover; the right cover remained visible to the right of the screen. Next, a hand reached behind the screen's right edge twice in succession, reappearing first with the cover and then with a small (possible event) or a large (impossible event) toy dog. Each dog was held next to the visible cover, so that their sizes could be readily compared. At 9.5 months of age, infants judged that either dog could have been hidden under the cover behind the screen. At 12.5 months of age, however, infants showed reliable surprise at the large dog's retrieval.

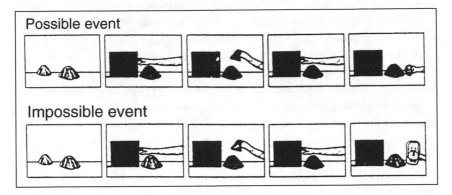

Figure 11.3 Paradigm for studying infants' understanding of unveiling phenomena. Infants first see two identical covers placed side by side; both covers display a small protuberance. Next, a screen hides the left cover, and a gloved hand reaches behind the screen twice in succession, reappearing first with the cover and then with a small (*top*) or a large (*bottom*) toy dog. Each dog is held next to the visible cover, so that their sizes can be readily compared

Together, these results suggest the following developmental sequence. When learning about unveiling phenomena, infants first form an initial concept centered on a distinction between protuberance and no protuberance. Later on, infants identify a continuous variable that affects this concept: they begin to appreciate that the size of the protuberance in the cover can be used to infer the size of the object under the cover.

Comments

How can the developmental sequences described in this section be explained? As I mentioned earlier, we assume that these sequences reflect not the gradual unfolding of innate beliefs, but the application of highly constrained, innate learning mechanisms to available data. In this approach, the problem of explaining the age at which specific initial concepts and variables are understood is that of determining (a) what data – observations or manipulations – are necessary for learning and (b) when these data become available to infants.

For example, one might propose that 3-month-old infants have already learned that objects fall when released in midair because this expectation is consistent with countless observations (e.g., watching their caretakers drop peas in pots, toys in baskets, clothes in hampers) and manipulations (e.g., noticing that their pacifiers fall when they open their mouths) available virtually from birth. Furthermore, one might speculate that it is not until 6.5 months that infants begin to appreciate how much contact is needed between objects and their supports because it is not until this age that infants have available pertinent data from which to abstract such a variable. Researchers have reported that the ability to sit without support emerges at about 6 months of age; infants then become able to sit in front of tables (e.g., on a parent's lap or in a high chair) with their upper limbs and hands relieved from the encumbrance of postural maintenance and thus free to manipulate objects.[10] For the first time, infants may have the opportunity to deposit objects on tables and to note that objects tend to fall unless significant portions of their bottom surfaces are supported. In the natural course of events, infants would be unlikely to learn about such a variable from observation alone because caretakers rarely deposit objects on the edges of surfaces. There is no a priori reason, however, to assume that infants could not learn such a variable if given appropriate observations (e.g., seeing that a box falls when released on the edge of a platform). We are currently conducting a "teaching" experiment to investigate this possibility; our preliminary results are extremely encouraging and suggest that very few observations may be necessary to set infants on the path to learning.

Second Pattern: Use of Qualitative and Quantitative Strategies

In the previous section, I proposed that when learning about a novel physical phenomenon, infants first develop an all-or-none initial concept and later identify discrete and continuous variables that affect this concept. The second developmental pattern suggested by current evidence concerns the strategies infants use when reasoning about continuous variables. Following the terminology used in computational models of everyday physical reasoning,[11] a strategy is said to be *quantitative* if it requires infants to encode and use information about absolute quantities (e.g., object A is "this" large or has traveled "this" far from object B, where "this" stands for some absolute measure of A's size or distance from B). In contrast, a strategy is said to be *qualitative* if it requires infants to encode and use information about relative quantities (e.g., object A is larger than or has traveled farther than object B). After identifying a continuous variable, infants appear to succeed in reasoning about the variable qualitatively before they succeed in doing so quantitatively.

To illustrate the distinction between infants' use of qualitative and quantitative strategies, I report experiments on the development of infants' ability to reason about collision phenomena (conducted with Laura Kotovsky), unveiling phenomena (conducted with Julie DeVos), and barrier phenomena.[3,5–7]

Collision phenomena

As I explained earlier, 5.5- to 6.5-month-old infants are surprised, after observing that a medium-size cylinder causes a bug to roll to the middle of a track, to see the bug roll farther when hit by a smaller but not a larger cylinder. Such a finding suggests that by 5.5 to 6.5 months of age, infants are aware that the size of the cylinder affects the length of the bug's trajectory.

In these initial experiments, the small, medium, and large cylinders were placed side by side at the start of each event, allowing infants to compare their sizes directly. In subsequent experiments, only one cylinder was present in the apparatus in each test event. Under these conditions, 6.5-month-old infants were no longer surprised when the small cylinder caused the bug to roll to the end of the track; only older, 7.5-month-old infants showed surprise at this event.

Our interpretation of these results is that at 5.5 to 6.5 months of age, infants are able to reason about the cylinder's size only qualitatively: They can predict the effect of modifications in the cylinder's size only when they are able to encode such modifications in relative terms (e.g., "this cylinder is smaller than the one used in the last trial"). When infants are forced to encode and compare the absolute sizes of the cylinders, because the cylinders are never shown side by side, they fail the task. By 7.5 months of age, however, infants have already overcome this initial limitation and succeed in the task even when they must rely on their representation of the absolute size of each cylinder to do so.[12]

Unveiling phenomena

In the previous section, I reported that 9.5-month-old infants are not surprised to see either a small or a large toy dog retrieved from under a cover with a small protuberance, even when a second, identical cover is present. Unlike these younger infants, however, 12.5-month-old infants are surprised when the large dog is brought into view. This last finding suggests that by 12.5 months of age, infants are aware that the size of the protuberance in a cloth cover can be used to infer the size of the object under the cover.

In our initial experiment, 12.5-month-old infants were tested with the second cover present to the right of the screen (see figure 11.3). Subsequent experiments were conducted without the second cover (see figure 11.4, top panel) or with the second cover placed to the left, rather than to the right, of the screen (see figure 11.4, bottom panel); in the latter condition, infants could no longer compare in a single glance the size of the dog to that of the cover. Our results indicated that 12.5-month-old infants fail both of these conditions: they no longer show surprise when the large dog is retrieved from behind the screen. By 13.5 months of age, however, infants are surprised by the large dog's retrieval even when no second cover is present.

These results suggest that at 12.5 months of age, infants are able to reason about the size of the protuberance in the cover only qualitatively: they can determine which dog could have been hidden under the cover only if they are able to compare, in a single glance, the size of the dog with that of a second, identical cover (e.g., "the dog is bigger than the cover"). When infants are forced to represent the absolute size of the protuberance in the cover, they fail the task. By 13.5 months of age, however, infants have already progressed beyond this initial limitation; they no longer have difficulty representing the absolute size of the protuberance and comparing it with that of each dog.

Barrier phenomena

Our experiments on barrier phenomena have focused on problems involving a moving object (a rotating screen) and a stationary barrier (a large box). In the test events, infants first see the screen lying flat against the apparatus floor; the box stands clearly visible behind the screen. Next, the screen rotates about its distant edge, progressively

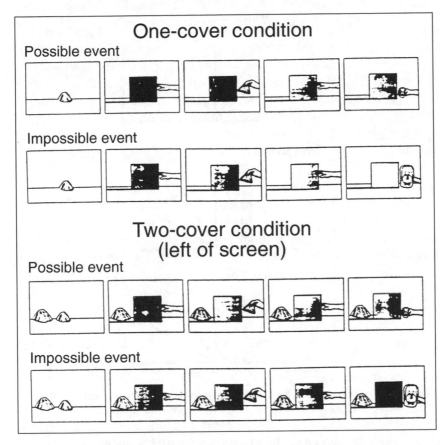

Figure 11.4 Further experiments examining infants' understanding of unveiling phenomena. These test events are identical to those depicted in Figure 11.3 except that only one cover is used (*top*) or the second, identical cover is placed to the left of the screen (*bottom*). In the latter condition, infants can no longer compare in a single glance the height of the dog to that of the second cover

occluding the box. At 4.5 months of age, infants expect the screen to stop when it reaches the occluded box; they are surprised if the screen rotates unhindered through a full 180° arc. However, infants are initially poor at predicting at what point the screen should encounter the box and stop. When shown a possible event in which the screen stops against the box (112° arc) and an impossible event in which the screen stops after rotating through the top 80% of the space occupied by the

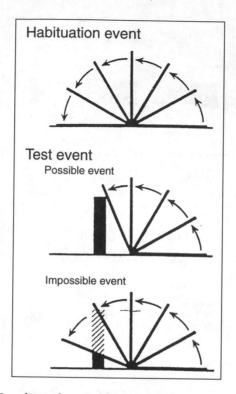

Figure 11.5 Paradigm for studying infants' understanding of barrier phenomena. Infants are first habituated to a screen that rotates through a 180° arc, in the manner of a drawbridge. Next, a large box is placed behind the screen. In the possible event, the screen stops when it encounters the box (112° arc); in the impossible event, the screen stops after rotating through the top 80% of the space occupied by the box (157° arc)

box (157° arc), 6.5-month-old infants give evidence of detecting this 80% violation, but 4.5-month-old infants do not: they judge both the 112° and the 157° stopping points to be consistent with the box's height and location (see figure 11.5).

In subsequent experiments, we examined whether 4.5-month-old infants would succeed in detecting the 80% violation if provided with a second, identical box. In one condition, this second box was placed to the right of and in the same frontoparallel plane as the box behind the screen (see figure 11.6, left panel). In the possible event, the screen stopped when aligned with the top of the second box; in the impossible

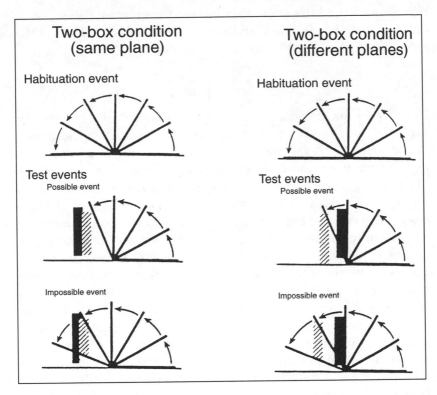

Figure 11.6 Further experiments examining infants' understanding of barrier phenomena. These events are identical to those depicted in figure 11.5 except that a second, identical box stands to the right of and in the same fronto-parallel plane as the box behind the screen (*left*) or to the right and in front of the box behind the screen (*right*)

event, the screen rotated past the top of the second box. In another condition, the second box was placed to the right of but slightly in front of the box behind the screen (see figure 11.6, right panel). In this condition, the screen rotated past the top of the second box in each test event. The infants succeeded in detecting the 80% violation in the first but not the second condition.

These results suggest that at 4.5 months of age, infants are able to reason about the box's height and location only qualitatively: they can predict the screen's stopping point only when they are able to rely on a simple alignment strategy (e.g., "the screen is aligned with the top of the visible box"). By 6.5 months of age, however, infants have already progressed beyond this point; they can use their representations of the occluded box's height and distance from the screen to estimate, within broad limits, at what point the screen will stop.

Comments

How should the developmental sequences described in this section be explained? We think it unlikely that these sequences reflect the maturation of infants' general quantitative reasoning or information processing because the same pattern recurs at different ages for different phenomena. What phenomenon-specific changes could account for the findings reported here? At least two hypotheses can be advanced. On the one hand, it could be that when first reasoning about a continuous variable, infants either do not spontaneously encode information about this variable or do not encode this information swiftly enough or precisely enough for it to be of use in the tasks examined here (e.g., infants do not encode the size of the protuberance in the cover and hence are unable to judge which dog could have been hidden beneath it). On the other hand, infants could encode the necessary quantitative information but have difficulty accessing or processing this information in the context of deriving new and unfamiliar predictions (e.g., infants encode the protuberance's size and realize that they must compare it with that of the dog, but are thwarted in performing this comparison by the added requirement of having to retrieve part of the information from memory). Future research will no doubt help determine which, if either, of these hypotheses is correct.

Concluding Remarks

I have argued that in learning to reason about a novel physical phenomenon, infants first form an all-or-none concept and then add to this initial concept discrete and continuous variables that are discovered to affect the phenomenon. Furthermore, I have proposed that after identifying continuous variables, infants succeed in reasoning first qualitatively and only later quantitatively about the variables.

This sketchy description may suggest a rather static view of development in which accomplishments, once attained, are retained in their initial forms. Nothing could be further from the truth, however. Our data suggest that the variables infants identify evolve over time, as do the qualitative and quantitative strategies infants devise. When judging whether a box resting on a platform is stable, for example, infants initially focus exclusively on the amount of contact between the box's bottom surface and the platform, and as a consequence treat symmetrical and asymmetrical boxes alike. By the end of the 1st year, however, infants appear to have revised their definition of this variable to take into account the shape (or weight distribution) of the box.[5] Similarly, evidence obtained with the rotating-screen paradigm suggests that infants' quantitative reasoning continues to improve over time (e.g., 6.5-month-old infants can detect 80% but not 50% violations, whereas 8.5-month-old infants can detect both), as does their qualitative reasoning (e.g., 6.5-month-old infants will make use of a second box to detect a violation even if this second box differs markedly in color from the box behind the screen, whereas 4.5-month-old infants will not).[3]

The model of the development of infants' physical reasoning proposed here suggests many questions for future research. In particular, what are the innate constraints that guide this development? Are infants born with core principles (e.g., intuitive notions of impenetrability and continuity) that direct their interpretations of physical events? Or are infants, as I suggested earlier, equipped primarily with learning mechanisms that are capable, when applied to coherent sets of observations, of producing appropriate generalizations? What evidence would help distinguish between these two views?

Some insight into this question may be gained by considering two predictions that proponents of the innate-principles view might offer. The first prediction is that when reasoning about a physical event involving a core principle, infants should succeed at about the same age at detecting all equally salient violations of the principle. Thus, researchers who deem impenetrability a likely core principle might expect infants who realize that a small object cannot pass through a gapless surface to understand also that a large object cannot pass through a small gap; provided that the two situations violate the impenetrability principle to a similar degree, they would be expected to yield identical interpretations. The second prediction is that infants should succeed at about the same age at reasoning about different physical events that implicate the same underlying core principle. Thus, it might be proposed that infants who are successful at reasoning about objects' passage through gaps should be just as adept at reasoning about objects' entry into containers, because both phenomena would trigger the application of the impenetrability principle.

The model presented here departs systematically from the two predictions just described. First, the model predicts explicitly that when reasoning about physical events, infants succeed in detecting certain types of violations before others. Thus, in contrast to the innate-principles view, the model would expect infants to recognize that a small object cannot pass through a gapless surface before they recognize that a large object cannot pass through a smaller gap. This developmental sequence would be cast in terms of the formation of an initial concept centered on a distinction between gap and no gap, followed by the identification of size as a continuous variable relevant to the phenomenon.

Second, the present model also diverges from the prediction that different physical events that implicate the same core principle should be understood at about the same age. The results summarized in the preceding sections and elsewhere[6] – such as the finding that unveiling tasks yield the same developmental patterns as rotating-screen tasks, but at much later ages – suggest that infants respond to physical events not in terms of abstract underlying principles, but in terms of concrete categories corresponding to specific ways in which objects behave or interact. Thus, according to our model, it would not be at all surprising to find that infants succeed in reasoning about gaps several weeks or months before they do containers; the order of acquisition of the two categories would be expected to depend on the content of infants' daily experiences. The model does not rule out the possibility that infants eventually come to realize that superficially distinct events – such as those involving gaps and containers, or rotating screens and cloth covers – can be deeply related; unlike the innate-principles view, however, the model considers such a realization a product, rather than a point of departure, of learning.

One advantage of the view that infants process physical events in terms of concrete categories focusing on specific types of interactions between objects is that this view makes it possible to explain incorrect interpretations that appear to stem from miscategorizations of events. Pilot data collected in our laboratory suggest that young infants expect a moving object to stop when it encounters a tall, thin box but not a short, wide box, even when the latter is considerably larger in volume than the former. We suspect that infants are led by the dominant vertical axis of the tall box to perceive it as a wall-like, immovable object, and hence categorize the event as an instance of a barrier phenomenon; in contrast, infants tend to view the wide box as a movable object, and hence categorize the event as an instance of a collision phenomenon, resulting in incorrect predictions.

The foregoing discussion highlighted several types of developmental sequences that would be anticipated in an innate-mechanisms view but not (without considerable elaboration) in an innate-principles view. To gain further insight into the nature and origins of these developmental sequences, we have adopted a dual research strategy. First, we are examining the development of infants' understanding of additional physical phenomena (e.g., gap, containment, and occlusion phenomena) to determine how easily these developments can be captured in terms of the patterns described in the model and to compare more closely the acquisition time lines of phenomena that are superficially distinct but deeply related. Second, as was alluded to earlier, we are attempting to teach infants initial concepts and variables to uncover what kinds of observations, and how many observations, are required for learning. We hope that the pursuit of these two strategies will eventually allow us to specify the nature of the learning mechanisms that infants bring to the task of learning about the physical world.

Notes

1 J. Piaget, *The Construction of Reality in the Child* (Basic Books, New York, 1954).
2 E. S. Spelke, Preferential looking methods as tools for the study of cognition in infancy, in *Measurement of Audition and Vision in the First Year of Postnatal Life*. G. Gottlieb and N. Krasnegor. Eds. (Ablex, Norwood, NJ, 1985).
3 R. Baillargeon. The object concept revisited: New directions in the investigation of infants' physical knowledge, in *Visual Perception and Cognition in Infancy*. C. E. Granrud, Ed. (Erlbaum. Hillsdale, NJ, 1993).
4 E. S. Spelke, K. Breinlinger, J. Macomber, and K. Jacobson, Origins of knowledge. *Psychological Review*. 99, 605–632 (1992).
5 R. Baillargeon, L. Kotovskv, and A. Needham. The acquisition of physical knowledge in infancy, in *Causal Understandings in Cognition and Culture*, G. Lewis, D. Premack, and D. Sperber, Eds. (Oxford University Press, Oxford, in press).
6 R. Baillargeon, A model of physical reasoning in infancy, in *Advances in Infancy Research*, Vol. 9, C. Rovee-Collier and L. Lipsitt, Eds. (Ablex, Norwood, NJ, 1996).

7   R. Baillargeon, Physical reasoning in infants, in *The Cognitive Neurosciences*. M. S. Gazzaniga, Ed. (MIT Press, Cambridge, MA, 1995).

8   E. S. Spelke, Physical knowledge in infancy: Reflections on Piaget's theory, in *The Epigenesis of Mind: Essays on Biology and Cognition*, S. Carey and R. Gelman, Eds. (Erlbaum, Hillsdale, NJ, 1991).

9   L. Alan, Core architecture and domain specificity, in *Mapping the mind: Domain specificity in cognition and culture*, L. Hirschfeld, S. Gelman et al., Eds. (Cambridge University Press: New York, NY, 1994).

10 P. Rochat and A. Bullinger, Posture and functional action in infancy, in *Francophone Perspectives on Structure and Process in Mental Development*, A. Vyt, H. Block, and M. Bornstein, Eds. (Erlbaum, Hillsdale, NJ, 1994).

11 K. D. Forbus, Qualitative process theory, *Artificial Intelligence*. 24, 85–168 (1984).

12 This example focused exclusively on the size of the cylinder, but what of the distance traveled by the bug in each event? It seems likely that infants encode this information not in quantitative terms (e.g., "the bug traveled x as opposed to y distance"), but rather in qualitative terms, using as their point of reference the track itself (e.g., "the bug rolled to the middle of the track"), their own spatial position (e.g., "the bug stopped in front of me"), or the brightly decorated back wall of the apparatus (e.g., "the bug stopped in front of such-and-such section of the back wall").

TWELVE

The A–not–B Error

Introduction

The A not B error is one of Piaget's most famous illustrations of the mistakes that infants can make when they are asked to search for objects. In this task the infant, usually in the age range 8- 12-months, is shown a toy which is then hidden (perhaps in a cup, or under a cover) in a location within reach of the infant. This location is either to the infant's left or right, and is called location A: the infant is then allowed to reach and retrieve the object. After the toy has been hidden and retrieved by the infant from location A, the toy is then, in full view of the infant, hidden in an identical manner, but this time in a new location on the infant's other side, called location B. When the infant is again allowed to search for the toy she will search at A, not B!

Piaget's interpretation of the error was that the act of reaching was part of the object's identity for the infant who expects it to reappear when reaching for location A. Since Piaget described the error there have been hundreds of studies describing variations on the task and attempting to understand the reason for the error. In this article Ayesha Ahmed and Ted Ruffman give an account of some of the explanations for the error. These include: problems with recall memory (remembering that the object is now at B, and not A); competition between two memories (those locating the object at A and at B); poor allocation of attention; difficulty in encoding information at B since it conflicts with the encoding of information at A; and difficulty in inhibiting a previously rewarded response (reaching at A).

Ahmed and Ruffman considered the question: do infants have any awareness that the toy is now at location B? They suggested that the answer might be "yes" – there existed anecdotal evidence that a small percentage of infants *looked* at B while at the same time they were *reaching* incorrectly at A. In order to investigate this possibility they used a "violation of expectancy" paradigm.

In Experiment 1 infants were tested in three conditions. In the first condition they replicated the standard reaching task and confirmed that infants made the error, especially if they had been prevented from reaching at B for a few seconds. They made no errors if they were allowed to reach as soon as the toy was hidden at B, which demonstrates that memory is involved in making the A not B error.

In the second condition they used a *nonsearch* task, in which the toy was hidden at A by the experimenter, and then retrieved from A, again by the experimenter. Then, the toy was hidden at B, and one of two events followed. For Event 1, the infant saw the toy retrieved by the experimenter from A – this was the "impossible" event, since the toy should have been in B. For Event 2, the toy was retrieved by the experimenter from B – this was the possible event. The rationale is that if infants knew, in some sense, that the toy was at B then Event 1 should have violated their expectancy and, thus should have been looked at for longer than Event 2.

In the third condition they used a *nonsearch one-location* task. The toy was hidden in one location (A) only and the infant saw it retrieved by the experimenter from either A or B. In this task the "impossible" event was seeing the toy retrieved from B, since it had not been seen to be hidden there.

The results from these three tasks are unambiguous, and demonstrate that when infants *search* for toys the A not B error was consistently made. However, when infants were *not allowed to search* and when *looking* was the dependent measure, greater looking at the toy occurred when it was being retrieved from the surprising, or impossible location, clearly indicating that the infant had some memory for the object's location.

Ahmed and Ruffman consider several interpretations of their intriguing findings. It may be that: (1) an inability to inhibit a prepotent response (reaching for A) is one cause of the infants' reaching problems; (2) different types of knowledge (implicit knowledge that is less accessible to guide conscious action than the explicit knowledge that is needed to ensure correct reaching) may be involved; or (3) the effects may be linked to the development of prefrontal areas of the brain. These, and other alternatives, are not mutually exclusive. Ahmed and Ruffman's findings help us to get closer to the real, and complex, explanation for why infants should make the A not B error.

Note: To save space only the first of the four experiments reported in Ahmed and Ruffman's paper is reproduced here. Experiments 2, 3 and 4 confirm and extend the findings from Experiment 1, using variations on the manual search and visual, nonsearch tasks. These experiments are not described here, other than to say that the main findings, of greater looking to the "impossible" events in the nonsearch tasks and inappropriate reaching to the B location in the search tasks (i.e., the classic A not B error), are consistently replicated.

Why Do Infants Make A Not B Errors in a Search Task, Yet Show Memory for the Location of Hidden Objects in a Nonsearch Task?

Ayesha Ahmed and Ted Ruffman

Object search tasks have been used widely to study infant development, with a great concentration of research on the *A not B error*, an object search error that occurs from approximately 8 months to 12 months of age. Piaget (1954) first investigated this phenomenon, which occurs when the experimenter hides a toy at location A, allows the infant to search, and then hides the toy at an identical location, B. If a certain delay between hiding and searching is imposed, 2s at 7.5 months, increasing by approximately 2s every month (Diamond, 1985), the infant will perseverate and search for the toy at A. The number of previous successful searches at A does not affect perseveration when the toy is hidden at B (Butterworth, 1977). If no delay is imposed, infants tend to search correctly at B for the toy (e.g., Diamond, 1985).

Piaget's (1954) explanation for the A not B error was that infants do not have a concept of object permanence. They do not understand that an object continues to exist when it is out of sight, and they therefore associate their search at A with bringing the object back into existence. However, studies by Baillargeon (e.g., Baillargeon, 1987) have shown that some infants as young as 3.5 to 4.5 months have at least some understanding of object permanence. Infants watching contrasting impossible and possible events involving hidden objects looked longer at impossible events, indicating that they were not expecting them to happen. This ability required an understanding that objects continue to exist when out of sight.

Alternative explanations for the A not B error have centered around a number of different factors. Diamond (1985) found that varying the delay between hiding and searching significantly affected occurrence of the error. She concluded from this that recall memory is a factor in causing the error. However, recall memory alone cannot be responsible for the A not B error. Butterworth (1977) used transparent covers to "hide" the toys in an A not B task, and infants still made the error even though the toy was fully in view at B, although errors were less frequent.

Perner (1991, pp. 313–315) argued for a variant of the memory hypothesis in combination with an attentional deficit. Horobin and Acredolo (1986) also argued that attention is a factor, and Harris (1989) proposed that infants make the A not B error because of a competition between two memory traces in combination with poor attention. In Harris's account, information about the object at A is held in long-term memory whereas information about the object at B is in a weaker short-term memory.

Other accounts of the A not B error have placed the difficulty at the encoding level. For instance, Bjork and Cummings (1984) suggested that encoding at B is more complex because it must be distinguished from A. Sophian and Wellman (1983) referred to information selection: prior information is mistakenly selected over current information either because infants forget current information or because they do not know that current information should take precedence.

The A not B task requires not only memory for the location of the toy, but it also requires the action of reaching for the toy. Memory and action must be integrated for the task to be performed correctly. One proposal is that infants know where the object is in the B trial, but it is the requirement for reaching which causes the error. Diamond (1985) suggested that the A not B error is due to a combination of memory difficulties and the habit of searching at a previously correct location. It appears that memory must be involved, because with no delay 8- to 12-month-old infants will not perseverate, but when a short delay is imposed, errors begin to occur. Diamond (1988) also proposed that infants will be less likely to err if habit or memory demands are lessened. This habit can be conceptualized as an inability to inhibit repetition of a previously rewarded response. Infants cannot inhibit repetition of their reach to A even when they know the object is at B, so they make the A not B error.

There is some evidence that tests that require a visual response in A not B tasks result in fewer errors than the standard search response. For instance, there is anecdotal evidence that a small percentage of infants gaze at location B, while reaching incorrectly to A (Diamond, 1988). In addition, Hofstadter and Reznick (1996) found that infants gazed toward the correct location significantly more often than they reached toward the correct location in a delayed response task, although only a small percentage of infants reached incorrectly whilst simultaneously gazing correctly. These findings are consistent with the idea that measuring performance with a response modality other than manual search may reveal some knowledge of the toy's location.

Another way of measuring responses in the visual modality is the violation-of-expectation paradigm, in which infants are shown two similar events, one possible and one impossible, and their looking times at these two events are compared. Baillargeon and Graber (1988) used this method, not in an A not B task, but in a study in which a toy was hidden behind screen A, and infants watched as it was retrieved either from behind screen A (possible event) or from behind screen B (impossible event). They found that infants looked significantly longer at the impossible event than at the possible event after delays of up to 30 s, and, in a later study (Baillargeon et al., 1989), after 70-s delays. The conclusion was that infants recognized the impossible event as a violation of what should have happened, and therefore knew where the toy should have been found.

The violation-of-expectation method has the advantage of not requiring an explicit response from the infant. The infant attends to the location at which an action is occurring, and watches as the object is revealed, either at the correct location or the incorrect location. The measure taken by the experimenter is the length of time the infant looks at that event. The infant is not making a visual response in the sense of the direction-of-gaze response, so perseveration of a previous response is not possible. In a direction-of-gaze task, infants must anticipate the location of the object whereas in a looking time task infants are merely reacting to an event that has already occurred. The lesser task demands of the looking time measure could enable it to provide a more direct method of assessing infants' conceptual knowledge than the traditional reaching measure, and even the direction-of-gaze measure, assuming looking time reveals the same type of knowledge as these tasks. However, it is important to note here that the violation-of-expectation paradigm may be revealing a different type of knowledge than that required to search correctly. This possibility will be addressed further in the General Discussion section.

For these reasons, we applied the violation-of-expectation paradigm to the A not B task. Infants were not allowed to search but merely watched the experimenter carry out a hiding and finding sequence that followed the A not B format. The toy was first hidden at A, retrieved from A, and then moved to B. After a delay there followed either an impossible event in which the toy was retrieved from the incorrect location, A, or a possible event in which it was retrieved from the correct location, B. This task involves the essential components of the standard A not B task, in which a toy is hidden and retrieved correctly from one location and is then visibly moved to the other location. The infant must remember not just a single location for the object, as in Baillargeon and Graber (1988) and Baillargeon et al. (1989), but also the most recent location. The possibility of interference from the initial memory trace therefore arises in the nonsearch A not B task but not in the tasks of Baillargeon and her colleagues.

The nonsearch A not B task could reveal whether infants have knowledge of the toy's location but are unable to demonstrate this knowledge in their search behavior. If infants look significantly longer at the impossible events than at the possible events this could indicate that they understand that the toy was retrieved from the wrong location, and therefore know where it should have been. The question arises whether infants can remember the location of the toy in a nonsearch version of the A not B task even after delays at which they would have made the error in a search task. If infants do show this memory ability, and if we assume that the search and nonsearch tasks involve the same type of memory and knowledge, it could be concluded that the requirement for a search response is critical in causing the A not B error. It is therefore important to carry out a study in which all infants participate in both the search and nonsearch A not B tasks.

Experiment 1

In Experiment 1, we tested these ideas by giving infants three tasks. The first task was a standard A not B search task modeled after that used by Diamond (1985). This provided us with a measure of the delay (d) at which a particular infant made the A not B error on a search task. The second task was a nonsearch A not B task in which the infant observed the experimenter hide the object at A, retrieve it, and hide it at B. After a delay of either zero, d (the delay at which the search error was made), or 15 s, the experimenter retrieved the object from either A (impossible event) or B (possible event). Infants' looking times at each event were recorded. The third task was a nonsearch one-location task modeled after the study by Baillargeon and Graber (1988). In this task, the infant observed while the object was hidden at A and then retrieved either from A or B after a delay of zero, d, or 15 s. This allowed us to compare the nonsearch A not B task with the task used by Baillargeon and Graber, and to compare infants' performances on both of these tasks with their performances on the A not B search task.

Note: As mentioned earlier, to save space only the first of the four experiments reported in Ahmed and Ruffman's paper is reproduced here. Experiments 2, 3 and 4 confirm and extend the findings from Experiment 1, using variations on the manual search and visual, non-search tasks. These experiments are not described here, other than to say that the main findings, of greater looking to the "impossible" events in the nonsearch tasks and inappropriate reaching to the B location in the search tasks (i.e., the classic A not B error), are consistently replicated.

Method

Participants.   Participants were 24 healthy, full-term infants ranging in age from 8 months 0 days to 11 months 28 days (*M* age = 9 months 15 days). In all experiments, parents volunteered to take part in studies at the Infant Study Unit at the University of Sussex and were contacted by telephone and visited in their homes where the study was carried out. The babies were given a small gift for participating.

Materials.   The apparatus for the search task consisted of two identical blue plastic pots, 15 cm in height and 10 cm in diameter, with blue lids. The toy used in the experiment was a red plastic rattle with a yellow handle. The rattle was 8 cm long and had a circular mirror under clear plastic, in which red, yellow, and blue beads were enclosed.

The apparatus for the nonsearch tasks consisted of two identical white plastic screens, 20 cm wide and 27 cm high. These were attached at their tops to a white plastic rail 130 cm long. The gap between the screens was 20 cm. The rail was supported on either end and could be slid across to move the screens from side to side. Two identical blue plastic placemats, 13 cm × 15 cm, were placed directly behind the screens, and lay 27 cm apart (see figure 12.1). In all experiments, the apparatus was always placed on the floor so that all of the babies were at a similar height to it and the parent sat with the baby on the floor. The experimenter sat behind the apparatus with a video camera positioned on a tripod so that the baby's eye movements could be recorded.

The placemats could be hidden and revealed from behind the screens, by pulling the rail from side to side. The toy used was the same rattle that was used in the search task. In the impossible event, another identical rattle was hung on a hook attached to the back of one of the screens. This allowed the experimenter to produce a rattle from behind one screen, even though the target rattle had been hidden behind the other screen, and to show both mats to be empty in between trials.

Procedure.   There were three tasks: an A not B search task, an A not B nonsearch task, and a one-location nonsearch task. Each infant participated in all three tasks. The search task was always carried out first, to establish the delay (d) at which the A not B error was made.

Search task.   The procedure for the search task was modeled after that used by Diamond (1985) to establish delays at which infants made the A not B error. The pots were placed 20 cm apart, a toy was placed in pot A, and the lids of both pots replaced simultaneously. The infant was allowed to search after a 2-s delay. Provided the infant searched correctly, the toy was then hidden in pot B, and the infant was again allowed to search after a 2-s delay. If the infant then made the A not B error (i.e., searched at A for the toy), the task was repeated once more with a 2-s delay. However if the infant searched correctly, the task was repeated with a 4-s delay. The task was continued, with delay being increased by 2 s after correct searches, until each infant searched incorrectly on two consecutive trials at a certain delay. That delay was then used as delay (d) in the nonsearch task. Infants were encouraged to look up at the experimenter during the delays, so that they could not fixate their gaze on the correct location.

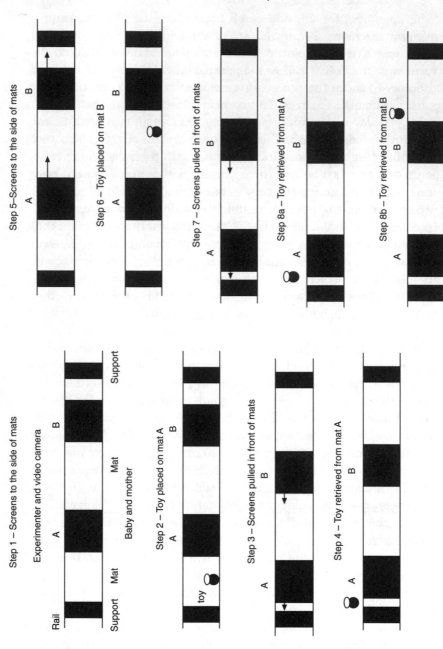

Figure 12.1   Apparatus and procedure for nonsearch tasks (Steps 1–8b)

Nonsearch A not B task.   Figure 12.1 provides a summary of the procedure for the nonsearch tasks. At the start, the screens were pulled aside to reveal two empty mats. The toy was placed on mat A, and the screens were then slid across to hide the mats. The toy was immediately retrieved by the experimenter from the outside edge of screen A (i.e., left edge, if A was the left screen). It was held there for 2 s while the infant looked. The screens were then pulled back to reveal two empty mats again. The toy was placed on mat B this time, and the screens slid across to hide the mats. After a delay of either 0, d (at which the search error was made), or 15 s, the toy was retrieved by the experimenter from behind screen A. This was the impossible event. The toy behind screen B was then placed on the hook without the infant's knowledge, and the screens were slid to the side to reveal two empty mats at the end.

For the possible event, the toy was first hidden behind screen B, then retrieved from B and hidden behind screen A. After the delay, it was retrieved from behind the correct screen, screen A, and two empty mats were revealed. In each case, the toy was held next to the screen from which it was found, until the infant looked away. During the delay in each event, the experimenter's hand, wearing a silvery glove, danced around in front of the apparatus for distraction, and the babies were encouraged to watch this glove to prevent them from fixating on one of the locations. The babies were allowed to play with the toy between trials. The task was recorded by a video camera placed on a tripod behind the experimenter.

Nonsearch one-location task.   The apparatus used for the nonsearch A not B task was also used for this task. In this task, Steps 4–7 were omitted (see figure 12.1). The toy was placed on mat A, and the screens were then slid across to hide the mats. After a delay of either 0, d, or 15 s, the toy was retrieved by the experimenter from behind screen B for the impossible event. For the possible event, the toy was retrieved from behind the correct screen after the delay. The only difference between this task and the nonsearch A not B task was that in the A not B version the infant always saw the toy being retrieved correctly from A first, and then being moved to B. The one-location task did not follow this A not B sequence of events.

Design.   All of the infants participated in the search task first. Half of the infants participated in the nonsearch A not B task second and half participated in the nonsearch one-location task second. Also, for half of the infants, location A was the left-hand screen; for the other half, location A was the right-hand screen. Each of the three delays and the impossible and possible events within each delay were carried out in a counterbalanced order. Infants saw a total of six events for each nonsearch task.

Results

Looking times at the impossible and possible events were measured directly from the videotape using a frame counter and were accurate to 1 frame, which was equivalent to 0.04 s. In addition to the primary observer, an independent observer, who was blind to the conditions, measured looking times for 25% of trials. Reliability was calculated by taking the average difference between looking times measured by each observer as a percentage of the total looking time measured by the primary observer. The average level of interobserver agreement was found to be 95%. The looking times recorded by the primary observer were used to determine the final measures.

The looking time measure was taken to be the time from when the infant saw the toy appear to when the infant looked away from the toy and location. Looking away usually involved looking at the experimenter or turning to look at the parent. Table 12.1 shows the mean looking times for the different tasks, events, and delays.

These data were analyzed using a repeated-measures analysis of variance (ANOVA) with looking time as the dependent variable, with event (impossible, possible), delay (0, d, 15 s), and task (nonsearch A not B, one-location) as within-subjects factors, and side of first hiding (left, right) and event order as between-subjects factors. There was a significant main effect of event, $F(1, 20) = 31.59$, $p < .001$, indicating that infants looked significantly longer at the impossible events than at the possible events. There was also a significant three-way interaction between delay, event, and hiding at the left side first, which we will not try to interpret, $F(2, 40) = 3.30$, $p < .05$.

To examine the effect of age on performance, we conducted a linear regression, with age as the independent variable and looking time as the dependent variable (time on the impossible condition at each delay − time on the possible condition at each delay). Age was not a significant predictor of performance in either the nonsearch A not B task, $t(23) = 0.74$, *ns*, or the one-location task, $t(23) = 0.01$, *ns*. Age was

Table 12.1   Mean looking times in the nonsearch tasks in Experiment 1

| | Delay (s) | | | | | |
| | *0* | | *d* | | *15* | |
Task	Impossible	Possible	Impossible	Possible	Impossible	Possible
A not B						
M	4.20****	2.27****	4.01**	2.21**	4.17*	2.95*
SD	2.54	1.84	2.52	1.06	2.26	1.87
One location						
M	4.78**	3.09**	4.22	3.09	4.41	3.78
SD	2.17	1.42	1.52	2.19	2.89	2.41

Notes: Significance tests are based on comparisons between impossible and possible looking times at each delay. d = delay at which the A not B error was made.
*p < .05. **p < .01. ****p < .001.

nonsignificantly correlated with looking time in both tasks ($r = -0.16$ and $r = 0.00$, respectively).

The same analysis was then carried out to examine the relation between age and the delay (d) at which children made the A not B error in the search task. In contrast to the above result, age was highly correlated with d, $r = 0.88$, $t(23) = 14.71$, $p < 0.001$. This result replicates that of Diamond (1985).

Contrasts between looking times at impossible and possible events for each delay in each of the nonsearch tasks were calculated using 1 *DF F* tests with a pooled error term. In the nonsearch A not B task, there was a significant contrast at 0 delay, $F(1, 20) = 17.37$, $p < .001$; at delay d, $F(1, 20) = 9.80$, $p < .01$; and also at the 15-s delay, $F(1, 20) = 5.02$, $p < .05$. Infants looked significantly longer at the impossible events than at the possible events at all three delays. In the one-location task, the effect was significant for 0 delay, $F(1, 20) = 8.54$, $p < .01$, but failed to reach significance at delay d, $F(1, 20) = 2.46$, *ns*, and the 15-s delay, $F(1, 20) = 0.73$, *ns*. Nevertheless, Table 12.1 shows that the means were in the same direction as in the nonsearch A not B task and our first analysis described above revealed no significant difference in looking times between the two nonsearch tasks, $F(1, 20) = 2.23$, *ns*, and no significant interaction overall between task, event, and delay, $F(2, 40) = 0.17$, ns.

Individual participants' looking times were then examined. In the nonsearch A not B task, the percentage of infants who looked longer at the impossible event than at the possible event was 83% for 0 delay (binomial test: $k = 20$, $n = 24$, $p < .001$), 75% for delay d (binomial test: $k = 18$, $n = 24$, $p < .05$), and 67% for the 15-s delay (binomial test: $k = 16$, $n = 24$, $p < .05$). The difference between looking times at impossible and possible events was significant even when individual data were examined. In the one-location task, 71% of infants looked longer at the impossible event after 0 delay (binomial test: $k = 17$, $n = 24$, $p < .05$), and 75% of infants looked longer at the impossible event after delay d (binomial test: $k = 18$, $n = 24$, $p < .05$), although only 42% did so after the 15-s delay (binomial test: $k = 10$, $n = 24$, ns).

Next, we compared each infant's performance on the nonsearch A not B task to his or her performance on the one-location task. To pass a task, infants had to look longer at the impossible than the possible event at a given delay. Five infants passed the nonsearch A not B task while failing the one-location task at 0 delay, and three infants obtained the opposite pattern (binomial test: $k = 5$, $n = 8$, ns). Six infants passed the nonsearch A not B task and failed the one-location task at delay d, and 6 infants obtained the opposite pattern, McNemar's $\chi^2(1, N = 12) = 0$, ns. Ten infants passed the nonsearch A not B task and failed the one-location task at the 15-s delay, and 4 obtained the opposite pattern, McNemar's $\chi^2(1, N = 14) = 2.57$, ns.

We then compared each infant's performance on the search task to his or her performance on the nonsearch A not B task. This was not done for 0 delay as this delay was not used in the search task, and it was not done for delay d because, by definition, all infants failed the search task at delay d. The criterion for passing the search task was correct search on the B trial. Nineteen infants failed the search task at delays of less than 15 s while passing the nonsearch A not B task with a 15-s delay, whereas none obtained the opposite pattern, McNemar's $\chi^2(1, N = 19) = 17.05$, $p < .001$, corrected. As all infants failed the search task at a delay less than 15 s, we assume that they would not have searched correctly after 15 s. This assumption is backed up by Diamond (1985) who reported deteriorated performance in the A not B task when delays are increased to 2 or 3 s more than the delay at which the infant makes the error. The mean delay at which infants made the A not B error on the search task was 4.64 s, which is much shorter than the 15-s delay at which infants looked longer at the impossible event in the nonsearch A not B task.

Discussion

The results show that infants of 8 to 12 months look significantly longer at a toy being retrieved from the incorrect location than at a toy being retrieved from the correct location in a nonsearch version of the A not B task. Most infants could remember the location of the hidden toy after a 15-s delay in an A not B task when they were not required to search. This is much longer than the average delay at which infants made the A not B error in the search task. In some sense, infants knew where the toy was hidden in the nonsearch A not B task, so the question that arises is whether they also knew where it was in the search version of the task, and if they did, why they searched incorrectly. This issue will be returned to in the General Discussion section.

We failed to replicate the results of Baillargeon and Graber (1988) and Baillargeon et al. (1989) perhaps because of minor methodological differences (e.g., the toy, the experimenter, or the method of coding). Nevertheless, looking times on the one-location task did not differ significantly from the nonsearch A not B task.

General Discussion

The results from all four experiments show that infants who make errors in an A not B search task look significantly longer at impossible events than at possible events in a nonsearch version of the A not B task. The violation-of-expectation paradigm used here is based on the assumption that infants will look significantly longer at an event that is unexpected than at a similar event that does not violate their expectations about the physical world. The infants were not expecting the toy to be retrieved from the wrong place, and from this we can conclude that in some sense they knew where the toy actually was in the nonsearch task.

Age was not significantly correlated with looking time in any of the four experiments, and correlations were negative in two of the experiments. This suggests that performance on the nonsearch task does not improve between 8 and 12 months of age, although Experiments 1 and

2 showed that performance on the search task clearly does. Similarly, the number of infants who passed the nonsearch tasks while failing search tasks was significant for most delays.

The discrepancy between search and nonsearch tasks raises the following question: do infants therefore know where the toy is in the search task even when they search incorrectly? Infants clearly remember the toy's location after a 15-s delay in a version of the nonsearch task that parallels the search version identically except for the search component (Experiment 3). This indicates that a memory trace for the object at the B location exists in the nonsearch task, and must also exist immediately before infants reach in the search task, even when they reach to A. What then makes the search task more difficult? Below we speculate on possible reasons for the dissociation between the two tasks. In general, theories can be divided into those that argue that infants have knowledge of the object at B but make search errors for other reasons, and those that argue that the form of knowledge that is needed for passing nonsearch tasks is qualitatively different than that required for search tasks.

First, we consider theories that our results do not support. Our results go well beyond those of Baillargeon and Graber (1988) and Baillargeon et al. (1989), as the memory demands in our nonsearch A not B tasks were likely to be considerably higher than they were in Baillargeon's one-location task. By using a task where the object was first placed at and retrieved from A we were able to assess theories that infants make the A not B error partly because of competition between a short-term memory trace for the object at B and a long-term trace for the object at A (Harris, 1989), and those that talk about interference from a previous response (Diamond, 1988). Unlike in the Baillargeon and Graber (1988) and Baillargeon et al. (1989) tasks, this competition was present in our looking time tasks, particularly in Experiment 3 in which the infants searched on the A trial of the nonsearch task yet clearly remembered the object's location after the B trial at delays of 15 s. Consequently, although the competition between A and B memory traces may hamper performance to some degree, it cannot be enough to cause the A not B error on its own. On the other hand, our results are consistent with Harris's (1989) claim that attention may be involved (i.e., that search errors occur because infants' attention wanders to A). Whereas in the search task infants must attend to the B location of their own accord, in the nonsearch task the experimenter draws infants' attention to the A and B locations. This may help account for the good performance on the nonsearch task.

Another theory that uses the notion of attention and memory is that of Perner (1991). He claims that the context markers designating the two memory traces (object at A, object at B) as past and present may fade with time. If the infant's attention wanders to A and the marker designating this trace as past has faded, the infant will search at A. Again, although there may be some fading of context markers, our results suggest that markers cannot have faded completely or infants would not have looked longer at the impossible event.

Our results can also be used to argue against a strong version of Bjork and Cummings's (1984) theory that encoding the information that the toy is at B is more complex than encoding the information that the toy is at A. Infants must have encoded at least some trace for the object at B to perform the nonsearch task correctly, and therefore they must have encoded this information in the search task also, before making the incorrect reach response.

Likewise, our results argue against the hypothesis of Sophian and Wellman (1983). They claim that prior information is mistakenly selected over current information either because infants forget current information, or because they do not know that current information should take precedence. Again, infants' performance on the nonsearch task shows that at some level they both remember current information (object at B) and understand that it takes precedence.

Horobin and Acredolo (1986) found that infants erred more often when the A and B locations were close together than when they were widely spaced. They also found that infants who did not make errors were more attentive to the B location. Their claim is that attentional abilities result in enhanced spatial encoding. Again, however, our results suggest that encoding is not by itself at the root of infants' difficulty. Although attention may be involved in a standard A not B task, it is not likely to have its effect through enhancing encoding.

Our results do however support Diamond's (1988) theory that the inability to inhibit a prepotent response is a partial cause of the A not B error. The violation-of-expectation task produces a looking reaction that is not vulnerable to perseveration in the same way as a reaching response. Our finding that the nonsearch task reveals some form of knowledge that is not revealed in the search task supports the idea that the requirement for a reach response may be preventing infants from

demonstrating any knowledge that they might have. Such a phenomenon is seen in the Wisconsin Card Sorting Task when, according to anecdotal evidence, adults with prefrontal cortex damage sort cards into the
incorrect category while saying out loud that they are wrong (Milner,
1964).

The notion that the prefrontal cortex is involved in perseveration is
supported by the neuropsychological literature. In particular, the dorsolateral region is involved in controlling interference from irrelevant
stimuli and selectively attending to relevant stimuli (Welsh and Pennington, 1988). Infants are therefore highly susceptible to interference,
due to the immaturity of the prefrontal cortex. Further support comes
from evidence that monkeys with lesions to the dorsolateral prefrontal
cortex perform perseveratively in the delayed response task (Diamond
and Goldman-Rakic, 1989). It has been suggested (Dempster, 1992)
that there may be a specific inhibitory mechanism that is not fully
mature in infants and is causing them to repeat the previously successful response of searching to A. The prefrontal cortex is maturing rapidly
during the 1st year of life, and its maturation may be linked to the developmental progression of performance on the A not B task (e.g., Bell and
Fox, 1992; Nelson, 1995).

Perseveration of response occurs when manual search is required,
but also seems to occur, to a lesser extent, when gaze responses are measured (Hofstadter and Reznick, 1996). There are various arguments for
why a gaze response may be less vulnerable to perseveration than a
reach response. The repetition of a manual response usually results in
increased skill at a task, and is therefore often appropriate. However,
when a visual response is repeated, this is often an inefficient use of
visual attention, as it reduces the total amount of information that is
taken in by the visual system (Abrams and Dobkin, 1994). Posner et al.
(1985) suggested the existence of a mechanism, which they call inhibition of return (IOR), that prevents such attentional perseveration in the
visual system. Evidence for IOR has been found in studies with infants
of only a few days old, provided the visual cues used in the task are interesting enough to attract the infant's attention at the start (Valenza
et al., 1994). It has also been suggested that functionally distinct
brain systems may be involved in visual and motor responses
(Bridgeman, 1992). There may be a difference in the transfer of information from the prefrontal cortex to the corpus striatum for a manual

response, and to the colliculus for a visual response, resulting in differences in abilities in manual and visual tasks (Hofstadter and Reznick, 1996).

However, the violation-of-expectation method used in the nonsearch A not B task may be immune to perseveration for a different reason. Once again, the measure taken is not the direction of the infant's response to having seen the toy being hidden, but it is instead the amount of attention the infant pays to the toy being retrieved from its location. This is a response after the toy has been retrieved and is therefore simply an indication of whether or not the infant was expecting the toy to come from that location. It is more of a reaction than a response, as the infants are not required to attend to the correct location themselves. If the looking time task involves the same type of knowledge as the search task, then the looking time measure may be more sensitive than the search response in assessing the infant's knowledge of the location of the toy, and it may even be preferable to a direction-of-gaze measure. Indeed, Hofstadter and Reznick (1996) found that only 14% of their pairs of gaze and reach responses were mismatched (i.e., gaze in one direction and reach in the other), with only 67% of these consisting of a correct direction-of-gaze and an incorrect direction-of-reach (9.4% of total response pairs). This contrasts with the percentage of children in our experiments who showed memory for the object's location in the looking time task but not the reaching task. The average percentage of children who showed this pattern of results across Experiments 2 and 3 was 56% at the 6-s delay. At the 15-s delay the average across Experiments 1 to 3 was 53%. Clearly, tasks that use a looking time measure seem more sensitive than tasks that use a direction of gaze measure.

Some of the views discussed above (e.g., Diamond, 1988) are consistent with the notion that infants may know that the object is at B when they search at A, and that interference from some other source masks their understanding. Such a view assumes that the knowledge required for success on the nonsearch task is identical or very similar to the knowledge required for success on search tasks. However, this may not be the case. Another possible explanation for the dissociation in performance between the violation-of-expectation task and the search and gaze tasks is that looking times in a violation-of-expectation task reveal a different form of knowledge, which may not be the full conceptual understanding needed for correct direction of reach or even gaze. The violation-of-expectation task involves a reaction to an event, using a form of recognition memory rather than a response using recall memory.

A graded representations theory (Munakata et al., 1994) offers an account of knowledge development in which the object concept is not an all-or-nothing construct that infants either have or do not have. Infants' knowledge consists of representations that vary in strength and in their accessibility to output systems, and it is the gradual strengthening of these internal representations that causes changes in behavior. When infants are looking at the impossible event, and look at it for longer than the possible event, this may indicate some degree of understanding of the object's location but not full conceptual understanding. There may be a lower threshold for looking responses, with reaching responses requiring stronger representations (Munakata et al., 1994). In other words, although there must clearly be a memory trace for the object at B in the search task, it may not be of the right type to result in correct search.

Another way of describing the different types of knowledge that may be involved in the search and nonsearch tasks relies on the distinction between implicit and explicit knowledge. Explicit knowledge is loosely defined as accessible to consciousness whereas implicit knowledge is less accessible. Dienes and Perner (1996) suggested four methodological criteria for assessing whether knowledge is implicit: (a) a lack of metaknowledge, (b) a lack of control over applying the knowledge, (c) knowledge that is not revealed in free recall, and (d) knowledge that shows itself only in indirect tests. In comparison to looking time, reaching seems to require more control over applying the knowledge, and more in the way of recall. It is possible, then, that looking time (and perhaps direction of gaze) draws to a greater extent on implicit knowledge. This does not mean that reach necessarily draws on explicit knowledge in the same sense as an adult's reach, but that search and looking time may differ in the degree to which they are implicit.

There is, however, one point that may favor the idea that despite committing the A not B error infants know where the object is. Diamond and Goldman-Rakic (1989) found that lesioning the DPC (dorsolateral prefrontal cortex) of monkeys led to the A not B error whereas lesions to the parietal cortex (Diamond and Goldman-Rakic, 1989) or hippocampal region (Diamond et al., 1989) do not produce A not B errors. Diamond's account is consistent with the idea that attentional or inhibitory abilities cause the error. The graded representations or implicit knowledge account would have to claim that at least a portion of the (perhaps distributed) representation involved in the A not B task happens also to be located in the DPC.

In conclusion, the A not B error may be explained by a number of different ideas, or by a combination of these ideas. For instance, infants' knowledge may develop as graded representations, which are also influenced by the maturational state of the brain. Although we cannot be certain of the precise nature of infants' difficulty on the A not B task, our results argue against some hypotheses, as described above. Further, our results suggest that infants do have some form of knowledge about the object's true location even when they search incorrectly. In sum, infants in some sense know where the toy is in the nonsearch task even though this knowledge is not demonstrated through their reaching behavior in the A not B task. We have argued that this dissociation occurs either because the nonsearch task taps a different type of knowledge, or because infants are prevented from using their knowledge when searching.

References

Abrams, R., & Dobkin, R. (1994). Inhibition of return: Effects of attentional cuing on eye movement latencies. *Journal of Experimental Psychology: Human Perception and Performance, 20,* 467–477.

Baillargeon, R. (1987). Object permanence in 3.5–4.5 month old infants. *Developmental Psychology, 23,* 655–664.

Baillargeon, R., DeVos, J., & Graber, M. (1989). Location memory in 8-month-old infants in a non-search A not B task: Further evidence. *Cognitive Development, 4,* 345–367.

Baillargeon, R., & Graber, M. (1988). Evidence of location memory in 8 month old infants in a non search AB task. *Developmental Psychology, 24,* 502–511.

Bell, M., & Fox, N. A. (1992). The relation between frontal brain electrical activity and cognitive development during infancy. *Child Development, 63,* 1142–1163.

Bjork, E. L., & Cummings, E. M. (1984). Infant search errors: Stage of concept development or stage of memory development? *Memory and Cognition, 12,* 1–19.

Bridgeman, B. (1992). Conscious vs unconscious processes: The case of vision. *Theory and Psychology, 2*(1), 73–88.

Butterworth, G. (1977). Object disappearance and error in Piaget's stage IV task. *Journal of Experimental Child Psychology, 23*, 391–401.

Dempster, F. N. (1992). The rise and fall of the inhibitory mechanism: Toward a unified theory of cognitive development and aging. *Developmental Review, 12*, 45–75.

Diamond, A. (1985). Development of the ability to use recall to guide action, as indicated by infants' performance on AB. *Child Development, 56*, 868–883.

Diamond, A. (1988). Abilities and neural mechanisms underlying AB performance. *Child Development, 59*, 523–527.

Diamond, A., & Goldman-Rakic, P. (1989). Comparison of human infants and rhesus monkeys on Piaget's AB task: Evidence for dependence on dorsolateral prefrontal cortex. *Experimental Brain Research, 74*, 24–40.

Diamond, A., Zola-Morgan, S., & Squire, L. R. (1989). Successful performance by monkeys with lesions to the hippocampal formation on AB and object retrieval, two tasks that mark developmental changes in human infants. *Behavioral Neuroscience, 103*, 526–537.

Dienes, Z., & Perner, J. (1996). Implicit knowledge in people and connectionist networks. In G. Underwood (Ed.), *Implicit cognition* (pp. 227–255). Oxford, England: Oxford University Press.

Harris, P. (1989). Object permanence in infancy. In A. Slater & G. Bremner (Eds.), *Infant development* (pp. 103–121). Hove, England: Erlbaum.

Hofstadter, M., & Reznick, J. S. (1996). Response modality affects human infant delayed-response performance. *Child Development, 67*, 646–658.

Horobin, K., & Acredolo, L. (1986). The role of attentiveness, mobility history, and separation of hiding sites on stage IV search behaviour. *Journal of Experimental Child Psychology, 41*, 114–127.

Milner, B. (1964). Some effects of frontal lobectomy in man. In J. M. Warren & K. Akert (Eds.), *The frontal granular cortex and behaviour* (pp. 313–334). New York: McGraw Hill.

Munakata, Y., McClelland, J. L., Johnson, M. H., & Siegler, R. S. (1994). *Now you see it, now you don't: A gradualistic framework for understanding infants' successes and failures in object permanence tasks.* Technical report, Carnegie Mellon University, Pittsburgh, PA.

Nelson, C. A. (1995). The ontogeny of human memory: A cognitive neuroscience perspective. *Developmental Psychology, 31*, 723–738.

Perner, J. (1991). *Understanding the representational mind.* Cambridge, MA: MIT.

Piaget, J. (1954). *The construction of reality in the child* (pp. 44–66). New York: Routledge.

Posner, M., Robert, R., Choate, L., & Vaughan, J. (1985). Inhibition of return: Neural basis and function. *Journal of Cognitive Neuroscience, 2*, 211–278.

Sophian, C., & Wellman, H. (1983). Selective information use and perseveration in the search behaviour of infants and young children. *Journal of Experimental Child Psychology, 35,* 369–390.

Valenza, E., Simion, F., & Umilta, C. (1994). Inhibition of return in newborn infants. *Infant Behaviour and Development, 17,* 293–302.

Welsh, M. C., & Pennington, B. F. (1988). Assessing frontal lobe functioning in children: Views from developmental psychology. *Developmental Neuropsychology, 4*(3), 199–230.

THIRTEEN

Predicting Later Intelligence

Introduction

Developmental psychology is as much interested in stability of development as it is in change. We wish to know whether, in spite of all the changes that occur in ontogenesis, there is some continuity of development so that, for instance, the bigger infants become the taller adults, the more cognitively aware infants become the more intelligent children, the more withdrawn infants become the shyest adults, and so on.

This interest in stability had particularly focused on our ability (or not!) to predict later IQ from measures taken in infancy. As McCall (1981, p. 141) has put it, "Some things are sacred. For developmental psychology, predicting later behavior from early behavior is sacred ... And so the search for early predictors of later IQ goes on."

From the 1970s it has become apparent that measures of infant attention, particularly to visual stimuli, display some moderate degree of (correlational) stability: thus, infants who process visual information more quickly (as indexed, perhaps, by rapid habituation, or decline of attention, to a repeatedly presented visual stimulus) are likely to become children with above average IQs.

In this article, Marian Sigman and her colleagues describe their predictive research and offer support to two possible causes of the observed continuity: (1) the speed with which infants are able to process information and; (2) their ability to inhibit and regulate attention. Note that the continuity observed is not simply genetically determined since it results, at least in part, from the responsiveness of the infant's caregivers.

Further reading

Slater, A. (1995). Individual differences in infancy and later IQ. *Journal of Child Psychology and Psychiatry, 36,* 69–110.

Bornstein, M. H., Slater, A., Brown, E., Roberts, E. and Barrett, J. (1997). Stability of mental development from infancy to later childhood: Three "waves" of research. In G. Bremner, A. Slater and G. Butterworth (eds.), *Infant Development: Recent Advances.* Hove, UK: Psychology Press.

Why Does Infant Attention Predict Adolescent Intelligence?

Marian Sigman, Sarale E. Cohen,
and Leila Beckwith

Numerous studies have demonstrated that infant attention predicts later intelligence (Bornstein and Sigman, 1986; Fagan and Singer, 1983; McCall and Carriger, 1993). Research investigations have moved from a concern with identifying relations between infant attention and childhood intelligence to a focus on explaining this continuity. Based on the assumption that some similar process must be tapped by both infant attention and childhood intelligence measures, one aim of current research is to identify this underlying process.

Three different characterizations of the shared underlying process have been proposed. One theory suggests that the process reflected in both effective attention by infants and intelligent behavior by children is speed or efficiency of information processing (Bornstein, 1985, 1989; Colombo, 1995). Infants who habituate rapidly, show short durations of attention to repeated or unchanging stimuli, or strong preference for novel stimuli are thought to be infants who either use efficient scanning strategies or form memory traces quickly. Children who can solve the kinds of language and perceptual problems that are tested on intelligence tests are known to have mastered these skills partly because of their strengths in encoding and retrieving information (Ceci, 1990; Dreary, 1995; Vernon, 1987).

A second theory suggests that the underlying process shared by the infant and childhood measures is the ability to inhibit responses to uninformative and familiar stimulation (McCall, 1994). Both infants who attend briefly and intelligent children are considered to be able to detect repetitive or irrelevant information and to turn their attention away from it towards more informative stimuli. The third theory, proposed by Berg and Sternberg (1985), is that an important characteristic is comfort with or a taste for novelty. Infants who have experienced a greater variety of stimulating conditions (within certain limits), may be better able to incorporate novel information into solutions than infants who have had more restricted novel experiences. Ease with novel stimuli may lead the child into more varied learning experiences, thereby improving his or her capacity to solve cognitive problems.

Research investigations of infant attention have provided support for the first hypothesis in that "long-looking" and "short-looking" infants differ in both the speed and nature of their processing. For example, Freeseman and her colleagues (Freeseman et al., 1993) have demonstrated that "short-looking" infants needed only about 10 s of familiarization time to demonstrate preference for a novel stimulus while "long-looking" infants needed 40 s to process the same stimulus. In these studies, "short-looking" infants began by attending to global features and moved to local features as exposure duration was increased, a pattern also employed by adults. In contrast, "long-looking" infants focused on local elements at familiarization times just beyond those required for discrimination of global features (Colombo, Freeseman et al., 1995). Furthermore, "long-looking" infants have been reported to inspect parts of stimuli for prolonged periods while "short-looking" infants engaged in more extensive scanning (Bronson, 1991).

Information processing has also been identified as important in longitudinal studies of preterm infants using multiple outcome measures to provide divergent validation. Rose and Feldman (1995) administered a battery of measures to 11–12 year old children whose preference for novelty and cross-modal transfer had been studied at 7 and 12 months of age. Speed of perceptual processing, as measured by the Colorado Perceptual Speed Test and an Educational Testing Service measure called Finding As, was the adolescent ability most consistently correlated with visual recognition memory tested in infancy with the preference for novelty paradigm.

Divergent validation was also used in our study of children born preterm after follow up assessments at 5 and 8 years of age had shown that children who were "long-lookers" in early infancy scored lower on intelligence tests than children who had been "short-lookers" in infancy. At 12 years, the children from English-speaking families were tested with a measure of information detection (the Span of Apprehension), sustained attention and inhibition of incorrect responses (the Continuous Performance Test), and ease in handling novel information (verbal analogies test: Marr and Sternberg, 1986) as well as standard tests of intelligence. The results showed that the infant measures were correlated with number of correct responses on one matrix of the Span of Apprehension but not the Continuous Performance Task or the novel relevant items of the verbal analogies task (Sigman et al., 1991). Thus, the results seem to support the first theory that infant fixation duration taps speeded information processing but not the third theory that infant fixation duration reflects facility with novel information.

The findings with respect to inhibition were more ambiguous. Two measures of inhibition were employed, only one of which was associated with infant fixation duration. The Continuous Performance Test was designed to include a task in which the target and nontarget stimuli were reversed after 400 trials. The child had to inhibit responding to the previously correct stimulus and begin responding to the previously incorrect stimulus. Infant fixation duration did not predict score on the reversal phase of the Continuous Performance Test. The other task that required inhibition was the verbal analogies test (Marr and Sternberg, 1986). Subjects had to incorporate novel relevant information into their responses and refrain from attending to irrelevant information. As mentioned above, infant fixation duration was not associated with score on incorporating relevant novel information into the verbal analogies solution, even when the adolescent was told that the information was relevant. However, when the cue was irrelevant and had to be ignored, verbal analogies score was associated with infant fixation duration. Thus, the child's capacity to inhibit responses on tasks requiring logical thinking was predicted by the infant's responses to the unchanging visual target.

The second issue addressed in the 12-year follow-up was whether the rearing environment mediated or moderated the relation between infant attention and childhood intelligence. Many theories of intelligence (e.g., Fagan, 1992) propose that both characteristics of the individual and rearing environments shape individual differences in intellectual capacities and studies of risk infants have supported these theories (Smith et al., 1994). In order to address this question, a measure of the caregiving environment, the frequency with which the mother talked to the infant during a home visit 1 month following the attention assessment, was used in analyses. Infant attention and maternal vocalizations were unrelated but both were independently associated with the children's intelligence at 12 years. The effects of the variables were additive in that the interaction was not significant so that both the infant's style of attending and the caregiver's style of interacting contributed to later intelligence.

To extend these findings, the sample was retested at age 18 with similar measures as had been used at age 12 years. It seemed important to reexamine these results to determine whether the link between early attention and later information detection was sustained over time. In addition, the sample was expanded to include 18-year-olds from all backgrounds, not just the children from English-speaking backgrounds as had been done at age 12 years. Because there had been no association between infant fixation duration and either ability to incorporate novel information into a solution or simple inhibition of response, these tasks were not readministered to the subjects. Instead, the subjects were administered a measure of executive function, the Tower of Hanoi, which is thought to require both the capacity to inhibit prepotent responses and strategic planning ability (Borys et al., 1982; Hayes et al., 1996; Welsh and Pennington, 1988). This task was substituted for the verbal analogies test used at 12 years in order to assess inhibition in a nonverbal context.

Based on the previous findings, the following hypotheses were proposed:

(1) infant fixation duration will be negatively correlated with 18-year intelligence;

(2) infant fixation duration will be negatively correlated with 18-year scores on the Span of Apprehension and the Tower of Hanoi, and these relations will be independent of intelligence;

(3) infant fixation duration will not predict 18-year score on the Continuous Performance Task; and

(4) infant fixation duration and maternal level of vocalization will contribute independently to the prediction of 18-year intelligence.

Method

Participants

The sample was composed of 93 adolescents who had been tested with the infant attention measure and, at least, one of the outcome assessments. Infants in the sample had a mean birthweight of 1895.5 gms. ($SD = 470.54$), mean gestational age at birth of 33 weeks ($SD = 3.2$), and a mean Hollingshead Index of 36.3 ($SD = 15.9$). The majority of subjects were Caucasian with 27 adolescents from families who were predominantly Spanish speaking during their infancy. The sample was not different in terms of birthweight, gestational age at birth, infant attention, or maternal vocalizations from the 33 children who were also followed from birth to two years but were not seen at 18 years of age. However, subjects who returned for testing at 18 years were from families with higher SES background on the Hollingshead index than those who were not tested at age 18 years, $t(124) = 2.57$, $p < .01$.

Procedure

Infant fixation duration.   The infant's attention to a single 2×2 checkerboard was observed for 60 seconds and recorded in half-second intervals when the infant reached expected date of birth (Sigman et al., 1973). In order to minimize the variations due to differences in state, all infants were first tested with a 10-min neurological assessment and then fed a small amount of milk. The interrater correlation in duration of fixation to the stimulus was $r(13) = .92$, $p < .001$.

Maternal vocalization rate.   Assessments of the rearing environment were derived from naturalistic home observations made when the infants were 1, 8, and 24 months of age, with age corrected for the length of prematurity (Beckwith and Cohen, 1984). For the purposes of this study, only the 1-month observation was used in order to keep both the infant and home assessment within the same time period. At 1 month, the infants were observed for an average of 73 min of awake time. The observer used a precoded check list, and every 15 s recorded the presence of a set of infant behaviors, caregiver behaviors, and events defined as contingent or reciprocal interactions between caregiver and child. Observer reliabilities were assessed during 30-min observations of 10 dyads by computing correlation coefficients for the total frequency of a specific behavior each observer had recorded in an observation. The coefficients ranged from .80 to .98 with the majority >.90.

Certain interactive events were selected a priori as indicators of attentive/responsive caregiving and were used in a total score at each age. At 1 month, these were maternal positive attentiveness to the infant, caregiver talks, mutual visual regard, maternal contingency to distress, and the infant held upright. For the purposes of this article, only the percentage of time that the caregiver engaged in talking was considered because this was the only 1-month variable associated with intelligence at 5 and 8 years of age (Beckwith and Cohen, 1984). Vocalization time at 1-month was significantly predictive of vocalization time when the infants were 8 and 24 months corrected age, r (90) = .62, p < .001, and with total caregiving scores at 8 and 24 months of age, r (89) = .44, p < .001 and r (80) = .44, p < .001, respectively. Mothers who vocalized more came from more advantaged families in that there was a significant association between maternal vocalization time and score on the Hollingshead Index, r (90) = .40, p < .001.

Adolescent intelligence.   Intelligence was tested at age 18 years with the WAIS-R (Satz mogel version). The mean IQ of the sample was 101.99 with a *SD* of 15.47 and a range from 71 to 134.

The Span of Apprehension.   The Span of Apprehension was used because it is thought to measure the individual's capacity to detect information that is exposed very briefly (Bartfai et al., 1991). A series of matrices of capital letters was tachistoscopically flashed on a computer screen for 50 ms. Each matrix contained a random array of letters, including either a "T" or an "F," but not both. The subject's task was to determine whether the predesignated target letter was present on each trial. Sets varied in the number of items displayed, including 3, 5, and 10 items, There were 16 matrices randomly presented over 96 trials for each task. The dependent measure was the percentage of trials on which the child was correct. Since there was little variability in scores for sets containing less than 10 items, only scores on the 10-item set were used in analyses.

The Continuous Performance Task.   The Continuous Performance Task seems to assess the capacity to sustain attention to a monotonous task over repeated trials in contrast to the Span of Apprehension which measures the accuracy of information detection with very brief presentations of complex stimuli (Neuchterlein, 1983). This measure was included to assess whether infant attention predicted general childhood attention capacities rather than specific information processing abilities. The subject was required to monitor a screen while a long sequence of rapidly presented random target stimuli was displayed. The paradigm involved the brief (50 ms.), rapid (every 1.0 s) presentation of randomly generated digits from 0–9 on the center of a viewing screen. The subjects's task was to attend and press a button when, and only when, a particular target digit appeared. The task was continued for 480 trials and the number of correct responses (hit rate) was calculated.

The Tower of Hanoi.   The Tower of Hanoi is a task on which the subject has to reproduce a pattern in as few moves as possible. This task is used frequently by neuropsychologists to assess executive function, which is thought to include inhibition, planning, and mental representation of tasks and goals (Eslinger, 1996). Two identical pegboards with three vertical pegs and four rings of different sizes and colors are set up and one is placed in front of the experimenter and one is placed in front of the subject. The subject has to transform his or her configuration to a configuration identical to that of the experimenter.

    The rings on the experimenter's pegboard are arranged on the experimenter's right hand peg to form a tower, with the largest ring on the bottom and the smallest ring on the top. The arrangement of rings presented to the subject differs for each problem. Only one ring can be moved at a time and a larger ring cannot be placed on a smaller ring. The subject has six trials to solve a problem and two consecutive successes are needed for correct solution. Inhibition is required on some of the more difficult problems because the subject needs to move some of the rings initially in the opposite direction from that required ultimately for the solution of the problem. Performance was scored on each problem so that a score of 6 was assigned if the subject succeeded on the first two trials, a score of 5 was assigned if the subject succeeded on the second and third trial, and so forth down to zero. Six different problems were administered to each subject. Subjects were told that this was a measure of how well they could plan or think ahead.

Results

Preliminary analyses were conducted to determine the extent to which abilities assessed on the Span of Apprehension and the Continuous Performance Task were stable across the six years. Results showed that scores on the two matrices of the Span of Apprehension were correlated with the 18 year score on the 10-item matrix, $r(76) = .40$, $p < .0003$, $r(76) = .36$, $p < .0001$ but there was no significant stability across age in scores on the Continuous Performance Task. Moreover, in contrast to 12 years when scores on the Span of Apprehension and Continous Performance Task were correlated, there was no significant association between these scores at 18 years of age.

Correlations were computed between infant fixation duration and scores on the measures administered to the adolescents with probability values based on one-tailed tests. As hypothesized, there was a negative association between fixation duration in infancy and score on the intelligence test, $r(91) = -.36$, $p < .0002$, and Span of Apprehension, $r(85) = -.26$, $p < .007$ administered at 18 years of age. The infant attention measure was not associated with hit rate on the Continuous Performance task. Thus, infant attention seems to be predictive of information detection and not of sustained attention at 18 years of age.

More intelligent 18-year-olds had higher scores on both the Span of Apprehension, $r(87) = .23$, $p < .015$ and the Continuous Performance Task, $r(85) = .25$, $p < .01$. The association between infant fixation duration and score on the Span of Apprehension was independent of intelligence; the correlation between the infant and adolescent scores remained significant even with adolescent intelligence covaried, $r(80) = -.20$, $p < .04$. Similarly, the correlation between infant attention and adolescent intelligence remained significant when score on the Span of Apprehension was covaried, $r(80) = -.31$, $p < .005$.

The Tower of Hanoi was administered to assess the adolescents' capacities for inhibition of prepotent responses and strategic planning in the context of a nonverbal task. Score on the Tower of Hanoi was strongly correlated with IQ, $r(89) = .54$, $p < .001$, but not with score on the Span of Apprehension. Infant fixation duration was negatively associated with score on the Tower of Hanoi, $r(91) = -.32$, $p < .002$, but the correlation was not significant when adolescent intelligence was covaried. However, the association between fixation duration and intelligence remained significant even when score on the Tower of Hanoi was covaried, $r(88) = -.25$, $p < .02$. In a hieracrchical multiple regression, infant fixation duration continued to contribute to the variance in adolescent IQ even after scores on the Span of Apprehension and Tower of Hanoi had been entered, $R^2 = .03$, $F(1, 89) = 3.86$, $p < .053$.

In order to determine whether adolescent intelligence was jointly predicted by infant attention and caregiver vocalizations, two hierarchical multiple regressions were calculated, one with infant fixation duration entered first and the other with rate of caregiver variable entered first. In both cases, the multiple regressions were significant and both variables contributed significantly to the regression, overall $R^2 = .22$. When the interaction term was added to these multiple hierarchical regressions, the interaction term added a small but significant amount, $R^2 = .04$, to the regression, $F(1, 89) = 3.88$, $p < .05$.

In addition, the sample was divided on both measures using a median split and a 2×2 ANOVA was conducted using IQ as the dependent measure. Significant main effects of both factors was modified by a significant interaction between the two, $F(1, 87) = 4.11$, $p < .05$. The caregiving environment clearly moderated the extent of prediction from infant attention to adolescent intelligence (see figure 13.1). Tests of simple main effects revealed that difference in intelligence as a function of infant attention only occurred for the children from homes where caregivers vocalized more to them, $F(1, 87) = 13.58$, $p < .001$, and not for the children from less stimulating homes. Similarly, the difference in intelligence as a function of maternal vocalizations was only significant for the children who showed brief fixation durations, $F(1, 87) = 13.13$, $p < .001$.

Discussion

A major aim of this investigation was to use divergent measures in adolescence to define the processes assessed in infancy. The accomplishment of this aim depends on the extent to which adolescent measures can be found that tap specific processes. However, the identification of the processes involved in most tasks is imprecise, particularly because most tasks measure more than one cognitive process. Moreover, multifaceted tasks are of inherent interest since successful adaptation usually

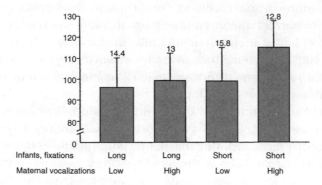

Figure 13.1   Mean IQs at age 18 years as a function of infant attention and caregiver behavior

requires the integration of various capacities. Given these considerations, the answers that can be given to the question in the title of this chapter are necessarily tentative.

Results from the current study replicate what was found previously with a smaller part of this sample, at a younger age, and with somewhat different measures. Infant attention was predictive of adolescent tasks thought to tap information processing ability but not of adolescent measures designed to test the capacity to sustain attention. Thus, the findings at age 12 years were not just chance associations. The association between infant fixation duration and adolescent information detection appears to be fairly specific in that the infant measure does not predict all forms of controlled attention.

The capacity for efficient information detection is clearly not the only form of processing that is shared by the infant attention and childhood intelligence measures. Intelligence continues to be correlated with infant attention even when score on the Span of Apprehension is controlled. The evidence that capacity for inhibition is a shared process cannot be ruled out. At both 12 and 18 years, infant attention was predictive of scores on measures thought to tap the capacity to inhibit prepotent responses in tasks requiring analogical and strategic thinking. The evidence that the association does not persist if intelligence is covaried does not disprove the inhibition hypothesis since intelligence very likely requires some capacities for inhibition of responses.

At the same time, the relation between infant fixation duration and inhibition only seems to hold for tasks that are intellectually challenging.

Infant attention did not predict the simple ability to inhibit responses to a previously correct stimulus and shift to a different stimulus at 12 years of age. Regulating attention to attractive targets may be a challenging task for the very young infant, comparable in degree of cognitive difficulty to a verbal analogies task at age 12 years and the Tower of Hanoi at age 18 years.

Long-term continuity has been identified most frequently in studies of preterm infants. About 20 years ago, we showed that preterm infants tested at term ('term' meaning the maturational age for preterm infants, e.g. for preterm infants born 1 month early, their term test would be at 1 month after birth) looked longer at a single stimulus than full-term infants, that preterm infants tested at four months corrected age showed less preference for novel stimuli when fixed familiarizations time were used, and that preterm infants tested at eight months corrected age explored a familiar object rather than novel objects for longer periods than full-term infants (Sigman, 1976; Sigman et al., 1977; Sigman and Parmelee, 1974). In addition, Rose (1980, 1983) demonstrated that preterm infants as a group required longer familiarization times than full-term infants in order to show preference for novel stimuli. These results suggest that there are more infants who process information slowly within preterm groups than within full-term groups. Followup studies of children born preterm demonstrate that, as a group, they have more learning problems than is true for children born full-term (for reviews, see Friedman and Sigman, 1992). Thus, continuity may be established best by studies of preterm infants because there are a greater number of children who are slow at processing information than is true within full-term groups. Indeed, preterm birth may constitute a risk factor for later cognitive development partly because it is associated with slower processing. Whether early birth causes this outcome, both are markers of some neurological deviance, or both stem from some associated event is completely unknown. However, infant attention measures may be particularly useful predictive tools in samples born preterm.

Early infant characteristics are clearly not the only predictors of later intelligence as shown by the differences in adolescent intelligence as a function of characteristics of the rearing environment. The spread in IQ is about half a standard deviation (98 vs. 106) when either the infants' fixation duration or the caregivers' vocalization rate is used to divide the sample into two parts. When both factors are taken into account, the spread in IQ between the lowest and highest groups becomes nearly 20 points, a very large effect indeed. Thus, the continuity in child abilities seems to be moderated by the environment.

Two explanations for the importance of caregiver vocalization rate seem likely. First, caregiver vocalization rate was a marker in this study for a home rearing environment that continued to be more responsive over the course of the next 2 years of the child's life. Evidence for this is the association between the rate of maternal vocalizations and the quality of the home environment when the infants were 8 and 24 months of age. In addition, caregiver vocalizations may be particularly important for infants in the early months of life. The mother's voice seems to become familiar to the fetus and is preferred over the stranger's voice soon after birth (DeCasper and Fifer, 1980). Thus, it is possible that verbalizations to neonates may have direct advantageous effects on the infants' capacities to organize themselves and respond to the environment.

The effects of variations in the environment on intelligence were only noted among the infants who showed shorter durations of attention. These infants may be more generally mature or specifically able so that they are able to take advantage of their environments, perhaps partly because of the superior abilities reflected in the infant measure. It was also true that infant abilities only differentiated the adolescent groups if the infants had been reared by mothers who vocalized more to them. Thus, infant fixation patterns did not predict later intelligence except for children reared in environments that provided potential advantages.

The evidence from this study shows that characteristics of both the infant and the rearing environment contribute to the individual's long-term intellectual competence (Cohen, 1995). The extent to which these characteristics reflect genetic proclivities or environmental influences is unknown. The attention patterns of infants in this study could have been shaped by genetic factors, fetal experiences or post-birth experiences in the hospital nursery or home, since all infants had been alive for at least one month when they were tested. Similarly, rearing conditions are likely to reflect genetic and nongenetic factors. While the study, then, cannot differentiate on this basis, the results do show that, early in life, the infant and home environment already have characteristics important for future development.

The fact that brief looking times were advantageous in early infancy to unchanging stimuli does not mean that brief fixations are advantageous at all ages and to all stimuli. Optimal attention times vary depending on the characteristics of the child, stimulus, and milieu. This is an important consideration for studies that use infant attention measures as outcomes of various environmental and nutritional interventions.

The issue of continuity has potential practical significance in identifying and intervening with infants at risk of later cognitive dysfunctions. The specification of "looking time" in infancy as a descriptor of information processing is an important first step. While only a small part of the variance in adolescent intelligence is predicted, the fact that a measure that tests preterm infants with the first few months of life is able to predict intelligence 18 years later is remarkable. Moreover, this measure was designed 25 years ago before much was known about infant cognition so it should be possible currently to design much more sensitive predictors. A necessary first step is to determine the extent to which infant looking time is related to speed of processing, efficiency of scanning, and inhibitory ability. The identification of the contributors to infant attention durations should have important implications for the design of assessment measures and possible early interventions.

References

Bartfai, A., Pedersen, N. L., Asarnow, R. F., & Schalling, D. (1991). Genetic factors for the Span of Apprehension: A study of normal twins. *Psychiatry Research, 28,* 115–124.

Beckwith, L., & Cohen, S. E. (1984). Home environment and cognitive competence in preterm children in the first five years. In A. W. Gottfried (Ed.), *Home environment and early mental development* (pp. 235–273). New York: Academic.

Berg, C. A., & Sternberg, R. J. (1985). Response to novelty: Continuity vs. discontinuity in the developmental course of intelligence. In H. W. Reese (Ed.), *Advances in child development and behavior* (Vol. 19, pp. 1–47). Orlando, FL: Academic.

Bornstein, M. H. (1985). How infant and mother jointly contribute to developing cognitive competence in the child. *Proceedings of the National Academy of Science, 82,* 7470–7473.

Bornstein, M. H. (1989). Sensitive periods in development: Structural characteristics and causal interpretations. *Psychological Bulletin, 50,* 130–133.

Bornstein, M. H., & Sigman, M. D. (1986). Continuity in mental development from infancy. *Child Development, 57,* 251–274.

Borys, S. V., Spitz, H. H., & Dorans, B. A. (1982). Tower of Hanoi performance of retarded young adults and nonretarded children as a function of solution length and goal state. *Journal of Experimental Child Psychology, 33*, 87–110.

Bronson, G. W. (1991). Infant differences in rate of visual encoding. *Child Development, 62*, 44–54.

Ceci, S. J. (1990). *On intelligence ... more or less: A bioecological treatise on intellectual development.* Englewood Cliffs, NJ: Prentice Hall.

Cohen, S. E. (1995). Biosocial factors in early infancy as predictors of competence in adolescents who were born prematurely. *Journal of Development and Behavioral Pediatrics, 16*, 36–41.

Colombo, J. (1995). On the neural mechanisms underlying developmental and individual differences in visual fixation in infancy: Two hypotheses. *Developmental Review, 15*, 97–135.

Colombo, J., Freeseman, L. J., Coldren, J. T., & Frick, J. E. (1995). Individual differences in infant fixation duration: Dominance of global versus local stimulus properties. *Cognitive Development, 10*, 271–285.

DeCasper, A. J., & Fifer, W. P. (1980). Of human bonding: Newborns prefer their mothers' voices. *Science, 208*, 1174–1176.

Dreary, I. J. (1995). Auditory inspection time and intelligence: What is the causal direction? *Developmental Psychology, 31*, 237–250.

Eslinger, P. J. (1996). Conceptualizing, describing, and measuring components of executive function: A summary. In G. R. Lyon & N. A. Krasnegor (Eds.), *Attention, memory, and executive function,* (pp. 367–395), Baltimore, MD: Paul Brookes.

Fagan, J. F. (1992). Intelligence: A theoretical viewpoint. *Current Directions in Psychological Science, 1*, 82–86.

Fagan, J. F., & Singer, L. T. (1983), Infant recognition memory as a measure of intelligence. In L. P. Lipsitt (Ed.), *Advances in infancy research* (Vol. 2, pp. 31–78). Norwood, NJ: Ablex.

Freeseman, L. J., Colombo, J., & Coldren, J. T. (1993). Individual differences in infant visual attention: Discrimination and generalization of global and local stimulus properties. *Child Development, 64*, 1191–1203.

Friedman, S., & Sigman, M. D. (Eds.). (1992). *The psychological development of low birthweight children.* Norwood, NJ: Ablex.

Hayes, S. C., Gifford, E. V., & Ruckstuhl, L. E. (1996). Relational frame theory and executive function; a behavioral approach. In G. R. Lyon & N. A. Krasnegor (Eds.), *Attention, memory, and executive function,* (pp. 279–305), Baltimore, MD: Paul Brookes.

Marr, D., & Sternberg, R. J. (1986). Analogical reasoning with nonentrenched concepts: Effects of conceptual novelty on gifted and nongifted students. *Cognitive Development, 1*, 53–72.

McCall, R. B. (1994). What process mediates predictions of childhood IQ from infant habituation and recognition memory? Speculations on the roles of inhibition and rate of information processing. *Intelligence, 18,* 107–125.

McCall, R. B., & Carriger, M. (1993). A meta-analysis of infant habituation and recognition memory performance as predictors of later IQ. *Child Development, 64,* 57–79.

Neuchterlein, K. H. (1983). Signal detection in vigilance tasks and behavioral attributes among offspring of schizophrenic mothers and among hyperactive children. *Journal of Abnormal Psychology, 92,* 4–28.

Rose, S. A. (1980). Enhancing visual recognition memory in preterm infants. *Developmental Psychology, 16,* 89–92.

Rose, S. A. (1983). Differential rates of visual information processing in full-term and preterm infants. *Child Development, 54,* 1189–1198.

Rose, S. A., & Feldman, J. F. (1995). Prediction of IQ and specific cognitive abilities at 11 years from infancy measures. *Developmental Psychology, 31,* 685–696.

Sigman, M. (1976). Early development of preterm and full-term infants: Exploratory behavior in eight-month-olds. *Child Development, 47,* 606–612.

Sigman, M., Cohen, S. E., Beckwith, L., Asarnow, R., & Parmelee, A. H. (1991). Continuity in cognitive abilities from infancy to 12 years of age. *Cognitive Development, 6,* 47–57.

Sigman, M., Kopp, C. B., Littman, B., & Parmelee, A. H. (1977). Infant visual attentiveness in relation to birth condition. *Developmental Psychology, 13,* 431–437.

Sigman, M., Kopp, C. B., Parmelee, A. H., & Jeffrey, W. E. (1973). Visual attention and neurological organization in neonates. *Child Development, 44,* 461–466.

Sigman, M., & Parmelee, A. H. (1974). Visual preferences of four-month-old preterm and full-term infants. *Child Development, 45,* 959–965.

Smith, L., Ulvund, S. E., & Lindemann, R. (1994). Very low birth weight infants (<1,501 g) at double risk. *Journal of Developmental & Behavioral Pediatrics, 15,* 7–13.

Vernon, P. A. (1987). *Speed of information processing and intelligence.* Norwood, NJ: Ablex.

Welsh, M. C., & Pennington, B. F. (1988). Assessing frontal lobe functioning in children: Views from developmental psychology. *Developmental Neuropsychology, 4,* 199–230.

Introduction to Part IV

Human infants are social beings from the start. They are reared in a social environment during the fetal period when their mothers talk to them and feel fetal movements that may appear to be responses to their mothers' stimulation (chapter 4). As soon as they are born, parents talk to their babies, touch them, and try to engage them in face-to-face conversations. Most infants are immersed in multimodal *social* stimulation during waking hours, especially when they are eating. Parents are delighted when their babies seem to react to their social stimulation by returning their gaze, imitating their facial gestures (chapter 9), and later on vocalizing and smiling at them (i.e., the face-to-face interaction procedures discussed in chapter 7).

The papers in this section present experiments on various aspects of social development and communication during infancy. In chapter 14, Papoušek et al. describe the special language adults use when they talk to infants, known as "baby talk." They discovered that by 4 months of age, babies not only prefer infant- over adult-directed speech, they would rather listen to "naturally approving" than "naturally disapproving" messages. By 6 months of age, infants show some comprehension of the meaning of words. Tincoff and Jusczyk (chapter 15) discover that infants associate at least two words selectively – the names that refer to each of their parents. Infants looked longer at the silent videos of their mothers' faces than videos of their fathers' faces when they heard a stranger repeating "mommy"; the opposite occurred when the stranger said "daddy."

Infants attend to their parents, and other adults, for a number of reasons. As shown in chapter 16, when infants are faced with an ambiguous situation they look at an adult to find out how they should proceed. This is called social referencing. Sorce, et al.'s classic study shows that when infants are uncertain about whether or not to cross a "visual cliff" they will stop if the mother poses a fearful facial expression and will cross the cliff if she poses joy. Social referencing helps the baby find out what is safe and what is dangerous without having to experience the outcome.

Infants also reference, or closely observe, adult activities for other reasons. For example, they learn language and various motor skills in part by imitation (e.g., mimicking words and using tools such as spoons and cups). In chapter 17, we learn that by 14 months of age, infants not only readily copy a stranger's actions on objects, but they are more likely to copy these actions if the act appears to be *intentional* rather than *accidental*. Carpenter et al. showed that infants could infer adult intentionality by the adult's verbal comments: "There" for a correct action and "Woops" for a mistake. Thus, infants may be able to "read another's mind" early in the second year of life.

While social infants are very interested in watching and learning from people in general, they develop a special relationship with their primary caregiver, usually the mother. According to Attachment Theory, mothers protect their infants and provide a secure base for them to explore a potentially dangerous world. When infants become afraid, they search for the mother to provide security and once they are reassured by her presence they are free to engage in exploratory behavior. While the onset of this selective attachment to a parent is not fixed, around 1 year of age most infants show their dependence on the caretaker by "making strange" (i.e., showing caution or fear when strangers approach them). Many infants will protest vigorously when their mothers leave them in an unfamiliar setting; when the mothers return, their infants usually approach them and want to be held (become physically attached) before resuming their play. Infants who respond this way (about $\frac{2}{3}$ of infants in normative samples) are considered to be *securely attached* to parents who are responsive to their needs. The other $\frac{1}{3}$ are insecurely attached: "Avoidant" infants ignore their parents while "Resistant" infants may not be easily consoled by the parent, alternating between clinging and crying and pushing the parent away. The different patterns of primary attachment relationships have been related to different types of parenting. Also they appear to have an important influence on future social relationships, including romantic relationships in adulthood. As shown by Benoit and Parker's study (chapter 18) the different types of attachment relationships may be transmitted from one generation to the next.

The last paper in this reader deals with a variety of infant social abilities including: the ability to use eye contact in social engagements, to exhibit joint attention and social referencing, to engage in various types of play, and to develop empathy. This paper compares the use of social cues by typical infants with infants having developmental delays and autism. The autistic infants are of particular interest because they usually are not identified until early childhood, when they fail to develop language and social skills. Their lack of language and seeming aversion to making eye contact with other people has led theorists such as Simon Baron-Cohen to suggest that they may be missing a neural module in the brain which specializes in reading and interpreting another person's eye-direction. This would make it difficult for autistic children to form a theory of mind. The search is now on to develop effective early diagnosis and treatment for this unusual group of infants, and in chapter 19 Charman et al. present one of the first prospective studies in pursuit of this goal.

FOURTEEN

Infant-Directed Speech

Introduction

In their classic chapter in the *Handbook of Infant Development*, Hanus and Mechthild Papoušek (1987) review their pioneering work on the nature of early caretaker-infant interactions and point out that the "social stimulation provided to the infant by caregivers is rich, multimodal, and reciprocal" (p. 674). Several aspects of caregiver responses to infants appear to be typical and automatic – part of a process the Papoušeks called "intuitive parenting."

One striking example of intuitive parenting is the form of speech adults use when they talk to infants during face-to-face interactions (which they do almost all of the time; e.g., Ellsworth et al., 1993), known as "baby talk," "motherese," or "infant-directed speech." The differences between infant- and adult-directed speech are numerous; they include a higher pitch, exaggerated pitch contours, slower tempo and a kind of sing-song rhythm (e.g., Bergeson and Trehub, 1999; Trainor and Zacharias, 1998). You can readily observe this when, for example, you see a baby in the check-out line in a grocery store – when parents and strangers (even children) approach the infant they will automatically address the infant in baby talk.

Young infants appear to be especially tuned into baby talk – when given the choice, they prefer to listen to it over adult-directed-speech (Fernald, 1985). In the paper selected for this book, Papoušck et al. (1990) demonstrate that by 4 months of age infants not only prefer baby talk, but they prefer baby talk that carries a particular message – approving over disapproving infant-directed speech. Papoušek et al. stripped away the linguistic content of exemplars of the two types of speech to produce prototypical *melodic* contours of each type. Infants were tested using a variation on the infant preferential looking procedure discussed earlier – they saw pictures of two different faces, next to each other.

Whenever infants looked at one face, the approving speech contour was played – looking at the other face turned on the disapproving speech type. They also included a clever control manipulation – both types of contours also were played backwards on some trials – giving melodic contour types with equal peak frequencies, frequency ranges, and durations, but opposite dynamic patterns of change. The results were clear-cut. Infants looked much longer at the faces associated with the approving speech contour than any of the other three contour types. Thus, melodic prototypes may carry meaningful affective messages for infants.

References

Bergeson, T., and Trehub, S. (1999). Mothers' singing to infants and preschool children. *Infant Behavior & Development*, *22*, 51–64.

Ellsworth, C., Muir, D., and Hains, S. (1993). Social competence and person-object differentiation: An analysis of the still-face effect. *Developmental Psychology*, *29*, 63–73.

Fernald, A. (1985). Four-month-old infants prefer to listen to motherese. *Infant Behavior & Development*, *8*, 181–195.

Papoušek, H., and Papoušek, M. (1987). Intuitive parenting: A dialectic counterpart to the infant's integrative competence. In Joy Osofsky (ed.) *Handbook of Infant Development. 2nd Edition.* (pp. 669–720). New York: Wiley.

Trainor, L., and Zacharias, C. (1998). Infants prefer higher-pitched singing. *Infant Behavior & Development*, *21*, 799–806.

Infant Responses to Prototypical Melodic Contours in Parental Speech

Mechthild Papoušek, Marc H. Bornstein,
Chiara Nuzzo, Hanuš Papoušek, and
David Symmes

Parents and other caretakers, across diverse cultures and languages, often use a special prosodic register when communicating with infants and even with newborns, who are not expected to process linguistic information (e.g., Ferguson, 1964; Fernald et al., 1989; M. Papoušek et al., 1985). Specifically, they raise and expand the range of their overall speech frequency and exaggerate intonation contours of individual utterances. Moreover, young infants appear to listen attentively to and prefer this infant-directed speech, especially its expanded melodic contours (Fernald and Kuhl, 1987).

The type and acoustic configuration of melodic contours in such speech also correlate with mothers' caregiving, particularly in relation to arousing/soothing, turn-opening/turn-closing, and approving/disapproving utterances (H. Papoušek et al., 1986). For instance, unidirectional rising contours prevail in contexts of encouraging infant visual attention or vocal response (Ryan 1978; Stern et al., 1982), and unidirectional falling contours at low pitch prevail in contexts of soothing distress (Fernald et al., 1989; M. Papoušek et al., 1985).

Kearsley (1973) reported that newborns display orienting responses to slower rise times in the intensity of auditory stimuli (as present in approving contours), whereas they display defensive reactions to faster rise times (as present in disapproving contours). Sullivan and Horowitz (1983) evaluated effects of rising and falling contours in female, male, and synthetic vocal signals on visual attention in 2-month-olds in an

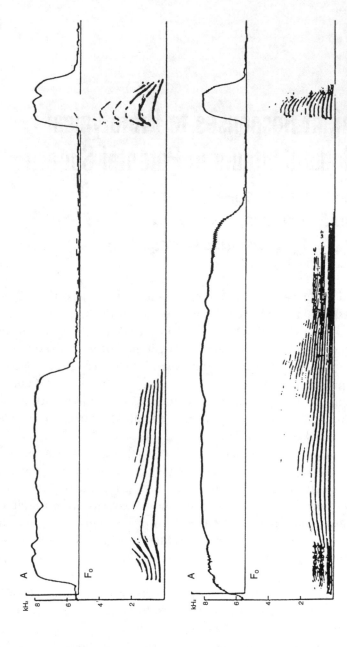

Figure 14.1 Spectograms (Kaye Elemetrics 7800 Digital Sonagraph, frequency range 0–8 kHz bandwidth 45 Hz) of the natural female (*top*) and male (*bottom*) approving (*left*) and disapproving (*right*) melodic contours. The amplitude contour (A) is displayed in the upper third of the spectogram

infant-control auditory-preference design. Only the female rising contour attracted infants. However, infants might also have been influenced by a wider pitch range and an elevated maximum pitch in that contour.

The present study analyzed whether visual behavior in 4-month-olds is influenced by specific types of rising-falling contours used by adults in "approving" and "disapproving" contexts. Based on mothers' pragmatic use of these contours in naturalistic contexts, infants were predicted to look longer at a picture of an adult face associated with an approving contour and shorter at an identical picture associated with a disapproving contour.

Thirty-two infants (17 male, 15 female) with a mean age of 123 days participated (range = 106–137; SD = 8.82). All were term and healthy at birth and had no known neurological or physical impairments (M birth weight = 3.66 kg; M birth length = 52.32 cm).

The experiment included two conditions identical in procedure; one used female and the other, male visual and auditory stimuli. Sixteen infants participated in each condition. Each condition was divided into two segments: One consisted of naturally occurring approving or disapproving sound contours, and the other consisted of temporally reversed equivalents of those same contours. Each of the two segments included a pretest, a 10-trial test, and a posttest.

The auditory stimuli were natural female and male adult vocal sounds without any linguistic segmental information (nasalized, central vowel-like sound /ə/). Each consisted of a rising-falling contour: one slow, as used in approving infant-directed speech, and one fast, as used in disapproving infant-directed speech. These sounds were produced by two of the authors (M.P. and H.P. – a mother and father who have the added benefit of many years' experience in the scientific study of babytalk) to an imagined infant after having been instructed, first, to praise the infant for pleasant cooing sounds and, next, to prevent the infant from carrying out a dangerous movement. Stimuli were digitized by computer; for sonagraphic displays, see figure 14.1. Peak frequencies were more than 1 octave higher in female approving (FA = 831 Hz) and disapproving (FD = 848 Hz) contours than in male approving (MA = 344 Hz) and disapproving (MD = 345 Hz) contours. Expressed in semitones, differences in frequency ranges were negligible (FA = 21; FD = 21; MA = 17; MD = 15). However, approving contours were longer (FA = 1287 ms and MA = 2267 ms vs. FD = 331 ms and MD = 235 ms), and disapproving contours showed steeper slopes (duration of rising slope: FA = 327 ms and MA = 389 ms vs. FD = 49 ms and MD = 36 ms) and more spectral energy above 2 kHz. Stimuli were copied onto a tape with 1.5-s ISIs, with approving contours on one track, disapproving contours on the other. Exact reverse copies served as controls. Reverse contours did not differ in peak frequency, frequency range, or in duration, however, they did differ in the dynamics of rising and falling slopes and spectral energy.

Alone in an experimental room, infants were placed in a standard infant car seat approximately 66 cm in front of a 90 cm × 75 cm white screen. The visual stimuli were slide pairs projected at infant eye level and subtending visual angles of approximately 21° each. The auditory stimuli were presented at normal conversational level through a speaker centrally located relative to the infant. The infant's face was photographed through a circular opening in the screen. The experimenter observed the infant's face on a TV monitor in an adjoining control room. A small signal light built into the projection screen was used to fixate the infant's gaze centrally before each trial. When the infant fixated, the visual stimuli were projected onto the screen.

The pretest stimulus, a black-and-white check pattern, was presented for 15 s and included no auditory signal. On each test trial, infants were shown a pair of adult faces for 15 s. Auditory stimuli were presented using an infant-control procedure: when the infant turned to the left image, the experimenter presented the auditory stimulus pre-matched to the left side; when the infant turned to the right image, the experimenter presented the auditory stimulus pre-matched to the right. If infants looked centrally or closed their eyes, no auditory stimulation was presented. After the tenth test trial, the posttest (identical to the pretest) was presented. There was then a pause during which the experimenter reset the apparatus and the parent played with the infant. Half the infants heard "normal contours" first, and half heard "reverse contours" first.

Each infant's visual regard was scored for total look time, first look time, and latency to first look for each stimulus on each trial, typical attention-holding and -getting measures (Cohen, 1973). Interrater reliabilities (r) for scoring 20% of the sample averaged .87.

These temporal variables were analyzed for the female and male voices separately and were combined by planned comparisons. Figure 14.2 shows the results for total looking. As can be seen, for the

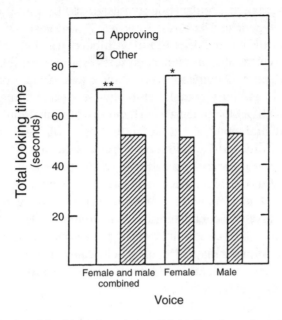

Figure 14.2 Total looking time (seconds) to female and male combined, female, and male naturally approving versus naturally disapproving, reverse-approving, and reverse-disapproving melodic contours (*$p \le .05$; **$p \le .01$)

female and male voices combined, the naturally approving pattern recruited more attention from infants than did the naturally disapproving and reverse-approving and reverse-disapproving patterns combined, $F(1,31) = 6.90$, $p = .01$. The same was true for the female voice, $F(1,15) = 5.40$, $p = .04$. The exact same patterns of results held for the durations of infants' first looks. Latency data showed the reciprocal trend: the naturally approving pattern showed a tendency to recruit infants' attention more quickly than the other patterns. Planned comparisons contrasting naturally disapproving with the other three patterns combined showed the reciprocal pattern of results.

Infants looked equally to the left and right on the pretest and posttest in the female and male voice conditions. Thus, the differential recruitment of attention during auditory stimulus presentations reflected stimulus control over infant visual behavior.

Prototypical approving and disapproving rising-falling contours from infant-directed speech differentially affected preferential visual behavior in 4-month-old infants independent of linguistic information and other contextual or acoustic features. Approving contours recruited infant looking, and disapproving contours inhibited it. The universality of these prototypical contours across sex (mothers and fathers) and cultures (German, American, and Mandarin Chinese mothers) was reported by H. Papoušek et al. (1986). These data extend existing evidence that high pitch and expanded melodic contours in infant-directed speech elicit and maintain infant attention (Culp and Boyd, 1975; Fernald and Kuhl, 1987). Such prototypes may also play a central role in infants' organization of speech categories (Bornstein, 1984, 1987; Grieser and Kuhl, 1989). The results further suggest that individual melodic prototypes may carry meaningful caregiving messages for infants. The fact that female contours were more effective than male contours might reflect lower sensory thresholds in infants for the frequency span of female voices (see Schneider et al., 1980) or more frequent, richer, or pleasant experiences with mothers during the first 4 months of life.

References

Bornstein, M. H. (1984). A descriptive taxonomy of psychological categories used by infants. In C. Sophian (Ed.), *Origins of cognitive skills*. Hillsdale, NJ: Erlbaum.

Bornstein, M. H. (1987). Perceptual categories in vision and in audition. In S. Harnad (Ed.), *Categorical perception*. New York: Cambridge University Press.

Cohen, L. B. (1973). A two-process model of infant visual attention. *Merrill-Palmer Quarterly, 19*, 157–180.

Culp, R. E., & Boyd, E. F. (1975). Visual fixation and the effect of voice quality and content differences in 2-month-old infants. In F. D. Horowitz (Ed.), *Monographs of the Society for Research in Child Development, 39* (Serial No. 158).

Ferguson, C. A. (1964). Baby talk in six languages. *American Anthropologist, 66*, 103–114.

Fernald, A., & Kuhl, P. K. (1987). Acoustic determinants of infant preference for motherese speech. *Infant Behavior and Development, 10*, 279–293.

Fernald, A., Taeschner, T., Dunn, J., Papoušek, M., Boysson-Bardies, B., & Fukui, I. (1989). A cross-language study of prosodic modifications in mothers' and fathers' speech to preverbal infants. *Journal of Child Language, 16*, 977–1001.

Grieser, D., & Kuhl, P. K. (1989). Categorization of speech by infants: Support for speech-sound prototypes. *Developmental Psychology, 25*, 577–588.

Kearsley, R. B. (1973). The newborn response to auditory stimulation: A demonstration of orienting and defensive behavior. *Child Development, 44*, 582–590.

Papoušek, H., Papoušek, M., & Koester, L. S. (1986). Sharing emotionality and sharing knowledge: A microanalytic approach to parent–infant communication. In C. E. Izard & P. B. Read (Eds.), *Measuring emotions in infants and children* (Vol. 2). New York: Cambridge University Press.

Papoušek, M., Papoušek, H., & Bornstein, M. H. (1985). The naturalistic vocal environment of young infants: On the significance of homogeneity and variability in parental speech. In T. M. Field & N. A. Fox (Eds.), *Social perception in infants*. Norwood, NJ: Ablex.

Ryan, M. L. (1978). Contour in context. In R. N. Campbell & P. T. Smith (Eds.), *Recent advances in the psychology of language*. New York: Plenum.

Schneider, B. A., Trehub, S. E., & Bull, D. (1980). High frequency sensitivity in infants. *Science, 207,* 1003–1004.

Stern, D. N., Spieker, S., & MacKain, K. (1982). Intonation contours as signals in maternal speech to prelinguistic infants. *Developmental Psychology, 18,* 727–735.

Sullivan, J. W., & Horowitz, F. D. (1983). The effects of intonation on infant attention: The role of the rising intonation contour. *Journal of Child Language, 10,* 521–534.

FIFTEEN

Early Word Comprehension

Introduction

In most textbooks the onset of true word comprehension, the association of a specific word with a specific object, is placed at about 12 months of age. However, this age milestone is derived from laboratory studies that test the ability of infants to apply verbal labels to immobile objects with varying degrees of familiarity. Tincoff and Jusczyk (1999) demonstrate that infants actually show some word comprehension at a much earlier age when one uses a familiar name which labels a very significant, animated object – their parents.

Tincoff and Jusczyk also used a variation of the preferential looking procedure. They presented infants with side-by-side, silent videotape replays of their mothers and fathers watching the news. Each trial lasted 10 seconds. The time infants spent looking at each parent on silent, baseline trials was compared to that for naming trials when an unfamiliar voice repeated "mommy" on some trials and "daddy" on other trials. Infants spent longer looking at the named parent, relative to baseline. When the experiment was repeated using videotapes of unfamiliar parents, the names failed to direct the infants' visual attention. These words appear to specify the infants' parents, rather than the general category of male and female.

Some Beginnings of Word Comprehension in 6-Month-Olds

Ruth Tincoff and Peter W. Jusczyk

Learning words is critical for acquiring language. Word learning depends on component skills such as the ability to perceive and represent objects and events, the ability to extract and remember sound patterns of potential words, and some capacity to link sounds and meanings appropriately. Considerable evidence shows that even infants between 3 and 6 months of age perceive and represent some objects and events (Mandler, 1997; Quinn and Eimas, 1996; Spelke, et al., 1992). As for the second skill, several recent investigations have reported that infants begin to demonstrate the capacity to segment words from fluent speech at about 8 months of age (Echols et al., 1997; Jusczyk and Aslin, 1995; Saffran et al., 1996). Moreover, infants at this age retain information about the sound patterns of words for as long as 2 weeks (Jusczyk and Hohne, 1997). However, when infants actually begin to link sound patterns with particular meanings is less clear.

Laboratory testing procedures typically fix the onset of word comprehension at 11 to 13 months (Oviatt, 1980; Thomas et al., 1981; Woodward et al., 1994). However, it has also been shown that 9-month-olds who hear a spoken word, as opposed to a tone, paired with a particular object are more apt to attend to other objects from the same category than to ones from a different category (Balaban and Waxman, 1997). The latter age is consistent with estimates of the onset of word comprehension derived from descriptions of when infants respond appropriately to verbal commands in naturalistic or semistructured settings (Benedict, 1979; Huttenlocher, 1974). However, because previous studies focused mostly on words referring to immobile objects of varying familiarity to infants, these investigations may underestimate early word-learning abilities. It is possible that younger infants associate words with objects when these words refer to animated individuals who are socially important to them, such as their own parents.

Infants appear to be especially attentive to sound patterns that are used in conjunction with highly salient social figures. Although they may not attach a referent to their own names yet, 4.5-month-olds listen significantly longer to repetitions of their own names than of other infants' names (Mandel et al., 1995). By comparison, they do not attend differentially to other frequently occurring words, such as "baby," until 6 months of age (Mandel and Jusczyk, 1997). Similarly, infants detect their own names in fluent speech sooner (6 months) than they can detect other kinds of familiarized words (7.5 months) (Mandel, 1996).

In the present study, we tested the hypothesis that the process of learning to associate sounds and meanings may occur sooner for words referring to salient social figures in infants' lives than for words referring to immobile objects. We examined whether 6-month-olds have learned to associate the labels "mommy" and "daddy" correctly to their own parents. We chose these labels because they are the ones parents visiting our laboratory report using most frequently. We used the intermodal preferential-looking paradigm (Golinkoff et al., 1987), presenting infants with side-by-side videos of their parents while audio presentations of the word "mommy" or "daddy" were played. We predicted that if the infants had already associated each of these sound patterns with the appropriate parent, they would attend longer to the video of the parent named on the audio than to the unnamed parent (i.e., when listening to repetitions of "daddy," they would look longer at the father's than at the mother's video, and when listening to repetitions of "mommy," they would look longer at the mother's video than at the father's video).

Experiment 1

Method

Participants. Twenty-four 6-month-olds (10 females, 14 males; mean age: 6 months, 11 days) from monolingual English-speaking homes were tested. Eight other infants were tested, but excluded because of crying ($n = 7$) or experimenter error ($n = 1$). Informed consent was obtained from the parents of all participants.

Procedure. Each parent was videotaped separately against a white background while watching the same videotaped news story in a small room. During testing, these videos were played on identical videotape players and monitors. A DECtalk speech synthesizer, in the voice of "Kit the Kid," produced the audio presentations of "mommy" and "daddy." This synthetic voice simulates that of a 10-year-old without discernible gender qualities. It was chosen because previous studies indicated that infants look more toward males when hearing a male voice and more toward females when hearing a female voice (Walker-Andrews et al., 1991). We surveyed the parents for the names they used to refer to themselves. The names for mother were "mommy" ($n = 19$), "mama" ($n = 3$), and "mom" ($n = 2$); the names for father were "daddy" ($n = 20$), "dad," ($n = 3$), and "papa" ($n = 1$).

During testing, each infant sat on a parent's lap facing a white wall with openings for two television monitors, a video camera, and a speaker. The parent wore a visor with a piece of thick black felt, which blocked any view of the monitors. The experimenter stood behind the wall to control the stimulus presentation and viewed the infant through the camera. She judged when the infant visually fixated a blinking orange light located between the television monitors to initiate a trial, raised and lowered an opaque screen that concealed the monitors from the infants' view between trials, and signaled the computer for the next trial. Both the parent and the experimenter were blind to the conditions of the video presentation. The test session was recorded on videotape for later off-line coding. The experimenter and another observer, also blind to the conditions of the video presentation, coded the videotapes of the infants' test sessions with the sound turned off. Fixations were measured from the onset of the first to the offset of the last auditory stimulus, indicated by illumination of a small light. Reliability checks for judging the amount of time an infant was oriented to each side (Monitor 1 or 2) on each trial yielded reliability coefficients greater than .90.

Infants were tested with videos of their own mothers and fathers. The experiment had three phases: four silent pretest trials, four silent baseline trials, and eight test trials with audio presentations (four with "mommy" and four with "daddy," randomized into two test blocks).

Each trial lasted for 10 s. The silent pretest trials acquainted the infant with the location of each parent's video (e.g., father on right, mother on left). Only one monitor was illuminated on these trials. By comparison, on silent baseline trials, both monitors were illuminated for the full trial duration. These trials served as a check on whether an infant displayed any inherent preference for one video over the other. Finally, on test trials, both monitors were illuminated, but with accompanying audio consisting of 10 acoustically varied tokens of either "mommy" or "daddy." The auditory stimuli emanated from a loudspeaker centered below the two video monitors. Side of presentation for each parent and location of the video presented first in the pretest were counterbalanced across infants.

Results

Because infants did not always look at the video displays during test trials, data analyses were based on the proportion of time on a given trial that infants spent looking at each parent. We calculated a baseline difference score for each infant based on the mean looking times on the four silent baseline trials (positive differences = preference for the mother's video; negative differences = preference for the father's video). An analysis of the baseline proportional looking times indicated that 15 of the infants looked longer at the mother ($M = .281$, $SD = .249$) and 9 looked longer at the father ($M = -.434$, $SD = .207$). An unpaired t test confirmed that these groups had significantly different looking biases, $t(22) = 7.387$, $p < .001$. Consequently, for the test trials, we compared infants' proportional looking times to the named and unnamed parents' videos, adjusting for an infant's preference during the silent baseline period. Therefore, the proportional looking times on the test trials (i.e., to mother's video when named, father's video when named, mother's video when unnamed, and father's video when unnamed) were divided by the corresponding proportional looking times on the silent baseline trials (i.e., to mother's video on baseline or to father's video on baseline).

We submitted these scores to a repeated measures analysis of variance (ANOVA) of a 2 (video: named parent vs. unnamed parent) × 2 (test item: "mommy" vs. "daddy") design. This analysis revealed a significant main effect of video $F(1, 23) = 5.339$, $p < .05$. As shown in figure 15.1, infants looked more at the parent being named than at the

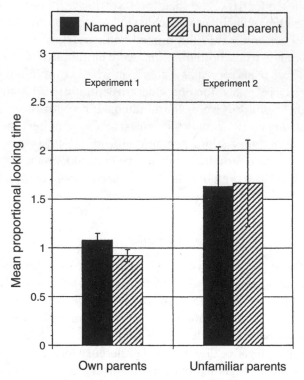

Figure 15.1 Mean proportional looking time (and standard error bars), adjusted for baseline preference, for the videos of named and unnamed parents in Experiments 1 and 2. Proportions greater than 1.0 indicate greater attention to the video in the test period compared with the baseline period

unnamed parent ($M_{named} = 1.077$, $SD = 0.473$; $M_{unnamed} = 0.921$, $SD = 0.437$). Neither the main effect of test item nor the interaction between video and test item was statistically significant. Overall, 18 of the 24 infants had longer looking times for the named than for the unnamed parent ($p < .025$ by a sign test).

Further confirmation that the infants associated each name with the appropriate parent comes from an examination of first-look data during the test trials. Across all eight trials, the tendency to look first toward the named parent did not significantly differ from chance, $t(23) = 1.320$, $p > .10$, $M = .536$, $SD = .135$. However, a finer breakdown of the data indicated that significantly more first looks were made to the named parent in the first half of the test session, $t(23) = 2.145$, $p < .05$, $M = .583$, $SD = .190$, but not in the second half, $t(23) = -.371$, $p > .70$, $M = .490$, $SD = .138$.

Experiment 2

The results of the first experiment indicated that infants responded to the auditory labels by looking more toward the named parent. However, before we could conclude that 6-month-olds have learned the correct links between "mommy" and "daddy" and their parents, we had to rule out another possibility. When infants begin producing words, they often overextend labels to objects not included in the adult category (Behrend, 1988; Clark, 1983). Thus, "dog" may be used to name sheep and cows, as well as canines. Is it possible that younger infants extend "mommy" to include all women, and "daddy" to include all men? To explore this possibility, we tested another group of 6-month-olds with the same parent videos used in Experiment 1. If 6-month-olds do overextend "mommy" and "daddy" to other women and men, the infants should have looked more toward the female in response to "mommy" and more toward the male in response to "daddy."

Method

Participants. Twenty-four 6-month-olds (12 females, 12 males; mean age: 6 months, 5 days) from monolingual English-speaking homes were tested. An additional 7 infants were tested, but excluded because of equipment failure ($n = 3$), crying ($n = 2$), failure to look at the displays ($n = 1$), and not being correctly centered on the parent's lap ($n = 1$). Informed consent was obtained from the parents of all participants.

Procedure. The procedure was the same as in the previous experiment. The names that parents used for mother were "mommy" ($n = 20$), "mama" ($n = 3$), and "mom" ($n = 1$); the names for father were "daddy" ($n = 21$), dada" ($n = 2$), and "dad" ($n = 1$).

Results

The data were scored and analyzed as in Experiment 1. The baseline proportional looking times indicated that 9 of the infants looked longer to the females ($M = .310$, $SD = .249$) and 15 looked longer to the males ($M = -.434$, $SD = .207$). The looking biases of these groups differed significantly, $t(22) = 7.91$, $p < .001$. Thus, the data were adjusted for the preferences shown during the baseline period. A repeated measures ANOVA indicated that neither main effect nor their interaction was significant. Most important, the main effect of video was not significant, $F(1, 23) < 1.00$, indicating that infants did not look more toward the unfamiliar father in response to "daddy" and the unfamiliar mother in response to "mommy" ($M_{named} = 1.63$, $SD = 2.93$; $M_{unnamed} = 1.66$, $SD = 3.19$; see figure 15.1). Overall, 10 of the 24 infants had longer looking times for the named than for the unnamed parent ($p > .50$ by a sign test). The lack of significant differences between the named and unnamed video occurred in all analyses of the first-look data (across all the test trials: $t[23] = 0.00$; in the first half of the test trials: $t[23] = 1.24$, $p > .20$; in the second half of the test trials: $t[23] = -1.55$; $p > .10$).

To confirm that the tendency to look toward the named video occurred only for infants' own parents, we combined the proportional looking-time data from both experiments for an ANOVA of a 2 (group: own parents vs. unfamiliar parents) × 2 (video: named parent vs. unnamed parent) × 2 (test item: "mommy" vs. "daddy") design. The critical interaction of Group × Video was marginally significant, $F(1, 46) = 3.753$, $p = .059$. None of the other interactions or main effects approached significance. Similarly, the overall number of infants with longer looking times to the named videos was significantly greater in Experiment 1 than in Experiment 2, $\chi^2(1, N = 48) = 4.2$, $p < .05$. Therefore, it appears that 6-month-olds initially attach the words "mommy" and "daddy" to their own parents, and not to women and men in general.

General Discussion

The present findings demonstrate that infants begin to link sound patterns with meanings at 6 months of age, considerably earlier than previously thought (Bates et al., 1992; Benedict, 1979; Huttenlocher,

1974; Oviatt, 1980; Thomas et al., 1981). A critical difference compared with earlier studies is that the words we used named salient social figures for the infants. Although it may take several more months for infants to attach labels more widely to other kinds of objects in their environment, our findings suggest that infants may begin to form their lexicons by linking sound patterns to socially significant figures, such as their parents.

Recent investigations have shown that early in the second half of their first year, infants have some prerequisites needed to develop a lexicon, such as the abilities to segment (Echols et al., 1997; Jusczyk and Aslin, 1995; Saffran et al., 1996) and encode (Jusczyk and Hohne, 1997) the sound patterns of words. Thus, infants are developing the capacities necessary for dealing with the sound patterns of words. The present findings indicate that 6-month-olds are beginning to take the next critical step in lexical development by linking sound patterns to specific meanings. Ultimately, the relation between sound patterns and what they name becomes considerably more abstract and complex than linking "mommy" and "daddy" to one's parents. Learners have to go beyond attaching a name to a specific individual; they must discover that linguistic labels apply to whole classes of objects. Nevertheless, the general principle that sound patterns can be used to symbolize meanings may be discovered by first learning to attach names to specific individuals, such as one's own parents. The full extent of 6-month-olds' abilities to attach labels to other significant individuals and objects in their environment remains to be determined, as does the point at which they begin to use labels to stand for classes of objects.

References

Balaban, M. T., & Waxman, S. R. (1997). Do words facilitate object categorization in 9-month-old infants? *Journal of Experimental Child Psychology, 64,* 3–26.

Bates, E., Thal, D., & Janowsky J. S. (1992). Early language development and its neural correlates. In S. J. Segalowitz & I. Rapin (Eds.), *Handbook of neuropsychology* (Vol. 7, pp. 69–110). New York: Elsevier Science.

Behrend, D. A. (1988). Overextensions in early language comprehension: Evidence from a signal detection approach. *Journal of Child Language, 15,* 63–75.

Benedict, H. (1979). Early lexical development: Comprehension and production, *Journal of Child Language, 6,* 183–200.

Clark, E. V. (1983). Meanings and concepts. In J. H. Flavell & E. M. Markman (Eds.), *Cognitive development* (Vol. III, pp. 787–840). New York: Wiley.

Echols, C. H., Crowhurst, M. J., & Childers, J. B. (1997). Perception of rhythmic units in speech by infants and adults. *Journal of Memory and Language, 36,* 202–225.

Golinkoff, R., Hirsh-Pasek, K., Cauley, K., & Gordon L. (1987). The eyes have it: Lexical and syntactic comprehension in a new paradigm. *Journal of Child Language, 14,* 23–45.

Huttenlocher, J. (1974). The origins of language comprehension. In R. L. Solso (Ed.), *Theories in cognitive psychology* (pp. 331–368). New York: Wiley.

Jusczyk, P. W., & Aslin, R. N. (1995). Infants' detection of sound patterns of words in fluent speech. *Cognitive Psychology, 29,* 1–23.

Jusczyk, P. W., & Hohne, E. A. (1997). Infants' memory for spoken words. *Science, 277,* 1984–1986.

Mandel, D. R. (1996). *Names as early lexical candidates: Helpful in language processing?* Unpublished doctoral dissertation, State University of New York, Buffalo.

Mandel, D. R., & Jusczyk, P. W. (1997, April). *Infants' early words: Familiar people and the changing nature of name representations.* Paper presented at the biennial meeting of the Society for Research in Child Development, Washington, DC.

Mandel, D. R., Jusczyk, P. W., & Pisoni, D. B. (1995). Infants' recognition of the sound patterns of their own names. *Psychological Science, 6,* 315–318.

Mandler, J. M. (1997). Representation. In D. Kuhn & R. S. Siegler (Eds.), *Handbook of child psychology: Vol. 2. Cognition, perception, and language* (5th ed., pp. 255–308). New York: Wiley.

Oviatt, S. L. (1980). The emerging ability to comprehend language: An experimental approach. *Child Development, 51,* 97–106.

Quinn, P. C., & Eimas, P. D. (1996). Perceptual organization and categorization in young infants. In C. Rovee-Collier & L. P. Lipsitt (Eds.), *Advances in infancy research* (Vol. 11). Norwood, NJ: Ablex.

Saffran, J. R., Aslin, R. N., & Newport, E. L. (1996). Statistical learning by 8-month-old infants. *Science, 274,* 1926–1928.

Spelke, E. S., Breinlinger, K., Macomber, J., & Jacobson, K. (1992). Origins of knowledge. *Psychological Review, 99,* 605–632.

Thomas, D. G., Campos, J. J., Shucard, D. W., Ramsay, D. S., & Shucard, J. (1981). Semantic comprehension in infancy: A signal detection analysis. *Child Development, 52,* 798–803.

Walker-Andrews, A. S., Bahrick, L. E., Raglioni, S. S., & Diaz, I. (1991). Infants' bimodal perception of gender. *Ecological Psychology, 3,* 55–75.

Woodward, A. L., Markman, E. M., & Fitzsimmons, C. M. (1994). Rapid word-learning in 13- and 18-month-olds. *Developmental Psychology, 30,* 553–566.

SIXTEEN

Social Referencing

Introduction

From birth, adults (especially parents) talk to their infants as though the infants actually understand what they are saying. In particular, adults try to tell infants which objects are safe (to be approached) and which are dangerous (to be avoided). But when do infants actually pay attention and use this information to regulate their behavior, an activity called "social referencing"? Sorce et al. (1985) conducted a classic social referencing study on 12-month-olds using an apparatus called the visual cliff (invented by Eleanor Gibson to study the development of infant depth perception). It consists of a clear, glass floor that covers a patterned floor having two levels. Infants are placed on the "shallow" side, where the patterned floor is just below the glass, and enticed by the adult to crawl across the glass, over a "visual" cliff, where the patterned floor is below the glass, to retrieve an attractive toy placed on the "deep" side.

In this study, when the infants reached the visual cliff, the mothers posed either a fear or an anger expression to encourage infants to stop, or a joy expression to encourage them to cross the cliff. The test conditions had to be just right to elicit social referencing from 1-year-olds. If the cliff was too shallow, all infants crossed; if it was too deep all avoided the cliff. Other important factors include using effective incentives for the infant to act (the attractive toy) and delivering a clear message for the infant to read (fear/anger facial expressions mean "stop"; joy means "go").

Social referencing effects can also be generated using toys (Klinnert, 1984) and by strangers (e.g., Klinnert et al., 1986). However, the story appears to be rather complex. Walden and Ogan (1988) studied a variety of social referencing behaviors exhibited by infants ranging in age from 6 to 22 months. They presented infants with "ambiguous" toys and the parents displayed either happy or fearful facial expressions of emotions (and appropriate comments such as "nice toy" or "scary toy") whenever the infant looked their way. Walden and Ogan found interesting age differences. For example, younger infants were most attentive to the parents' positive messages, older ones to their fearful expressions. Only 10- to 13-month-olds' instrumental behavior toward the toys matched the parent's message (approaching happy and avoiding fear toys). In fact, older infants seemed to prefer toys associated with the fearful message!

Baldwin and Moses (1994) studied social referencing using a different procedure. Pairs of objects were presented to infants and an experimenter expressed happiness or disgust toward one of the objects either while the infant was looking at the same object (joint attention) or at the other object. Infants as young as 12 months of age varied their behavior appropriately toward the object the adult was looking at, however the results were complicated by the tendency for infants to generalize their response to the nontarget object as well.

Infants even seem to get the adult's social cues about hidden objects. Repacholi (1998) found that infants as young as 14 months of age varied their search for and exploration of novel toys hidden in containers, as a function of an experimenter's affective expression. In this case, the experimenter used multiple cues including direction of gaze and action to convey the message. The pair of boxes were shown to the infant and the experimenter shook a box, and then looked inside and expressed happiness (and said "Wow!") and then did the same thing to the other box while expressing disgust (and said "Eww!"). When the infants were presented with the boxes, they touched both boxes but preferred to search for and explore the happy object. Baldwin (1993) also has shown that infants reference adults when they attach names to novel objects, illustrating the importance of this phenomenon in language acquisition.

Clearly, at the beginning of the second year of life, infants appear to use information about objects provided by adults to regulate their behavior. A good review of recent social referencing research is provided by Repacholi (1998).

References

Baldwin, D. (1993). Early referential understanding: Infants' ability to recognize referential acts for what they are. *Developmental Psychology*, 29, 832–43.

Baldwin, D. A., and Moses, L. J. (1994). Early understanding of referential intent and attentional focus: Evidence from language and emotion. In C. Lewis and P. Mitchell (eds.), *Origins of one understanding of mind* (pp. 133–156). Hillsdale, N.J.: Erlbaum.

Klinnert, M. (1984). The regulation of infant behavior by maternal facial expression. *Infant Behavior & Development, 7*, 447–65.

Klinnert, M., Emde, R. N., Butterfield, P., and Campos, J. (1986). Social referencing: The infant's use of emotional signals from a friendly adult with mother present. *Developmental Psychology, 22*, 427–32.

Repacholi, B. M. (1998). Infants' use of attentional cues to identify the referent of another person's emotional expression. *Developmental Psychology, 34*, 1017–25.

Walden, R., and Ogan, T. (1988). The development of social referencing. *Child Development, 59*, 1230–40.

Maternal Emotional Signaling: Its Effect on the Visual Cliff Behavior of 1-Year-Olds

James F. Sorce, Robert N. Emde,
Joseph Campos, and Mary D. Klinnert

In human psychological research, emotional expressions are generally treated as behavioral responses or as outcomes of cognitive appraisal processes. Thus, they are viewed as external indexes of internal states. Relatively little attention has been given to the function of such displays as regulators of interpersonal behavior. This lack of attention contrasts sharply with clinical experience and everyday life, wherein the emotional reactions of another can have powerful effects on the perceiver, such as in eliciting empathy or inducing moods. It also contrasts sharply with studies in nonhuman primates where emotional signaling has been a topic of considerable interest. Facial expressions such as fear, anger, and playfulness, as well as the intensity of emotion, serve communicative functions among monkeys, as has been reviewed by Chevalier-Skolnikoff (1967) and Hinde (1974). Furthermore, the development of responsiveness to maternal facial signals among infant chimpanzees in the wild has been documented (Lawick-Goodall, 1967); in this, infants responded to postural and facial expression variations in their mothers, which indicated the moods and subsequent behavior of the latter. More recently, some theoreticians have speculated about the "catching of fears" (Bowlby, 1973) and about emotional expressions as parameters of observational learning (Bandura, 1977; Campos and Sternberg, 1981).

A major turning point for human emotions research occurred when two separate teams of investigators demonstrated the apparent universal communication value of specific emotional expressions. Cross-cultural studies of adult facial expression have shown that particular patterns are recognized reliably (such as joy, fear, anger, sadness, surprise, and disgust) and, correspondingly, there also seems to be a species-wide, intuitive capacity to express these emotions (Ekman et al., 1969; Izard, 1971). These findings have generated a number of lines of investigation. Among them is research leading to measurement advances in specifying the facial patterning involved in emotional signals that are recognized. In addition, it has led to research demonstrating that discrete emotional expressions occur in response to specific eliciting circumstances (Hiatt et al., 1979; Stenberg et al., 1983).

We believe the latter two lines of research have made possible the empirical study of the communicative and regulatory functions of emotional expressions. Our logic is as follows. If the observer can identify emotional expressions and can assume that the expressing person is reacting to relevant environmental circumstances, then it seems quite likely that the attitude and/or behavior of that observing person will be influenced by noting the other's emotional expressions (i.e., a communicative function). Beyond this, to the extent that emotional expressions influence the behavior of the observer, they can be said to be serving a *social regulatory* function.

Our human infancy research has begun to investigate the developmental roots of the social regulatory functions of facial expression. We have come to realize that a process we have called social referencing occurs when an infant is confronted with an ambiguous circumstance: the infant looks to the face of another in order to search for emotional information to help appraise or evaluate the ambiguity. The infant's subsequent behavior then reflects a revised appraisal of the environment. Accordingly, the following series of studies investigates social referencing using one ambiguous circumstance, namely a modified visual cliff. We sought to determine whether 1-year-olds confronted with this kind of ambiguous circumstance would (a) look to mother's face and (b) use the emotional information in the mother's experimentally manipulated facial pose to guide their subsequent exploratory behavior.

Method

Subjects were middle-class volunteers who had been recruited from birth announcements in the neighborhoods of the University and the Health Sciences Center and whose infants were normal at birth. In response to postcard inquiries, they had expressed an interest in participating in studies of normal psychological development. Subjects coming to our laboratory were included in the study if (a) they did not become distressed at any time *prior* to noticing the drop-off, (b) they spontaneously referenced mother's face after observing the drop-off (defined as an uninterrupted sequence of looking *down* at the depth and *up* to mother's face), and (c) the mother's facial signal adequately represented the pose taught during pretraining as verified by a manipulation check.

In the first three studies to be reported below, of 145 infants coming into the lab, 11% were unable to be included in the study because of distress during the warm-up, 21% because they did not engage in visual referencing of mother's face, and 8% because mother's pose was judged as inadequate when scored by an observer naive to the hypothesis of the study.[1] Overall, therefore 40% of the original infants were not included. Because of the question being asked, criteria for subject inclusion from Study 4 were different; these data will be presented with the results from that study.

To create an ambiguous circumstance, we chose to manipulate depth – a physical dimension that can be varied to elicit avoidance of heights in infants, no avoidance at all, or a threshold of uncertainty. The visual cliff apparatus permits this manipulation of height quite readily (Walk, 1966). The cliff is a plexiglass-covered table divided into two halves: a shallow side under which a patterned surface is placed immediately beneath the plexiglass, and a deep side under which is placed a similar surface some varying distance beneath the plexiglass. Pilot testing revealed that setting the depth at 30 cm and placing an attractive toy (a Fisher-Price musical ferris wheel toy, model no. 969) on the deep side elicited infant pauses at the edge and frequent looks to the mother but no clear avoidance of the depth.

Before each trial, infants were placed on the shallow side of the cliff and entertained there by a previously familiarized experimenter, while mother positioned herself on the far (deep) side of the table. A second experimenter, monitoring the infant's behavior on a videotape screen from an adjacent room, was able to provide mother with instructions by means of a wireless earphone. Mother placed the attractive toy directly on the deep surface (to increase the ambiguity concerning the tactual solidity and visual transparency of the deep side) and began smiling to encourage her infant to approach the drop-off. When the infant advanced to within 38 cm of the drop-off, oriented toward the depth, and looked up to mother's face, the mother was instructed to signal her infant with one of the discrete emotions designated below.

Mothers had been trained in posing the desired facial expression in accordance with the descriptions of Izard (1980) and Ekman and Friesen (1975); they used no words, sounds, or gestures. For fear, the facial expression manipulation involved raising and drawing together of the brows, eyes open wide with sclera showing, and the mouth opened and the lips pulled back. For anger, the brows are drawn down and together, the upper eyelids are lowered, and the mouth is either open and square-shaped, or the lips are pressed together. For interest, there is a slight raising of the eyebrows, the eyes are widened slightly, and the mouth is closed and the face relaxed. For happiness, the corners of the lips are drawn back and up, the cheeks are raised, and the lower eyelids are raised but not tense. For sadness, the inner corners of the eyebrows are drawn up, the skin below the eyebrow is triangulated with the inner corner up, and the corners of the lips are drawn down.

Maternal facial expressions were scored independently by a naive rater who had achieved reliability on MAX training (Izard, 1980). All expressions during times of visual referencing were scored for the presence of components that would be expected for the given emotion according to Ekman and Friesen's *Unmasking the Face* (1975). Facial expressions met criteria of having predicted components in two or three facial zones and no components belonging to other target emotions. On those unusual occasions when only one facial zone met the predicted pattern, the posed feature had to be an indicator of the intended emotion and no other (for example, a smile or "sad brows").

A trial was terminated when the infant either crossed the deep side (touching the toy, mother, or the end wall) or when 120 s elapsed from when the infant entered the region of the drop-off. All trials employed split-screen videotape recordings, with one camera constantly focused on the infant's face and body and a second camera on the mother's face.

Tapes were scored for three infant behavioral categories: (a) *hedonic tone* – rated every 10s on a 5-point scale ranging from a broad smile (rating of 1) through neutral interest to overt distress (rating of 5), (b) *maternal referencing* – the total number of times an infant looked at mother's face after an initial instance of looking from the depth immediately to mother's face, and (c) *coping behavior* – the presence or absence of crossing the deep side, and the frequency of retreat back onto the shallow side, defined as turning his or her back to mother and moving back onto the shallow side. Reliabilities for each of these dependent variables, calculated as exact agreement between two naive judges, ranged from .80 to 1.00, with a mean of .94.

Results

First study: happy versus fear signal

The first study compared infant responses to this uncertain situation when mothers signaled either happiness or fear. Thirty-six middle-class mothers and their 12-month-old infants were randomly assigned to a smiling condition ($N = 10$ males, 9 females) and to a fear condition ($N = 9$ males, 8 females).

The mother's emotional signaling had three dramatic effects on the infants' behavior. First, it significantly influenced the infant's tendency to cross the cliff or not. When mother posed a fearful expression *none* of the 17 infants ventured across the deep side. In sharp contrast, 14 of the 19 infants who observed mothers' happy face crossed the deep side, $\chi^2(1) = 20.49$, $p < .0001$. Second, the fear pose created a negative motivational valence: 11 of the 17 infants in the fear condition retreated, whereas only 3 of the 19 infants in the joy condition retreated, $\chi^2(1) = 5.38$, $p < .03$. Infants in the fear condition usually vacillated back and forth in the midzone of the cliff and then moved back to the shallow side. Third, the fear expression generated a significantly more negative hedonic tone in the infants, $F(1, 34) = 4.03$, $p < .05$. These findings are summarized in table 16.1.

Second study: interest versus anger signal

A second study was conducted to determine whether the regulatory effect of social referencing could be observed with different emotions.

Table 16.1 Effect of mothers' facial expressions on infant behavior

	Study 1		Study 2		Study 3
Variable	Joy (N = 19)	Fear (N = 17)	Interest (N = 15)	Anger (N = 18)	Sadness (N = 19)
Percentage of infants crossing deep side	74%	0	73%	11%	33%
Mean number of retreats per minute to shallow side	0.420	1.08	0.420	0.72	0.660
Mean rating of hedonic tone	1.62	2.12	2.00	1.92	1.92
Mean number of references per minute	3.60	2.46	5.70	2.94	4.59

Two different emotional signals, interest and anger, were used. These emotions were selected because they not only represented a positive and negative emotional signal but, like enjoyment and fear, they both seemed to provide situationally relevant messages concerning the appropriateness of crossing versus not crossing the cliff.

Thirty-three 1-year-old infants and their mothers comprised the sample for the second study, with 15 randomly assigned to the interest condition (8 males, 7 females) and 18 to the anger condition (11 males, 7 females). The instructions, training, and trial procedures as well as the subsequent data scoring techniques were identical to those reported for the first study.

Results again revealed a powerful effect of mothers' emotional signaling on infant crossing behavior (again, see table 16.1). When mother posed an anger expression, only 2 of the 18 infants ventured across the deep side, while 11 of the 15 infants who observed mother's interest expression crossed the deep side, $\chi^2(1) = 13.29$, $p < .001$. Infants who saw mother's angry expression while at the visual cliff edge tended to actively retreat by moving back onto the shallow side: 14 of the 18 infants in the anger condition retreated, and only 5 of the 15 infants in the interest condition did so, $\chi^2(1) = 5.22$, $p < .05$. Unlike the results of the initial study, there were no significant differences in infant hedonic tone.

As discrete emotional expressions, fear and anger appear to be situationally relevant in the child's appraisal of the deep side of the cliff. Fear provides a warning that there is danger and the infant should avoid the drop-off to insure his or her safety. Anger serves as a restraint, prohibiting the infant from approaching further. Both fear and anger, however, also convey a negative hedonic tone, which might be the mediator of the avoidance behavior in both cases, independently of the discrete emotional information (Izard, 1977).

Third study: sadness signal

A third study was conducted to look at the effects if mothers signaled sadness. Sadness is a fundamental emotion, which conveys a negative hedonic tone, but its discrete emotional information does not imply avoidance or prohibition. In a third study we, therefore, investigated the reactions of an additional eighteen 12-month-old infants (6 males and 12 females) on the visual cliff while their mothers posed sadness. Results indicated that 6 of the 18 infants successfully crossed the deep side when mother's face conveyed sadness. The mean number of references by infants from this group was higher than any other, suggesting that these infants might be puzzled or uncertain about the facial signal itself or its meaning in the present context, among other possibilities.

A comparison of the crossing behavior in the negative emotion conditions revealed a significant difference between sadness and fear (Fisher Exact Probability Test, $p = .01$) and a nearly significant difference for sadness and anger ($p = .09$); the difference between fear and anger was not significant ($p = .26$). These findings suggest that the appropriateness of the context for an emotional signal must be taken into account; the most contextually appropriate emotion (fear) elicited the most consistent avoidance of heights.

Fourth study: fear signal without uncertainty

The final study in the series addressed a separate issue related to the importance of context. In order to determine whether the expressions influenced the infant's evaluation of an ambiguous situation, or whether they were effective in controlling behavior merely because of their discrepancy or unexpectedness, we tested an additional 23 infants (11 males and 12 females) with the visual cliff table modified to consist of two shallow sides separated by a center strip .3 m wide. The mothers were instructed exactly as they had been in the fear condition described above. They smiled broadly until the infant reached the center of the table, then shifted to a previously trained fear facial pose. The results obtained in this condition were quite different from the earlier study, revealing very little referencing and no effect of the facial expression on crossing behavior. Seventeen of the infants tested in this condition did not look to the mother at all and merely continued crossing to reach her or the toy. Among the six babies who referenced, two of the mothers gave poor signals, and the infants were eliminated from the study. Those four babies who looked to the mother and received a fear signal crossed to the toy in spite of her fear pose. This behavior was in marked contrast to that of the babies who saw the mothers' fear face after noticing the slight drop-off (Fisher Exact Probability Test comparing for fear in the two contexts, $p = .0004$). The findings described earlier, therefore, seem interpretable as a social referencing process – the infant must seek out emotional information for that information to be maximally effective in regulating behavior.

Discussion

The form of emotional communication we have referred to as social referencing appears to have a powerful and consistent effect on infant behavior. Social referencing, as we have defined it, is a process whereby an individual seeks out emotional information in order to make sense of an event that is otherwise ambiguous or beyond that individual's own intrinsic appraisal capabilities (Campos and Stenberg, 1981; Klinnert et al., 1982). Under the conditions of our experiment, the tendency to visually reference mother and to respond according to an emotional message is already well established at 12 months of age, and it appears rather dramatic to mothers and researchers alike who view our videotapes. Under other conditions, such as the entry and approach of a stranger, social referencing effects have been shown at 10 months of age (Feinman and Lewis, 1983). Two sorts of experimental questions remain to be answered before any general application of findings about social referencing. These questions have to do with the role of *selection* of subjects and the role of *context* for social referencing.

First for selection factors. Our experiments looked at a relatively narrow set of infants. Volunteers were middle-class, and not all children were able to complete the testing. We did not include children who were crying during the warm-up phase or children who never looked at mother (except for the fourth experiment). Because of selection factors our results may, therefore, represent children who are functioning at a relatively high capacity. We need to understand more about individual differences among children who do and do not reference (e.g., Feinman and Lewis, 1983). Related to this, we need to know more about individual differences concerning internal "state" factors affecting children who may or may not attend or who may or may not be involved in appraisal. Furthermore, are there subtle differences in social referencing based on individual differences and the history of the relationship between mother and infant? A series of studies is planned to explore these questions, some of which use heartrate as a sensitive measure of change related to attentional processes and emotional state.

Now for the questions regarding context. We need to know more about situations generating "uncertainty." In our experiments, we did a considerable amount of pilot work to develop a definitive zone of uncertainty. If the "deep side" of the visual cliff was deeper, infants showed fear and avoidance; if it was shallower, they showed no uncertainty and crossing to the toy occurred without referencing. This precise adjustment was necessary to establish our experimental condition. But it is important to realize that the visual cliff is a situation that is highly controlled and one in which the infant has relatively few options, considering his or her complex behavioral repertoire. We need research involving more complex experimental situations – situations in which there are richer opportunities for behavioral regulation and coping. Recent work of Gunnar and Stone (1983) has underscored the importance of uncertainty in social referencing tasks involving unfamiliar toys. We are currently doing experiments in a variety of other uncertainty situations, which include a toy robot, a collapsing house, the approach of strangers, and a variety of social situations.

In addition to contextual questions about the setting, there are contextual questions about the emotional signal, including appropriateness. Again, it seems important to emphasize that, for reasons of experimental control, we limited the signal to a manipulation of the face alone. We now need to study other channels of communication besides the facial channel. Emotional signaling occurs through the vocalic channel of emotional communication, and it is likely that posture and gestures are also important. Research also needs to be done in more complex contexts – those in which emotional signaling occurs in multiple channels at the same time, as would be the usual case in the infant's world.

There are other interesting questions that arise from this line of research. What is the developmental onset of social referencing? What is the role of learning? Of maturation? Do emotional expressions regulate behavior by eliciting feelings in the perceiver, or are they merely cues that guide behavior? What is the relationship of social referencing to the past history of individual infants in relationship to attachment and to particular socialization experiences? What is the relationship of social referencing to empathy? What happens in situations of conflicting emotional signals?

We have emphasized future experimental approaches, but the latter questions indicate that we also need to explore naturalistic settings for the occurrence of social referencing and related phenomena. Social referencing is only one form of emotional signaling. Whatever else, these experimental effects that seem so impressive need to be understood in terms of their real-life significance.

Note

1   The breakdown according to numbers of subjects eliminated for the first three studies is as follows: infant distress during warmup (12, 2, and 2); no maternal referencing (7, 15, and 8); inadequate mother pose (6, 2, and 3).

References

Bandura, A. (1977). *Social learning theory*. Englewood Cliffs, NJ: Prentice-Hall.

Bowlby, J. (1973). *Attachment and loss. Vol. II: Separation*. New York: Basic Books.

Campos, J., & Stenberg, C. (1981). Perception, appraisal and emotion: The onset of social referencing. In M. E. Lamb & L. R. Sherrod (Eds.), *Infant social cognition* (pp. 273–314). Hillsdale, NJ: Erlbaum.

Chevalier-Skolnikoff, S. (1967). In D. Morris (Ed.), *Primate ethology*. London: Weindenfeld & Nicholson.

Ekman, P., & Friesen, W. (1975). *Unmasking the face*. Englewood Cliffs, NJ: Prentice-Hall.

Ekman, P., Sorensen, E., & Friesen, W. (1969). Pancultural elements in facial displays of emotion. *Science 164*, 86–88.

Feinman, S., & Lewis, M. (1983). Social referencing at ten months: A second-order effect on infants' response to strangers. *Child Development, 54*, 878–887.

Gunnar, M. R., & Stone, C. (1983, April). *The effects of maternal positive affect of one-year-olds reactions to toys: Is it social referencing?* Paper presented at meetings of the Society for Research in Child Development, Detroit.

Hiatt, S., Campos, J., & Emde, R. N. (1979). Facial patterning and infant emotional expression: Happiness, surprise and fear. *Child Development, 50,* 1020–1033.

Hinde, R. A. (1974). *Biological bases of human social behavior.* New York: McGraw Hill.

Izard, C. (1971). *The face of emotion.* New York: Meredith and Appleton-Century Crofts.

Izard, C. (1977). *Human emotions.* New York: Plenum.

Izard, C. (1980). *Maximally discriminative facial movement coding (MAX).* Newark, DE: University of Delaware Press.

Klinnert, M. D., Campos, J., Sorce, J., Emde, R. N., & Svejda, M. (1982). The development of social referencing in infancy. In R. Plutchik & H. Kellerman (Eds.), *Emotion: Theory, research and experience, Vol. 2: Emotion in early development.* New York: Academic Press.

Lawick-Goodall, J. van. (1967). Mother–offspring relationships in chimpanzees. In D. Morris (Ed.), *Primate ethology* (pp. 287–346). London: Weidenfeld and Nicholson.

Stenberg, C., Campos, J., & Emde, R. N. (1983). The facial expression of anger in seven-month-old infants. *Child Development, 54,* 178–184.

Walk, R. (1966). The development of depth perception in animals and human infants. *Monographs of the Society for Research in Child Development, 31,* (Whole No. 5).

SEVENTEEN

Infant Understanding of Others' Intentions and Theory of Mind

Introduction

In previous chapters, we learned that by 4 months of age infants can detect emotional information in an adult's vocal message (chapter 14) and display social responses more when an adult makes eye-contact (chapter 7). By 6-months they can associate their parents' names with their faces, an early form of word comprehension (chapter 15). The onset of clear social referencing responses appears around 12 months of age, when infants begin to seek out and use another person's vocal and non-verbal messages about third parties (other objects and people) to regulate their instrumental behavior (chapter 16). At the same time, at birth, infants imitate a few adult facial expressions (chapter 9); this imitation is a very potent social cue for adults. As they grow older, infants continue to imitate adult facial expressions and begin to reproduce simple words modeled by caretakers such as "ma ma" and "da da." Indeed, imitation learning is a major kind of social learning in all developmental theories.

Carpenter, Akhtar and Tomasello (1998) note that although young infants may imitate gestures and sounds, it may be simple mimicry of the action without an appreciation of the model's goal or intentions for producing the acts. Parrots mimic human speech without understanding the speaker's intentions (meanings). But how do we assess the infant's understanding of another person's intention when we cannot question them directly? Meltzoff (1995) developed a clever procedure to answer that question. He had an adult repeatedly try, and fail, to complete an action on an object that the infant never had seen before (e.g., pushing a button with a stick that never made contact). When 18-month-olds were given a chance, they successfully completed the action, indicating that they knew the adult's intention.

In the present selection, Carpenter et al. used what appears to be an even more challenging task with younger infants to see if they would selectively imitate novel intentional, but not accidental, actions. Their procedure involved several steps and control conditions. Simply put, the experimenter demonstrated several two-action sequences that led to interesting events, such as a light display, and infants willingly imitated the model's actions. Then, the model displayed several two-action sequences to the infants in different orders. In one order, they said "Woops" to indicate a mistake; in the other order they said "There" to indicate a correct response. The results were very clear-cut. Infants imitated many more intentional, than accidental, actions. This ability to infer adult intentions about their actions is related to language acquisition and the operation of adult-like social cognition.

Reference

Meltzoff, A. (1995). Understanding the intentions of others: Re-enactment of intended acts by 18-month-old children. *Developmental Psychology, 31*, 838–50.

Fourteen-Through 18-Month-Old Infants Differentially Imitate Intentional and Accidental Actions

Malinda Carpenter, Nameera Akhtar,
and Michael Tomasello

Understanding others' intentions is one of infants' first steps toward a theory of mind, that is, an understanding that other people have mental states such as desires, knowledge, and beliefs. Older children clearly understand a great deal about others' intentions. When 5- to 6-year-old children make moral judgments, they take into account the intentions of the people involved: even when unintended actions result in the same amount of damage as intended actions, they are viewed as less "naughty" (e.g., Karniol, 1978). In addition, children as young as 3 years of age have been found to be able to distinguish intentional actions from mistakes, reflexes, and passive movements (Shultz et al., 1980; see also Shultz and Wells, 1985; Smith, 1978).

Whereas studies of older children's understanding of others' intentions involve explicit, linguistic explanations of behavior, studies of this understanding in children 2 years old and younger must involve more implicit measures. Several studies of young infants have used measures of habituation-dishabituation (e.g., Gergely et al., 1994; Gergely, et al., 1995) or gaze direction (Phillips et al., 1992). These studies have found that by 9 months of age, infants are sensitive to rational, goal-directed action, and that they engage in "goal detection" following ambiguous actions by looking to the actor's face. Because such studies rely solely on infants' patterns of gaze, many studies of very young children's understanding of intentions use imitation paradigms.

There are several types of social learning by means of which one individual may end up reproducing the actions of another individual (see Galef, 1988; Whiten and Ham, 1992). Tomasello (1996; Tomasello et al., 1993) has singled out imitative learning as the only type of social learning that involves some understanding of the intentions behind others' actions. That is, the process of mimicking, as in parrots mimicking human speech, involves reproducing the means only, or topography of others' motor activities without an understanding of their goal or intention. Conversely, processes such as local enhancement or emulation learning involve reproducing the end only, or the change of state in the world produced by others, but doing so without any regard for their actual behavior or behavioral strategies. Imitative learning consists of reproducing the intentional actions of others, including both the end result or goal at which they are aiming and the behavior or strategy by means of which they are attempting to accomplish that goal (Tomasello, 1996).

Infants as young as 6 months of age can reproduce others' actions on objects (e.g., Barr et al., 1996). However, it is not until age 13 or 14 months that there is evidence of imitative learning. In a study by Meltzoff (1988), 14-month-old infants watched, along with other demonstrations, an adult bend at the waist and touch a panel with his forehead, thus turning on a light. The infants followed suit even though they might also have turned on the light by simpler means (e.g., with their hands) – implying that they were indeed reproducing the adult's behavioral act. To test the possibility that infants at this age were only mimicking the adult, that is, reproducing the adult's action without also trying to achieve the same goal as the adult, Carpenter et al. (1998) included similar actions in a longitudinal study of 24 infants from 9 to 15 months of age. Results showed that at an average age of 13 months infants began not only to reproduce an adult's "arbitrary" action to achieve an effect – for example, knocking on or touching their head to a plain wooden box to activate a light – but they also accompanied their behavioral reproductions with a look to the light, in apparent anticipation that their behavioral act would produce the same effect as had the adult's. Bauer and Hertsgaard (1993) also have shown that 13.5-month-olds can reproduce novel sequences of two or three actions on objects in order to meet a goal (in that study, the goal of the actions was verbally stated by the experimenter during the demonstration and response periods).

In perhaps the most direct test of infants' understanding of others' intentions, Meltzoff (1995) showed 18-month-old infants an adult trying but failing to perform several actions on objects. When given an opportunity to play with the objects themselves, the infants reproduced what the adult was trying but failing to do, an action they had never seen in its entirety. They did this more often than infants in various other control conditions (and as often as infants who saw successful performance of the act).

Tomasello and colleagues also have used imitative learning paradigms to investigate 18- to 24-month-olds' understanding of others' intentions, although in these studies what is imitated is a piece of language instead of actions on objects. Tomasello et al. (1996) reported a study of 18-month-old infants in which an adult used a novel word in announcing her intention to "find the *toma.*" Infants then watched as the adult searched a series of buckets for the toma, picking up and rejecting objects on the way (scowling and replacing them) before picking up another object with obvious glee. Children learned (i.e., imitated) the word "toma' for the object reacted to with glee (and not for the rejected objects), presumably indicating their ability both to understand that the adult's goal was to find the toma and to tell when she had fulfilled that goal.

What is perhaps a more stringent test of young children's ability to understand intentional actions was employed by Tomasello and Barton (1994) with 24-month-old children. In this study, an adult announced to 24-month-olds her intention to produce an action ("Let's *meek* Big Bird") and proceeded to an apparatus where two novel actions were possible. In one condition she first produced an accidental action (saying "Woops!") followed by an intentional action (saying "There!"), with appropriate vocal intonations in both cases. In another condition the order of accidental and intentional actions was reversed (and there was counterbalancing of actions and conditions). In both conditions children learned the new word to refer to the intentional action (i.e., irrespective of the order in which the two actions were performed), indicating both their ability to discriminate intentional from accidental actions and their tendency to reproduce intentional actions. This discrimination is different from the one required in the experimental paradigms in which infants only had to see certain behaviors or emotional reactions as indicative of a certain intentional action in a certain context (as in the Meltzoff, 1995, and Tomasello et al., 1996, studies). In this study, two actions were performed before the child had an opportunity to act, and the child then had to choose which one (or both) the adult intended to perform – using an entirely different set of cues than in the other studies of infants' understanding of intentional action. This is arguably a more difficult task.

Studies of infants' understanding of accidental and unfulfilled intentions are particularly important when assessing infants' understanding of others' intentions, because they involve the understanding that others may have intentions that may not match with the current state of affairs. This advanced level of understanding may be contrasted with simply understanding persons in terms of their intentions and understanding that others may have intentions that differ from one's own (Tomasello, 1995); the latter two, earlier levels of understanding may be seen in infants as young as 9 to 12 months of age (see Tomasello, 1995 for further discussion). Indeed, studies of accidental and unfulfilled intentions are analogous to studies of false belief, as they involve deviations from the true state of affairs, and thus may be considered an "acid test" of understanding of others' intentions. So far, this level of understanding has been studied only in 18-month-old and older children (e.g., Meltzoff, 1995; Tomasello and Barton, 1994).

In the current study, we sought to test for this level of understanding in infants 14 through 18 months of age. In particular, we tested infants' ability to distinguish between accidental and intentional actions, using an action imitation paradigm. Infants observed an adult demonstrate actions on objects which afforded two actions. Some infants saw an intentional action followed by an accidental action, some saw an accidental action followed by an intentional action, and some saw two intentional actions. The major discriminative cue was the adult saying "Woops!" or "There!" with the appropriate intonation as she produced a particular action. We chose vocal cues knowing that by age 12 months, infants use adults' vocal emotional signals more reliably than their visual-facial cues to regulate their own behavior, at least in social referencing situations (Mumme et al., 1996). The hypothesis was that infants as young as 14 months would preferentially reproduce intentional over accidental actions in this situation – although reproduction of accidental actions might occur at some frequency as well as they would still suggest to the infants things that might be done to objects irrespective of adult intentions. Demonstration of such a preference would indicate both infants' ability to discriminate intentional from accidental actions and their tendency to reproduce mainly the intentional actions of adults.

Experiment

Method

Participants.   Twenty infants (mean age = 16 months, 6 days; range = 14 months, 1 day to 18 months, 29 days) participated in the study. Twelve of the infants were male, 8 were female; all were from middle and upper-middle class families. No infants were dropped from the study. Infants were recruited by telephone from a file of names of parents who had volunteered to participate in studies of child development. Compensation for participation included a book or a t-shirt.

Materials.   Eight objects were constructed specifically for the study (two were used to warm up the infants and, if necessary, to train them – see "Training procedure" section below; the other six were used in the test). Pictures of the test objects are presented in figure 17.1. Objects consisted of wooden boxes or other supports (e.g., a plastic newspaper recycler turned upside down and a wooden bird feeder), each of which had two parts or attachments that could be moved (e.g., on the top of one of the boxes, there was a hinge and a spinner; for the bird feeder, the top moved up and down and a string with a ring on it attached to the middle could be pulled). Also attached to each object was an end result (i.e., colored Christmas-tree lights, a small toy that popped out of a box and dangled on a string and then was pulled back into the box, or an air-powered party favor); end results were activated surreptitiously by an experimenter (i.e., with her hand behind a curtain, she unobtrusively switched on the lights, jiggled the string attached to the small toy, or pressed repeatedly on a pump attached to the party favor). End results were activated for a few seconds after the other experimenter's demonstrations, and after any reproductions of the target (i.e., intentional) actions by infants. A list of the objects, the actions performed on them,

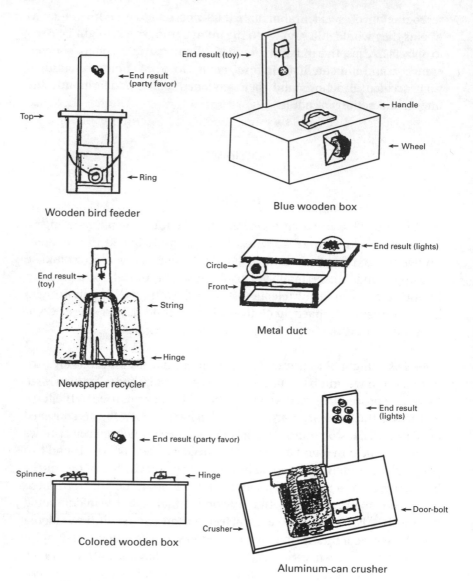

Figure 17.1   The test objects (note: drawings are not to scale)

and their respective end results is presented in the Appendix at the end of this chapter.

In addition, at the end of the session, parents were asked to complete the short form of the MacArthur Communicative Development Inventory (Reznick and Goldsmith, 1989). This measure of infants' vocabulary production was collected in order to determine whether there was a correlation between infants' reproduction of intentional actions and their verbal abilities.

Experimental design.   Two actions in sequence were modeled on each of the six test objects. There were two types of actions: Accidental actions and Intentional actions. Demonstrations of Accidental actions were immediately followed by the word "Woops!" and demonstrations of Intentional actions were immediately followed by the word 'There!" — both with the appropriate intonation. There were three conditions, corresponding to the order and type of actions modeled: Accidental-Intentional (A-I), Intentional-Accidental (I-A), and Intentional-Intentional (I-I). The A-I and I-A conditions served as controls for each other: if infants reproduced only one of the two actions and they differentially reproduced the intentional action, regardless of its position in the sequence, it would indicate that they discriminated between the two types of actions and chose to imitate the intentional one. The I-I condition provided an additional test of infants' intentional understanding. If infants could reproduce a sequence of two actions and they understood something about intentional behavior, they should reproduce both actions only when it was appropriate to do so, that is, when both actions were modeled intentionally. Thus, if infants reproduced both actions in the I-I condition more frequently than they reproduced both actions in the A-I and I-A conditions, it would indicate that they were imitating, rather than mimicking the adult's actions. The I-I condition also served to reduce the number of consecutive accidents infants saw modeled.

Each infant participated in each condition twice (i.e., there were two A-I objects, two I-A objects, and two I-I objects for each infant). For each infant, objects were assigned to conditions randomly, and the order of presentation of objects also was random, with the stipulation that no two identical conditions would be presented consecutively. Whereas the two actions associated with a given object (e.g., for the bird feeder, lifting the top and pulling the ring) always were the same for all infants, both the order in which the actions were modeled and the condition to which they were assigned were randomized.[1] Thus, for the bird feeder, for example, approximately half of the infants saw the top being lifted first and the ring being pulled second; the other infants saw these actions in the reverse order. In addition, some of the infants in each of these cases saw the top being moved accidentally and some of them saw it being moved intentionally.

We designed the actions to look as similar as possible when modeled as accidental or intentional, but also to be credible in both cases. Thus, the two attachments for each object were positioned such that, in the case of accidents, E1's hand could plausibly get caught on or brush against one attachment on the way to or back from the other (although with enough distance between them to reduce the likelihood that infants would themselves perform the actions truly accidentally). However, the same action (e.g., pull ring, in the case of the bird feeder) was performed in a similar manner in both the Intentional and Accidental conditions. That is, in both conditions E1 pulled the ring with her index finger in such a way that could be seen as either intentional or accidental – she did not, for example, merely brush against it in the Accidental condition and tug on it very deliberately in the Intentional condition.

In natural accidents, several bodily cues are usually available: besides the vocal cues (which include not only just a word such as "Woops!", but also a characteristic intonation), there also may be a startled facial expression, the actor's body may jump slightly, and the actions them-selves may be quicker and interrupted. In the current study, we mini-mized all but the vocal cues, although we did not eliminate the other cues completely. For example, during accidents, the experimenter's upper body often jumped up slightly. There also were minimal facial cues, although infants were watching the actions, not the experi-menter's face, during demonstrations. The main difference between accidental and intentional actions in this study was the "Woops!" or "There!" vocalization. It was expected that vocal cues would be sufficient based on results of Mumme et al.'s (1996) social referencing study in which it was found that infants used adults' vocal emotional signals to regulate their behavior by age 12 months.

Procedure.   Infants were seen in a Psychology Department playroom for one visit lasting approximately 30 to 45 minutes; visits were videotaped. Infants sat on the floor with a parent facing a curtain which hid the objects. Parents were instructed not to provide hints or feedback to their infants but were asked to encourage infants to approach the objects if necessary. There were two female experimenters, E1 and E2. E1 sat next to the infants, interacted with them, and modeled the actions; E2 sat to one side of the curtain, facing infants, and surreptitiously activated the objects' end results with one hand behind the curtain. She also coded infants' responses.

Training procedure.   A training phase was included for two reasons. First, this phase was used to expose infants to the objects and the general procedure of watching E1's demonstrations to learn how to activate the objects' end results. It was also used to provide a measure of whether individual infants were able to reproduce a sequence of two actions.

The procedure of the training phase was as follows. After a brief warm-up period, the first of the two training objects was brought out from behind the curtain and placed in front of it, facing the infant and E1. In both the training phase and the test, infants were prohibited from touching the objects until after the adult's demonstrations. The first training object was a decorated wooden box with a silent doorbell and a large spring attached to the top; a set of colored Christmas-tree lights was the end result. For this object, E1 announced, "Watch, I'm going to show you how this works," and then modeled a single, simple action: pressing the doorbell several times. During the training phase, E1 performed actions very deliberately (unlike during the tests) and she modeled actions without vocally marking them as accidental or intentional (i.e., without saying "Woops!" or "There!") – there were no accidents during this phase (but E1 did not mark the actions as intentional either). We thus were not training infants to reproduce intentional actions; we were training them to watch E1's demonstrations to learn how to operate the objects. E2 then unobtrusively switched on the lights for several seconds, during which time E1 shared in the infant's interest and excitement about the lights. When the lights went off, E1 encouraged the infant to take a turn, using language that did not refer to the action performed (e.g., "Now you try. Can you make it work?"). If infants reproduced the modeled action, the end result was activated for a few seconds by E2 and then E1 proceeded to the second of the two training objects. If infants did not successfully reproduce the modeled action, it was modeled again (several times, if necessary). If infants still did not reproduce the modeled action after several demonstrations, E1 taught them, using verbal and manual coaching, to perform the action (this was only rarely necessary for the first training object). Infants were then encouraged to perform the action (and receive the end result) several times before going on to the next object.

The same procedure was followed with the second of the two training objects (a different decorated wooden box), with one exception. A sequence of two actions was modeled on this object: raising and lowering a doorstop and then twanging a small spring. In order for infants to succeed on this object, they had to reproduce both of the modeled actions in the modeled order. If, as often was the case, on their first attempts infants reproduced only one action (or they reproduced both in the incorrect order), E1 provided feed-back until they correctly reproduced both actions or until they showed signs of frustration.[2] During the training period, demonstrations consisted of one and two actions, respectively, so as not to bias infants toward reproducing one or both actions during the test.

Test procedure.   During the test phase, the same general procedure of E1 modeling actions and then giving infants a turn to respond was followed. During the test, however, demonstrations always consisted of two actions, and individual actions were modeled either intentionally or accidentally, depending on the condition, as discussed above. In addition, infants received only two demonstration and response trials for each test object, with no hints or training from E1. E1 modeled the first actions, gave the infant a response period, modeled the same actions again (in the same way) during a second trial, and gave the infant a second response period before moving on to the next object. Actions were performed only once per demonstration, in order to avoid repeated presentations of accidental actions. Again, following demonstrations, infants were asked, for example, "Can you make it work? Your turn," (but never "Can you do what I did?").

Response periods had no fixed length; if infants did not respond immediately, they were encouraged verbally and nonverbally to approach and interact with the test object until they responded in some way or until they made it clear (e.g., by walking away or fussing) that they were not going to respond. During response periods, only infants' first response was scored. If infants reproduced just one action and then paused and perhaps looked expectantly to the end result, their response was scored as one action, even if they later proceeded to perform a second action. Conversely, if infants reproduced two actions with no obvious pause in between, they were scored as having reproduced two actions. There were six objects (two in each condition), with two demonstration and response periods each, for a total of 12 trials (four in each condition).

During E1's demonstrations, the end result was activated approximately .5 to 1 sec after the second action. During infants' responses, the procedure for activating the end result differed slightly depending on the condition but always depended on whether infants reproduced the intentional action(s). In the I-I condition, the end result was activated if infants reproduced both actions in the modeled order. In the A-I condition, the end result was activated only if infants reproduced the intentional (second) action, regardless of whether or not they reproduced the accidental (first) one. In the I-A condition, the end result was activated only if infants reproduced the intentional (first) action, regardless of whether or not they reproduced the accidental (second) action, but it was done so a full 2 sec after infants performed the intentional action. This delay was implemented in order to give infants a chance to perform the accidental action.

Scoring and reliability.   Infants' responses were coded live by E2 and also from the videotapes by E1. For each trial, infants were scored as reproducing the First Action Only of the demonstration, the Second Action Only, Both Actions in Order, Both Actions in Incorrect Order, or Neither Action. If infants clearly were attempting to reproduce an action but were unsuccessful due to lack of strength or dexterity, they were given credit for reproducing that action as long as they did more than simply touch the object in the appropriate location.

E1's coding was used for analyses (E2's live coding was used when an action could not be seen clearly on the videotape). Interobserver reliability was assessed for six (30%) randomly chosen infants in the following way. Because E1's coding was not blind to experimental condition (although usually she did not watch the demonstrations), a videotape was made by an independent research assistant of only the response periods for these six infants so that the reliability coder, E2, would be blind to condition. For each response period on this videotape, E2 recorded the action(s) she saw the infant produce. Following coding, these actions were matched with the order of the actions of the corresponding demonstrations (yielding codes of First Action Only, Second Action Only, etc.) and then this blind coding was compared to E1's original coding from the videotapes. Reliability was excellent: Cohen's kappa using these coding categories was .92.

Results

Following coding of infants' responses (i.e., First Action Only, Second Action Only, Both Actions in Order, Both Actions in Incorrect Order, or Neither Action), the responses were matched with the condition of the demonstration (i.e., A-I, I-A, or I-I) and various measures of the percentages of intentional versus accidental actions reproduced were calculated (see below). Percentages were used instead of frequencies because in a few cases individual infants did not complete a total of 12 trials.[3] Trials during which infants made no response or responded with actions other than the modeled actions were not included in analyses because we were interested not in whether infants could imitate, but, instead, in whether when imitating they would differentiate between accidental and intentional actions. We also assumed that infants' motivational or attentional states were not ideal for these trials.[4] The first analysis investigated infants' tendencies to reproduce intentional versus accidental actions overall, regardless of whether or not infants' responses were "correct," that is, whether or not they reproduced the intentional actions only. The second set of analyses investigated the nature of infants' responses more precisely.

The first analysis compared the overall percentage of intentional versus accidental actions reproduced by infants, regardless of whether or not infants responded correctly (that is, this analysis includes correct as well as other types of responses, i.e., responses which included accidental actions). Because no accidental actions were modeled in the I-I condition, only the A-I and I-A conditions were used for this analysis. For each infant, we counted the number of intentional actions the infant reproduced in each condition (possible range = 0–4 for each of the two conditions) and divided these numbers by the total number of intentional actions modeled in the condition (usually 4, i.e. one intentional action in each of two trials for each of the two objects in the condition) to yield the percentage of intentional actions reproduced. Similarly, the percentages of accidental actions reproduced in each condition were calculated by dividing the number of accidental actions (range = 0–4) infants reproduced by the total number of accidental actions (usually 4) modeled. Thus, the percentage of intentional actions and the

Table 17.1 Mean percentages and standard deviations (in parentheses) of intentional and accidental actions reproduced in the Accidental-Intentional (A-I) and Intentional-Accidental (I-A) conditions

Condition	Intentional actions	Accidental actions
Accidental-Intentional (A-I)	74.6 (27.5)	45.4 (26.7)
Intentional-Accidental (I-A)	81.7 (20.5)	39.2 (33.5)

percentage of accidental actions reproduced were calculated independently and, when added together, could equal more than 100% because during any given trial infants could have reproduced both of the modeled actions.

Table 17.1 presents the mean percentages and standard deviations of intentional and accidental actions reproduced in each condition. A Wilcoxon signed-rank test comparing the percentage of intentional versus accidental actions reproduced in the A-I plus I-A conditions yielded significant results, $z = 3.07$, $p < .01$, with infants reproducing a significantly greater percentage of intentional actions (overall $M = 77.7\%$ of the total intentional actions seen across these two conditions) than accidental actions (overall $M = 42.7\%$ of the total accidental actions seen). Tests of this comparison in both the A-I and I-A conditions individually also were statistically significant, $z = 2.26$, $p < .05$ for A-I and $z = 2.88$, $p < .01$ for I-A, with no significant differences in infants' percentage of intentional or accidental actions reproduced across conditions, $z = .79$ for intentional actions and $z = .73$ for accidental actions. This finding was obtained on the level of individual infants as well: 18 of the 20 infants reproduced a greater percentage (as calculated above) of intentional than accidental actions in the A-I and I-A conditions combined, $p < .001$, binomial test. Infants thus imitated more of the intentional actions than the accidental ones overall.

The next set of analyses investigated infants' responses in more detail. Figure 17.2 presents the mean percentage of trials in which infants produced each type of response for each of the three conditions separately. To calculate these percentages, for each condition we divided the number of times infants produced each type of response (possible range

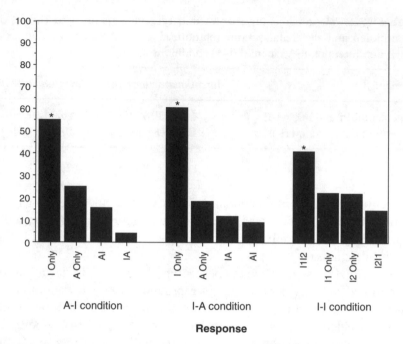

Figure 17.2 Mean percentage of trials in which infants produced each type of response for each of the three conditions: Accidental-Intentional (A-I), Intentional-Accidental (I-A), and Intentional-Intentional (I-I).

= 0–4) by the total number of trials in the condition (usually 4); infants' responses added to 100 in these analyses. For each condition, there was only one type of response that was considered correct: when infants reproduced *only* the action(s) marked in the demonstration as intentional. Thus, in the A-I and I-A conditions, the correct response was Intentional Action Only (*I Only* in figure 17.2) and in the I-I condition, the correct response was Both Actions in the Modeled Order (I_1I_2 in figure 17.2). Wilcoxon tests comparing correct responses to each of the other types of responses were used.

As can be seen in figure 17.2, in the A-I condition, the percentage of infants' correct (*I Only*) responses ($M = 54.6\%$) was significantly greater than the percentages of each of the other (incorrect) types of responses (each of those means was less than 26%), Wilcoxon tests, $p < .05$ in each case. Similar results were obtained in the other two conditions. In the I-A condition, the percentage of infants' correct (*I Only*) responses ($M = 60.8\%$) was significantly greater than the percentages of each of

Table 17.2 Mean percentages for each type of response and results of Wilcoxon tests for each comparison in figure 17.2

Condition	Comparison (mean percentage of that type of response is in parentheses)		z and p values
Accidental-Intentional	I Only* (54.6%) versus:	A Only (25.4%) $AI^\dagger$ (15.8%) IA (4.2%)	$z = 2.26, p < .05$ $z = 3.38, p < .001$ $z = 3.70, p < .001$
Intentional-Accidental	I Only* (60.8%) versus:	A Only (18.3%) $IA^\dagger$ (11.7%) AI (9.2%)	$z = 2.88, p < .01$ $z = 3.41, p < .001$ $z = 3.54, p < .001$
Intentional-Intentional	$I_1I_2^{*\dagger}$ (41.3%) versus:	I_1 Only (22.1%) I_2 Only (21.7%) I_2I_1 (15.0%)	$z = 2.09, p < .05$ $z = 2.14, p < .05$ $z = 2.86, p < .01$

Notes: *This is the correct or imitative learning response. †This is the mimicking response.

the other types of responses (each of those means was less than 19%), $p < .01$ for each Wilcoxon test. In the I-I condition, the percentage of infants' correct (I_1I_2) responses ($M = 41.3\%$) was significantly greater than the percentages of each of the other types of responses (each of those means was less than 23%), $p < .05$ for each Wilcoxon test (see table 17.2 for individual means for each type of response and z and p values for each comparison). Infants thus reproduced the correct, intentional actions significantly more often than they produced any other type of response in each of the three experimental conditions.

Of particular theoretical interest is the comparison between infants' tendencies to engage in imitative learning versus mimicking. In the previous analysis, a correct response (reproduction of the intentional actions only) indicated imitative learning. A mimicking response was a response in which infants reproduced both actions in order in the A-I and I-A conditions, without regard for the intentionality of the actions. Recall that infants responded correctly (i.e., engaged in imitative learning) significantly more often than any other type of response, including mimicking (see table 17.2 for mean percentages). Whereas in the I-I condition, imitative learning could not directly be distinguished from mimicking, a comparison of infants' tendencies to reproduce both of the modeled actions in order in the I-I versus in the A-I and I-A conditions sheds some light on what they were doing in the I-I condition. Infants reproduced both actions in order in the I-I condition ($M = 41.3\%$ of their total responses in this condition) significantly more often than they did so in either the A-I ($M = 15.8\%$, $z = 2.86$, $p < .01$) or I-A ($M = 11.7\%$, $z = 3.41$, $p < .001$) conditions. Thus, infants imitated the sequence of two actions significantly more often when it was appropriate to do so, that is, when both actions were marked as intentional. They thus engaged in imitative learning more often than they mimicked throughout the experiment.

Other analyses.   To rule out other explanations for the results presented above, a final set of analyses was conducted in which the effects of various methodological factors were investigated.

Practice effects.   Because infants received a total of 12 demonstration and response trials, 8 of which included accidental actions, it was important to make sure that the finding of differential imitation of intentional and accidental actions was not due solely to practice or training effects. That is, because infants were rewarded only for performing the intentional actions, they may have learned over the course of the session to discriminate and reproduce these actions for reasons other than the intentionality behind them. Two sets of analyses were conducted in order to address this potential concern.

First, a comparison was made of infants' responses on the first versus second trial for each object. The number of correct responses for each infant collapsing across all six test objects (and all three conditions) was computed for the first and second trials separately. Infants responded correctly on average 50.4% of the time following the first demonstration and 52.7% of the time following the second demonstration. This difference was not statistically significant, $z = .45$. A second analysis investigated whether the percentage of infants' correct responses improved across the entire session by comparing infants' best responses (i.e., if infants responded correctly on one of the two trials, their best response would be correct) on the first versus last object they saw. Infants' best responses were correct 83.3% of the time for the first object, on average, and 63.2% of the time for the last (sixth) object, a finding in direct opposition to a hypothesis of practice effects. This difference was marginally significant, $z = 1.63$, $p = .052$.

Infants thus did not improve significantly either after repeated exposure to individual objects or after repeated exposure to different objects. They thus were not trained or conditioned to respond correctly but instead apparently came into the study with the ability to discriminate intentional from accidental actions. Indeed, if anything, they did more poorly at the end of the session than at the beginning. It is possible that this was due to the relatively high rate of "accidents" infants witnessed. That is, because infants saw a total of eight accidents throughout the course of their visit, their attention may have been called to these actions more than it would have been in a more natural setting and the accidental status of these actions may have decreased. If this were the case, infants might be expected to reproduce more of the accidental actions at the end of the session as compared with the beginning. This is indeed what we found: on average, infants reproduced significantly more accidental actions on the last object in the A-I or I-A condition (55.0% of the accidental actions modeled) than on the first one (35.0%), $z = 1.90$, $p < .05$.

Blind coding of demonstrations. Midway through the study, a blind coding was done of the actions to determine whether a naive adult could tell whether the action was modeled intentionally or accidentally without using E1's vocalization. An independent research assistant watched a tape of the demonstration periods for six randomly selected infants with the sound off and made a forced choice as to whether each action was intentional or accidental. The coder, like the infants, had only one chance to watch each demonstration. The adult's coding provided the opportunity to see whether possible visual differences in the ways accidental and intentional actions were performed affected infants' responses. That is, if infants reproduced more of the actions that *looked* intentional and fewer of the actions that *looked* accidental, irrespective of the condition in which they were modeled, an explanation involving the saliency of the actions based on temporal or other surface features instead of intentionality would be possible.

The adult was able to guess correctly using only visual information on 75.4% of the actions (this is more than chance, binomial test, $p < .01$). He incorrectly identified 26.1% of the intentional actions as accidental and 21.7% of the accidental actions as intentional. To address the issue of whether infants responded correctly based purely on visual aspects of the demonstrations, an analysis was conducted in which the correctness of infants' responses was compared for when the blind coder was correct versus incorrect. A 2 (coder correct vs. incorrect) × 2 (infant correct – i.e., reproduced the action when it was modeled as intentional and did not reproduce it when it was modeled as accidental – vs. incorrect) chi-square analysis yielded significant results, $\chi^2 = 6.81$, $p < .01$. There was an *inverse* relation between the correctness of the coder and the infants, however. When the coder correctly identified the condition of the action, infants responded correctly ($M = 51.0\%$ of their responses) as often as incorrectly ($M = 49.0\%$). When the coder was incorrect, however, infants responded correctly ($M = 76.5\%$ of their responses) more often than incorrectly ($M = 23.5\%$). Infants thus responded correctly more often than not even when it was not obvious from a visual standpoint alone what type of action was being modeled. Infants' actions thus were likely influenced more by the way in which the adult's actions were marked vocally ("Woops!" or "There!") than by the way they looked.

Correlations with age and language level.   Finally, analyses were conducted to determine 1) whether there were any differences in the way the younger and older infants responded and 2) whether there was any relation between infants' imitative abilities and their level of vocabulary production. Infants' age in days at the time of testing was correlated with each of the measures discussed above (i.e., percentage of intentional and accidental actions overall and by condition, and percentage of each type of response in each condition). There were no significant correlations, indicating that there was no clear developmental trend during this age range. There also were no significant correlations between infants' scores on the vocabulary checklist and their performance on the imitation tasks.

Discussion

Infants in this study watched an adult perform sequences of two actions on objects which were followed by interesting results. Some of the adult's actions were marked vocally as intentional, some were marked as accidental. Results indicated that the infants imitated significantly more of the intentional than the accidental actions. These results thus provide evidence of an ability to distinguish intentional from accidental actions at a younger age than previously demonstrated (i.e., in Tomasello and Barton's, 1994, study of 2-year-olds). In addition, the infants in this study were, on average, two months younger than Meltzoff's (1995) 18-month-olds, who showed evidence of under-standing intentional actions in a different paradigm (and some of the successful infants were four months younger).

In order to succeed at the current task, as in Meltzoff's (1995) study, infants had to 1) interpret the adult's overall behavior as intentional (e.g., the adult was acting with the goal of turning on the light), and 2) reproduce only the adult's intended actions without mimicking exactly her "surface behavior," or what she actually did. That is, infants in this study could have reproduced the adult's actions exactly (even with the words she used) *and still produced the end result* because the result was activated if infants reproduced the intentional action(s), regardless of whether they reproduced the accidental ones as well. However, they chose instead to reproduce for the most part only those actions the adult had marked as intentional, skipping over her accidental actions. Whether the infants made a choice following the demonstration (i.e., "she didn't mean to do A so B must be what I should do") or whether infants did not really "see" or register the accidental actions in the first place (as is sometimes the subjective experience of adults) is unknown. What is clear is that infants seem to understand something about the intentions of others before age 18 months and that they use this under-standing to make sense of others' behavior.

Whereas infants imitated more of the adult's intentional than acci-dental actions, they nonetheless did reproduce some of the accidental actions. There are several reasons why this might be the case. For example, because infants were not given a chance to interact with the objects before the adult's demonstrations, they may have reproduced some of the adult's actions simply because they looked like fun, irre-spective of the adult's intentions and/or the relation between the actions and the end result. Because the conditions to which actions were assigned were randomized, infants' tendencies to reproduce actions for fun would not have affected their differential imitation of the intentional actions across experimental conditions. Infants also saw a total of eight "accidents" during the course of their visit. The high rate of accidents may have called infants' attention to the accidental actions and decreased their perceived status as accidental.

Another procedural factor that may have increased the number of accidental actions infants reproduced was the relative subtlety of the dif-ferences between the accidental and intentional versions of the modeled actions. In natural situations, accidental actions may be quicker, less definite, and thus less salient than intentional actions. We attempted in this study to reduce these differences somewhat by making actions look very similar across conditions, with the main difference being the vocal markers used. This was done for purposes of experimental control, so that any differences found in infants' tendency to imitate intentional versus accidental actions could not be attributed to the timing or saliency of the actions. Given the barely verbal status of these infants, the lack of obvious or exaggerated physical cues about the adult's intentions (which normally are present in more natural situations) may have made it more difficult for infants to distinguish between them. Whereas an adult who was blind to the condition of the modeled actions often could guess whether the actions were modeled accidentally or intentionally using only visual cues, it appears as though infants did not use this information, as their rates of responding correctly and incorrectly were almost identical when the adult was correct. Infants thus seemed to be relying primarily on the vocal markers of intentionality provided by the experimenter.

There are several other methodological factors that may have affected our results. First, this was a difficult task in that whereas many previous studies of imitation (e.g., Carpenter et al., 1998; Meltzoff, 1995) gave infants three demonstrations of a single action before each response period, infants in this study responded after seeing a demonstration composed of two actions only once. There also were several indications that reproducing a sequence of two actions, as opposed to a single action, was difficult for these infants (as it is for most infants of this age, Bauer and Hertsgaard, 1993). During the training period, most of the infants had more trouble reproducing two actions than one and during the test trials, too, infants in the majority of their responses – 67.6% across all three conditions – imitated only one of the two modeled actions. Still, when infants reproduced only one of the two modeled actions in the A-I and I-A conditions, it was significantly more often the intentional one. In addition, even though reproducing a sequence of two actions was difficult for these infants, they nevertheless responded in this way more often when it was the correct response (in the I-I condition) than when it was not (in the other two conditions).

The combination of different patterns of responding in different conditions and the fact that infants did not improve across the session or across repeated presentations of individual objects makes purely methodological explanations of our results implausible. It thus appears that before age 18 months, infants have a relatively advanced understanding of others' intentions. During the 9 to 12 month period, they first show evidence of understanding that others have intentions and that these intentions may differ from their own (see Tomasello, 1995 for a review). The earliest evidence we have of the more complex understanding that others' intentions may differ from the reality of the situation (an understanding that is analogous to that of false belief), is in 14- through 18-month-olds.

This understanding of others' intentions is one of the first steps in the development of a theory of mind and an adult-like understanding of other persons (Tomasello, 1995). Moreover, the results demonstrate that when attempting to reproduce the actions of others, infants at this age quite often are able to "screen out" others' unintentional, meaningless actions. This is an important ability because many of the most significant cultural skills that children must master during the toddler and preschool periods – including language and other cultural conventions – can only be acquired via the imitative learning of the intentional actions of other persons.

Notes

1 Because conditions and actions were randomized and not counterbalanced, we checked to make sure that actions were evenly distributed in terms of order and condition for each object. They were: all six 3 (condition) × 2 (order of actions) χ^2s were not statistically significant.

2 During the training period, most of the infants had more trouble reproducing two actions than one: whereas 15 of the 20 infants reproduced the single action modeled on the first training object without teaching, only 6 infants reproduced the sequence of two actions modeled on the second training object without teaching. After teaching, however, all 20 infants reproduced one action and 18 of the 20 reproduced two.

3 At least one trial was dropped for six of the infants, with a total of nine dropped trials. Five of the dropped trials were due to procedural errors (mechanical failures and experimenter error) and in one case an infant was frightened by the end result. The first three trials of another infant's visit were dropped because his mother informed us at that point that they used "Uh oh" for accidents instead of 'Woops!" ("Uh oh" was used for the rest of that infant's visit).

4   No Response trials (i.e., trials in which infants did not reproduce either of the modeled actions) made up only a small percentage of the total trials: on average, the overall percentage of no response trials was 6.3% (5.0% for the A-I condition, 8.8% for the I-A condition, and 5.0% for the I-I condition). Including these trials in the total trials resulted in an identical pattern of statistically significant results to those reported below.

References

Barr, R., Dowden, A., & Hayne, H. (1996). Developmental changes in deferred imitation by 6- to 24-month-old infants. *Infant Behavior and Development, 19,* 159–170.

Bauer, P. J., & Hertsgaard, L. A. (1993). Increasing steps in recall of events: Factors facilitating immediate and long-term memory in 13.5- and 16.5-month-old children. *Child Development, 64,* 1204–1223.

Carpenter, M., Nagell, K., & Tomasello, M. (1998). Social cognition, joint attention, and communicative competence from 9 to 15 months of age. Monographs of the Society for Research in Child Development.

Galef, B. G. (1988). Imitation in animals: History, definition, and interpretation of data from the psychological laboratory. In T. R. Zentall, & B. G. Galef, Jr. (Eds.), *Social learning: Psychological and biological perspectives* (pp. 3–28). Hillsdale, NJ: Erlbaum.

Gergely, G., Csibra, G., Bíró, S., & Koós, O. (1994, June). The comprehension of intentional action in infancy. Poster presented at the 9th International Conference on Infant Studies, Paris, France.

Gergely, G., Nádasdy, Z., Csibra, G., & Bíró, S. (1995). Taking the intentional stance at 12 months of age. *Cognition, 56,* 165–193.

Karniol, R. (1978). Children's use of intention cues in evaluating behavior. *Psychological Bulletin, 85,* 76–85.

Meltzoff, A. N. (1988). Infant imitation after a 1-week delay: Long-term memory for novel acts and multiple stimuli. *Developmental Psychology, 24,* 470–476.

Meltzoff, A. N. (1995). Understanding the intentions of others: Re-enactment of intended acts by 18-month-old children. *Developmental Psychology, 31,* 1–16.

Mumme, D. L., Fernald, A., & Herrera, C. (1996). Infants' responses to vocal and facial expressions in a social referencing paradigm. *Child Development, 67,* 3219–3237.

Phillips, W., Baron-Cohen, S., & Rutter, M. (1992). The role of eye contact in goal detection: Evidence from normal infants and children with autism or mental handicap. *Development and Psychopathology, 4,* 375–383.

Reznick, J. S., & Goldsmith, L. (1989). A multiple form word production checklist for assessing early language. *Journal of Child Language, 16*, 91–100.

Shultz, T. R., & Wells, D. (1985). Judging the intentionality of action-outcomes. *Developmental Psychology, 21*, 83–89.

Shultz, T. R., Wells, D., & Sarda, M. (1980). Development of the ability to distinguish intended actions from mistakes, reflexes, and passive movements. *British Journal of Social and Clinical Psychology, 19*, 301–310.

Smith, M. C. (1978). Cognizing the behavior stream: The recognition of intentional action. *Child Development, 49*, 736–743.

Tomasello, M. (1995). Joint attention as social cognition. In C. Moore, & P. Dunham (Eds.), *Joint attention: Its origins and role in development* (pp. 103–130). Hillsdale, NJ: Erlbaum.

Tomasello, M. (1996). Do apes ape? In B. Galef, & C. Heyes (Eds.), *Social learning in animals: The roots of culture* (pp. 319–346). New York: Academic Press.

Tomasello, M., & Barton, M. (1994). Learning words in nonostensive contexts. *Developmental Psychology, 30*, 639–650.

Tomasello, M., Kruger, A. C., & Ratner, H. H. (1993). Cultural learning. *Behavioral and Brain Sciences, 16*, 495–552.

Tomasello, M., Strosberg, R., & Akhtar, N. (1996). Eighteen-month-old children learn words in nonostensive contexts. *Journal of Child Language, 23*, 157–176.

Whiten, A., & Ham, R. (1992). On the nature and evolution of imitation in the animal kingdom: Reappraisal of a century of research. In P. J. B. Slater, J. S. Rosenblatt, C. Beer, & M. Milinski (Eds.), *Advances in the study of behavior* (Vol. 21, pp. 239–283). New York: Academic Press.

Appendix

	Training objects	
Object	*Action(s)*	*End result*
Wooden box	Press doorbell	Lights
Wooden box	Lift doorstop, twang spring	Toy appears

	Test objects	
Object	*Actions*	*End result*
Wooden bird feeder	Hit top up, pull ring	Party favor
Blue wooden box	Pull handle up, spin wheel	Toy appears
Metal duct	Lift front, hit attached circle	Lights
Newspaper recycler	Push hinge, pull string	Toy appears
Colored wooden box	Spin spinner, lift hinge	Party favor
Aluminum-can crusher	Slide attached door-bolt, depress front of crusher	Lights

Note: Lights were sets of colorful Christmas-tree lights that were turned on for several seconds; toys were small toys (e.g., balls with bells inside) that were lowered from their hiding place (an inverted box – see figure 17.1) by a string, dangled, and then suddenly pulled back up into the hiding place by the string; party favors were air-powered poppers that were inflated by a pump several times. Each wooden box, toy, light set, and party favor was decorated differently.

EIGHTEEN

Social Attachments

Introduction

Perhaps the most dramatic and important social phenomenon in infancy is the development of an infant's attachment to its primary caregiver (although others can serve in this capacity, mothers usually are the primary attachment figures in the Western culture). Although babies may discriminate between mothers and strangers at an early age, most begin to show a fear of strangers around 6 months of age. By 12 months, most babies become very upset when they are left with strangers, or alone in a strange room (in the lab). This is readily apparent to a new babysitter who is left with a child who begins to cry after the mother's departure and continues to do so until her return.

Mary Ainsworth and co-workers (Ainsworth et al., 1978) developed an experimental assessment of this attachment response in infants between 12 and 18 months of age, the Strange Situation Test (SST). It involves several brief periods in which the mother leaves her infant in a play-room alone or with a stranger. Four types of infants have been classified based in part on their behavior when the mother returns to the room. *Secure* infants greet the mother, make visual or physical contact, and then settle down to independent play. Three *insecure* categories have been defined. "Avoidant" infants ignore their mothers. "Resistant" infants may alternate between clinging to their mothers and pushing them away, or show prolonged crying. "Disorganized" infants have been identified recently; they appear to be disoriented during the procedure and sometimes show fear of the mother. These different patterns of response have been related to different histories of parent-child interactions, although the relationship is not perfect. Secure infants' mothers tend to be warm, consistent, and attentive; avoidant infant's mothers are more distant; resistant infant's mothers are more ambivalent and inconsistent; and disorganized infants' mothers may be depressed or abusive.

According to attachment theory (initially formulated by Bowlby, 1969), these different attachment types have developed different "working models" or mental schemas of their primary attachment relationship which influence future social relationships with peers, teachers, spouses, and eventually with their own children. For example, a disproportionate number of children (e.g., Goldberg, 1997) and adults with various behavioral problems (including criminal behavior; Wand et al., 1996) have a history of insecure attachments.

Recently, investigators have begun to ask the question: are patterns of attachment passed on from one generation to the next? Benoit and Parker have conducted an impressive longitudinal study on three generations, infants, mothers, and grandmothers, to provide an answer to this question. They found an 88% agreement in the attachment classifications of the mothers and the infants. The relationships between all three generations are clearly illustrated in figure 18.1 which traces the attachment type of each grandmother, mother and infant. This finding, at the very least, underlines the importance of early social relationships.

Benoit and Parker's paper is necessarily brief and thus does not provide detailed information on attachment theory and how working models are measured in people of different ages. Goldberg (1991; in Slater and Muir, 1999) provides an excellent short review of attachment theory and a more detailed description of the adult attachment scale is given by Main et al. (1985). An up-date on recent theoretical and empirical work on attachment is presented by Waters et al. (1995).

References

Ainsworth, M., Blehar, M., Waters, E., and Wall, S. (1978). *Patterns of attachment*. Hillsdale, NJ: Erlbaum.

Bowlby, J. (1969). *Attachment and Loss: Attachment*. New York: Basic Books.

Goldberg, S. (1991). Recent developments in attachment theory and research. *Canadian Journal of Psychiatry*, *36*, 393–400. In A. Slater, and D. Muir (eds.) (1999). *The Blackwell Reader in Developmental Psychology*. Oxford, UK: Blackwell.

Goldberg, S. (1997). Attachment and childhood behavior problems in normal, at risk, and clinical samples. In L. Atkinson and K. J. Zucker (eds.) *Attachment and Psychopathology* (pp. 171–95). New York: Guilford Press.

Main, M., Kaplan, N., and Cassidy, J. (1985). Security in infancy, childhood, and adulthood: A move to the level of representation. In I. Bretherton and E. Waters (eds.). Growing points in attachment theory and research (pp. 66–104), *Monographs of the Society for Research in Child Development, 50* (1–2, Serial No. 209).

Waters, E., Vaughn, B., Posada, G., and Kondo-Ikemura, K. (eds.) (1995). Caregiving, Cultural, and Cognitive Perspectives on Secure-Base Behavior and Working Models: New Growing Points of Attachment Theory and Research. *Monographs of the Society for Research in Child Development. 60,* (2–3, Serial No. 244).

Wand, T., Hudson, S. and Marshall, W. (1996). Attachment Style in Sex Offenders: A preliminary study. *Journal of Sex Research, 33,* 17–26.

Note: To save space some discussions of interest to the specialist concerning methodological details, interrater reliability, and alternative attachment classifications in the original paper were removed by the authors from the version reproduced here.

Stability and Transmission of Attachment across Three Generations

Diane Benoit, and Kevin C. H. Parker

Bowlby (1969/1982) suggested that *internal working models* are dynamic mental processes that influence an individual's affect, behavior, and perceptions of the self, others, and relationships. He also contended that working models have a propensity for stability within individuals and across generations. One of the major methodological breakthroughs in attachment research was the development of empirical means for "measuring" working models of attachment in infants, using the Strange Situation (SS; Ainsworth et al., 1978), and *states of mind* with respect to attachment in adults, using the Adult Attachment Interview (AAI; George et al., 1985).

The scoring system of the AAI is similar to that of the SS in that *patterns* of responses are considered to categorize an adult's *state of mind* with respect to attachment. In other words, the scoring of the AAI relies primarily on qualitative aspects of the adult's descriptions rather than on factual information provided by the adult. Based on patterns of responses to the AAI, the adult's state of mind is then classified as *autonomous, dismissing, preoccupied,* or *unresolved*.

Adults classified as autonomous are generally thoughtful, value attachment experiences and relationships, and freely examine the effects past experiences have had on personal development. They either provide balanced, noncontradictory descriptions of one or both parents as loving during childhood, or if they had unfortunate experiences such as rejection, role reversal, or abuse, they have convincingly forgiven their parent(s) for the maltreatment.

Individuals classified as dismissing tend to dismiss attachment experiences as unimportant in influencing their personal development and their approach to their own children. They may insist that they cannot remember early events. The memories they do recall often contradict or fail to support their generally idealized descriptions of early experiences.

Individuals classified as preoccupied are often entangled with their early experiences and relationships with their family. They rarely have difficulty remembering early events but have difficulty presenting a coherent and succinct report of childhood experiences. They may be still dependent upon their parents and want to please them inordinately. Some preoccupied individuals may still be intensely angry with their parents.

The discourse of individuals classified as unresolved may show characteristics of any of the three other classifications but a primary unresolved classification is assigned when there is evidence of significant lapses in *metacognitive monitoring* of discourse or reasoning processes when discussing loss or trauma (Main and Hesse, 1990). These lapses may take the form of confusion or disorientation when loss of a loved one through death or experiences of sexual and/or physical abuse are discussed. Reports of behavioral disorganization in response to loss or trauma are also considered for unresolved classification (Main and Hesse, 1990).

Studies that have used both the AAI and the SS have documented an impressive 66%–82% correspondence between patterns of mothers' responses to the AAI and patterns of infants' behavior toward the mothers in the SS, whether the data are examined prospectively, retrospectively, or concurrently (e.g. Fonagy et al., 1991; Zeanah et al., 1993). The specific adult-infant pairings are: autonomous-secure, dismissing-avoidant, preoccupied-resistant, and unresolved disorgnized/disoriented.

Findings from these studies provide indirect evidence of the validity and cross-generational stability of adults' states of mind with respect to attachment. Nonetheless, the psychometric properties of the AAI (unlike those of the SS) are still unclear. Specifically, there are no published reports on the stability of AAI classifications within individuals. However, Ward et al. (1992) recently presented preliminary data on 18 adolescent mothers indicating a 78% correspondence between AAI classifications during pregnancy and about 18 months later (using the four-category classification system). In addition, a correspondence between mothers' and their own mothers' AAI classifications has never been documented. Finally, studies that have examined the transmission of attachment across generations have been limited to two generations (parent and infant).

The present study contributes to our understanding of the AAI in three ways. First, it examines the stability of AAI classifications within individuals, from pregnancy to 11 months after delivery, in a stable, middle- to upper-middle-class sample. Second, it examines the correspondence between mothers' and their own mothers' attachment classifications. Finally, it explores the transmission of patterns of attachment across *three* generations.

Method

Subjects and procedures

One hundred and ten expectant mothers were recruited. Criteria for inclusion were that the expectant mother be at least 18 years old and have an uncomplicated pregnancy and that her mother agree to participate in the study.

Of these 110 mothers, 14 (13%) either miscarried or decided not to participate after more information about the project was provided. Of the 96 remaining mothers, 12 (13%) completed only parts of the study.

During a final sample (see table 18.1 for details), informed consent and general demographic information were obtained from the 96 mothers of the final sample. The mothers were interviewed twice with the AAI: once during the last month of pregnancy and once 2 to 4 weeks before they were seen with their 12-month-old infants in the SS.

The maternal grandmothers were interviewed at any time during the course of the study (i.e., whenever they were available) after informed consent was obtained. Interviews with the mothers and grandmothers were conducted in the lab or in the subjects' homes. However, eight grandmothers who lived out of town and were not expected to visit during the course of the study were interviewed over the telephone.

Table 18.1 Characteristics of the sample

	M	SD	Range	%
Mothers ($N = 96$):				
Age (years)	29.17	4.08	20–39	...
Education (years)	15.58	2.99	9–27	...
SES computed score	44.52	13.57	14–66	...
% Married	...	...	...	98
Infants ($N = 96$):				
Gestational age (weeks)	40.19	1.87	34.5–43.0	...
Birthweight (kilograms)	3.56	.53	2.3–4.6	...
% Firstborn	...	...	...	46
% Male	...	...	...	55
Maternal grandmothers ($N = 81$):				
Age (years)	57.26	7.68	41–75	...
Education (years)	13.24	3.48	5–23	...
Marital status:				
% Married	...	...	...	77
% Widowed	...	...	...	13

Measures

Adult Attachment Interview (AAI; George et al., 1985). This 1-hour structured interview inquires about an adult's recollection and evaluation of early attachment experiences. The interview is audiorecorded, and verbatim transcripts are then rated using 14 9-point scales to measure the adult's *probable experience* with each attachment figure during childhood (three scales) and his or her current *state of mind* with regard to attachment (11 scales).

 Interrater reliability was examined using 32 transcripts from this study and 10 transcripts from another study. Overall agreement was 74% and 83% for the major classifications in the three- and four-way classifications, respectively (kappa = .61 and .74).

 Strange Situation (SS; Ainsworth et al., 1978). This is a well-known laboratory paradigm consisting of a series of 3-min episodes designed to be increasingly stressful for 12–18-month-old infants. The procedure was videotaped and infant behaviors were coded using four 7-point anchored rating scales for proximity seeking, contact maintaining, avoidance, and resistance and one 9-point anchored rating scale for disorganization (Main and Solomon, 1986, 1990).

Based on patterns of infant behavior directed toward the caregiver, the quality of infant-caregiver attachment was classified into one of four categories: secure, avoidant, resistant, or disorganized/disoriented. In the three-category version of the SS, infants classified as disorganized/disoriented are force-classified into one of the other three categories. The reliability and validity of this procedure have been well documented in numerous investigations. Both raters received training in the coding of the SS from Alan Sroufe and Mary Main.

Interrater reliability was examined using 28 procedures from this study and 10 procedures from a related study using the same children with their fathers instead of their mothers. Overall agreement was 86% and 84% for the major classifications in the three- and four-way classifications, respectively (kappa = .61 and .69).

Results

First, we present the results pertaining to the stability of the AAI classifications within mothers over a 12-month period. In the second section, we examine the transmission of attachment across generations. The AAI and SS data are presented in two ways: (a) the four-category classification system produced by including the AAI unresolved and SS disorganized/disoriented classifications, and (b) the original three-category classification system.

Stability of AAI classifications within individuals

As seen in table 18.2, 84 mothers responded to the questions of the AAI both during pregnancy and about 12 months later. When the four-category classification system is used, the concordance between maternal classifications obtained at pregnancy and 12 months later is 77%, compared to 38% expected by chance alone ($\chi^2 = 104.38$, $df = 9$, $p < .001$, kappa = .63). With one less category, both the observed and expected concordance rates should increase. Indeed, the three-category AAI classifications obtained during pregnancy remained stable 12 months later in 90% of the mothers, compared to 55% expected by chance alone ($\chi^2 = 101.10$, $df = 4$, $p < .001$, kappa = .79).

Table 18.2 Stability of mother's AAI four- and three-category classifications

| | Pregnancy AAI Classifications | | | | | | | | | |
| | Autonomous | | Dismissing | | Preoccupied | | Unresolved | | Total | |
11-month AAI classifications	N	(N)	N	(N)	N	(N)	N	(N)	N	(N)
Autonomous	38	(57)	1	(1)	1	(2)	3	(–)	43	(60)
Dismissing	0	(0)	4	(6)	0	(0)	0	(–)	4	(6)
Preoccupied	1	(2)	1	(3)	5	(13)	1	(–)	8	(18)
Unresolved	7	(–)	3	(–)	1	(–)	18	(–)	29	(–)
	46	(59)	9	(10)	7	(15)	22	(–)	84	(84)

Notes: Values in parentheses are for the three-category system. Observed match = 77% (90%) vs. 38% (55%) expected by chance alone. Kappa = .63 (.79), p < .001 (p < .002). Chi-square = 104.38 (101.10), df = 9 (4), p < .001 (.001). Cramer V = .64 (.78).

Transmission of attachment across generations

Grandmother-mother. The concordance between grandmothers' and mothers' attachment classifications was examined in the 81 dyads for whom data were available. As seen in table 18.3, the concordance between mothers' AAI classifications during pregnancy and their own mothers' AAI classifications was significant when the data were examined using the three-category classification system ($\chi^2 = 43.95$, $df = 4$, $p < .001$, kappa = .51, $p < .05$) but not when the four-category classification system was used ($\chi^2 = 25.09$, $df = 9$, $p < .003$, kappa = .18, N.S.) Note that 44 grandmothers (54%), compared to 24 mothers (30%), were classified as unresolved, and 23 of the unresolved grandmothers had autonomous daughters. Both the three- and four-category chi-squares are significantly different from the expected values. The three-category kappa is significantly different from zero but not the four-category kappa. The failure of the four-category kappa is due to the large number of unresolved grandmothers with autonomous daughters.

Mother-infant. The concordance between mother and infant attachment classifications was examined prospectively (pregnancy AAI and

Table 18.3 Correspondence between maternal grandmothers' AAI and mothers' (pregnancy) AAI classifications, four- and three-category systems

	Maternal grandmothers' AAI classifications									
	Autonomous		Dismissing		Preoccupied		Unresolved		Total	
Mothers' AAI classifications	N	(N)	N	(N)	N	(N)	N	(N)	N	(N)
Autonomous	16	(45)	2	(8)	0	(3)	23	(–)	41	(56)
Dismissing	3	(3)	4	(5)	1	(2)	1	(–)	9	(10)
Preoccupied	2	(3)	0	(1)	1	(11)	4	(–)	7	(15)
Unresolved	5	(–)	1	(–)	2	(–)	16	(–)	24	(–)
	26	(51)	7	(14)	4	(16)	44	(–)	81	(81)

Notes: Values in parentheses are for the three-category classification system. Observed match = 46% (75%) vs. 34% (49%) expected by chance alone. Kappa = .18 (.51), N.S. ($p < .05$). Chi-square = 25.09 (43.95), $df = 9$ (4), $p < .003$ (.001). Cramer $V = .32$ (.52).

SS) on 88 mother-infant dyads (three infants with a primary disorganized/disoriented classification were dropped from the three-classification analyses because their behavior in the SS was unclassifiable using the three-calssification system) and concurrently (11-month AAI and SS) on 82 mother-infant dyads.

As seen in table 18.4, there was a 68% match (vs. 41% expected by chance alone) between pregnancy AAI and infant SS when the prospective data of mother-infant dyads were examined with four classifications ($\chi^2 = 56.60$, $df = 9$, $p < .001$, kappa = .46). The match between maternal and infant classifications increased to 81% (vs. 58% expected by chance alone) when the three-category classification system was used ($\chi^2 = 47.59$, $df = 4$, $p < .001$, kappa = .55).

The concordance rates between maternal AAI and infant SS attachment classifications measured concurrently (about 2 weeks apart) was 74% (vs. 41% expected by chance; $\chi^2 = 71.20$, $df = 9$, $p < .001$, kappa = .56) with the four-classification system and was 82% (vs. 58% expected by chance alone; $\chi^2 = 49.17$, $df = 4$, $p < .001$, kappa = .57) with the three-classification system.

Table 18.4   Correspondence between mothers' (pregnancy) AAI and infants' SS classifications, four- and three-category systems

	Autonomous		*Dismissing*		*Preoccupied*		*Unresolved*		*Total*	
Infants' SS classifications	N	(N)	N	(N)	N	(N)	N	(N)	N	(N)
Secure	40	(56)	4	(4)	0	(0)	8	(–)	52	(65)
Avoidant	0	(1)	2	(4)	1	(1)	1	(–)	4	(6)
Resistant	1	(3)	1	(2)	4	(9)	1	(–)	7	(14)
Disorganized	7	(–)	2	(–)	2	(–)	14	(–)	25	(–)
	48	(60)	9	(10)	7	(15)	24	(–)	88	(85)

Mothers' (pregnancy) AAI classifications

Notes: Values in parentheses are for the three-category systems, without the adult unresolved and the infant disorganized/disoriented classifications. Observed match = 68% (81%) vs. 41% (58%) expected by chance alone. Kappa = .46 (.55), $p < .05$ (.05). Chi-square = 56.60 (47.59), df = 9 (4), $p < .001$ (.001). Cramer V = .46 (.53).

There were no statistically significant effects of infant birth order or sex on SS classifications.

Grandmother-mother-infant. Data from 77 grandmother-mother-infant triads were available and were used for analysis.[2] Figure 18.1 illustrates the complete distribution of three-category attachment classifications among the members of the 77 triads. In order to develop a statistical model of the transmission of attachment from one generation to the next, we used data from the three-category classification system. We began with a model consisting of a $3 \times 3 \times 3$ (grandmother × mother during pregnancy × infant three-category attachment) matrix containing 27 cells. The values in the 27 cells correspond to the values in the final numeric column of figure 18.1. The use of the three-category classification system was driven by the obvious sparseness of the data, with 77 triads dispersed amongst 27 cells for a mean cell frequency of 2.85. With 64 cells, the cell frequency would drop to 1.2.[3] Using log-linear analysis, we added predictive information in a stepwise cumulative manner until the distribution of observations among the 27 cells was predicted with no significant departure from goodness of fit.

Grandmothers   Mothers (pregnancy)   Infants

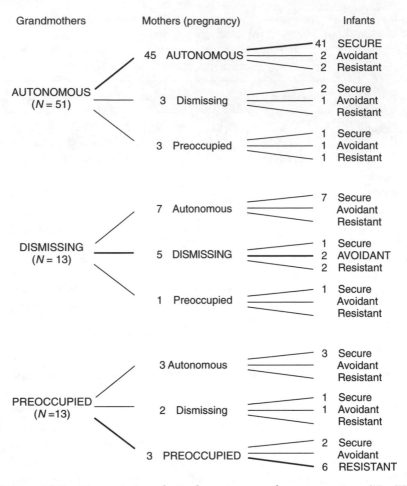

Figure 18.1   Transmission of attachment across three generations ($N = 77$)

In stage one, the distribution of the triads was predicted using the simple distribution of attachment in each of the three triad members: grandmother, mother (pregnancy), and child. This model assumes that there is no significant relationship between one generation's attachment and that of any other. The predicted values were significantly different from the observed values for both the three-category (likelihood ratio $\chi^2 = 73.21$, $df = 20$, $p < .001$) and the four-category (likelihood ratio

$\chi^2 = 94.18$, $df = 54$, $p < .001$) classification systems. This suggests a significant failure of the predictive model. When the mothers' 11-month AAI classifications are used, comparable results are obtained for both the three-category (likelihood ratio $\chi^2 = 70.3$, $df = 20$, $p < .001$) and the four-category (likelihood ratio $\chi^2 = 95.6$, $df = 54$, $p < .001$) classification systems.

In stage two, the distribution of triads was predicted using the assumption that the mother's attachment classification during pregnancy has a significant impact on the child's attachment classification. This applies from grandmother to mother, and from mother to infant. This model assumes that any attachment correspondence between grandmother and infant is an indirect effect mediated through the mother. There was no significant difference between the predicted and observed values for the three-category (likelihood ratio $\chi^2 = 11.05$, $df = 9$, N.S.) and four-category (likelihood ratio $\chi^2 = 30.61$, $df = 22$, N.S.) classification systems. This indicates that the predictive model is successful.

Note that when mothers' 11-month AAI classifications were used in stage two, there was no significant difference between the predicted and observed values for the three-category classification system (likelihood ratio $\chi^2 = 5.01$, $df = 9$, N.S.), but there was for the four-category system (likelihood ratio $\chi^2 = 19.78$, $df = 10$, $p < .05$). However, these significant results are considered to be untrustworthy because more than half of the grandmothers were classified as unresolved and more than one-third were classified as autonomous, leaving 11 subjects distributed among 32 cells. The extreme sparseness of the data renders the chi-square values questionable at best.

Information limited to the distribution of attachment classifications *within* generations fails to account for the joint distribution of attachment classifications *across* generations. However, the knowledge of the joint distribution of attachment classifications of mother and child (i.e., both the grandmother-mother classification and mother-infant classification) is sufficient to explain the distribution of the entire data set, including the correspondence between grandmother and infant classifications, as well as among all three generations. In other words, when the pattern of relationships between grandmothers and mothers or else between mothers and infants is known, one can infer all the other relationships among the family members to the limit of the accuracy of the data.

Figure 18.2 illustrates this point using the four-category classification systems of the AAI and SS. Indeed, one can see how the prediction of the infant's actual attachment classification improves when the mother's attachment classification is known by comparing the base rate and the actual rate. For example, the base rate indicates that 28%, 59%, 5%, and 8% of infants in this sample should be classified as disorganized/disoriented, secure, avoidant, and resistant, respectively. However, compared to the expected base rates, infants of unresolved mothers are 2.07 times more likely to be classified as disorganized, 1.79 times less likely to be classified as secure, 1.25 less likely to be classified as avoidant, and 2.00 times less likely to be classified as resistant. Similarly, compared to the expected base rates, infants of autonomous mothers are 1.86 times less likely to be classified as disorganized/disoriented, 1.41 times more likely to be classified as secure, and 4.00 times less likely to be classified as resistant (no infants of autonomous mothers were classified as avoidant when the four-category classification system was used). Compared to expected base rates, infants are 4.40 times more likely to be classified as avoidant when their mothers are classified as dismissing, and are 7.13 times more likely to be classified as resistant when their mothers are classified as preoccupied.

Discussion

An important finding from this study is that maternal AAI classifications remained stable from pregnancy to 11 months after delivery in 90% and 77% of cases when the three- and four-category classification systems were used, respectively. These findings suggest that states of mind with respect to attachment are very stable during adulthood. Although the high rate of stability may reflect, in part, the skew in our sample of the distribution of attachment classifications toward security, the preoccupied classification was stable (87% and 71% using the three- and four-classification systems, respectively). Similarly, 76% of mothers classified as unresolved during the pregnancy were also classified as unresolved 12 months later. The dismissing classification was less stable within mothers in our sample (60% and 44% using the three- and four-classification systems, respectively).

Possible mediators of stability within individuals of three-category adult attachment were examined in the 64 mothers for whom complete

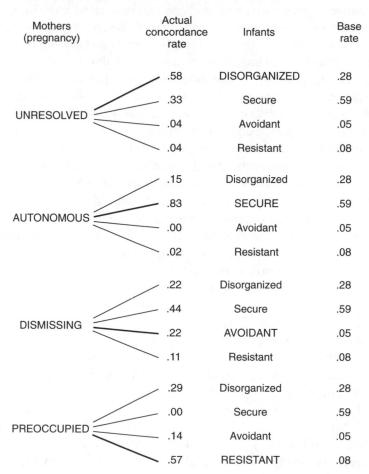

Mothers (pregnancy)	Actual concordance rate	Infants	Base rate
UNRESOLVED	.58	DISORGANIZED	.28
	.33	Secure	.59
	.04	Avoidant	.05
	.04	Resistant	.08
AUTONOMOUS	.15	Disorganized	.28
	.83	SECURE	.59
	.00	Avoidant	.05
	.02	Resistant	.08
DISMISSING	.22	Disorganized	.28
	.44	Secure	.59
	.22	AVOIDANT	.05
	.11	Resistant	.08
PREOCCUPIED	.29	Disorganized	.28
	.00	Secure	.59
	.14	Avoidant	.05
	.57	RESISTANT	.08

Figure 18.2 Prediction of infants' four-category SS attachment classifications from base rates and actual concordance rates ($N = 85$)

data sets were available. Questionnaire and interview measures of possible mediators of stability, including life stresses, social support, self-esteem, and marital satisfaction, were obtained during pregnancy and 12 months later. We found no significant mediators of stability of adult attachment among these variables. The most likely cause for these negative findings was the low power of any statistic measuring change in the context of high stability. Only five of the 64 subjects in this subsample changed attachment classification over 12 months, leaving little scope for measurement and analysis of change. Populations at risk for unstable adult attachment should be sought and studied in order to assess the nature and impact of mediators of stability.

In summary, although our data show evidence for the stability of attachment classifications within individuals, the stability rests primarily in the autonomous classification, while insecure classifications are four times as likely to be involved in changes. The determination of unresolved classifications seems to depend on a number of factors. Such factors may be subject-related (e.g., whether the subject reports the loss and trauma warranting an unresolved classification), interviewer-related (e.g., whether interviewer probes as extensively as necessary for every death and trauma), rater-related, and system-related.

Our data on the stability of AAI classification within individuals suggest that unresolved status may be quite unstable within some individuals, although the reasons for this remain unclear. Further, the unresolved classification is only weakly predictive across generations.

The finding that 54% of grandmothers, compared to 30% of mothers, were classified as unresolved was somewhat unexpected, although not surprising in hindsight. This finding may reflect the fact that, by virtue of their older age, the grandmothers have experienced more losses, including losses of significant attachment figures such as parents and spouses. In fact, the grandmothers in our sample experienced almost twice as many losses as their daughters ($M_{grandmothers} = 4.062$, SD = 1.826 vs. $M_{mothers} = 2.340$, SD = 1.695; paired $t = 7.683$, $df = 80$, $p < .001$). The individuals lost through death were often one or both parents, siblings, spouses, and even children. The number of losses through death, combined with the significance of the individuals lost, seem to make older adults more prone to unresolved mourning.

The AAI scoring system does not allow for the determination of when the grandmothers became unresolved following the loss or trauma that led to the unresolved classification. It would be interesting to discover whether the correspondence between grandmothers' and mothers' attachment classifications would be affected if one knew when the grandmothers became unresolved. This observation is especially pertinent when examining the transmission of attachment patterns across generations and it also raises questions about the applicability and meaning of unresolved classifications in older adults (especially unresolved mourning which seems to be so prevalent in the older adults in our sample). Indeed, one could argue that "being" unresolved while raising one's children might impact the children, quality of caregiving, and transmission of attachment across generations quite differently from "becoming" unresolved later in life. Future research should examine these questions and look for possible factors that might place individuals at risk for or protect them against unresolved mourning and trauma.

Because the presence of an unresolved classification is dependent on the occurrence of a *specific event* (loss or trauma) in a person's life, one should not expect the unresolved status *per se* to be transmitted across generations. Whereas the other three classifications (autonomous, dismissing, and preoccupied) assess states of mind with respect to attachment, the unresolved status may be more properly described as a reaction to a specific event in one's life. Indeed, unless the specific event leading to the unresolved status in one individual was shared and similarly experienced by another individual, the impact of the event is not likely to be transmitted from one generation to the next. Further, the event leading to an unresolved status is located in time; once it has occurred, there is no other necessary connection in time between when the event occurred and when the person achieved unresolved status. In the end, while unresolved status in caregivers predicts disorganization in their infants, the absence of a specific event precludes the development of unresolved status. The question of whether and how disorganization in infancy predisposes to unresolved classification later in life should be addressed in future research.

It is worth noting that most of our subjects were from intact, middle- to upper-middle-class families. As was demonstrated with SS classifications in infants from families under stress (Vaughn et al., 1979), it is possible that AAI classifications of adults from more stressed and impoverished backgrounds would be less stable.

Nonetheless, our finding of 90% stability of AAI three-category classifications over 12 months in this middle-class sample is compelling. The 90% stability is in keeping with the 73%–96% stability reported in studies examining the stability of SS three-category classifications in middle- to upper-middle-class samples (Main and Weston, 1981, Waters, 1978, 1983). Together, the findings from these and the present study provide strong empirical evidence for Bowlby's (1969/1982) contention that working models of attachment have a propensity for stability within individuals.

Another important finding from this study is that when the three-category systems are used, the mother's AAI classification obtained during pregnancy successfully predicted her infant's SS classification at infant's age 12 months in 82% of cases. This impressive concordance is somewhat higher than the 66% match recently reported by Fonagy and colleagues (1991), also using the three-category systems. The discrepancy between our results and those of Fonagy et al. is quite consistent with the difference in the distribution of three-category attachment classifications in the two samples. More mothers were classified as autonomous in our sample (71%) than in Fonagy et al.'s (61%). Such increased skew toward the largest classification tends to increase stability as a statistical artifact. Using log-linear analysis, we tested the correspondence between Fonagy et al.'s matrix of mother-child attachment and our own. When the different distribution of attachment classifications in the two studies is taken into account, there is no significant difference between the two matrices (likelihood ratio $\chi^2 = 4.35$, $df = 4$, N.S.). A larger number of insecure AAI classifications in our sample would probably have led to a lower concordance rate.

Our findings concerning the stability of adult attachment and the predictive value of maternal attachment assessed during pregnancy on infant attachment assessed at 12 months have implications for the early identification of those mother-infant dyads at risk for the development of relationship problems. Indeed, insecure maternal attachment – as assessed by the three-category classification system – has been overrepresented in clinical infant populations (van IJzendoorn, 1993; 1996). This suggests that maternal security of attachment may act as a factor protecting against the development of a variety of clinical problems in infants, whereas insecure maternal attachment may act as a risk factor (Benoit et al., 1992). The relation between parental unresolved attachment classifications and the clinical status of infants remains to be examined.

Another significant finding from the present study provides compelling evidence for Bowlby's (1969/1982) contention that internal working models of attachment tend to be perpetuated across generations (i.e., cross-generational stability). When the three-category adult and infant attachment classifications were examined across three generations, 65% of 77 grandmother-mother-infant triads had corresponding attachment classifications in all three generations. These results must be viewed cautiously because of the skewed distribution of attachment toward security in the sample. Our protocol did not permit the direct exploration of factors that might account for the movement between categories of attachment across generations. Future research in the field should address these important questions.

Several limitations of the present study must be stressed. First, the skewed distribution of attachment classifications toward security and the demographic characteristics of the sample, in particular high maternal education and socioeconomic status, are not representative of the general population. Thus, generalization of our findings to individuals with other demographic characteristics must be cautious. Future studies examining the stability of adult attachment and the transmission of attachment across generations should include subjects who are less educated and are from stressed and impoverished environments. Second, the psychological characteristics of the mothers and grandmothers were not examined in depth in the present study. Evidence about intellectual, personality, and other individual characteristics of parents as they relate to adult attachment would be valuable.

Bowlby (1980, 1969/1982) suggests that what may be transmitted across generations is an internal working model of attachment relationships. Caregivers' states of mind with respect to attachment may be derived from actual and perceived childhood experiences with attachment figures and may influence behavior in caregiving situations. This model of transmission suggests that what may be transmitted across generations may be a state of mind, which is communicated to the child via parental behavior, especially parental response at times of stress (when the attachment system is activated). We hope to explore in future research the questions of whether and how states of mind with respect to attachment relate to parental behavior in "noncaregiving" situations (e.g., play, teaching) or in situations where the attachment system is not activated. Although our study did not directly examine mechanisms of transmission of attachment across generations, the findings add one more link to the chain of evidence that tends to support Bowlby's contentions about attachment. Studies examining both the mechanisms of transmission across generations and the mediators of stability of attachment within individuals and across generations are needed.

Notes

1   Mothers' pregnancy AAIs were used for data analysis because more pregnancy than 11-month AAIs were available ($n = 81$ vs. $n = 74$). The concordance between mothers' (11-month) and their own mothers' AAI

classifications was significant when the data were examined using the three-category classification system ($\chi^2 = 34.93$, $df = 4$, $p < .001$, kappa = .49, $p < .001$) but not when the four-category classification system was used ($\chi^2 = 18.38$, $df = 9$, $p < .031$, kappa = .14, N.S.).

2   Results of analyses using data from mother's pregnancy AAIs are presented because more maternal AAIs (in the context of three-generational data) were available during pregnancy than at 11 months ($n = 77$ vs. $n = 74$).

3   The four-category data will be made available upon request to the first author.

References

Ainsworth, M. D. S., Blehar, M. D., Waters, E., & Wall, S. (1978). *Patterns of attachment*. Hillsdale, NJ: Erlbaum.

Benoit, D., Zeanah, C. H., Boucher, C., & Minde, K. K. (1992). Sleep disorders in early childhood: Association with insecure maternal attachment. *Journal of the American Academy of Child and Adolescent Psychiatry, 31,* 86–93.

Bowlby, J. (1980). *Attachment and Loss: Vol. 3. Loss, sadness and depression*. New York: Basic.

Bowlby, J. (1982). *Attachment and Loss: Vol. 1. Attachment*. New York: Basic. (Original work published 1969.)

Fonagy, P., Steele, H., & Steele, M. (1991). Maternal representations of attachment during pregnancy predict the organization of infant-mother attachment at one year of age. *Child Development, 62,* 891–905.

George, C., Kaplan, N., & Main, M. (1985). *The Adult Attachment Interview*. Unpublished manuscript, University of California at Berkeley, Department of Psychology.

Main, M., & Hesse, E. (1990). Parents' unresolved traumatic experiences are related to infant disorganized attachment status: Is frightened and/or frightening parent behavior the linking mechanism? In M. T. Greenberg, D. Cicchetti, & E. M. Cummings (Eds.), *Attachment in the preschool years* (pp. 161–182). Chicago: University of Chicago Press.

Main, M., & Solomon, J. (1986). Discovery of an insecure-disorganized/disoriented attachment pattern: Procedures, findings, and implications for the classification. In M. Yogman, & T. B. Brazelton (Eds.), *Affective development in infancy* (pp. 95–124). Norwood, NJ: Ablex.

Main, M., & Solomon, J. (1990). Procedures for identifying infants as disorganized/disoriented during the Ainsworth Strange Situation. In M. T. Greenberg, D. Cicchetti, & E. M. Cummings (Eds.), *Attachment in the preschool years* (pp. 121–160). Chicago: University of Chicago Press.

Main, M., & Weston, D. R. (1981). The quality of the toddler's relationship to mother and to father: Related to conflict behavior and the readiness to establish new relationships. *Child Development, 52,* 932–940.

van IJzendoorn, M. H. (1993). *Associations between adult attachment representations and parent-child attachment, parental responsiveness, and clinical status: A meta-analysis on the predictive validity of the Adult Attachment Interview.* Unpublished manuscript.

van IJzendoorn, M. H. (1996). Attachment representations in mothers, fathers, adolescents, and clinical groups: A meta-analytic search for normative data. *Journal of Consulting & Clinical Psychology, 64,* 8–21.

Vaughn, B., Egeland, B., Sroufe, L. A., & Waters, E. (1979). Individual differences in infant-mother attachment at twelve and eighteen months: Stability and change in families under stress. *Child Development, 50,* 971–975.

Ward, M. J., Carlson, E. A., & Altman, S. C. (1992). Stability of the Adult Attachment Interview for adolescent mothers. Abstracts of Papers Presented at the Eighth International Conference on Infants Studies. *Infant Behavior & Development, 15,* 242.

Waters, E. (1978). The reliability and stability of individual differences in infant-mother attachment. *Child Development, 49,* 483–494.

Waters, E. (1983). The stability of individual differences in infant attachment: Comments on the Thompson, Lamb, & Estes contribution. *Child Development, 54,* 516–520.

Zeanah, C. H., Benoit, D., Barton, M., Regan, C., Hirshberg, L. M., & Lipsitt, L. P. (1993). Representations of attachment in mothers and their one-year-old infants. *Journal of the American Academy of Child and Adolescent Psychiatry, 32,* 278–286.

NINETEEN

Infants with Autism

Introduction

Autism is a rare developmental disorder, affecting some 1 in 2–5,000 children. Estimates of its incidence vary given that autistic symptoms vary from mild to severe so that it can be difficult to classify a child as being clearly autistic. Nevertheless, the primary symptoms of autism have been well established, and they constitute a triad of impairments, in socialization, communication, and imagination. The child with these autistic symptoms usually has them throughout life. Autism is not normally diagnosed until around 2 or 3 years of age, though anecdotal reports of the parents of autistic children suggest that they may have behaved differently from non-autistic children from birth.

Given that autism may have its origins in early infancy it may be possible to detect those infants who are (or will become) autistic, and Simon Baron-Cohen and his colleagues (1996) describe a screening devise, called the CHecklist for Autism in Toddlers (CHAT) that can be used in the identification of autism in infancy. In this study Tony Charman and his colleagues describe the results of a massive epidemiological study in which CHAT was given to a population of 16,000 18-month-olds. They discovered a small number of infants with autism – those who failed to use social gaze in joint attention tasks, showed poor empathy, engaged in little pretend play, and were usually unable to imitate actions they saw others perform. These infants have the classic autistic symptoms, and Charman et al. comment that "the identification of autism-specific impairments in early social cognitive abilities may have important clinical implications for the early diagnosis of the disorder and for the setting of goals and monitoring of progress in early intervention programs."

Reference

Baron-Cohen, S., Cox, A., Baird, G., Swettenham, J., Nightingale, N., Morgan, K., Drew, A., and Charman, T. (1996). Psychological markers of autism at 18 months of age in a large population. *British Journal of Psychiatry*, 168, 158–163.

An Experimental Investigation of Social-Cognitive Abilities in Infants with Autism: Clinical Implications

Tony Charman, John Swettenham, Simon Baron-Cohen, Antony Cox, Gillian Baird, and Auriol Drew

Theoretical accounts of psychopathological development in individuals with autism emphasize the role of various social and cognitive factors that emerge during infancy in typical development. However, to date, research has mostly been conducted with school-age children, adolescents, or young adults with autism (for a review, see Baron-Cohen et al., 1993). This is because the disorder is rarely diagnosed before the age of 3 (Gillberg et al., 1990). Research with school-age children, adolescents, and young adults with autism has demonstrated autism-specific impairments in a variety of infantile social-cognitive abilities, including empathic response (e.g., Sigman et al., 1992), pretend play (e.g., Mundy et al., 1986; Wetherby and Prutting, 1984), joint attention behaviors (e.g., Baron-Cohen, 1989; Mundy et al., 1986) and imitation (e.g., Dawson and Adams, 1984; Rogers et al., 1996). These impairments have been cited as support for the theoretical accounts of psychopathological development put forward by various authors and, in turn, they have been linked to the later problems in social understanding and social communication that characterize autism (Baron-Cohen, 1993, 1995; Hobson, 1993; Leslie, 1987, 1994; Meltzoff and Gopnik, 1993; Mundy, 1995; Mundy et al., 1993; Rogers and Pennington, 1991).

To summarize briefly the research findings with older school-age children, adolescents, and young adults with autism:

1   Individuals with autism show poor coordination of affective response in that they are less likely than controls to combine smiles with eye contact and to smile in response to smiles from their mother (Dawson et al., 1990; Kasari et al., 1990), and are impaired in their *empathic responses* to signals of distress (Sigman et al., 1992).

2   In unstructured or free-play conditions, children with autism produce significantly less *pretend* play, but intact functional play, compared to chronological or mental age-matched comparison groups (Baron-Cohen, 1987; Lewis and Boucher, 1988; Mundy et al., 1986; see Jarrold et al., 1993, for a review).

3   There is substantial experimental evidence for impairments in the production and comprehension of *joint attention* behaviors in children with autism. Many studies have shown, for example, that while children with autism are able to use eye contact and gestures to request objects (protoimperative gestures) or to engage in social action routines, they nevertheless do not use eye contact and gestures to share interest in objects or their properties (protodeclarative gestures) (e.g., Baron-Cohen, 1989; Mundy et al., 1986; see Charman, 1997, 1998, for reviews).

4   While most studies have demonstrated impaired *imitation* – in particular of complex and novel sequences of actions – in children with autism (Dawson and Adams, 1984; Rogers et al., 1996, see Smith and Bryson, 1994, for a review), a few studies have found that school-age children with autism are able to produce simple, basic-level imitation of gestures, actions on objects, and facial expressions (e.g., Charman and Baron-Cohen, 1994; Loveland et al., 1994; Morgan et al., 1989).

The opportunity to study these social-cognitive abilities in younger children with autism would be of great clinical value, for several reasons: First, while it would be expected that infants with autism would demonstrate impaired development of empathy, pretend play, joint attention, and imitation – because these have previously been found to be specifically impaired in older children, adolescents, and adults with autism – information about the specificity of these impairments to autism in infancy (compared to infants with developmental delay without autism) would aid differential diagnosis between autism and other developmental and language delays in very young children. Second, early intervention programs typically focus on increasing skills in the areas of functional and pretend play, imitation, and the understanding and production of joint attention gestural communication behaviors (Bondy and Frost, 1995; Rogers, 1996; Rogers and Lewis, 1989). Systematic measurement of which aspects of these skills are *intact* and which are *impaired* in infants with autism will inform the content and design of intervention programs, and the development of sensitive outcome measures, which would enable progress over time to be monitored.

In the present study, infants aged 20 months were tested on experimental measures of the following abilities: empathic response to a display of distress, spontaneous functional and pretend play, joint attention and requesting behaviors, and imitation. The present study is an advance on previous work in this area in a number of ways: first, the present research takes advantage of a recent prospective method of identification of autism (Baron-Cohen et al., 1996) to investigate the development of these social communicative abilities in *infants* with autism. Baron-Cohen et al. (1992) developed a screening instrument for childhood autism (the CHecklist for Autism in Toddlers; CHAT). The CHAT checks for the presence of pretend play and joint attention behaviors, as well as unrelated developmental accomplishments such as rough-and-tumble play. Studying a "high risk" sample of 18-month-old siblings of children already diagnosed as having autism, Baron-Cohen et al. (1992) found that only the four children who went on at age 3 to receive a diagnosis of autism failed *both* pretend play and joint attention at 18 months. A similar screening method has been used on a large population of 18-month-olds (see Baron-Cohen et al., 1996, for details). This enabled prospective identification of 8 infants with autism, 13 infants with atypical autism, Asperger's syndrome or pervasive developmental disorder, and 8 infants with developmental delays (primarily language delays) but without autism (see Baird et al., forthcoming, for details). Thus, we have been able to study a younger sample of individuals with autism than has previously been possible. Second, the present study compares the performance of infants with autism to those who show developmental impairments in the three recognized domains of autistic impairment of reciprocal social interaction, communication, and repetitive and restrictive interests, but who do not meet the full diagnostic criteria for autism – but rather meet criteria for the related disorders of pervasive developmental disorder not otherwise specified,

Asperger's syndrome or atypical autism (ICD-10; World Health Organization, 1993). While there is some disagreement about the nosological validity of the concept of an autistic continuum, or spectrum (Volkmar, 1997; Wing, 1988), information on whether and in what ways individuals with autism differ from those with atypical autism, Asperger's syndrome, or pervasive developmental disorder in aspects of social-cognitive behavior in infancy and beyond will provide evidence against which the concept of a continuum with valid diagnostic subgroups can be judged. Third, previous experimental work has largely adopted between-group comparisons to identify specific delays in these social-cognitive abilities in groups of individuals with autism, compared to groups of individuals with developmental delay without autism. This strategy can lead to the erroneous assumption that no individuals with autism show any of the behavior of concern at any particular age. Documenting the proportion of infants with autism, and those with related pervasive developmental disorders, who show some aspects of these behaviors, and comparing this to the proportion of infants with developmental delay without autism who show such behaviors, is an important database on which clinicians can draw when making decisions regarding differential diagnosis. Thus, because this is the first opportunity to study infants with autism, the findings of the present study represent important information at a descriptive level, as well as at the level of looking for between-group differences in the behaviors measured.

Method

Participants

The present research was part of the first epidemiological study to attempt early screening for autism. It used the CHAT on a population of 16,000 18-month-old children (Baron-Cohen et al., 1996). The epidemiological aspects of the larger study are reported elsewhere (Baird et al., forthcoming; Baron-Cohen et al., 1996; Cox et al., 1997) and will not be considered here. Following identification of children considered at risk of developing autism according to their performance on the CHAT at 18 months – by failing items measuring the production and comprehension of protodeclarative pointing (pointing for interest), gaze monitoring, and the production of pretend play (see Baird et al., forthcoming; Baron-Cohen et al., 1996, for details) – the infants were tested on a series of experiments in the clinic at age 20 months. While tentative ICD-10 (World Health Organization, 1993) diagnoses were made at this age, the children were followed up at age 42 months when full confirmatory ICD-10 diagnoses were made. The performance of participants in the present experiments at age 20 months is presented according to individuals' final diagnosis made at 42 months.[1] Autism group: 8 children (7 boys, 1 girl) met ICD-10 (World Health Organization, 1993) criteria for autism at age 42 months. Pervasive Developmental Delay group: 13 children (11 boys, 2 girls) met ICD-10 criteria for atypical autism (2), Asperger's syndrome (2) or pervasive developmental delay not otherwise specified (9) at age 42 months (hereafter know as the PDD group). Developmental delay group: 8 children (3 boys, 5 girls)[2] met ICD-10 criteria for either expressive or mixed receptive-expressive language disorder, and of these 3 also had a nonverbal mental age 3 or more months below their chronological age (of approximately 20 months).

The descriptive data – chronological age (CA), nonverbal mental age (NVMA) measured by the A (motor development), D (eye-hand coordination), and E (performance) scales of the Griffiths Scale of Infant Development (Griffiths, 1986), and language ability measured by raw scores[3] on the Verbal Comprehension (VC) and Expressive Language (EL) subscales of the Reynell Language Scale (Reynell, 1985) – for the three participant groups is shown in table 19.1. The groups were matched on all measures. Although there was a nonsignificant trend on the Reynell VC measure, with the autism group scoring lower than the other two groups (Analysis of variance: ANOVA; $F (2,26) = 2.80$, $p < .08$), post-hoc Scheffe tests revealed that no two groups differed from each other at the $p = .05$ significance level.

The testing session

The experiments were conducted in a single session, and there was no fixed order of administering the tasks, except that the beginning of the testing sessions were invariant: the spontaneous play session was conducted first to avoid spontaneous play being contaminated by the other tasks. Due to noncompliance, not all children took part in all the trials. However, the drop-out was very low and is reported below for each

Table 19.1 Chronological Age (CA) and Griffiths Nonverbal Mental Age (NVMA) in months, and raw Reynell Verbal Comprehension (VC) and Expressive Language (EL) scores for the autism, Pervasive Developmental Delay (PDD) and developmental delay groups

	Autism mean SD (N = 8)	PDD mean SD (N = 13)	Developmental delay mean SD (N = 8)
CA	21.4 (1.8)	20.5 (1.7)	20.5 (1.0)
NVMA	17.5 (1.9)	17.5 (1.6)	18.3 (2.0)
VC	3.1 (1.1)	6.4 (3.8)	6.9 (3.7)
EL	6.1 (2.8)	8.4 (3.8)	9.4 (1.1)

individual task. The total testing time varied from child-to-child, but was usually between one-and-a-quarter hours and one-and-a-half hours. The sessions were videotaped and analyzed subsequently. The raters were blind to the diagnoses of the children. A subset of all tapes were rated by a second rater and inter-rater reliability calculated. Agreement was moderate to high, with kappa values between .75 and 1 for over three quarters of the variables coded, and on only 1 variable did kappa fall below .50 – pointing during the joint attention tasks (.47) (see Charman et al., 1997, for details).

Empathic response. A measure of affective and attentional response to a display of distress by an adult, based on earlier work by Sigman et al. (1992) and Zahn-Waxler et al. (1992), was used. The experimenter (in all cases T.C. or J.S.) played jointly with the child, with a plastic pounding toy and hammer. During this, at a point when the child was actually touching the toy, the experimenter pretended to hurt himself by hitting his thumb with the hammer. For 10 s the experimenter displayed facial and vocal expressions of distress (i.e., cries of pain), without using words, and stopped touching the toy. After a further 10-s period of neutral affect, the experimenter showed the child that his finger did not hurt any more, and resumed playing with the toy. Following the protocol employed by Sigman et al. (1992), it was recorded whether during the first 10 s of the trial the child: looked to the experimenter's face; looked to the experimenter's hand; and stopped playing with, or touching, the toy. In addition, the child's own facial affect was coded as either: (1) concerned/upset; (2) indifferent/neutral; or (3) positive.

Spontaneous play task. When the child entered the room the following sets of toys were available (all at once), spread out on the floor: a toy teaset; a toy kitchen stove with miniature pots and pans, spoon, pieces of green sponge; and junk accessories (e.g., brick, straw, rawplug, cottonwool, cube, box) and conventional toy accessories (toy animals, cars, etc.). This combination of objects was based on the earlier studies by Baron-Cohen (1987) and Lewis and Boucher (1988). The child's parents and the experimenters remained seated, and offered only minimal and nonspecific responses to child-initiated approaches. Each child was filmed for 5 min. Each different play act produced by the child during the 5-min session was coded into the following four mutually exclusive categories according to the definitions used by Baron-Cohen (1987): sensorimotor; ordering; functional play; and pretend play. If there was uncertainty over which rating to make, the action was scored conservatively (i.e., the lower developmental categorization was scored: sensorimotor < functional < pretend; ordering play was not considered part of this hierarchy).

Joint attention tasks. A series of three active toy tasks based on those described by Butterworth and Adamson-Macedo (1987) were conducted. Although these tasks are similar to social referencing paradigms (e.g., Klinnert et al., 1986), social referencing behavior was not coded as the target variable was joint attention. The child stood or sat between the mother and the experimenter. A series of mechanical toys, designed to provoke an ambiguous response – that is, to provoke a mixture of attraction and uncertainty in the child – were placed one at a time onto the floor of the room 1 to 2 meters from the child. The toys were a robot, which flashed and beeped and moved around in circular sweeps; a car, which followed a circular path around the room; and a pig, which made "oinking" noises and shunted backwards and forwards. The toys were controlled by the experimenter via a control box and an electrical lead that ran from the box to the toy. They were active for a period of 1 min, during which time they stopped and restarted twice. The following actions were scored as either present or absent for each trial: (1) infant switched gaze between toy and adult (experimenter or parent) and back to toy, (2) infant looked to control box, (3) infant pointed to target object, (4) infant reached toward target object, and (5) infant vocalized.

Goal detection tasks. A series of tasks described by Phillips et al. (1992) were conducted at different times throughout the testing session: *(1) The blocking task*: When the child was manually and visually engaged with a toy, the experimenter covered the child's hands with his own, preventing the child from further activity, and held the block for 5 s. This was repeated four times during the session. *(2) The teasing task*: The experimenter offered the child a toy. When the child looked at the toy and began to reach out for it, the experimenter withdrew the toy and held it out of reach for 5 s. The experimenter then gave the toy to the child. This was repeated four times during the session. The key behavior recorded on each trial was whether the child looked up toward the experimenter's eyes during the 5-s period immediately after the block or the tease. While in previous studies we have regarded a look to the experimenter's face following the ambiguous blocking or teasing action to indicate a declarative gesture on the part of the infant (Charman et al., 1997; Phillips et al., 1992), we are now persuaded by the argument that they in fact *may* be measuring a form of imperative, or requesting, gesture – because the look to the experimenter when an object is held out and then removed may well have an instrumental function ("give me that back") (Peter Mundy, personal communication, 1997; see Charman, 1998, for discussion).

Imitation. The materials and method for the procedural imitation task followed those used with normally developing infants by Meltzoff (1988), and used with older subjects with autism by Charman and Baron-Cohen (1994). The child sat opposite the experimenter. Four actions were modelled, all on objects designed to be unfamiliar to the child. Each act was performed three times. At the end of the modelling period (about 2 min in all), the objects were placed, in turn, in front of the child. One nonspecific prompt ("What can you do with this?") was given if the child failed to pick up or manipulate the object at once. The response period was 20 s, for each object. Rigorous scoring criteria for imitation of each action, as set out by Meltzoff (1988), were adopted.

Results

Empathic response task

All subjects took part in this task. The results are summarized in table 19.2. While all eight infants with developmental delay and all but two of the infants with PDD looked to the experimenter's face, only half of

Table 19.2 Percent of children in the autism, Pervasive Developmental Delay (PDD), and developmental delay groups who produced the key behaviors on the empathy task

		Look face (%)	Look hand (%)	Continue to touch toy (%)	Show facial concern (%)
Autism	(N = 8)	50	25	88	13
PDD	(N = 13)	85	62	46	46
Developmental delay	(N = 8)	100*	38	50	38

*p < .05.

the infants with autism did so [$\chi^2(2, N = 29) = 6.50, p < .04$]. The post hoc group-by-group comparison reached significance between the autism and developmental delay groups (post-hoc Fisher's exact test; $p < .04$), but failed to reach statistical significance for autism versus PDD comparison. Only one infant with autism showed facial concern at the feigned distress, compared to nearly half the infants with PDD and developmental delay, although this comparison did not reach significance [$\chi^2(2, N = 29) = 2.53, p = ns$]. There were no significant differences in the proportion of infants in each group who looked to the experimenter's "injured" hand, nor in those who continued to touch the toy, although fewer infants with autism looked to the experimenter's "injured" hand and all but one continued to touch the toy – compared to approximately half of the infants in the PDD and developmental delay groups.

Spontaneous play task

One infant from the PDD group did not take part in this task. The percentage of children in each group producing at least one example of play in each of the four categories – sensorimotor, ordering, functional, and pretend – is shown in table 19.3. All participants across all three groups produced some examples of sensorimotor play, with few subjects showing ordering play. Over half the infants in all three groups

Table 19.3 Percentage of children in the autism, Pervasive Developmental Delay (PDD), and developmental delay groups who produced each category of play in the spontaneous play task

		Sensorimotor (%)	Ordering (%)	Functional (%)	Pretend (%)
Autism	(N = 8)	100	25	63	0
PDD	(N = 12)	100	0	92	25
Developmental delay	(N = 8)	100	25	63	50

produced some functional play acts. However, no infants in the autism group and only three in the PDD group produced any examples of pretend play, compared to half the infants in the developmental delay group – a trend that did not reach statistical significance [$\chi^2(2, N = 28)$ = 5.33, $p < .10$). However, post hoc group-by-group comparison reached significance for the autism versus developmental delay group comparison (post hoc Fisher's exact test; autism × PDD = ns; autism × developmental delay $p < .04$; PDD × developmental delay $p = $ ns).

Joint attention tasks

The groups of participants with autism, PDD, and developmental delay completed a mean of 2.6, 2.7, and 2.8 out of 3 possible trials, respectively. The percentage of completed trials on which the infants produced the key behaviors are shown in table 19.4. The data were analyzed in two ways: first the group mean proportion of trials on which the critical behavior was observed was analyzed by analysis of covariance (ANCOVA), with CA, and NVMA entered as covariates. Second, the proportion of participants who produced at least one example of each behavior across the trials completed was analyzed nonparametrically using the chi-square test. On the critical declarative joint attention behavior of gaze switch between the toy and an adult, infants with PDD and developmental delay produced gaze switches on approximately two thirds of trials, compared to only approximately one quarter of trials for the infants with autism. This comparison produced a significant main

Table 19.4 Percentage of trials on which children in the autism, Pervasive Developmental Delay (PDD), and developmental delay groups produced the key behaviors on the joint attention task

	Look to adult Mean SD (%) (%)		Look to box Mean SD (%) (%)		Point Mean SD (%) (%)		Reach Mean SD (%) (%)		Vocalize Mean SD (%) (%)	
Autism (N = 8)	23	(37)	33	(31)	0	(–)	4	(12)	4	(12)
PDD (N = 13)	64	(44)	53	(35)	18	(32)	28	(40)	26	(27)
Developmental delay (N = 8)	71	(38)*	54	(43)	6	(18)	8	(15)	17	(36)

*$p < .05$.

effect for group [ANCOVA; $F (2, 24) = 3.89$, $p < .04$], and no covariate effects. Post hoc group-by-group ANCOVA comparisons revealed that infants with autism gaze switched less than the infants from both the PDD and the developmental delay groups [ANCOVA; $F (1, 17) = 6.46$, $p < .03$; and ANCOVA; $F (1, 12) = 5.39$, $p < .04$; respectively]. All but three of the infants with PDD and all but one of the infants with developmental delay produced *at least one* gaze switch, compared to only three of the infants with autism, although this trend just missed statistical significance [$\chi^2(2, N = 29) = 5.37$, $p < .07$]. Across all three groups, participants looked to the box which controlled the mechanical toys on between one third and one half of trials. Across all three groups, participants pointed and reached towards the toy, and produced vocalizations, on relatively few trials and across these variables, there were no significant differences between the groups.

Goal detection tasks

The groups of participants with autism, PDD, and developmental delay completed a mean of 3.6, 3.8, and 3.8 out of four possible blocking trials, and 3.3, 3.1 and 3.5 out of a possible four teasing trials, respectively. The mean percentage (standard deviation in parentheses) of completed blocking trials on which the infants looked to the experimenter's face (taken to indicate an imperative or requesting gesture) was 20% (SD = 35%) in the autism group, 56% (SD = 44%) in the PDD group, and 62% (SD = 44%) in the developmental delay group. On the teasing trials the mean (SD) percentages were 13% (19%), 52% (50%), and 53% (39%), respectively. However, despite the fact that infants with autism looked to the experimenter on fewer trials than the infants in the two other groups, there were no significant main group effects on either the blocking or the teasing trials, and no covariate effects [ANCOVA, $F(2, 24) = 1.76$, p = ns; and ANCOVA, $F (2, 24) = 2.52$, p = ns; respectively]. Similarly, when analyzed in terms of the proportion of participants in each group who produced a look to the experimenter on *at least one trial* there were no significant group differences on either task, with 38% of the infants with autism, 77% of the infants with PDD, and 75% of the infants with developmental delay producing at least one look on the blocking trials, and 38%, 62% and 75% in the teasing trials, respectively [both $\chi^2(2, N = 29)$, $p > .10$].

Imitation task

The groups of participants with autism, PDD, and developmental delay completed a mean of 3.9, 4.0, and 3.4 out of four possible imitation trials, respectively. The mean percentage of imitation trials on which the infants successfully imitated the modelled actions were 22% (SD = 25%) in the autism group, 56% (SD = 34%) in the PDD group, and 65% (SD = 26%) in the developmental delay group. This comparison produced a significant main effect for group [ANCOVA; $F (2,24) = 3.47$, $p < .05$], and no covariate effects. Post hoc group-by-group ANCOVA comparisons revealed that infants with autism gaze switched less than the infants from both the PDD and the developmental delay groups [ANCOVA; $F (1,17) = 5.27$, $p < .04$; and ANCOVA; $F (1,12) = 8.32$, $p < .02$; respectively]. When analyzed nonparametrically, in terms of the proportion of participants in each group who produced *at least one* imitative action, there was also a significance difference, with only 50% of the infants with autism producing at least one imitative action, compared to 85% of the infants with PDD, and 100% of the infants with developmental delay [$\chi^2(2, N = 29) = 6.50$, $p < .04$]. The post hoc group-by-group comparison reached significance between the autism and developmental delay groups [post hoc Fisher's exact test; $p < .04$], but failed to reach statistical significance for autism versus PDD comparison (post hoc Fisher's exact test; p = ns).

Discussion

As indicated in the introduction, the strategy used to analyze the present dataset took into account analysis of between-group differences *and* the absolute level of performance of individual subjects within each group. This dual strategy is important in terms of providing some database against which clinical decisions can be made regarding the significance of the presence, or absence, of a particular behavior in any individual infant on similar experimental measures conducted in the clinic. Such useful descriptive information can easily be masked by adopting a between-group analytical strategy only, which can lead to an incorrect impression that all individuals with autism do not produce *any* examples of certain behaviors, because their group mean is significantly less than that of a comparison group. Thus, throughout this discussion, both differences between the groups, and the degree of variability in performance of the behavior of concern within any particular diagnostic group, will be considered.

Across the different aspects of social-cognitive development measured, the group of infants with autism showed low production of some behaviors, in contrast to the infants with PDD and developmental delay. For instance, only half the infants with autism looked at the experimenter during their feigned distress in the empathy task and only one was rated as showing facial concern. Thus, while some individuals with autism noticed the cry of distress, only one showed any clear evidence of an empathic response (Sigman et al., 1992; Zahn-Waxler et al., 1992). This is in contrast to the infants with PDD and developmental delay, nearly all of whom noticed the "distress" and half of these showed active facial concern.

Similarly, while all but three of the infants with PDD and one infant with developmental delay produced at least one example of a gaze switch of visual attention in response to ambiguous toys on the joint attention task – and did so consistently with gaze switches occurring on nearly two thirds of trials in both groups – only one third of the infants with autism produced even one example of a gaze switch. In contrast, they produced as many "nonsocial" looks at the box that controlled the toys. Thus, it seems clear that the infants with autism were interested in the mechanical toys (indeed all children looked intently at the ambiguous toys), and were able to use gaze to investigate physical aspects of the paradigm (by looking to the control box through which the experimenter stopped and started the toy), but did not use gaze to share aspects of the situation with an adult, in contrast to both the PDD and developmental delay infants. This concurs with previous experimental findings that difficulties in the declarative aspects of the eye gaze behavior, particularly when it involves the triadic switching of attention from person to object and back to person, is one of the most pronounced social communicative impairments in individuals with autism (e.g., Baron-Cohen, 1989; Mundy et al., 1986; see Charman, 1997, 1998; Mundy et al., 1993; Mundy, 1995, for reviews).

A similar pattern also emerged on the imitation task, with the infants with autism imitating on only one fifth of the trials, in contrast to infants with PDD and developmental delay infants, who imitated on over half the trials. While this contrasts with a recent study with school-age children with autism using the same tasks that found no autism-specific deficit (Charman and Baron-Cohen, 1994), it is in line with the majority of studies that find impairments in imitation in autism (see Rogers et al., 1996; Smith and Bryson, 1994, for reviews), and it suggests that while some simple, basic-level imitation abilities may present by school-age in children with autism, they are not in place by age 20 months.

In contrast to this, on the goal-detection tasks – taken as measures of imperative or requesting behavior – one third of the infants with autism looked to the experimenter following the ambiguous action on at least one trial. Thus, while as a group the individuals with PDD and developmental delay produced more than twice as many looks to the experimenter as the individuals with autism across all the trials completed, these differences did not reach statistical significance because at least *some* of the infants with autism were producing *some* imperative looks on at least some trials.

A different pattern of results was found on the spontaneous play task. Here no infants with autism and only three with PDD produced any examples of pretend play, in contrast to half the infants with developmental delay. However, two thirds of subjects in all three groups produced some examples of functional play. These findings are similar to the majority of studies that have previously looked at spontaneous pretend play in autism (Baron-Cohen, 1987; Lewis and Boucher, 1988; Mundy et al., 1986; see Jarrold et al., 1993, for a review).

While the poor performance of the infants with autism was expected – indeed in all cases older samples had been previously shown to be impaired on similar tasks – more surprising was the relatively *intact* performance of the PDD group on the empathy, joint attention, goal-detection, and imitation tasks. Their performance was close to that of the infants with developmental delay without an autism spectrum diagnosis on all tasks, with the exception of spontaneous pretend play. While little experimental data are available that pertain to differences between individuals with autism and PDD on such measures, we expected that the individuals with PDD would perform similarly to the individuals with autism – or at least somewhere between the individuals with autism and those with developmental delay without autism. Because the most recent revisions of the two classification systems used in international research – ICD-10 (World Health Organization, 1993) and DSM-IV (American Psychiatric Association, 1994) – clarified the status of individuals who meet most, but not the full, diagnostic criteria for autism, researchers are increasingly dividing participants who fall into the autistic continuum into those with "core" childhood autism versus those with related PDDs. Further research will confirm whether our unexpected finding – that infants with PDD performed more similarly to infants with developmental delay without autism than to infants with autism – is replicable.

This highlights one important caution in the interpretation of these experimental findings: while the performance of the infants with PDD was similar to that of the infants with developmental delay in these structured experimental measures conducted at 20 months, their observed and reported behavior in the full clinical assessments conducted at age 42 months (on the basis of which ICD-10 clinical diagnoses and assignment to experimental groups was made) did distinguish the groups. From the present data we are unable to conclude whether this represents some change in the behavior shown by the infants with PDD between 20 months and 42 months when the final clinical diagnosis was made (see Baird et al., forthcoming; Cox et al., 1997, for discussion), or whether it reflects a discrepancy between everyday interactions and performance on such structured experimental tasks. We are currently analyzing data from structured interactions with the present sample collected at age 20 months and 42 months to help answer this question. One clear caution is warranted, isolated examples of pretend play, gaze switching, and imitative behavior in clinical diagnostic assessments of infants or preschool children cannot rule out a diagnosis of PDD nor indeed of autism because many individuals with PDD and, a few individuals with autism, did produce examples of all the target social communication behaviors (with the exception of spontaneous pretend play).

The present findings are also of relevance to theoretical accounts of the psychopathological development in autism. Studying the pattern of intact abilities and impairments shown by infants with autism and PDD in these early-emerging social-communicative abilities may contribute to the delineation of which early social-communication behaviors are functionally related to later-emerging skills, such as theory of mind development, which previous research has demonstrated are impaired in school-age children with autism (see, Baron-Cohen, 1993; for a review). This will have implications for our understanding of the abnormal development of social communication in autism, and further our understanding of the developmental trajectories of empathy, play, joint attention, and imitation in the normal case. However, the theoretical conclusions that can be drawn from the present cross-sectional study alone are limited, and we must await the outcome of longitudinal and training studies (Bradley and Bryant, 1983) to better understand the relationship between impairments in the early social communicative abilities studied here and the characteristic pattern of social-communicative impairments seen in school-age children with autism.

To return to the present focus on the clinical utility of studying infants with autism: the present results could help inform the content and strategy of intervention programs. For example, the fact that some infants with autism *are* able to produce functional play is an important consideration when designing an intervention program with a play element, which aims to increase the repertoire of symbolic play activity in which the child can engage. Reinforcement and shaping of the functional use of objects, and the introduction of similar- and near-shaped nonfunctional objects into the play routine (Jarrold et al., 1996), might increase the development of truly symbolic, or pretend, play. Similarly, the fact that half the infants with autism noticed the experimenter's feigned cries of distress – while only one actually showed any affective empathic response – is a starting point for teaching and shaping behavioral responses to the emotional displays of others. It may be that more basic deficits in conceptual or affective ability in individuals with autism will eventually undermine such enterprises, but research evidence is beginning to emerge that early intervention programs that take such a step-by-step to the development of social communication skills can bear significant benefit over time (Bondy and Frost, 1995; Rogers and Lewis, 1989; see Rogers, 1996, for a review). The fact that *some* 20-month-old infants with autism were found to have *some* intact social communication behaviors in the domains of empathy, joint attention, pretend play and imitation studied, and further that many of those who did not showed some (perhaps earlier emerging) related behaviors – such as functional play, noticing distress, and imperative requests – gives a starting point for intervention programs with even the youngest children seen in child development clinics for autism. Experimental measures that are quick to conduct and that can be given in a relatively standardized and repeated manner (with different materials in some cases where learning might be expected to occur over repeated presentations, e.g., in the imitation task), such as those used in the present study, have the potential to be used to monitor the progress of individuals in intervention studies.

The opportunity to study this unique sample of infants with autism and PDD has given us the opportunity to document their profile of infantile social cognitive abilities around the time that these abilities emerge – rather than years later, as is the case with much research into autism. We hope to fill out this developmental account of autism by following the sample into their preschool and school-age years, and then may be able to answer with more certainty questions about the typical development of social cognitive abilities in infancy, their relationship to later social cognitive abilities, and the atypical course of this developmental trajectory in individuals with autism and related disorders.

Notes

1 Portions of these data have been presented in a previous paper (Charman et al., 1997). However, when this earlier paper was written only the diagnoses of autism made at 20 months had been confirmed at age 42 months. Further, in Charman et al. (1997), data are not presented separately on children who do not meet ICD-10 criteria for childhood autism but rather meet criteria for atypical autism, Asperger's syndrome, or pervasive developmental disorder not otherwise specified. In the present study, all children

had been followed up at age 42 months and ICD-10 (World Health Organization, 1993) diagnoses had been made at this age. See Baird et al. (forthcoming) and Cox et al. (1997) for discussion of the stability of diagnosis between 20 months and 42 months.

2 Although the groups were not matched for gender, and as would be expected the majority of participants in the autism and PDD groups were male, analysis of the performance of boys and girls in the developmental delay group revealed no differences and data are presented for all participants seen.

3 Raw scores were used because some subjects scored below the floor for assigning a language age equivalent.

References

American Psychiatric Association. (1994). *Diagnostic and statistical manual of mental disorders. (4th Ed.) (DSM–IV)*. Washington, DC: American Psychiatric Association.

Baird, G., Cox, A., Baron-Cohen, S., Swettenham, J., Charman, T., Drew, A., & Nightingale, N. (forthcoming). What are the rates of false positives and negatives in detecting autism at 18 months of age using the CHAT? Unpublished manuscript. University of London.

Baron-Cohen, S. (1987). Autism and symbolic play. *British Journal of Developmental Psychology, 5*, 139–148.

Baron-Cohen, S. (1989). Perceptual role-taking and protodeclarative pointing in autism. *British Journal of Developmental Psychology, 7*, 113–127.

Baron-Cohen, S. (1993). From attention-goal psychology to belief-desire psychology: The development of a theory of mind and its dysfunction. In S. Baron-Cohen, H. Tager-Flusberg, & D. Cohen (Eds.), *Understanding other minds: perspectives from autism* (pp. 59–82). Oxford: Oxford University Press.

Baron-Cohen, S. (1995). *Mindblindness: An essay on autism and theory of mind*. Cambridge, Massachusetts: MIT Press.

Baron-Cohen, S., Allen, J., & Gillberg, C. (1992). Can autism be detected at 18 months? The needle, the haystack and the CHAT. *British Journal of Psychiatry, 161*, 839–842.

Baron-Cohen, S., Cox, A., Baird, G., Swettenham, J., Hightingale, N., Morgan, K., Drew, A., & Charman, T. (1996). Psychological markers of autism at 18 months of age in a large population. *British Journal of Psychiatry, 168*, 158–163.

Baron-Cohen, S., Tager-Flusberg, H., & Cohen, D. (1993). *Understanding other minds: Perspectives from autism*. Oxford: Oxford University Press.

Bondy, A. S., & Frost, L. A. (1995). Educational approaches in preschool: Behavior techniques in a public school setting. In E. Schopler & G. B. Mesibov (Eds.), *Learning and cognition in autism*. (pp. 311–333). New York: Plenum.

Bradley, L., & Bryant, P. E. (1983). Categorizing sounds and learning to read – a causal connection. *Nature, 301*, 419–421.

Butterworth, G. E., & Adamson-Macedo, E. (1987). The origins of pointing: A pilot study. Paper presented at the Annual Conference of the Developmental Psychology Section of the British Psychological Society. September 1987, York, UK.

Charman, T. (1997). The relationship between joint attention and pretend play in autism. *Development and Psychopathology, 9*, 1–16.

Charman, T. (1998). Specifying the nature and course of the joint attention impairment in autism in the preschool years: Implications for diagnosis and intervention. *Autism: The International Journal of Research and Practice, 2*, 61–79.

Charman, T., & Baron-Cohen, S. (1994). Another look at imitation in autism. *Development and Psychopathology, 6*, 403–413.

Charman, T., Swettenham, J., Baron-Cohen, S., Cox, A., Baird, G., & Drew, A. (1997). Infants with autism: An investigation of empathy, pretend play, joint attention and imitation. *Developmental Psychology, 33*, 781–789.

Cox, A., Klein, K., Charman, T., Baird, G., Baron-Cohen, S., Swettenham, J., Wheelwright, S., & Drew, A. (1997). What is the primary abnormality in autism? Evidence from the ADI-R at 20 months and 42 months. Paper presented at the Biennial Conference of the Society for Research in Child Development. April 1997, Washington DC.

Dawson, G., & Adams, A. (1984). Imitation and social responsiveness in autistic children. *Journal of Abnormal Child Psychology, 12*, 209–226.

Dawson, G., Hill, D., Spencer, A., Galpert, L., & Watson, L. (1990). Affective exchanges between young autistic children and their mothers. *Journal of Abnormal Child Psychology, 18*, 335–345.

Gillberg, C., Ehlers, S., Schaumann. H., Jakobsson, G., Dahlgren, S. O., Lindblom, R., Bagenholm, A., Tjuus, T., & Blinder, E. (1990). Autism under age 3 years: A clinical study of 28 cases referred for autistic symptoms in infancy. *Journal of Child Psychology and Psychiatry, 31*, 921–934.

Hobson, R. P. (1993). *Autism and the development of mind*. London: Lawrence Erlbaum Associates.

Jarrold, C., Boucher, J., & Smith, P. (1993). Symbolic play in autism: A review. *Journal of Autism and Developmental Disorders, 23*, 281–308.

Jarrold, C., Boucher, J., & Smith, P. (1996). Generativity deficits in pretend play in autism. *British Journal of Developmental Psychology, 14*, 275–300.

Kasari, C., Sigman, M., Mundy, P., & Yirmiya, N. (1990). Affective sharing in the context of joint attention interactions of normal, autistic and mentally-retarded children. *Journal of Autism and Developmental Disorders, 20*, 87–100.

Klinnert, M. D., Emde, R. N., Butterfield, P., & Campos, J. J. (1986). Social referencing: The infant's use of emotional signals from a friendly adult with mother present. *Developmental Psychology, 22,* 427–432.

Leslie, A. M. (1987). Pretence and representation: The origins of "theory of mind." *Psychological Review, 94,* 412–426.

Leslie, A. M. (1994). Pretending and believing: Issues in the theory of ToMM. *Cognition, 50,* 211–238.

Lewis, V., & Boucher, J. (1988). Spontaneous, instructed and elicited play in relatively able autistic children. *British Journal of Developmental Psychology, 6,* 325–339.

Loveland, K., Tunali-Kotoski, B., Pearson, D. A., Brelsford, K. A., Ortegon, J., & Chen, R. (1994). Imitation and expression of facial affect in autism. *Development and Psychopathology, 6,* 433–443.

Meltzoff, A. N. (1988). Infant imitation and memory: Nine-month-olds in immediate and deferred tests. *Child Development, 59,* 217–225.

Meltzoff, A. N., & Gopnik, A. (1993). The role of imitation in understanding persons and developing theories of mind. In S. Baron-Cohen, H. Tager-Flusberg, & D. Cohen (Eds.), *Understanding other minds: Perspectives from autism* (pp. 335–366). Oxford: Oxford University Press.

Morgan, S. B., Cutrer, P. S., Coplin, J. W., & Rodrigue, J. R. (1989). Do autistic children differ from retarded and normal children in Piagetian sensorimotor functioning? *Journal of Child Psychology and Psychiatry, 30,* 857–864.

Mundy, P. (1995). Joint attention and social-emotional approach behavior in children with autism. *Development and Psychopathology, 7,* 63–82.

Mundy, P., Sigman, M., & Kasari, C. (1993). The theory of mind and joint attention in autism. In S. Baron-Cohen. H. Tager-Flusberg, & D. Cohen (Eds.), *Understanding other minds: Perspectives from autism* (pp. 181–204). Oxford: Oxford University Press.

Mundy, P., Sigman, M., Ungerer, J. A., & Sherman, T. (1986). Defining the social deficits of autism: The contribution of non-verbal communication measures. *Journal of Child Psychology and Psychiatry, 27,* 657–669.

Phillips, W., Baron-Cohen, S., & Rutter, M. (1992). The role of eye-contact in goal-detection: Evidence from normal toddlers and children with autism or mental handicap. *Development and Psychopathology, 4,* 375–384.

Rogers, S. J. (1996). Brief report: Early intervention in autism. *Journal of Autism and Developmental Disorders, 26,* 243–246.

Rogers, S. J., Benetto, L., McEvoy, R., & Pennington, B. F. (1996). Imitation and pantomime in high-functioning adolescents with autism spectrum disorders. *Child Development, 67,* 2060–2073.

Rogers, S. J., & Lewis, H. (1989). An effective day treatment model for young children with pervasive developmental disorders. *Journal of the American Academy of Child and Adolescent Psychiatry, 28,* 207–214.

Rogers, S. J., & Pennington, B. F. (1991). A theoretical approach to the deficits in infantile autism. *Development and Psychopathology, 3,* 137–162.

Sigman, M. D., Kasari, C., Kwon, J. H., & Yirmiya, N. (1992). Responses to the negative emotions of others by autistic, mentally retarded, and normal children. *Child Development, 63,* 796–807.

Smith, I. M., & Bryson, S. E. (1994). Imitation and action in autism: A critical review. *Psychological Bulletin, 116,* 259–273.

Volkmar, F. (1997). Ask the editor. *Journal of Autism and Developmental Disorders, 27,* 103–105.

Wetherby, A. M., & Prutting, C. A. (1984). Profiles of communicative and cognitive-social abilities in autistic children. *Journal of Speech and Hearing Research, 27,* 364–377.

Wing, L. (1988). The continuum of autistic characteristics. In E. Schopler & G. B. Mesibov (Eds.), *Diagnosis and assessment in autism* (pp. 91–110). New York: Plenum.

World Health Organization. (1993). *Mental disorders: A glossary and guide to their classification in accordance with the 10th revision of the International Classification of Diseases (ICD-10).* Geneva: WHO.

Zahn-Waxler, C., Robinson, J. L., & Emde, R. N. (1992). The development of empathy in twins. *Developmental Psychology, 28,* 1038–1047.

Index